The Ethics of Remembering and the Consequences of Forgetting

New Imago: Series in Theoretical, Clinical, and Applied Psychoanalysis

Series Editor: Jon Mills, Adler Graduate Professional School, Toronto

New Imago: Series in Theoretical, Clinical, and Applied Psychoanalysis is a scholarly and professional publishing imprint devoted to all aspects of psychoanalytic inquiry and research in theoretical, clinical, philosophical, and applied psychoanalysis. It is inclusive in focus, hence fostering a spirit of plurality, respect, and tolerance across the psychoanalytic domain. The series aspires to promote open and thoughtful dialogue across disciplinary and interdisciplinary fields in mental health, the humanities, and the social and behavioral sciences. It furthermore wishes to advance psychoanalytic thought and extend its applications to serve greater society, diverse cultures, and the public at large. The editorial board is comprised of the most noted and celebrated analysts, scholars, and academics in the English speaking world and is representative of every major school in the history of psychoanalytic thought.

Titles in Series

Transgenerational Trauma and the Aboriginal Preschool Child: Healing through Intervention, edited by Norma Tracey

The Ethics of Remembering and the Consequences of Forgetting: Essays on Trauma, History, and Memory, edited by Michael O'Loughlin

Fragments of Trauma and the Social Production of Suffering: Trauma, History, and Memory, edited by Michael O'Loughlin and Marilyn Charles

Relating to God: Clinical Psychoanalysis, Spirituality, and Theism, by Dan Merkur

The Uses of Psychoanalysis in Working with Children's Emotional Lives, edited by Michael O'Loughlin

Psychodynamic Perspectives on Working with Children, Families, and Schools, edited by Michael O'Loughlin

Working with Trauma: Lessons from Bion and Lacan, by Marilyn Charles

In Freud's Tracks: Conversations from the Journal of European Analysis, edited by Sergio Benvenuto and Anthony Molino

Desire, Self, Mind, and the Psychotherapies: Unifying Psychological Science and Psychoanalysis, by R. Coleman Curtis

Hypocrisy Unmasked: Dissociation, Shame, and the Ethics of Inauthenticity, by Ronald C. Naso

Searching for the Perfect Woman: The Story of a Complete Psychoanalysis, by Vamık D. Volkan with J. Christopher Fowler

The Ethics of Remembering and the Consequences of Forgetting

Essays on Trauma, History, and Memory

Edited by
Michael O'Loughlin

ROWMAN & LITTLEFIELD
Lanham • Boulder • New York • London

Published by Rowman & Littlefield
A wholly owned subsidiary of The Rowman & Littlefield Publishing Group, Inc.
4501 Forbes Boulevard, Suite 200, Lanham, Maryland 20706
www.rowman.com

Unit A, Whitacre Mews, 26-34 Stannary Street, London SE11 4AB

British Library Cataloguing in Publication Information Available

Library of Congress Cataloging-in-Publication Data

The ethics of remembering and the consequences of forgetting : essays on trauma, history, and memory / edited by Michael O'Loughlin.
pages cm. — (New imago : series in theoretical, clinical, and applied psychoanalysis)
Includes bibliographical references and index.
ISBN 978-1-4422-3187-0 (cloth : alk. paper) — ISBN 978-1-4422-3188-7 (electronic)
1. Psychic trauma. 2. Collective memory. 3. Recollection (Psychology)
4. History—Psychological aspects. I. O'Loughlin, Michael.
BF175.5.P75E84 2015
155.9′ 35—dc23 2014037852

∞™ The paper used in this publication meets the minimum requirements of American National Standard for Information Sciences—Permanence of Paper for Printed Library Materials, ANSI/NISO Z39.48-1992.

Printed in the United States of America

Contents

List of Figures

Foreword

Claude Barbre

> How repetitive and unfree we are as well as the remarkable way in which we can change, and in this kind of self-transcendence, we do not move beyond the world but more deeply into it, and in being affected by the others we reconnect with ourselves as subjects who have some measure of freedom. In these moments we do not turn away from the precariousness of existence but embrace all of who we are as we more fully partake of life. (Halling, 2008, p. 3)

In Greek mythology, Mnemosyne, the Titan goddess of memory and remembrance, is also the creator of language. As the daughter of Ouranos (Heavens) where creation moves in the cycles of day and night, she is also the goddess of time, and thus represents the oral tradition and narrative memorizations before the introduction of writing—language skills that preserved the stories of history and cultural sagas. In this capacity, Mnemosyne is represented as the mother of the nine Mousia (Muses), in part reflective of her original role as patron goddess of the poets and musicians. Hence, we can see in the foundational attributes of this archetypal figure how memory, history, and language, twinned with the offspring forces of literature, science, and the arts, are deeply intertwined in a relational web of meanings and affinities.

There is another side of Mnemosyne's legacy that is often overlooked. In addition to her attributes, we must also remember that although Apollo was later placed as the leader of the Muses in Greek mythology, it is Hermes, the trickster god and notorious thief of Apollo's cattle, who is associated with language and interpretation, and thus heir to the language creator, Menmosyne, or personified memory. This association is telling. For the etymology of "Hermes" is connected to the Greek *hermeneus*, meaning "interpreter," reflecting Hermes' function as a divine messenger who discerns and reveals sacred correspondences and delivers them to the world. But as a trickster god, Hermes as interpreter may deliver messages that are unpredictable and dangerous, difficult to receive, and often filled with multifaceted meanings and possibilities. He is the lord of the in-between and the powers of the road. As Lewis Hyde says, trickster figures "pass through the halls of stability and order to enliven each place with mischief and change. They are the spirits of the doorway leading out, and of the crossroad at the edge of town" (Hyde, 1998, p. 17), and these boundary-crossing, ambit-breaching figures also convey a spirit road which all of us will travel and traverse. As spiritual phenomena, they move between heaven and earth, the living and the dead, and govern the spaces of heightened uncertainties. They appear to summon contradiction and paradox, ambiguity and question, and the internal tensions of right and wrong, sacred and profane, clean and dirty, young and old, male and female—in every case the trickster will cross the familiar lines and confuse the distinction in order to open us to life again. In particular, the word "hermeneutics," which is the study and theory of interpretation, is derived from *hermeneus*, and thus associated with this trickster god. Thus, interpretation has its roots in revelation, epiphany, and discernment of the spirits, and is itself kindred to the sacred arts. But Hermes, as a trickster god, is also the mythic embodiment of ambiguity and ambivalence, doubleness and duplicity, and is always lurking in how we interpret meaning in the language worlds we inhabit.

C. G. Jung remarked that "archetypes were, and still are, living psychic forces that demand to be taken seriously, and they have a strange way of making sure of their effect" (Jung, 1959, p. 156). Reading these remarkable and evocative essays about the ethics of remembering and the consequence of forgetting in regard to trauma, history, and memory, the archetypal forces of Menmosyne and Hermes take wing, hovering above our words, informing our individual and collective worlds with the trickster nature of memory and language, history and time, arts and sciences, and the complexities of interpretation and meaning. For, as we have seen, memory and interpretation have trickster elements, and this is no less true in these extraordinary meditations on intergenerational suffering that deconstruct the more familiar views of trauma studies in order to challenge our assumptions and to open the reader to unexpected peripheries and visions. As Lewis Hyde said, the trickster "is the spirit of the road at dusk, the one that runs from one town to another and belongs to neither. There are strangers on that road, and thieves, and in the underbrush a sly beast whose stomach has not heard about your letters of safe passage" (Hyde, 1998, p. 31). These essays lead us along the dangerous road of tragic anamnesis, the underbrush of unspoken testimonies riddled with broken symmetries—and, in doing so, paradoxically lift us, as in Hermes's flight, to new interpretations of trauma knowledge and therapeutic directions for individuals and communities who suffer without voice or identity.

If the interpretation of language worlds is archetypally imbued with trickster qualities, what about memory? Writing about the development of memory, psychiatrist Daniel Stern points out that from infancy our subjective world includes a mental construction that emerges from the interaction between "actuality" and the mental processes that encounter that actuality, and distorts and refashions it into subjective psychic reality. Our object-related preferences and tendencies unfold in conjunction to intrapsychic givens that influence the construction of reality. As we grow and develop, the working of the mind in considering and organizing its own history concerning lived-events become memories, and these memories are organized into representations—representations that, in turn, help interpret, construct, distort, and create the psychic reality of the next encountered lived-event of interpersonal reality (Stern, 1988). Stern calls this dynamic the "prototypic memory," a memory that is no longer a complete and accurate record of what "actuality" happened. In short, the prototype is a construction from "reality," an abstraction, but also represents reality as multiply experienced. Thus, psychic representations that we create from life events are abstracted accumulations of historical events. However, Stern notes that not all specific memories get absorbed in the formation of a prototype: "Sometimes memory will act as a more potent guide for interpreting the currently encountered interpersonal reality than the representation. In this form, a singular event among many will stand for all and will guide the interpretation of an event which is better represented and guided by the prototype" (Stern, 1988, p. 511). Stern calls this event the "specific memory"—a powerful memory that he maintains contain reticles of the representations and hence is constructed to a degree.

We can see in Stern's developmental description of memory as constructed by prototypic representations and in-breaking, specific memories, the trickster dance that questions actuality and historical reality in order to refashion interpersonal life. But what if one introduces the phenomenon of trauma into the construction of memory and recollection, as many of the authors do in this rich volume about remembering and forgetting? As Michael O'Loughlin remarks, "Perhaps the most vexed question in addressing trauma is the role of memory," reminding us of Freud's concept of *nachträglichkeit*, a term emphasizing "that it is not the objective impact of the supposedly traumatic event that causes injury, but the delayed memory of that event that is reactivated at a later time." Along these lines Freud noted that often delusions borne of trauma and annihilation anxiety "are found applied like a patch over the place where originally a rent had appeared in the ego's relation to the external world" (Freud, 1924, p. 151; quoted in Sklar, 2011, p. 8). As Jonathan Sklar points out,

> The gap, in time, can become the "split" in the ego. However, this is more complicated than it seems as the German for "split" is *Einreiss,* which leans more to a meaning of a "tendency to tear." This throws another perspective on to Freud's meaning because a "tendency" includes the idea that despite being fragile, the tear may not worsen. It is not a break. This is less critical than a *Reiss*, which is an actual tear and is more a term to delegate to psychosis." (Sklar, 2011, p. 8; Danckwardt and Wegner, 2007, p. 1118)

Drawing from Freud, Sklar notes that in regard to the *Einreiss* "things are both really known and quite unknown simultaneously, like a life lived in a concurrent parallel way. The patch covering the tear in the mind like a dream or a symptom attempts reconnection with reality" (Sklar, 2011, p. 9). As Freud points out, "*That which we take to be the pathological product, is in reality an attempt at recovery, a process of reconstruction*" (Freud, 1911, p. 71, italics in original; Sklar, 2011, p. 9). In essence, we see that in regard to the tear in the psyche, and the attempts to patch the tear:

> The delusion is a patch, thereby directing attention to the delusions, imaginary constructs, as well as fixities of the body that enable life apparently to continue on the surface as if there is no mental gap or tear. The symptoms are there as a covering structure to enable some sense of not fragmenting. The patch over the ego does not have a healing function; it is an unconscious phantasy because the deeper mental structures held apart from each other do not grow together. Instead, the patch can become more organized, such as a delusional system quietly enlarging to take account of the different unconscious narrative and relational affects on either side of the tear. (Sklar, 2011, p. 9)

Freud's view of the traumatic rents in the psyche that are consequently patched by delusions leads us to ponder if there can also be a tear in the collective psyche due to cultural terrors and sufferings that incur societal patches—cultural structures that obfuscate the memory of trauma, erasing the possibility of recovery by silencing trauma narration and fossilizing identity formation? A response to this question is at the heart of this collection of essays—significant writings that speak to the dangers of overbearing silences of traumatic repression that often accompanies unacknowledged tragedy. For example, Scott Boehm points out the way that post-dictatorship Spain depicts itself as the country of *mucha alegria*, even as it "patches" over, effaces its recent genocidal past—a type of cultural forgetting and historical negligence; Clara Valverde and Luis Martin-Cabrera also explore the intergenerational consequences of Francoist Spain, and the nature of historical erasure; Reinhold Stipsits' personal accounts of his visits to memorials in present-day Romania, Lithuania, and Moldova explore the trickster nature of collective memory where "a museum tells us more about the present than the past" (Browning, 2013, p. 153). Justina Kaminskaitė Dillon writes of the life narratives of Lithuanian women who were deported to Siberia during the Soviet occupation—stories that challenge the unacknowledged history of these traumatic events. Billie Pivnick and Tom Hennes examine approaches to managing traumatic collapse reflected in the relational designs of the 9/11 Memorial Museum. Angie Voela writes of the artwork that arises from *lieux de memories* (sites of memories) and historical ruptures of humanity. Nigel Williams' essay examines the German Diaspora and ethnic cleansing in post–World War I Britain, and the foreclosure of this history from cultural memory.

Along the dangerous and disturbing roads leading from traumatic experiences and loss, a primary theme in these essays is the possibility of healing through the search for identity and personal context. For instance, Mari Ruti, drawing from the writings of philosopher Susan Brison who in her book *Aftermath*, speaks about surviving rape and attempted murder, writes of the tensions between autonomy and relational ontology in the context of trauma. In contradistinction to the writing of Judith Butler on the ethics of precarity, Ruti, echoing Brison, underscores that "being able to recover a sense of autonomy is an essential part of surviving trauma . . . even though this autonomy will always be incomplete, will always encounter various obstacles, but it is also life-preserving." Minh Truong-George describes her flight from war-torn Vietnam and her return thirty years later, offering us a detailed account of the experience of flooding memories and emotions associated with childhood recollection. Writing in concert with Aboriginal artist Graham Toomey, who speaks of a profound rediscovery of his identity years after being separated from his Aboriginal roots, Norma Tracey contextualizes the collective trauma of Aboriginal people through a powerful historical overview, adding that the hope for Aboriginal recovery resides in the way a people can find "a new way of being that has their 'old' soul in it." A granddaughter of immigrants from Eastern Europe, Hannah Hahn writes of the intergenerational effects on children of the great migration of 1880–1924, and her own search to understand the impact of these events on future generations. The search for meaning in the traumatic space of loss is also a theme in Nirit Gradwohl Pisano's account of the effects of the Holocaust on third-generation descendants, where mourning and traumatic memories are repressed yet transmitted to the subsequent generations. Russ Truscott writes of a genealogy of post-apartheid empathy and forgiveness in South Africa, exploring colonial inheritances and the lingering affects of cultural disavowal of its traumatic history, while Ricardo Ainslie explores the violence of lynching in the Southern United States. Naama De La Fontaine and Kate Szymanski explore the transmission of Jewish/Israeli collective memory in narratives of Israeli soldiers who participated in the 2006 Second Lebanon War, articulating how collective identity deeply influences the self-images of Israeli participants in these conflagrations. All of these essays are introduced beautifully by Michael O'Loughlin, whose own chapter points out how reductionist and essentialist arguments in trauma discourses have distorted our discussions "to the extent that our understanding of traumatic experience has become interpolated with utilitarian, positivist, biologized, and often medicalized language that undoubtedly takes us away from the existential understanding of the experience of, and the social and political production of, human suffering." These essays offer an opportunity, echoing the work of Davoine and Gaudillière, to also "see beyond the difficulties of the individual as embodying individual disorder or lack, and instead pay attention to the gaps and ruptures of individual experience because they are symptoms pointing us precisely to the moments of history that have been erased," a history of breakdown in the social order and historical context. As O'Loughlin notes, "the role of the analyst as *annalist* refers to the role of the analyst as recuperator of memory and history"—the hallmark of these unflinching studies in this important volume.

James Joyce once remarked that he had a crossroad mind, indicative of the way writers engage the trickster nature of language worlds and interpretation. These essays capture the spirit of the *hermeneus* in that they subvert and disturb privileged and one-sided views found in trauma and historical discourses. They are parabolic in the sense that they deconstruct ideologies not to eradicate meaning, but to create a potential space for life to burgeon—what John Crossan has called "interior apocalypses" (Crossan, 1975). In short, these essays invite us to greater depths of awareness and vision by challenging our assumptions about the way life is—our dogmas and definitions, our inflated certainties—and do so in a creative way which encourages our imaginations to transcend expectations. These essays are about our actions, our motivations, and our omissions. In turn, they stimulate action, curiosity, periphery, and plenum. And like the trickster and parabolic spirit of interpretation that subverts and shatters the deep structure of our accepted perspectives, these essays show us the seams and edges of reality. They resist the quick complacency of a cursory regard. In the chaos of this subversion, new, creative voices can find a transformed space to speak, and we are all better for it.

REFERENCES

Browning, C. R. (2013). Reply to Daniel Fulda. In N. Frei and W. Kansteiner, (Eds.), *Den Holocaust erzahlen* (pp. 151–64). Weimer: Wallstein Verlag.

Crossan, J. D. (1975). *The dark interval: Towards a theology of story.* Salem, OR: Polebridge Press.

Danckwardt, J. F., and Wegner, P. (2007). Performance as annihilation or integration? *International Journal of Psychoanalysis*, 88: 1117–138.

Freud, S. (1911). Psychoanalytic notes on an autobiographical account of a case of paranoia (dementia paranoides). *Standard Edition*, 12: 1–82.

Halling, S. (2008). *Intimacy, transcendence, and psychology: Closeness and openness in everyday life.* New York: Palgrave-Macmillan.

Hyde, L. (1998). *Trickster makes this world: Mischief, myth, and art.* New York: Farrar, Straus, and Giroux.

Jung, C. G. (1959). Archetypes and the collective unconscious. In G. Adler and R. F. C. Hull (Eds.), *The collected works of C. G. Jung*, Vol. 1. Princeton, NJ: Princeton University Press.

Sklar, J. (2011). *Landscapes of the dark: History, trauma, psychoanalysis.* London: Karnac Books.

Stern, D. (1988). The dialectic between the "interpersonal" and the "intrapsychic": With particular emphasis on the role of memory and representation. *Psychoanalytic Inquiry* 8(4): 505–12.

Acknowledgments

I wish to thank all of the authors for their outstanding contributions to this volume. Thanks to Jon Mills for accepting this book and its companion volume, *Fragments of Trauma and the Social Production of Suffering: Trauma, History, and Memory* in the New Imago Series. Amy King, my editor at Rowman & Littlefield, and her assistant Francinia Williams managed all aspects of the book production process with grace and ease. Thanks also to Meaghan White, production editor for this book. Special thanks to Dr. Errol Rodriguez from the Derner Institute of Advanced Psychological Studies at Adelphi University who has graciously assigned students from the master's program as graduate assistants. These students, Katrina Florio, Jacqueline Hrzich, Caitlin Lapine, Brendan McGann, Bri McMahon, Dolores Paul, and Melodie Piciullo assisted willingly with proofreading, index preparation, etc., and we are very grateful to them. I am grateful too to Claude Barbre and Marilyn Charles, who graciously agreed to author the Foreword and Afterword, respectively.

Introduction

The Ethics of Remembering and the Consequences of Forgetting

Michael O'Loughlin

This book brings together scholars from a variety of disciplines who draw on multiple disciplinary perspectives to address issues that arise at the intersection of trauma, history, and memory. The writers include critical theorists, feminist theorists, critical historians, psychoanalysts, psychotherapists, a museum designer, and a working artist. The methodologies brought to bear include personal narrative, autoethnography, microhistory, psychosocial studies, critical theory, psychoanalysis, film and art criticism, and critical historical inquiry. The book has a geographic reach that includes discussions of the legacy of the Franco era in Spain; post-apartheid South Africa; the fate of the German diaspora in Great Britain after World War I; Jewish migration at the turn of the twentieth century; the construction of a memorial to the victims of the 9/11 disaster at the World Trade Center in New York City; the legacy of the Holocaust in the third generation; Lithuania and other East European states in the post-Soviet era; collective memory among the Israeli Defense Forces; migration as a refugee from Vietnam, contemporary racial violence in East Texas and the return of the ghosts of lynching; and the legacy of colonialism for Aboriginal people in postcolonial Australia. While many authors use a variant of intergenerational trauma theory in their work, rather than coalesce around a single orthodoxy, the authors push and pull at the edges of conventional understandings of how trauma is defined and the nature of the intersectionality between trauma, history, and memory. What unites the work is a respect for the importance of the recuperation of memory and the creation of interstitial spaces where trauma might be voiced. The writers are consistent in showing a deep respect for context, and for the sociohistorical situatedness of subjective formation, and many, too, are deeply concerned with the political importance of recuperating dangerous memory—the kind of memory that some authorities go to great lengths to erase. This work will be of interest to critical historians and critical social theorists interested in the intersection of trauma, history, and memory; to psychoanalysts and psychotherapists interested in understanding the ancestral, historical, and latent aspects of human experience and how they may gain expression; to psychosocial theorists looking for illustrations of liberatory methodologies of inquiry; and to persons interested in the possibilities of life as the practice of freedom

Mari Ruti opens up discussion on the problematic of trauma narration in chapter 1 with the story of an attack on American philosopher Susan Brison in France:

> Dartmouth philosopher Susan Brison tells us, in *Aftermath*, that in the summer of 1990, she went for a morning walk on a country road in Southern France. She was attacked from behind, dragged into a nearby ravine, raped, and beaten and strangled unconscious four times. Her assailant tried to kill her to keep her from reporting the rape, responding to her attempts to assure him that she would not report it by an insistent "il le faut"—"it must be done." When Brison regained consciousness after the fourth attack, she pretended to be dead, and her assailant left her in the ravine. She climbed back onto the road, flagged down a farmer on a tractor, and was taken to the hospital where she was treated for serious injuries. Her assailant was apprehended quickly—he lived in the neighborhood—and was eventually sentenced to twelve years in prison for rape and attempted murder. Brison reports that, unlike many rape survivors, she was treated relatively well by the French legal system, presumably in part because she was a white middle-class married woman, and in part because the attack was so grievous that it left no doubt about what had happened. The bulk of her book outlines the aftermath of the attack: her lengthy, and in many ways only partially successful, battle against severe symptoms of post-traumatic stress disorder.

Mari uses this story as a launching pad for an exploration of the possibility of an ethics of autonomy among trauma victims, contrasting it with the limitations of an ethics of precarity (i.e., insecurity), as advanced by Judith Butler. Brison and Butler would agree, Mari notes, that there is no essential self that can give a coherent account of the self. She suggests, however, that Butler goes too far by eliminating any notion of agency and thereby ends up failing to acknowledge a human capacity for autonomy that is essential for recovery. She notes that Brison, in contrast, argues for the importance of trauma narration as a critical step toward her recovery and her capacity to reclaim her sense of autonomy and control:

> More specifically, Brison confirms what countless other survivors have reported, namely that their repeated efforts to tell their stories are, among other things, an attempt to establish a measure of agency over lives that have been torn apart. Because there is a performative element to self-narrativization—so that

> in saying something about the trauma one acts on the memory of that trauma—narrativization helps the survivor externalize the trauma; rather than being a passive victim of another's violence, she becomes the (tentatively) active subject of her story. Brison in fact tells us that her recovery would not have been possible without the presence of others willing to respond to her story: "Each time someone failed to respond I felt as though I were alone again in the ravine, dying, screaming." (p. 16)

This is not to suggest that narrating trauma, alone, can be fully reparative, but Mari views it as a vital step toward regaining a claim on subjectivity after traumatic violation of personhood. Addressing Butler's theory, Mari suggests that reacting to the Enlightenment subject as a hoax, posthumanists, Butler among them, argue that

> you are not as powerful as you think you are; precariousness is the underpinning of your existence and this is how things should stay; any effort you might make to become more autonomous is essentially unethical (because the worst you could ever do would be to begin to resemble the agentic subject of Enlightenment humanism).

Butler, she suggests, attempts to combine Levinasian phenomenology with psychoanalysis to argue—contra-Kantian rationalism—that we are thoroughly interpellated by the other and thereby necessarily traumatized by impingement from the other. Instead of subjectivity as autonomous, Butler argues for a relational ontology that causes us to recognize the fundamental vulnerability of all human suffering. While Mari is admiring of the political project underlying Butler's work—a project that recognizes the unjustness of a world in which some people live more precarious lives than others due to social inequities—she is nevertheless adamant that when it comes to severe traumatization, Butler's work leads to theoretical dead-ends—throwing out the baby with the bath water, so to speak. In addition to deligitimating autonomy as a possibility, she argues that Butler errs, too, by pushing the notion of self-responsibility so far "that she finds it difficult to condemn those who inflict harm on others." Instead, Mari notes, Butler "adopts Levinas's somewhat problematic notion that we are irrevocably responsible for the other regardless of how the other behaves." She argues that in using psychoanalytic concepts that delineate the unconscious underpinnings of human behavior, Butler ends up adopting a morally relativistic position about victim and perpetrator, and thus endorsing "an ethics of leniency" when it comes to addressing violent acts. Mari argues for a space in which autonomy and rationality are juxtaposed, and she reaches toward the argument that recollection and memorialization are both socially and ethically necessary to the healing process:

> [T]here is also a great deal to be said for the idea that the commemoration of collective traumas—through public acts of grieving, official apologies and attempts at restoration, museums, monuments, and various artistic interventions, and so on—is both ethically necessary and socially curative.

In chapter 2, I explore the obstacles to critical trauma work that might lead to the possibility of recuperating and working with dangerous memory in the interests of promoting personal and political freedom. I begin the paper with a discussion of the dominance of reductionist and medicalized notions of post-traumatic stress disorder (PTSD). The conundrum is that while PTSD has gained tremendous purchase as what Fassin and Rechtman call "the language of the event," the prevailing narrow definition of trauma is highly limiting as a trope for human suffering, and shapes discursive understandings of trauma and violence—and even human subjectivity—in limiting and reactionary ways. In this section of the chapter, I also explore the absence of the unconscious in trauma discourse. A focus on symptoms (e.g., PTSD) and symptom removal through interventionist therapies, such as cognitive behavioral therapy (CBT), has led to the disappearance of the unconscious from contemporary discourses of trauma. Using Ruth Leys' genealogical work on trauma, I explore how trauma has shifted from an internal process to an emphasis on external events and the traces they leave on the psyche, and more recently, through the study of epigenetics, to traces left on the body itself.

Next I offer a critical exploration of the history of psychoanalysis, focusing particularly on the departure of contemporary psychoanalysis from its roots in radical social action in Freud's Vienna to become the bourgeois psychoanalysis that is dominant today—a psychoanalysis that risks defining human subjectivity in essentialist ways and that dovetails all too well with operational definitions of trauma that are symptom-focused or, at best, intrapsychic. Countering this trend, I present the work of El Salvadorean psychologist and priest Ignacio Martín Baró. Martín Baró was assassinated by the military junta due to the principled stand he took for his beliefs. He was clear that psychology had an obligation to recuperate dangerous memory:

> Martín Baró (1994) recognizes ahistoricism and individualism as significant faults in contemporary psychology (pp. 22–23) and he argues for a psychology that focuses on the recovery of memory: "Thus, the recovery of a historical memory supposes the reconstruction of models of identification that, instead of chaining and caging the people, open up the horizon for them, toward their liberation and fulfillment" (p. 30). He speaks of ways in which mass media and the state apparatus obfuscate the working of ideology, and he points to the need for facilitators who can de-ideologize everyday experience so that it can be exposed to scrutiny. He says each person needs "to say the word of one's own existence" (p. 40) and, following Freire, he suggests that "[t]hrough the

> gradual decoding of their world, people grasp the mechanisms of oppression and dehumanization." "This," Martín Baró says, "crumbles the consciousness that mythifies the situation as natural, and opens up the horizon to new possibilities for action" (p. 40). What is crucial here, and this is most relevant to any discussion of the possibilities of liberatory psychoanalysis as Erich Fromm and others understood, is that the intrapsychic feelings of the individual are understood within the context of sociohistorical circumstance, as opposed to in isolation from the social.

Then, drawing on Davoine and Gaudillière's *History beyond trauma*, I explore the possibility of developing a psychoanalysis that is focused not on narrative recuperation, but on developing an attuned capability to listening to the historical silences and ruptures in discourse so that the unspoken past may be rendered present. Borrowing the metaphor of analyst, as annalist, I note that "[t]he role of the analyst as *annalist*, therefore, refers to the role of the analyst as recuperator of memory and history, 'the chronicler who keeps the records of a gesture that has been silenced'" (p. 28). This leads to an attunement with buried signifiers or "fossil messages" in the life of the trauma sufferer:

> This "meeting" in the presence of a sensitive analyst, attuned to "fossil messages" in the being of the patient, eventually leads to the possibility of finding tattered remnants of those severed social links and stitching together a patch in the ruptured narrative of a person or community of people.

In the concluding section of the chapter I begin with an exploration of moral genealogy, drawing on Fassin and Rechtman's discussion of the effects on subjectivity when all of trauma is reduced to a mere mark on the body or on the psyche, and I conclude, following Agamben and Margalit, with the possibility of moral witness as a potentially liberatory path toward engaging in the kind of work around dangerous memory that might render us fully human.

Angie Voela, author of chapter 3, takes as her entry point, a painting by Barbara Loftus, *Hildegard under the Table,* part of a series of artworks inspired by Loftus's mother Hildegard, who fled from Nazi Germany to England as a refugee. Using her discomfiture with her own personal pleasurable associations to the painting, while simultaneously aware of the connection of the work to Holocaust trauma, Angie begins to interrogate the uses of art to evoke and work through traumatic memory. She draws on the work of Bracha Ettinger to offer a theory of subjective response to trauma that is much more expansive and cocreated than conventional trauma theory, and, that, in its reliance on Ettinger's matrixial borderspace and theory of transsubjectivity rather than Lacan's phallic theory, offers a very different kind of space for engaging with places, spaces, and chronologies of memory:

> An encounter with Hildegard's childhood brings up a host of theoretical concerns regarding memory, truth, subjectivity and spectatorship. For instance, how does a narration of events turn into a visualisation of spaces? What is the value of that product? Whose truth does it speak? If it is not a "real" piece of the past and therefore of historical-archival interest, how does it operate as a commemoration of an event like the Holocaust?

Using Pierre Nora's concept *lieux de mémoires* (sites of memory), Angie speaks of the power of art to create evocative memorial spaces where the memories of past traumas can be evoked, once a point in time is reached when literal memories and actual witnesses to those traumas are no longer available to provide testimony to the actual events. She suggests that Barbara Loftus's works are *lieux de mémoires* because, instead of attempting to provide literal representations of events, they are works that offer a sense of nonplace and nonbelonging, thus preventing the viewer from reaching for literal narrative allusions, and instead developing a receptivity to knowledge that makes its presence felt *après coup*:

> The same applies to the artist's treatment of time and place: the interiors Loftus envisages *too late* are situated at a time *before* the big historical event and form an imaginary past of a past, useless to the historian but no less true and traumatic. The interiors are hers and her mother's; witnessing scenes that might not have been witnessed by Hildegard; events related to them—the confiscation of valuables—have been narrated, but that is the only fact we can verify; the paintings announce an event yet to come, too early too late, leaving the house, the latter to become a site of loss, of property and then of life. These simultaneities of places and times, suggest that between the viewer, the artist and the work we may need to situate a revised and much more "generous" and "inclusive" conceptualisation of the Real.

Angie argues that works like this allow for a poetic reworking of traumatic memory and this is where she draws on Bracha Ettinger's notion of co-constructed meaning and transsubjectivity to articulate a theory of memory that illustrates why works like those produced by Barbara Loftus have the potential to reclaim memory and to create an address to trauma. Before moving on to explicate Ettinger's theory and contrast it to Lacan's, Angie offers a pointed critique of a host of problems associated with the commodification of "trauma," the simplistic, instrumental binaries that have arisen with the popularization of trauma as a concept, and so on:

> At the same time, various concerns are raised in the field of cultural studies: about the transcendentalisation of trauma and the loss of its historical specificity when turned into "trauma for all" (Mowitt, 2007); about the contemporary glut of information surrounding the Holocaust which triggers a surge of derivate

> mental images (Baer, 2000, p. 44); about the sensualisation of the other's pain which preys on the conflation of testimony and confession (Modlinger and Sonntag, 2011); about the dark glamour of trauma, the limits of empathy and the disavowal of the victim in the act of identification or in the language of sympathy (Modlinger, 2011); about the near-impossibility of giving an account of oneself, let alone telling the other's story (Davis, 2011). Radstone highlights the oxymoronic popularity of trauma today and critiques the Manichean binaries of "inside" and "outside," "trauma" and "normality," "victims" and "perpetrators" (2007, p. 19) currently favoured in the field of Trauma Studies. She finds that the topological "flattening out" of the psyche blunts the distinction between intrapsychic and inter-subjective processes (2007, p. 20). Radstone emphasises the unconscious processes in the production of mind's scenes and meaning, drawing attention to the activities of condensation, displacement and symbolization fundamental to the Freudian model (2007, p. 18). She also recommends admitting into the reckoning "the darker side of the mind," such as sexual phantasies, that trauma theory usually sees only as coming from outside. (2007, p. 19)

In the remainder of the chapter, Angie explores facets of Ettinger's theory in detail, exploring the matrixial borderspace, metramorphosis, transsubjectivity, and the important idea that the knowledge we construct, for instance, in responding to a work of art, is constructed as a form of *co-naissance* because of the trans-subjective nature of our being as *partial subjects*. She concludes by exploring points of correspondence between Lacanian theory and Ettinger's work, which seeks to articulate a new epistemophilic openness.

Minh Truong-George is an ethnically Chinese person who was born in Vietnam, and who had to flee from there during a Communist purge in the 1970s. She and her family made a perilous voyage to a refugee camp in Malaysia, and, a year later, she was part of the first wave of "boat people" to arrive in New Zealand, where she practices therapy today. More than thirty years later, feeling a strong urge to reconnect with her roots, Minh decided to visit Malaysia and Vietnam with her brother and a friend to seek some answers. In chapter 4, Minh invites us along for the journey and allows us to bear witness as her imaginings of her childhood, and her longing for a homeland, come face-to-face with the realities of Malaysia and Vietnam today, and face-to-face too, with the flood of memories and emotions that the return triggers for her. The account gains depth and complexity due to Minh's training both in psychotherapy and in Buddhist teachings. Minh takes us to the stretch of beach in Malaysia where she landed—a beach now covered in tourist cabins—hoping to find remnants of the beached fishing boat on which she journeyed. What she did experience, much to her surprise, was a return of her eight-year-old self, with its accompanying emotions: "It was a palpable moment as my guide and friend fell into silence with me, and, almost ghost-like, I felt with relief the child and her sadness melding into me." As she began speaking with locals, Minh experienced extreme confusion and rage, because, instead of offering a narrative of the boat's arrival that would flesh out her memories, she was surrounded by a cacophony of voices, all proffering different truths about the event.

Reentering Vietnam provoked a roller coaster of emotions in Minh, as she tried to stitch herself into a narrative and a streetscape that was truly hers yet was also truly alien. Minh was overcome with an extraordinary desire to revisit her childhood home, yet she felt a tremendous sense of trepidation, sparked by her father's warnings against exhuming troubled memories, and also by the skepticism of the woman who controlled access to the house:

> At first she tried to talk me out of it, but eventually she found a key, and with terror pounding in my ears I was able to step inside my childhood home for the first time in 35 years. I had an out of body experience in which I was aware of my voice telling me to breathe deeply and to stay open to the experience. Everything seemed so much smaller, and the house was narrower than I had remembered. As I walked towards the back I recognised the kitchen, and with it the water-well making gentle lapping noises. My tears flowed as I was reminded of the nightly sounds the water-well used to make. I remembered instantly how it used to soothe my sadness and fear of not knowing where my father was, and how it used to lull me to sleep. Seeing my tears, the woman who let me in asked whether I was feeling sad, not realising the indebtedness I felt to her for the opportunity to know whether what I remembered was real. It felt as if I had entered a forgotten place inside my heart and body that I had not known existed, and drank deeply from its well. Reentering the physical space of my childhood has also enabled the unlocking of a forbidden space in the psyche of my family.

In the remainder of the chapter, Minh gives a phenomenologically near description of the return of her traumatic memories, and she describes the spiritual struggle that ensued as she wrestled with these spectral memories, as well as with disapproval from some family members and friends who pressed her to leave the past buried: "'You shouldn't have gone back to Vietnam and stirred all of that up' or 'They went back last year and they didn't suffer from PTSD' or even 'I thought all of your training as a psychotherapist would have helped you instead of making you worse.'" Minh explores her struggle with these traumatic memories and explains how her understanding of the Four Noble Truths finally led her on a path toward healing through embracing rather than fleeing from her painful losses.

Norma Tracey is the head of Gunawirra (Gunawirra.org.au), an organization that provides services for Aboriginal mothers and children in New South Wales, Australia. In chapter 5 she partners with Aboriginal artist Graham Toomey (grahamtoomey.com) to explore healing processes for Aboriginal people. Graham showed up at Gunawirra seeking employment as a part-time bus driver to support himself through school as an adult student. He has since become an established Aboriginal artist and a key contributor to the healing work pursued by Gunawirra. Cate Osborn's chapter in the accompanying volume (Osborne, 2014) provides some details of the critical importance of Graham's work in assisting Aboriginal mothers in expressing their feelings, hopes, and suffering. This chapter is composed partly of Graham's story, spoken in his own words, and partly of Norma's contextualization of the healing process for Aboriginal families—a process that can be understood in terms of a combination of Aboriginal healing practices and psychoanalytic understandings of psychic suffering. Norma begins by summing up the appalling collective trauma to which Aboriginal people have been subjected:

> With the new colonial settlement of Australia came not only physical disease but a serious uprooting of all that was familiar for the Aboriginal people. It was a violent, annihilating situation ending in total subjugation of a proud nomadic people with their spirituality, their intrinsic connection to earth and nature, and their survival of 40,000 to 80,000 years. With the coming of early "whites," Aboriginal people were moved off their sacred land, dispersed from their normal communal life, robbed of their hunting grounds, and left dependant on the white man for their daily subsistence. Through the claims of a law, called *Terra Nullius*, or land belonging to no one, they were denied existence as a people. Then they had their children born of white men taken from them and given to white families as a matter of law. The damage caused by this flowed down through the generations.

Norma notes that "recovery" for Aboriginal people requires

> finding their spiritual roots through the aesthetic, not as an expression of the old world but as part of finding a new way of being that has their "old" soul in it. The sounds through music, the sight through art, the experience through drama and literature, all resonate with the pain of others to create a universally shared empathic witnessing, not only for this ancient race, but as a template of what can happen to any traumatised people.

Graham, Norma notes, considers himself "a seeker in a spiritual sense." Born of a white mother and an Aboriginal father, Graham's parents separated when he was just five, and although he had some contact with his father during his childhood years, Graham now recognizes that he was raised in what Australians call whitefella's ways for the first thirty years of his life. He had no concept of himself as an Aboriginal man. Here is a brief extract from Graham's poignant narrative:

> I grew up in a time where Aboriginal people were seen as rubbish, as vermin, as a nothing. I think we were so ashamed and afraid, terrified to speak up, to have a voice, that we accepted that we were nothing people. My grandmother was part of the *stolen generation*. We were instructed by our parents to be

> afraid—just don't say too much because they are fearful of the response. Things will get back to the welfare or the police. They were pretty mixed up themselves because it's been generation after generation where you are told not to speak up, not to be heard, because of the fear of reprisals. Well my father didn't really come across much of that. When he was 14 he went and started work but his mother and father, they would have grown up with a sense of terror. They were moved on from place to place. They started in Nyngan and were forced down the Bogan river to different reserves until they reached a place called Albert. This was a really little place back in the 1920s. Albert was where my dad was born in a tin shack on the Bogan River. Some years later my people were forced to move to Dandaloo and then eventually into a house in Trangie, Narromine. It was where I was born because Trangie did not have the proper medical services to deliver children. They were moved on from place to place. They started in Nyngan and were shuffled down the river to different reserves until they reached a place called Albert. This was a really little place back in the 1920s. Dandaloo in Trangie, Narromine, really little places on the rivers in the reserves. My mother's family came from Pilliga forest around Mudgee. They were a mixture of Irish and English families. They were very hard people and my mother doesn't talk very much about it, but they were very hard and that is how they had to grow up there. There was love there but it was nothing like the Aboriginal side and it was very different. From when I was 6 or 7 I just didn't ever have a dad around, and now I look back and I see there was no encouragement, no guidance—those valuable things you look to from a father like "Good onya son!" I was only able to go home to my dad on weekends once a fortnight. I kind of lost touch with my father's community in the end, and I was left to just make up my own mind. I could see them with my own eyes walking around the street. I didn't see them as bad because of the fighting. Mostly that was because they just were drinking all the time, not doing anything with their lives, just sitting around. I understand now that it was a bit of a statement, in a way, that they didn't belong. They had nowhere to go. Maybe some tried to get work but the white people took one look, saw they were Aboriginal, and wouldn't give them any work. It was a terrible history. Actually people were scared to employ Aboriginal people because there was so much prejudice that they feared people wouldn't go to them because they employed Aboriginals.

After Graham's moving narrative, Norma explores Aboriginal concepts, such as *Dadirri* and *The Dreaming*, as well as western psychoanalytic concepts, to illuminate both the terrible injury that has been done to Aboriginal people, as well as healing paths that are respectful, that honor ancestry and the land, and that allow Aboriginal people to chart meaningful futures.

Nigel Williams (chapter 6) brings his considerable skills in psychosocial studies and autoethnography to bear in studying the acute crisis produced for the German diaspora in Britain by the onset of World War I. His goal, as he notes, is to "focus on the role of memory, its erasure, and the construction of post-traumatic narratives of identity." There had been a significant German presence in Britain since the Edwardian period, and the decimation of this population was as intentional as it was catastrophic:

> How many Germans were affected? No one really knows as migration had been essentially unregulated since the start of the German royal lines in Britain, but estimates vary somewhere between 30,000 and 50,000. Some, including my direct family, managed to hide. Most could not. This largely invisible and unacknowledged ethnic cleansing has had, and continues to have, consequences in our world today.

Nigel offers a multilevel account of the events leading up to the ethnic cleansing, culminating in the internment of many Germans in a wave of xenophobia as World War I broke out, and to its long-term traumatic consequences. One strand of his account is academic in tone, weaving together historical details and concepts from psychoanalysis and from intergenerational trauma theory to document the psychic consequences of the dislocations. Simultaneously, Nigel pursues archival research into his own family's German origins. Nigel's tracing of the movements of family members, the changes in family names as the pressure to anglicize increased, and the discovery of a lost strand of his family line, makes for compelling reading and adds immeasurably to the illustrative power of his argument about trauma, memory, and erasure. The significance of this multidisciplinary work cannot be understated, and Nigel, perhaps, sums it up best:

> Do I feel different as a result of a decade of research and inquiry? If anyone had told me before any of this broke into my consciousness that I would be working at migrant identities and their implications for relations between nations I would have said no, I am a psychotherapist, I do not do the social, it is too ephemeral. Now I feel enormously increased by it. There seems to be more of me, and I have met many new people. More than anything else I have become more confident that if I look steadily at this new field it will gradually be possible to do what Norbert Elias (1978) in *The Civilising Process* proposed, which is to establish a practice for and sensibility of the long term, so that the complex histories that make up our conflicted migratory and war torn planet can be acknowledged as the seed for conflict resolution in neighbourhoods, nations and between nations. Norbert Elias' sociology is an intergenerational project, an evolving commitment to understand and develop practices both now and in the future that counter splitting and non-connectivity.
>
> Of course I would be the first in the queue to tell me that this idea is largely illusory and grandiose, but even to have the wish is an achievement and reconnects with my ancestors' conviction that a different and radically better life was possible. I think that tackling intergenerational dynamics in this way has to be in the spirit that the world itself is redeemable, and that the biggest and most profound problems can be solved. The contribution that an understanding of

intergenerational dynamics might make is that each person's and each group's past interacts with and in some way articulates contemporary problems. Every attempt at conflict resolution, or, in the therapeutic arena, any attempt to work through a problem, brings pressing opportunities to heal old hurts as well as current ones. Mourning loss is all well and good, but one person's mourning is another's loss and oppression, when it comes to war, civil conflict and ethnic cleansing. Care over the detail helps a lot; in fact it is the difference between solution and repetition. But first we have to have the courage to look and continue looking; we have to think it is worth it.

Nirit Gradwohl Pisano completed her doctoral dissertation on the effects of the Holocaust on third-generation descendants, under my direction, and she subsequently published her research as a book, *Granddaughters of the Holocaust* (Pisano, 2012). The case study presented in chapter 7 is drawn from this work. Nirit begins with a review of relevant issues from Holocaust studies and particularly from research in intergenerational effects of the Holocaust and other catastrophic events, posing the question: "Can future generations heal the pain of a past they did not personally endure?" She explores processes by which mourning is foreclosed and how history may be unconsciously reenacted by future generations. Drawing on Louise Kaplan and Judith Kestenberg, she focuses particularly on processes of transposition—those processes by which the child unconsciously takes up the unspoken or unspeakable emotions of the parent(s) and absorbs them. Difficulties in a parent's capacity for empathic attunement can cause the child to become excessively attuned to these parental gaps and lead the child to absorb unsymbolized parental trauma.

Applying these concepts to a particular narrative, Nirit describes the case of Leah, a child whose grandparents had experienced unspeakable trauma:

> I know that my grandparents . . . they had a five-year-old son and he was shot on the street by a Nazi soldier in front of my grandmother. My mom wasn't born yet . . . this would've been my mom's brother . . . my mom wasn't born, she never met him . . . so he was killed when he was five and my grandparents were both taken . . . they were already married and had a family . . . they were both taken to Auschwitz, separated, lost each other, and ended up finding each other afterwards.

Nirit offers a fine-grained analysis of Leah's character and probes for evidence of the ways in which her particular obsessions and defenses offer evidence for a lineage descending from the losses her grandparents experienced. Consider, for example, this description and analysis of Leah's aunt (her father's brother), who resided with her survivor parents until their death:

"Oh, I mean like crazy. . . . She hadn't been taking her medications; she had been eating all the wrong things. Like, there was old food thrown around the house. It reeked when my parents first got there. They found something like over $20 in change just in one day strewn about the house. She had bags and bags of, for instance, leather gloves that she had bought, never opened, never worn. She had an entire bag of different pairs of silver earrings. . . . As if you were going out and you wanted a pair of silver hoop earrings so you bought every one you could find and figured you could decide later and return them, and she just never returned them. She never cleaned out the house from her parents' stuff, but after my grandfather passed away she moved out of her bedroom into what was their master bedroom, but she so cluttered her own bedroom that they couldn't even open the door. She would go on like business trips and she wouldn't unpack her suitcase when she came home, so she just went and bought another suitcase and packed it with new clothes. She had dozens of packed suitcases with the tags still on them so my parents could tell where she'd been and where she'd gone."

Clearly, this daughter of Holocaust survivors spent a lifetime mired in the internal devastation of her parents' experience. Never having found a place within language, her family's unmourned suffering flooded her post-Holocaust life. One can only fantasize about the significance of silver hoop earrings and leather gloves; do such accessories represent fragments of knowledge, in an existence that unfolds outside of language? What of the numerous packed suitcases, which suggest a preparedness to flee yet an inability to truly escape one's baggage? "She just never returned them," Leah says of the earrings, speaking volumes about her aunt's incapacity to "return" and rework the original trauma.

Justina Kaminskaitė Dillon, a doctoral candidate at Adelphi University, is a recent migrant from Lithuania, and her dissertation research, directed by Michael O'Loughlin, brings her back to her home country to investigate the life narratives of Lithuanian women who were deported to Siberia during the Stalinist period of Soviet occupation. In chapter 8, Justina and Michael lay out the background this way:

The Soviet Union invaded Lithuania in 1939. The occupation was accompanied by a crackdown on dissent and decimation of the Lithuanian elite. People who belonged to banned "anti-Soviet" organizations or had been employed in "undesirable" positions (e.g., leadership roles in the former judicial system, government, etc.) were secretly placed on lists of people seen as objectionable. Soviet law also recognized collective responsibility for illegal activity, which meant that family members of an offender were considered equally guilty (Anušauskas, 1996). By June 1941, the NKVD (Soviet police) and NKGB (Soviet secret police and intelligence) had registered thousands of "undesirable elements of society" and their families. On June 14, in the middle of the night, NKVD operatives burst into the homes of people to be deported and informed the families that they were being moved to other parts of the Soviet Union. Often the operatives would not allow the families to pack even the most essential items. Anybody who tried to escape was shot (Anušauskas, 1996). Under the two Soviet occupations of Lithuania (1940–1941 and 1944–1990), one in six Lithuanians, a total of 456,000 people, experienced some kind of repression, including imprisonment, deportations, and killings (Anušauskas, 1996; Vardys & Sedaitis, 1997). A total of 132,000 Lithuanians (not including political or criminal prisoners), 70 percent of them women and children, were forcibly deported to Siberia, the Arctic Circle, and Central Asia (Kuodytė & Tracevskis, 2004). During the deportation of 1941, the men were immediately separated from their families and dispatched to the Gulag to replenish the free labor force there. The majority of women, children, and elderly persons were transported to the Altai mountain region, in the west of present-day Mongolia. The trip, in cramped cattle cars, similar to those used for Holocaust transport, took weeks. There was not enough water and food, and the deportees struggled to breathe in the overheated, fully enclosed cars. Upon arrival at labor camps, the deportees had any valuables confiscated, were settled in uninsulated wooden barracks—usually several families per room—and employed in timber harvest, salt mining, brick production, and other labor-intensive industries. For their labor, the deportees were given fourteen ounces of white bread per day, but even that was not guaranteed. Children, elderly persons, and sick persons were allocated six ounces of bread per day. The living conditions were highly unsanitary and unfit for the cold winters of the Altai mountains, during which the temperatures reached as low as −76°F and featured heavy snowstorms (Anušauskas, 1996; *Encyclopedia Britannica*, 2013). More than half of the deportees died during the trip or shortly after arrival (Kuodytė & Tracevskis, 2004).

In the summer of 1942, almost half of the Lithuanian deportees from the Altai region were uprooted again and transported to the Arctic regions in the general Yakutsk area, about 2000 miles further north (Anušauskas, 1996). According to the survivor Dalia Grinkevičiūtė, "They transported us at a time when we were just getting used to the climate and conditions of the new place, and after we had traded our belongings for potatoes, planted gardens, and the potatoes were just starting to bloom, giving us hope that next winter we would not have to starve. (1990, p. 2)."

After a grueling trip of about three months in crammed train cars, trucks, and barges, the deportees were dropped off on uninhabited islands in the Arctic Circle by the Laptev Sea.

Only a handful of the deportees were able to return to Lithuania after Stalin's death, and even then they were not greeted with open arms by the Soviet government that deported them in the first place. In the eyes of the government, they and their families were viewed as "bandits," even though most of the survivors had been children at the time of deportation. They were barred from education, jobs, and housing. Many found their homes destroyed or confiscated. Settling down was a struggle the survivors had not anticipated when contemplating the return to their longed-for land. Until Lithuanian Independence in 1990, survivors were forced to hide their traumatic histories, and now, many feel that the younger generation no longer cares to listen (J. Puodžius, personal communication, January, 2013).

To begin her investigation, Justina spent the summer of 2013 in Lithuania and engaged in lengthy life-history interviews with eight women survivors of the deportations, who had been taken from Lithuania as children. For the purposes of this chapter, our presentation focuses on a detailed account of the narrative of one of those survivors. Justina documents the normality of Janina's middle-class life as a child, the seizure of her family, the dispatch of her father to certain death, and the deportation of herself, her mother, and her brother, first to the Altai region, and then to the far north of Siberia (by the Laptev Sea). The depths of the privation and suffering beggar description. At first, Janina, her family, and a couple of other families lived in a tiny yurt that was made of moss, with ice in place of a window. She describes their living conditions:

> Ice yurt with ice walls with one burning thread [candle wick]. . . . I, for example, lie between brother and mommy, let's say, on one side—35 centimeters belong to me. I lie on sticks which are not icy on top, but there is ice at the bottom. My head is by black ice. It's –4°C (24.8°F) inside, without a blanket. But mommy because she could no longer walk, they let her mend fishermen's nets. So, she stole piece after piece, piece after piece, piece after piece, piece after piece: stole, stole, stole . . . and made this little ball. . . . I was the only one who had a pillow under my head under my ear on those sticks that softness. They put their heads directly on those sticks.

As in so many survivor stories, amid appalling deprivation there was evidence of resilience and apparently a will to survive as homage to her mother's fortitude:

> Each person had a quota of bread that they could buy every day. Janina's family, like most others, did not have enough money to buy the full quota, which was a few slices per day. And even when they had saved up and could buy a piece of bread, the process was not simple. They would have to line up by the bakery two hours before work and stand in the wind and the blizzards waiting for the few slices of bread. As a result of starvation, grueling work, and inadequate clothing, people died every day. The deaths of Janina's colleagues and friends were a daily experience: "[During that] very first, very deathly, first period full of horror, [that] very frost . . . and from my children's work brigade a portion died. One already does not arrive in the morning, so you don't know if he is unable to get up, if he is already pulled out onto the snow lying outside, because there was no funeral. Then everyone floated away with those ice floes in 1943 and it is not clear. And maybe, maybe those feral foxes, maybe, gnawed them up. On one of the islands . . . one Russian used to chop those frozen dead into traps for those white foxes."
>
> Janina emphasized that her mother tried to ensure that her daughter was sheltered from the horrors surrounding them. Thus, Janina felt that she was able to remain a child until her mother died: "I was no longer shy only when

> mommy died. . . . Mommy had said . . . either alive here or dead, whoever dies first, but that my brother and I would not be burdened by figuring out how to get that piece of bread, when to eat it. . . . And she said, already in the Arctic, she said "When I die, that will be time enough to grow up." And we struggled, worked [despite] deadly exhaustion, but my brother and I—when mommy died, I know, we were watching a pot and asking each other how to know that water is boiling. . . . We used to be protected by that invisible care, that concern."
>
> For Janina and her brother, the death of their mother signified the end of their childhood, and the heartache from this point in her life remains with Janina till this day. In 1989, Janina was able to go back to the Arctic and retrieve her mother's remains. She was quite surprised that eight men, warmly clothed and well-fed, struggled to dig out her mother's grave in the summer. She understood that her brother had carved the grave out of ice in the winter with a "bleeding soul, with bleeding hands, with . . . a bleeding heart . . . in a horrible hopelessness, in the black night." When she returned, she found her mother completely preserved in her icy grave just as she used to be: "That's why I found mommy—my frozen beautiful young mom."

As this work is in its early stages, no definite conclusions are offered, but we conclude the chapter by examining questions about the erasure and recuperation of memory posed by Janina's story. These are exquisitely complex questions: The returnees returned to a Sovietized society with all of the cultural connotations associated with that ideology. It was also a society in which they were received with great ambivalence, and it is also a society where, since renewed independence in 1990, the possibility of speaking these truths activates a whole new round of memory suppression. This, and all the connotations of the intergenerational transmission of individual and communal trauma, make for a rich, complex and deeply layered story of the intersection of trauma, history, and memory—a story that surely needs to be exhumed for all East European post-Soviet countries. Lithuania's story is merely the tip of this iceberg of post-Soviet traumatic residue and erased memory.

Hannah Hahn, a granddaughter of immigrants from Eastern Europe who fled during the great migration wave of 1880–1924, begins chapter 9 on a note of regret, recalling her incomprehension during her childhood of the odd ways of her East European Jewish grandparents. It is clearly no coincidence, then, that Hannah has set out on a quest to understand the experiences of loss surrounding this great migration. Hannah balances a careful discussion of mechanisms of intergenerational transmission among this Jewish disapora, with discussion of the profound dislocative effects of forced migration. As Hannah notes, this was no ordinary migration. Poverty, anti-Semitism, and pogroms created a climate of extreme violence for East European Jews in the late nineteenth century, a time when fully one-third of East European Jews fled:

> In this atmosphere of economic uncertainty, the Russian government allowed, or perhaps instigated, attacks on the Jewish community (Epstein, 2007, pp. 3–4). Russian soldiers passing through a town would randomly seize, rape, or kill young Jewish women. Jewish boys were subject to conscription, sometimes as young as age eight. After the assassination of Tsar Alexander II in 1881, discrimination and violence towards Jews worsened, and organized pogroms began. Pogroms were widespread between 1881 and 1906; in 1881 alone 20,000 Jewish homes were demolished (Epstein, 2007, p. 9; Dawidowicz, 1984, p. 13). Furthermore, in 1881, Alexander III, who hated the Jews, instituted the "May Laws," which attempted to destroy the Jews' shtetl way of life by forbidding Jews to live in towns of populations under 10,000. Jewish access to higher education was greatly restricted (Epstein, 2007, p. 11), and various edicts were passed restricting the ability of Jews to earn a living.

Hannah's chapter recounts the experience of the children of such immigrants, based on in-depth psychosocial interviews. Their stories are suffused with both the losses of migration and the losses experienced through persecution, poverty, and in many cases, surviving the Russian Revolution or World War I. In terms of the rich material Hannah uncovers and interprets, consider just the issue of how much parents shared with their children of their own history and suffering. First, Jacob:

> Jacob, a highly intelligent and curious scientist, said, "They told us kids nothing. They wanted to make a marked transition to the U.S. and dump all that stuff. We're here. Let's forget that." Jacob knew only a few details about his family's life in Europe and was unable to speculate about his parents' psychological transition to the U.S. He conveyed to me that, for his family, survival was paramount, and, consequently, there was no room for thoughts of happiness.

And then, Rose:

> Rose, an astute professional woman in her 60's, seemed overwhelmed by her parents' massive sense of loss and trauma, and she felt that her parents communicated in opposite manners about their pasts. Rose's mother, Leah, spoke in detail and repetitively about her own mother's frightening experiences during World War I. When displaced with her young children, including Leah, she courageously chose living with them in an isolated barn rather than living with sick families. In contrast, Rose's father never once spoke of his experiences. As a teen-ager, Rose begged her father to tell her at least one story; he told her about a recurrent traumatic experience from his childhood. Each day when he and the other Jewish boys from his village walked to school, they formed a circle with one boy walking inside the circle. They were stoned by gentile boys, but the boy in the middle was protected from stoning. Rose sensed that this was probably the least troubling of the experiences her father might have told her.

And, Elaine:

> Elaine's mother, at the opposite end of the continuum from Jacob's father, spoke a great deal about the family she had left behind in Europe. Like Rose's mother, she spoke in detail about the past. In fact, she flooded Elaine with her story of loneliness and trauma. Another similarity was Elaine's father's silence about much of his past. . . . Elaine's mother also told her about her father's early death from cancer and about the anti-Semitic violence, including a pogrom, which took place in her mother's small city. She made clear to Elaine its traumatic impact on her, emphasizing her hate for everything Polish. Elaine felt this hate deeply. Significantly, the dreadful feelings of loss and emptiness which Elaine's mother experienced during her early years in New York may have been worsened because of the effects of the accumulation of everything that had happened to her before her arrival.

In the concluding section of her chapter, Hannah offers a detailed analysis of interviews she conducted with two of the women she interviewed and concludes by again weaving this important narrative analysis with her own personal story:

> This concept of necessary loss reminds me of a memory my grandfather related to my father. As my grandfather was departing from his very poor Galician village, thinking that he would never again see his parents or his remaining siblings, *his* father accompanied him for part of the journey. His father said, "If you remain here, you will not be a human being." My great-grandfather meant that emigration was a necessity because in Galicia there was no way for my grandfather to make a living. Without that, my grandfather would be, in effect, less than human. Thus my grandfather's loss of his family, and his father's loss of a son, was necessary for economic survival. Indeed, though no one knew it at the time, this loss was necessary for my grandfather's physical survival. Those family members who remained were killed in the Holocaust. Thus this loss was profoundly ambiguous for the family.

In chapter 10, Clara Valverde and Luis Martin-Cabrera address the transgenerational consequences of the Francoist dictatorship for contemporary Spain. They begin with a statement of the appalling state of memory in Spain today:

> Unlike other countries in the world that went through similar social traumas such as Chile, Argentina, El Salvador, or South Africa to name a few, in Spain there are no truth commissions, no trials for perpetrators of human rights abuses, and very little State sponsored memorial sites or reparatory justice measures of any kind. As we will explain below in detail, the structure of power established during the forty years of the dictatorship (1939–1975) has remained intact. For instance, in Spain the State has abdicated its responsibility to exhume the bodies of those who were executed during the war and its aftermath.

Clara and Luis divide their chapter into three parts: the first focusing on the Spanish Civil War as a sociohistoric trauma; the second is a detailed exploration of unprocessed trauma based on interviews with third-generation survivors; and the final part offers a look at movements in Spain seeking to create reparative opportunities by restoring links to lost memory thereby disrupting the apparent perpetual reenactment of trauma. The story begins with the declaration of the Second Spanish Republic in 1931 and a brief period of unprecedented liberal opening. This was followed by forty years of the brutal Francoist dictatorship, a government, Clara and Luis argue, that was modeled on a marriage of Spanish colonial technique and the principles of fascism. The list of violations is appalling, including arbitrary detentions; "disappearance" of dissidents; forced labor; abduction of children who were then raised by supporters of the regime; torture; censorship, and the kind of "social death" that froze all suspected opponents of the regime out of public life and career advancement. Drawing on intergenerational trauma theorists, Abraham and Torok, Clara and Luis offer an analysis of the kinds of intergenerational symptoms that might be expected from survivors of such a regime who were never provided opportunities to process their experiences. The authors close the first section by noting that in 1997, the new "democratic" government passed a law "explicitly prohibiting the opening of legal prosecution against those responsible for human rights violations and crimes against humanity." The government, in effect, blessed a policy of amnesia. Even the "so-called Law of historical memory, approved in 2007 during the government of José Luis Rodríguez Zapatero . . . is the first explicit recognition of this traumatic past on the part of the State, it is also, in many ways, a law that perpetuates impunity and oblivion in Spain." All of the movements for the exhumation of mass graves and organizations that are seeking to recuperate historical memory, restore "the disappeared," and provide opportunities to process frozen grief, are civic associations, not official government bodies.

The authors note that a recent presentation by Clara on transgenerational consequences of political violence in Spain was received with gasps of surprise by the audience. The novelty of the work Clara and Luis are doing (and see also Scott Boehm's chapter in this volume) suggests that the importance of this work cannot be overstated. In the second part of the chapter Clara reports on interviews she has conducted with members of the third generation around issues of trauma and memory. Here are some brief illustrative highlights.

On the pervasive presence of anger:

> My father gets really angry and is violent. But he can't help it. He is very angry about what they did to his father during the war (first they imprisoned him, then they sent him by force to the front lines to fight on Franco's side always being

> watched and then they murdered him). My father gets out of control very easily. Well, I also have quite a temper and I can't control it either.

And another:

> It's become more obvious to me with time that I don't forgive those criminals (my uncle was killed in the war and my grandfather was murdered after) . . . it eats me up. I can't stop thinking about all that, with anger, with pain . . . now more than ever.

On pervasive fear about speaking out:

> My grandfather was executed at the end of the Civil War. My father was in prison during the Dictatorship. And my friends criticize me because I won't go to demonstrations with them. They say I am a chicken. . . . If they knew that what I have is not fear . . . it's panic!

On confusion caused by the inability to grieve due to a blanket of silence:

> My grandfather died when I was 6 years-old. Although I was little, I remember that each Christmas he would start crying and he would stay in bed. It did not seem like Christmas. I asked why he was crying and my mother would say that it was because of "those who are not here. No one explained to me who were those who were "not here" and why they were "not here." I don't know why, but I thought that it had something to do with those ghosts I thought were under my bed at night (although I always checked before going to bed. [NMN, male, 41 years old]

On blindness as somatic symptom:

> My mother (who did not wear glasses), once a year for a few days, she said that her eyes were blurry and she could not read. I checked out the dates and it always coincided with the date that her father was taken away during the war. I told her but she told me that my idea was ridiculous and that I paid too much attention to psychology. [ANT, female, sixty-two years old]

The authors conclude by examining stigmergic movements such as 15M, in Spain, and offer some thoughts as to what it will take to create a reparative movement that will finally lay the ghosts of the fascist era in Spain.

Eugene de Kock, who, as I write this, had his application for parole deferred pending consultation with families of his victims, was commander at Vlakplaas, a farm where a counterinsurgency unit of the Apartheid South African government that was essentially a hit squad, charged with eliminating enemies of the government, was based. Being the only relatively high official in the apartheid apparatus to be convicted of atrocities, de Kock has become an archetype of the evil that the apartheid government personified, and in so doing, has inevitably contributed to the reduction of the apartheid era to a simple binary of good and evil. Pumla Gobodo-Madikizela met with de Kock in prison for a series of interviews, and Ross Truscott, author of chapter 11, uses her book, *A Human Being Died That Night: A South African Story of Forgiveness* to trouble this binary and engage in an incisive examination of what he calls "a genealogy of post-apartheid empathy." He introduces the problematic of Gobodo-Madikizela's enterprise this way:

> De Kock was commanding officer at Vlakplaas—a farm outside Pretoria where, from the 1970s onwards, apartheid's counterinsurgency police unit interrogated, tortured and murdered anti-apartheid activists, frequently disposing of bodies by burning, burying or blowing them up—between 1985 and 1993. Gobodo-Madikizela, a clinical and academic psychologist, visited de Kock on behalf of the Truth and Reconciliation Commission of South Africa (TRC) in the Pretoria Central prison where he is currently serving two life sentences and 212 years. As one would expect, Gobodo-Madikizela expresses dread and anxiety over meeting de Kock, but in contrast to the media generated image of a cold hearted psychopath, she finds a vulnerable, remorseful man, a man suffering. "His world," she states, "was a cold world where eyes of death stared accusingly at him, a world littered with corpses and graves—graves of the unknown dead, dismembered or blown up bodies" (p. 47). Indeed, Gobodo-Madikizela finds a man with whom she—much to her horror—comes to identify and empathize. The identification between Gobodo-Madikizela and de Kock is set in motion, and plays itself out over an incident wherein she, moved by his vulnerability, touches his hand during an interview and encounters "a human being capable of feeling, crying and knowing pain." (p. 38)

Gobodo-Madikizela's work opens up the complex childhood of de Kock, postulating his barbaric behavior as a repetition; she demonstrates the power of the talking cure as de Kock gropes toward reconciliation; and through her portrayal of de Kock as a human being with feelings, she challenges the fundamental denial and splitting in South African society that allows people to project all of the evil of apartheid into de Kock thereby disavowing their own complicity, a posture that seems quite consistent with the official ideology of amnesia and reconciliation that the post-apartheid government has adopted.

Ross explores Gobodo-Madikizela's account of de Kock's childhood origins in some details, and while evincing some sympathy for the psychoanalytic explanation that difficulties and disappointments in de Kock's relationship with his father may have motivated his penchant for violence, he worries about the reductionism and depoliticized nature of such an argument:

> There is much to take issue with in this formulation, most notably, as I have already suggested, the risk of psychological reductionism, a risk Gobodo-Madikizela is not unaware of and yet one she takes. We might also say, in Gilles Deleuze's (2009) words on psychoanalysis on fascism, that, in reducing the cause of violence to the father, psychoanalysis has "crushed phenomena of desire on a familial stage, crushed the whole political and economic dimension of the libido" (p. 89). Let us try, then, to locate the violence of identification within a wider frame.

Drawing on Fuss's work on colonial identifications, as well as on Freud's and Butler's writings on loss, Ross draws the lens back further to look at the colonial inheritances that might have contributed to de Kock's subjectivity, and he explores, particularly, the role of heteronormativity and anxieties around masculinity as a motivating force in the desire to dominate and annihilate sexualized black male bodies. Certainly the ferocity of the attacks, reminiscent of the violence of lynching in the southern United States, as Ricardo Ainslie details in chapter 15 of this volume, suggests that some deep reenactment is at play:

> If counterinsurgency operations were performed with the *manifest* objective of protecting a vulnerable feminine subject against the threat of a sexually rapacious, dangerous black male body—dissimulating a scene where the young de Kock protected his mother from his father, or failed to do so (Gobodo-Madikizela, 2003)—treating the black body as an object, a prop in the staging of white masculinist identity—many of these scenes entailing not only violence, but also, crucially, homosociality, and, frequently, nudity among men and the application of torture instruments onto the genitals of suspected "terrorists"—then the erasure of the erotics of male bonding is one of the *latent* effects condensed in the act of destroying a body that has become the refuse of the unconscious pursuit of revenge on the father, who never loved that way, and whom one never loved that way.

In the last part of the chapter, Ross turns to a radical critique of empathy. He uses as his staring point the moment when de Kock reaches out his hand and Gobodo-Madikizela takes it in hers, and realized that, at that moment, she experienced an identification with the evil of de Kock. Ross goes on to develop an argument that rhetorics such as *empathy* and *forgiveness* become "displaced sites for colonial violence," in which the forgiver, by exerting the privilege of forgiveness may become complicit because all empathy is grounded in identification. Drawing on Sitze, Ross then opens this up into a critique of the ways in which the Truth and Reconciliation Commission itself, and, indeed, the very field of psychoanalysis valorize certain hegemonic forms of narration, reparation, and "healing," which are vestiges of colonialism.

Scott Boehm (chapter 12) also takes up the legacy of the Franco era in Spain. His chapter complements the work of Clara and Luis, discussed above. Scott does not hesitate to label the Franco era as a period of genocide, noting that 114,266 certified cases of enforced disappearance occurred during that period; that at least 30,000 babies born to *los rojos* (i.e., "the reds," a racialized political identity invented by Spanish fascists to justify their mass extermination) were ripped from their mothers—many of whom were summarily executed—and given to fascists to ensure they were raised in an ideologically "pure" environment; and he cites a conservative estimate that 150,000 quasi-judicial deaths (executions) occurred during the fascist era. In addition, "tens of thousands of *los rojos* were deported to Nazi camps; more than 7,000 of them were sent to Mauthausen in Austria, where a large percentage of them died." In the first part of the chapter Scott focuses on la Transición, the Spanish transition to democracy during the post-Franco period, and particularly "the country's institutionalized refusal to deal with the specters of genocide created by the Francoist state." Essentially the government mandated "silence and forgetting" and they resisted the movement toward the exhumation of mass graves because "exhumations disrupted celebratory narratives of the Transition." Scott notes that while monuments to Franco and his cohort are widespread in Spain, there has been no official/state attempt to memorialize the victims of genocide. Consider, for example the case of psychiatrist Antonio Vallejo Nájera:

> A symbolic example of how these divisions have not been erased during the post-dictatorship period is that Antonio Vallejo Nájera, the Nazi-trained psychiatrist who led the search for the "red" gene and was responsible for initiating the theft of at least 30,000 "red" babies as part of a state-sponsored eugenics policy, still has a street named after him in the center of Madrid. Like other key figures of the dictatorship—including Franco himself—the memory of Vallejo Nájera lives on in Spain's capital while street names that mark the memory of those who resisted fascism and the dictatorship are noticeably absent.

Scott has been actively involved in the exhumation movement, seeking "the return of the disappeared." He brings us to the precipice of horror and the ghosts of the past this way:

> There are few things as horrifying as peering into the depths of a mass grave. Bones piled randomly on top of each other elicit primal fears of arbitrary death, abandonment and post-mortem anonymity. Skulls gaze back at you, eerily interrogating your stare with their unspeakable knowledge. Bullet holes in the back of craniums bear witness to human brutality, scenes of which are involuntarily imagined through the instant recall of black and white images of summary executions and concentration camps, collective memories fixed by film footage

> of atrocities committed during the long twentieth century. Femurs, tibias and vertebra strewn haphazardly in the dirt testify to the violence and disdain with which those deemed undesirable were made to disappear. Fragments of ribs and tiny finger bones reveal the fragility of the human skeletal structure hidden beneath the surface of our seemingly impenetrable skin. Teeth still sparkling among the dirt become uncanny reminders that such prostrate remains were once full of life—life abruptly denied the right to exist by a firing squad. Standing at the edge of a mass grave is to find oneself on the precipice of the real lurking in everyday experience, where a picturesque field of wheat is suddenly transformed into a crime scene. A frightening abyss is exposed beneath the apparently peaceful pastures where sheep roam oblivious; picturesque rural landscapes take on a sinister, haunted appearance. Such proximity to the remains of violent death incites feelings of dread because it explodes notions of personal security and cultural stability. Looking closely at a mass grave is to risk putting comforting notions about historical progress in jeopardy. It is a precarious act, in which traumatic memories of the past flash up, revealing the present as a moment pregnant with the seeds of danger, sown with hate.

With this quote Scott opens up a lengthy discussion on the erasure of memory in Spain, the possibilities for retributive justice, and the need for an ethics of remembering "that is nothing less than the praxis of hospitality that Jacques Derrida prescribes in *Specters of Marx*."

In the final section of the chapter, Scott documents a rather subtle and uncanny *revenant* of these haunted memories that has occurred via the genre of a new wave Spanish horror film which he argues is inextricably tied up with the cultural trauma of genocide. For illustrative purposes, consider his concluding analysis of Juan Antonio Bayona's *El orfanato*:

> Following Lowenstein's appropriation of Walter Benjamin, I see remnants of *Trauerspiel*, the Baroque German mourning plays that Benjamin used to formulate his thoughts of allegory, in this sequence of *El orfanato* and in much of recent Spanish horror (Benjamin, 1998). Benjamin claimed that in those German tragic mourning plays, allegory represented history as a "petrified, primordial landscape" of "decay," best encapsulated by the recurring symbol of the "death's head" (Benjamin, 1998, p. 166). I would argue that within the Spanish horror renaissance, a subgenre of "Spanish tragic mourning films" reflect a similar view of haunted history that employ many of the tropes and the specific melancholic mood of allegory that Benjamin describes. Additionally, for Benjamin, an allegorical moment is also "a moment of danger" in which an image—a memory—of the past flashes up suddenly, momentarily making evident the ways in which the past and the present are linked (Benjamin, 1955, p. 255). Like Laura's act of breaking through the oven door, an allegorical moment cuts through the blinders of ideology that prevent us from recognizing how the present is structured by past historical tragedies and traumas.

In chapter 13, Reinhold Stipsits takes us to three pockets of Eastern Europe to peer through windows into trauma. Reinhold's chapter is a form of cultural historiography, in which the author, much like an archeologist, focuses in on artifacts and probes them for their secrets. As Reinhold notes, "the memorials speak, lest we forget." Reinhold's chapter consists of three vignettes, in each of which he visits a place and allows the memories to speak. The first is a university in Transylvania where Reinhold is assigned to teach a course. As it happens, he is assigned accommodations in the villa of former dictator Nicolae Ceausescu. He sleeps restively in Ceausescu's bed, roams the villa, pokes in the closets, and inhales the gloomy and paranoid vapors of oppression:

> As a guest professor, I was given the privilege of sleeping for two nights in the bed of the dictator! The advantage of this compared to ordinary citizens was disputable; I hardly found rest or sleep at all. Hallucinations and visions haunted me. Anxiety has never been a good counselor or instructor. Eerie daydreams, horrible nightmares were, to put it mildly, sensations I experienced. Did I step into the lion's den? Certainly the paranoia of the "Conducător," the "Great Leader," had an immense impact on the aura of this villa. And, I cannot deny the lingering impact on my awareness.

Reinhold then recounts the traumatic history of the Sathmar Swabians, pawns in the contest for empire, bounced repeatedly between German, Hungarian, and Romanian identities. The story of Sandor, one of his students, captures a tiny fraction of this complexity:

> In 2006, here in the premises of Dictator Ceausescu, a place full of haunting visions, I remembered a student sharing his experience of fleeing with his mother when he was nine years old. Sandor was raised in a trilingual environment. He learned Romanian from his mother, Hungarian from his friends at elementary school, and a childlike German from his father's side. Ceausescu had planned to steamroll the farmhouses of all non-Romanian minorities in the villages to build huge agricultural production cooperatives. Local farmers were forced to leave their homes and were promised work places in factories. The megalomaniac dream of a despot instilled trembling fear. Sandor's family was forced to leave home. So, they tried to escape. Sandor's mother carried him piggyback when they waded through a river to the western border, to freedom in Hungary. But Sandor fell off and as he fell, he yelled for help, in Romanian! The getaway ended in an asylum camp in Austria. That was where his Christmas memory was anchored. Being traumatized, he refused to talk, as he spoke no language of any use. But he had to start to learn German. As his parents did not find a permanent job in the area, they moved to the south of Germany where Swabian was spoken. At school, he mastered German quickly. Then his father lost his job and again, the family moved back to Romania. There he had to start afresh, with the old languages, Romanian, and for the first time, he had to learn

> to write in Hungarian. He intended to study journalism, in Cluj-Napoca, at the department of German Language. And—traumatized by his childhood years—he still fervently expressed one wish: "Please do not talk about this background story in a negative way that might make somebody think badly of Romania. I forgive them, since the State of Romania provides me an opportunity, gives me an education!" What a noble mind, shaped by traumatic events.

For the second vignette, Reinhold takes us to the Museum of Genocide, in Vilnius, Lithuania, a building with many ghosts:

> Under the Russian occupation, when Lithuania was part of the Russian Empire, the building was intended to impress as a courthouse of the Russian province of Vilnius. It quickly changed and served the occupying German institutions from 1915 to 1918. Then, under the occupying Polish regime, it changed from a conscription center to a remand prison. Then, under the Soviet Government until the Nazis took over, it went from a remand prison to a prison for mass reprisals. Under Hitler Germany's Special Unit for the City of Vilnius, mass executions of Jews were ordered on those premises. From that building which then housed Gestapo headquarters, Nazi henchmen pursued local Jews as well as thousands of people from other nations. In that same building, bloodhounds killed patriots from Lithuania whenever regimes changed. In 1944, the Soviets took over and the instruments and chambers of torture remained in operation until 1991. The building served as the Lithuanian branch of KGB headquarters. From 1959, when it was renamed as a prison, the facilities were used as interrogation cells. Today, the death chamber is still there in the basement. Where victims stood on sand before being shot, there is now a glass bottom. Visitors walk in and see traces of shoes in the sand. The torture rack in the basement can almost be touched, as if a museum is likely to be more convincing if there is a realistic experience.

As Reinhold takes us on a tour of the building, he asks probing questions about the preservation of collective memory and, particularly, about the role of museums in enabling "our eyes to see what they can no longer see." In speaking of the war of resistance in the early days of the Communist takeover, for example, he describes the abandonment of the partisans by the West and questions how we are to hold on to and work through the collective memory of such losses:

> The resistance hoped for liberation by the West, trusting that the Atlantic Charta would be implemented and would demand freedom for the occupied nations. The disappointment of the partisans became acute. From 1944 to 1953, Lithuania fought its war entirely alone. The West did not dare raise a voice in protest against the destruction of the Lithuanian nation. Partisans came to be known as forest brothers and about 20,000 people died as local heroes in the

> guerrilla war within one year (Kuodytė & Tracevskis, 2006). A nation cried for help but, alas, that cry went unheard. Another trauma occurred. But the question remains the same as in the case of the Holocaust: How is the collective memory of a population to be managed if we are to be able to understand the situation of the partisans, those volunteers who fought for freedom? Like Christopher Browning, I support the idea of the representation of micro-history. Micro-history covers everything. In a way, one may claim that general history is embedded in the history of a single person.

Finally, Reinhold take us to Pirita, in Moldova, to visit the City of Children—an institution for "leftover children" whose parents became desperate economic migrants when the Soviet Union devastated the Moldovan wine industry, the mainstay of the economy. Here again, through micro-history, Reinhold illustrates how focusing in on one singular detail explodes the traumatic history of a whole society. The ghosts are everywhere in the lives of these orphaned children:

> In no other country in Europe are there as many real orphans or so-called social orphans as in Moldova. Street kids are a by-product of state monopoly capitalism in less developed countries. In an independent state, as Moldova declared itself to be, resistance against Western or foreign help is prevalent. Both major players in the European scene, Germany and the long arm of Russia, are met with distrust among the population. Too deep are the wounds from when the German *Wehrmacht* occupied the banks of the River Dnjestr (today Nistru). The Russian Front was right there in the nowhere lands of Moldova, along the River Nistru with its Moldovan name. The Red Army, too, has left but memories remain. A camp for young pioneers was established in Pirita, with a fortified wall to avoid direct contact with the local village people. In the hot Moldovan summer days, young pioneers were proud to have an outdoor swimming pool for relaxation. A red brick wall at the pioneer camp bears the inscription in Russian and in Cyrillic letters: *Nation's pride*. Involuntarily or forced, the heyday is now gone, leaving today the remnants of an outdated ruin.

Naama dela Fontaine and Kate Szymanski invite us, in chapter 14, to consider a particular aspect of the anxiety over memory in Israel. The "Never forget" imperative post-Holocaust, and the rise of Zionism as a defensive response to the vulnerability Israelis felt in a hostile Arab world, have both been formative in shaping the ideological approach of modern Israel to the issue of memory. Naama and Kate explore this by focusing on the workings of ideology in the Israeli Defense Force (IDF). The IDF, with its mandatory military service (orthodox Jews excepted), occupies a valorized place in Israeli society, and, in this chapter, Naama and Kate report on interviews conducted with soldiers who served in the Second Lebanon War to ascertain the ways in which Israel's inherited memory and imperative for survival work as ideological motivating forces for soldiers. This is a complex issue to disentangle as all armies, except those comprised of reluctant conscripts, indoctrinate their soldiers with mantras of patriotism and binary notions of good and evil. Likewise, soldiers under stress appear to develop cohesiveness and resolution from the Band of Brothers phenomenon, where loyalty to comrades provides the most powerful imperative for combat and survival. Is there something more at work in the case of the IDF?

Naama and Kate suggest that memories of persecution of the kind that are pervasive in Jewish history, together with an ongoing external threat, provide a particularly potent force for motivating mechanisms of defense of the kind the IDF represents for Israelis, as one soldier participant noted:

> I'll tell you what that drive is . . . after the war we were told not to return our equipment, that we were going for a second tour. And I asked my commander, "What will happen? Again, the same story?" . . . So he said, I'll summarize it for you: "They want to kill you because you are a Jew on the land of Israel." Suddenly, he spoke to me in terms of the land of Israel, of Jews. . . . I recalled that on the yellow flag of the Hezbollah it says that they're also releasing Jerusalem, so, it's like something I can fight for . . . it gave me perspective. I recall suddenly feeling confidence . . . gaining perspective: You are now fighting for your land, for your identity. They're not just fighting over territory somewhere, they are fighting for Jerusalem.

The IDF explicitly teaches soldiers that Jews have the right to live as a free nation, safe in their own country, a concept known as "Righteousness of the Way." This was mentioned by some participants as an explicit motivator for combat:

> [After the war] the IDF realized that it's not enough to be a professional military now . . . with the most innovative missiles, it's not what works. An internal drive is needed. That will provide values that would provide some type of reason to fight, Righteousness of Way, whatever you want . . . this subject is so important to me because I think it's the secret of our existence here. If it will end . . . we will not remain here . . . [we've become a] hedonistic society and are supposed to be an idealistic society. Under these conditions, there's no chance that we'll succeed. It'll take a year, two years, 10 years, but they have patience and belief in whatever they believe.

Another soldier explicitly referenced Holocaust trauma as a motivator:

> I watch military shows . . . of the American air force, or the American military and it disgusts me, it repels me damn. . . . Rambo, that's not at all the thing. That there is a soldier, and an Israeli soldier, who defends the land of Israel, . . . his

> nation, after the awful Holocaust . . . the memory of the Holocaust is very powerful for me, not because I have family from there, I'm Sephardic [it] doesn't relate to me. And suddenly you're a soldier, after 60 years that . . . that we were under the incinerators, suddenly you wear the IDF uniform and defend your nation. Wow. That's like a thing that you have to be part of.

Naama and Kate go on to explore the dissonance Israeli soldiers experience when these beliefs are called into question either by questionable operations initiated by the army, or due to public criticism of the military in Israeli mass media. There is an irony in democracies needing indoctrinated armies that are willing to lay down their lives for democratic principles, but needing, nonetheless, to protect the military from the cacophony of democratic disputation in the name of cohesiveness and discipline.

Ricardo Ainslie (chapter 15) explores the tragic murder of James Byrd Jr. in Jasper, Texas, as a window into "the architecture of memory." James Byrd Jr., an African American man, was walking home from a party when he accepted a ride from three men in a pickup truck. The men, two of whom were members of a white supremacist organization, brutally beat Mr. Byrd. They then chained him to the rear of the truck and dragged his body for close to three miles. This is how the episode concluded:

> Huff Creek Road is home to a small, rural community, the majority African American, and many of whom had lived in the area for several generations. The area is pastoral in its beauty and lush with wildflowers and dense woods. An African American cemetery and church anchor the end of the narrow country road. The brutally disfigured and, by then, decapitated remains of James Byrd were left early on a Sunday morning in front of that African American church, presumably to be discovered as families arrived for services later that morning. A distinct trail of blood covered some two miles of Huff Creek road, beginning at the point where the men had dragged Mr. Byrd from a clearing in the woods onto the paved road.

Ricardo's work is an ethnographic inquiry into "spectral horror" in the history of the Jasper community that provides a backdrop to the murder of Mr. Byrd, leading to his argument that, due to archaic echoes from the time of slavery and the subsequent period of lynching, this brutal crime has spectral undertones:

> In east Texas, race relations are predominantly shaped by the legacy of slavery, the Civil War, Reconstruction, and Jim Crow and thus governed by the psychodynamics attendant to slavery and white oppression, including violence directed toward African Americans. In other words, the reigning paradigms for race relations in different parts of Texas have been shaped by distinct historical and cultural contexts.

Ricardo uses intergenerational trauma theory to make the case that African Americans in Jasper—living appropriately in a poor all-black community named The Quarters in reference to its history as the slave quarters of that community—are a community that, following Varvin, he says suffers from collective traumatization. While Ricardo draws on Kai Erikson's now classic definition of collective trauma, a novel contribution of his work here is the argument that, while parallels can be drawn between individual and collective trauma, repair of collective trauma is distinct in demanding memorialization:

> My argument in this chapter is that because collective trauma is organized along different lines, it plays a different role in psychic life. In particular, rather than psychodynamics that revolve around the repression and dislocation in memory of traumatic experience that we see in relation to individual trauma, I hope to illustrate that in collective trauma we often witness the opposite: a compelling need to remember and a demand for acknowledgement and memorialization of those traumatic experiences. In other words, not all trauma is unsayable or unknowable (except in the sense that all representations of experience are incomplete and elusive), much less unconscious.

This argument echoes Avishai Margalit's (2002) argument in *The Ethics of Memory* of the imperative of moral witness to the healing process for communities.

Ricardo sketches a history of lynching in East Texas and then goes on to describe a series of ethnographic interviews he conducted with white and African American residents in Jasper, including family members of two of the three perpetrators, finding significant evidence of trauma in the narratives, and particularly, archaic echoes of earlier lynchings in the area. As Ricardo notes, there was nothing novel about the architecture of Mr. Byrd's murder:

> In this respect, the murder of James Byrd Jr., as a collective experience, represents a variation on Freud's notion of the uncanny (1919). The hate crime was simultaneously profoundly shocking and in this sense foreign, while also psychologically deeply familiar as an action that perfectly fit the mold of historical acts of terror against the black community. A collective history of brutal violence was forced into awareness by the act of three white men who murdered a black man on a whim fueled by deep racial hatred. Byrd's murder made present something that was supposed to be past. It was impossible to separate the understanding of the brutal murder from the broader context in which this incident of racial violence had taken place. Both African Americans and whites spontaneously and instinctively drew the parallel. Thus, the hate crime was immediately recognizable as something familiar and known, yet foreign, as something that was supposed to be past. That past was brutally enacted in the present, tearing

> off the protective layers of distance and time. The protective illusion of lynching as something of the past was shattered by the Sunday morning horror of a black man chained and dragged to his death behind a pickup truck.

In the final section of the chapter, Ricardo explores mechanism of intergenerational trauma transmission, and then concludes with a discussion of the contestation of memory, culminating in the unsurprising tale that the only acceptable place in which a memorial to Mr. Byrd could be erected was in The Quarters, where it would be viewed by African Americans, and where members of the white community of Jasper could be protected from any feelings of guilt or any possibility that archaic vulnerability might be aroused had the memorial been placed in the public square.

In the final chapter, psychoanalyst Billie Pivnick and museum designer Tom Hennes describe their work where, as members of *Thinc* (http://thincdesign.com/), Tom's design firm, they played a leading role in the design of the National September 11 Memorial and Museum in New York (http://www.911memorial.org/museum). Early on, they offer a stark reminder of the collapse:

> Over mass media, we watched in rapt horror the endless replay of the second impact, captured from every imaginable angle, and then the video of the first impact that emerged later in the day, serendipitously captured by a film crew traveling with a fire company not far from the World Trade Center. And we watched the collapse, over and over again, of the two towers. It was surely the collapse itself, with its unfathomable force, the uncountable number of souls within it, and the utter destruction of these icons of American bravado, that most shocked us, making us numb and yet compelling us to rush in, each of us in our way, to do something, anything, to help. We waited for the wounded to be pulled out and brought to St. Vincent's Hospital, where hundreds of medical personnel were awaiting the ambulances that never came. Instead, missing posters, by the thousands, appeared on walls and fences and lampposts across New York. Vigils assembled spontaneously. But with the exception of 23 survivors pulled from the vast pile of wreckage, almost nothing of the 2763 missing victims of the New York attack ever emerged from the wreckage of the Towers.

Tom allows that he approached the project with skepticism, fearing that it "could easily become a jingoistic remaking of the events and their aftermath into a two-dimensional caricature, similar to the rhetoric around the wars in Afghanistan and Iraq." The challenge they set themselves, working as it turned out within a babel of competing voices, and at the vortex of a struggle between political and ideological forces, and a very large set of grieving families, many very vocal in their demands—who, themselves, were by no means unanimous in conceptualizing a suitable memorial to their loved ones—was to hold on to some purity of ideals and to figure out how to forge some consensus in the midst of this maelstrom. Museums, at their core, represent struggles about representation and about who gets to control the narrative(s), and nowhere is this more evident than in the gripping story Billie and Tom narrate.

The complexity of managing the representation of "collapsed time" first became monumentally clear to them when they visited Hangar 17 at Kennedy Airport, where potential artifacts for a future museum were stored:

> We were alerted to the importance of collapsed time to the design process during our first visit to Hangar 17, the repository of the artifacts that included, among many other things, eighty thousand square feet of steel, sorted by type and stacked neatly on wooden blocks. The effect of all these rusty, often twisted beams standing guard over objects like a torqued bicycle rack minus its bike riders left viewers nearly speechless. The maimed remnants of the giant antenna that stood atop the North Tower looked like the Skylab space station from the same era as the Towers. Fire trucks, some crushed and twisted, one of them shiny and nearly intact at one end, burned and rusted at the other, sat among flattened cars and an ambulance whose roofless interior was burned away and filled with ash. Remnants of a huge Calder sculpture were laid out along with fragments of Rodin figures that seemed like actual blackened, torn bodies. The conservator of these objects greeted us by saying, "This will not be your first visit. . . ." We assumed he meant, "This will not be your last visit" since most of us were there for the first time. We mused that the narrative pancaking pointed to by his confusion of temporal terms could, if opened, become a space where we would see history emerging—and where the nascent story of 9/11 would begin, scaffolded in now-wounded steel that told a story devoid of verbs.

The vision they nurtured, following Margalit, was the construction of an ethical community of memory, one in which, as many authors in this volume have noted, the artifacts and their judicious placement allow for the activation of archival memory and the working through to a place of reparation through a process of contemplative immersion. Their chapter will take you through the theoretical underpinning of their work in "relational design"; their understanding of uses of narrative theory in artifact representation; their struggles with representing absence metaphorically; the attempt to maintain a narrative arc, yet allow multiple narratives to be told; their desire to engender deep reflection yet protect viewers from retraumatization; the significance of the *Last Column*, the *Signing Steel* and the *In Memoriam* exhibits; the struggle over *The Composite* exhibit; and the challenge of convincing other stakeholders of the possibility of constructing an intersubjective space that allows for the possibility of facilitating the creation of an ethical community:

> We were in fact able to realize a museum that admits mixed feelings while incorporating many of the features of 9/11 that emerged in the process of making it. These include presence and absence; physical and symbolic loss; the collapse of time; the multiplicity of perspectives on the events; the potential of overwhelming affect and narrative incoherence arising from split off aspects of experience; and a history that is indeterminate, evolving, and contested. . . . Our guiding principles have the primary objective of supporting a wide-ranging relational field in which all of the participants—those who contribute objects and narrative, those who organize the experience, and those who participate in the course of a visit—attain the means to come to know their own experience more fully and to more confidently locate themselves within the larger field of collective experience.

If you find the writings in this book useful, I hope you will also consider consulting the companion volume, *Fragments of Trauma and the Social Production of Suffering: Trauma, History, Memory*, which I edited with my colleague Marilyn Charles, and which is also published by Rowman & Littlefield.

REFERENCES

Margalit, A. (2002). *The ethics of memory*. Cambridge: Harvard University Press.

Osborn, C. (2014). A Good Little Group: Recovering Lost Connections between Aboriginal Mothers and Children. In M. O'Loughlin & M. Charles (Eds.). *Fragments of trauma and the social production of suffering: Trauma, history, memory*. Lanham, MD: Rowman & Littlefield.

Pisano, N. G. (2012). *Granddaughters of the holocaust: Never forgetting what they didn't experience*. Boston: Academic Studies Press.

Part I

ETHICS OF MEMORY

Chapter 1

Is Autonomy Unethical?

Trauma and the Politics of Responsibility

Mari Ruti

Autonomy does not consist of putting walls around oneself . . . but instead, of forming essential relationships with others.

—Susan Brison, *Aftermath* (2002)

JUDITH BUTLER MEETS SUSAN BRISON

Dartmouth philosopher Susan Brison tells us, in *Aftermath*, that in the summer of 1990, she went for a morning walk on a country road in Southern France. She was attacked from behind, dragged into a nearby ravine, raped, beaten and strangled unconscious four times. Her assailant tried to kill her to keep her from reporting the rape, responding to her attempts to assure him that she would not report it by an insistent "*il le faut*"—"it must be done." When Brison regained consciousness after the fourth attack, she pretended to be dead, and her assailant left her in the ravine. She climbed back onto the road, flagged down a farmer on a tractor, and was taken to the hospital where she was treated for serious injuries. Her assailant was apprehended quickly—he lived in the neighborhood—and was eventually sentenced to twelve years in prison for rape and attempted murder. Brison reports that, unlike many rape survivors, she was treated relatively well by the French legal system, presumably in part because she was a white middle-class married woman, and in part because the attack was so grievous that it left no doubt about what had happened. The bulk of her book outlines the aftermath of the attack: her lengthy, and in many ways only partially successful, battle against severe symptoms of post-traumatic stress disorder. Her memoir does not end on a triumphant note, for she writes, in its final pages:

> I wasn't surprised that my recovery wasn't linear—no one led me to expect that—but by the fact that whatever trajectory my life was on didn't seem to *be* one of recovery. There was (and is) no discernible pattern. I'd like to be able to tell a story of trauma and recovery in a more "conventional" sense. . . . [But] recovery no longer seems to consist of picking up the pieces of a shattered self (or fractured narrative). It's facing the fact that there never was a coherent self (or story) there to begin with. No wonder I can't seem to manage to put myself together again. I'd have to put myself, as the old gag goes, "together again for the first time." (pp. 111, 116)

Brison's overall vision of subjectivity and self-narrativization thus agrees with the one that Judith Butler (2004, 2005, 2010, 2012) has advocated in the context of the ethics of precarity that she has developed during the last decade: because there is no coherent self, there is no way to give a coherent account of oneself. Yet Brison repeatedly stresses what Butler would find difficult to integrate into her approach, namely that being able to recover a sense of autonomy is an essential part of surviving trauma. This autonomy will always be incomplete, will always encounter various obstacles, but it is also life-preserving. If trauma results in a loss of control, in utter helplessness, then, as Brison maintains, the seemingly impossible "task faced by the trauma survivor is to regain a sense of control over her or his life" (p. 73). More specifically, Brison confirms what countless other survivors have reported, namely that their repeated efforts to tell their stories are, among other things, an attempt to establish a measure of agency over lives that have been torn apart. Because there is a performative element to self-narrativization—so that in saying something about the trauma one acts on the memory of that trauma—narrativization helps the survivor externalize the trauma; rather than being a passive victim of another's violence, she becomes the (tentatively) active subject of her story. Brison in fact tells us that her recovery would not have been possible without the presence of others willing to respond to her story: "Each time someone failed to respond I felt as though I were alone again in the ravine, dying, screaming" (p. 16). There is no illusion, in Brison's text, that the narrativization of trauma will lead to complete self-mastery. But she recognizes that trauma survivors often urgently need to rebuild a sense of self. Comparable calls for self-determination can be found in texts, such as Frantz Fanon's *The Wretched of the Earth* (1961), that address the need of a traumatized collectivity to reestablish its viability in the face of oppression. Given that this is the case, my question in this essay is whether Butler is correct in positing that ethics is (or should be) a matter of contesting "sovereign notions of the subject" (2012, p. 9)—notions that, as Adriana Cavarero argues, are based on "individualistic doctrines, which are too preoccupied with praising the rights of the *I*" (quoted in Butler 2005, p. 32).

I understand the reasons for Butler's attack on "the ontology of individualism" characteristic of the humanist subject, particularly of the self-contained Enlightenment subject (2010, p. 33), for the critique of the violent exploits of this subject—including its imperialist aspirations—has always been central to posthumanist theory. And in recent years, this critique has found a new target: the narcissistic neoliberal subject for whom the fantasy of impermeability and self-sufficiency is foundational. However, the impulse to crush this subject has arguably grown to be so habitual in contemporary progressive theory—including Butler's work—that it has become difficult to remember that not all attempts to gain autonomy are synonymous with arrogant individualism, that trauma survivors, for instance, often pursue autonomy not because of an aggressive desire to dominate the world but because of a desperate need to render the self moderately functioning. More generally speaking, because posthumanist theory is on a mission to discredit the overly confident humanist subject, it cannot always adequately address the struggles of less robust subjects; even when it recognizes the psychic realities of vulnerability—as Butler's ethics of precarity certainly does—it tends to talk as if all efforts to surmount this vulnerability were intrinsically deplorable, with the consequence that it may unwittingly end up further disempowering the very subjects who most need to overcome their disempowerment. That is, the message of much of posthumanist theory seems to be the following: you are not as powerful as you think you are; precariousness is the underpinning of your existence and this is how things should stay; any effort you might make to become more autonomous is essentially unethical (because the worst you could ever do would be to begin to resemble the agentic subject of Enlightenment humanism).

This is not to say that I do not appreciate many components of Butler's ethics of precarity, including its attempt to replace Kantian rationalism by a combination of Levinasian phenomenology and psychoanalysis. Both of these sources reveal the Enlightenment subject to be a hoax by focusing on the subject's social, relational ontology. If Levinas (1998) sought, as he put it, to break "the obstinacy of being" (p. 202) by showing that we owe our very existence to the other, and that we are therefore irrevocably responsible for this other, psychoanalysis reveals the ways in which our primary infantile relationships linger into adulthood, repeatedly interrupting any sense of coherence we might attain. In other words, psychoanalysis reminds us that the other dwells within the self—through the unconscious, through the repetition compulsion, and even through our bodily drives—in ways that render us constitutionally incomplete, disoriented, out-of-joint, and riven by alterity. Most importantly for Butler's purposes, our early exposure to the other—what she describes, following Jean Laplanche, as our primordial impingement by the other—is involuntary and always potentially traumatizing. Even when we are not treated badly, we are treated unilaterally, which means that we are completely at the mercy of others. And when we *are* treated badly, our masochism is inevitable in the sense that we are forced to cathect to those who harm us; our very survival depends on such wounded attachments, with the result that being injured—and injurable—becomes the status quo of our lives.

Butler thus replaces the metaphysical model of subjectivity as autonomous and self-generating with a psychoanalytic model of relational ontology. This relational ontology, in turn, becomes the foundation for her ethics of precarity—an ethics that postulates that our recognition that vulnerability is a shared human condition functions (or, ideally, should function) as a resource for our resolve to protect others against all attempts to exploit their helplessness. That is, there is something about vulnerability—particularly about bodily vulnerability—that offers a potentially universal platform for opposing violence in its various forms. Like any good poststructuralist, Butler feels conflicted about this universality, taking care to specify that precariousness, while being a general condition of human life, is always experienced in singular ways, so that it is impossible to draw an easy analogy between one experience of suffering and another. Nevertheless, the fact that all of us are defenseless in the face of suffering allows us, on a very basic level, to connect to the suffering of others.

Furthermore, Butler prompts us to become aware of the biopolitical and necropolitical power structures that distribute precariousness unevenly, so that some individuals and populations are much more precarious than others. I find her arguments about grievability—about the unequal ways in which some people are deemed worthy of being mourned while others are not—quite compelling and I discuss them at length elsewhere.[1] There is absolutely no question that Butler's ethics aims at a more just world—a world where economic, racial, and other social inequalities would be leveled so that everyone's vulnerability would count equally and everyone would be equally protected. However, I would like to propose that Butler's categorical flight from the humanist subject leads to two theoretical dead ends that, ironically enough, neutralize her capacity to speak to the complexities of acute traumatization. First—as I have already started to suggest—she fails to validate the legitimate need for autonomy that many trauma survivors express. Second, because she starts from the assumption that the very possibility of autonomy is ethically questionable, she finds it difficult to condemn those who inflict trauma on others, as Susan Brison's assailant did. That is, Butler deems the notion of self-responsibility—which is what autonomy on some level implies—so unpalatable that she constructs an ethical model completely devoid of normative content, with the result that she loses the capacity to distinguish between right and wrong, just and unjust, actions. Instead, she adopts Levinas's somewhat problematic notion that we are irrevocably responsible for the other regardless of how this other behaves. I will proceed by discussing the Levinasian outlook first, before circling back to the considerations about traumatization and autonomy that constitute the central preoccupation of this essay.

WHEN FORGIVENESS IS NOT ENOUGH

Levinas argues that our responsibility for the other is unconditional and inescapable, that the other as "face" is inviolable and that, unfortunately for us, even the executioner, even the Nazi guard, has a face. We may feel tempted to attack such a face, but ethics demands that we resist this temptation. So far so good: I do not have a problem with the idea that I should not counter murder with murder, particularly as Levinas emphasizes that it is the task of justice—as opposed to ethics—to arbitrate between different faces. But things become more troublesome when Butler combines Levinas with psychoanalytic insights about the intrinsically opaque nature of subjectivity to promote an ethics of leniency whereby I am exhorted to forgive those who wound me. According to this ethics, I need to recognize that others are driven by unconscious motivations that remain beyond their reach, which means that they do not always know what they are doing. Nor are they capable of giving a full account of their actions, which means that my request for such an account constitutes a form of ethical violence. On the flip side, I can expect similar leniency from others. As Butler proposes, "I will need to be forgiven for what I cannot have fully known, and I will be under a similar obligation to offer forgiveness to others, who are also constituted in partial opacity to themselves" (2005, p. 42). In this way, Butler turns my inner opacity—which is, among other things, an indicator of the extent to which I am *not* an autonomous being—into a semiautomatic grounds for forgiveness. To be sure, she admits that this opacity should not be seen as a license to do whatever I want to do. But, in principle, it deserves the patience, forbearance, and forgiveness of others. Even more pointedly, Butler proposes that because my prehistory—the part of my infantile formation that I cannot, as an adult, reconstruct—keeps interrupting any story I tell of myself, it constitutes "my failure to be fully accountable for my actions, my final 'irresponsibility,' one for which I may be forgiven only because I could not do otherwise" (2005, pp. 78–79). As a result, she concludes, "If we speak and try to give an account from this place [of opacity], we will not be irresponsible, or, if we are, we will surely be forgiven" (2005, p. 136).

Might this not be a little too convenient for us? Butler reads the psychoanalytic insight about our inner opacity to mean that we cannot be held fully responsible for our actions but will, instead, "surely" be forgiven. I would say that this is a fairly self-serving, even dangerous, way to interpret the consequences of the fact that we are often motivated by unconscious currents that we do not entirely understand. I would indeed be tempted to reverse Butler's formulation to argue that I am fully responsible for my actions even when I cannot comprehend how the ghosts of my formative experiences goad me to these actions. Freud's point about making the unconscious conscious, after all, was not that I should resign myself to riding the pulse of the repetition compulsion for the rest of my life; rather, his point was that by developing an active relationship to my unconscious, I might be able to foster the capacity to intervene in this compulsion whenever it threatens to hurt either me or others. By this I obviously do not mean that I expect to master my unconscious. If nothing else, I remain a good Lacanian. But I believe that psychoanalysis teaches me that I am responsible for my actions even—and perhaps *particularly*—when they are unconsciously motivated. In this sense, my opacity does not absolve me of responsibility but rather asks me to become more vigilant in relation to my unconscious patterns. That I have a prehistory that I cannot control does not mean that I have no say over my actions in the present. Nor does my lack of self-transparency mean that I cannot attain a degree of self-understanding. This is why I cannot see my opacity as a get-out-of-jail card; rather, I see it as an invitation to a radical form of self-responsibility.[2]

"My unconscious made me do it" may be a tempting excuse, but it places a potentially unbearable burden on those who have been harmed by my actions. Likewise, though I appreciate Butler's inclination to remain generous with the inner opacities of others, I am not as quick to absolve them of their wrongdoings as Butler is. If anything, I think that there is something questionable about Butler's call for patience, forbearance, and forgiveness in a biopolitical context where some people—say, women—are already expected to offer such patience, forbearance, and forgiveness more than others. I am not at all certain that uncritical charity with respect to others is either ethically prudent or psychoanalytically sound. Indeed, nothing is easier than abusing this charity. From the neoliberal subject who cannot commit to anything, and who therefore expects others to tolerate his ambivalences indefinitely, to the rapist who claims that his victim "provoked" him, as Brison's rapist tried to do, the world is full of people who are used to getting away with more than they should. The refusal to condemn them in the name of a more capacious ethics merely gives them permission to continue their hurtful behavior; indeed, this refusal directly contradicts Butler's own view that we should oppose any and all attempts to exploit human vulnerability. Moreover, looking back, one might ask whether feminism, the Civil Rights movement, anticolonial struggles, and so on, would have been possible if those involved had decided to be forgiving rather than angry. Butler argues that "it may be that only through an experience of the other under conditions of suspended judgment do we finally become capable of an ethical reflection on the humanity of the other, even when that other has sought to annihilate humanity" (2005, p. 45). Does this mean that if I condemn a person who has "sought to annihilate humanity," as Brison's assailant did, I fail at the task of being ethical?

The Levinasian-Butlerian ethical model shifts the ethical burden from the victimizer to the victim. Because this ethics places no normative limits on the behavior of the victimizer—because it starts from the premise that we are responsible for the other regardless of how brutally he or she behaves—it translates the infant's primordial masochism into a moral virtue. As Butler writes in *Precarious Life* (2004), "our responsibility is heightened once we have been subjected to the violence of others" (p. 16). Consider also the following statement from *Parting Ways* (2012): "The responsibility that I must take for the Other proceeds directly from being persecuted and outraged by that Other. Thus there is violence in the relation from the start: I am claimed by the other *against my will*, and my responsibility for the Other emerges from this subjection" (p. 59; emphasis added). This assertion is not as crazy as it may seem when taken out of context, for what Butler is getting at is the Levinasian connection between my relational ontology and my ethical responsibility. The basic idea is that because the other "interrupts" the coherence of my being, impeding my self-closure, I am, in a sense, always "persecuted" and "outraged" by the other; at the same time, because the other is always already an ingredient of my self, I cannot denounce my responsibility for this other. In this model, responsibility is the reverse of being impinged upon by the other in ways that sometimes feel persecuting and outrageous. As Butler reminds us, according to Levinas, "precisely the Other who persecutes me has a face" (2005, p. 90). Consequently, "I cannot disavow my relation to the Other, regardless of what the Other does, regardless of what I might will." Responsibility, in this sense, is "not a matter of cultivating a will, but of making use of an unwilled susceptibility as a resource for becoming responsive to the Other": "Whatever the Other has done, the Other still makes an ethical demand upon me, has a 'face' to which I am obliged to respond" (2005, p. 91). Simply put, if the individualistic ethical theories that Butler resists praise the "rights of the *I*," Butler's relational ethics, like its Levinasian counterpart, values the other's well-being over the subject's self-preservation. In Butler's words, "One of the problems with insisting on self-preservation as the basis of ethics is that it becomes a pure ethics of the self, if not a form of moral narcissism" (2005, p. 103).

I understand why Butler's relational alternative represents an effective decentering of the Enlightenment subject. But does it not swing too far to the other extreme? Is there not, particularly from a feminist perspective, something quite uncomfortable about the idea that I am responsible for others who violate me "against my will." Indeed, how would Butler account for Brison's admission that, after her ordeal, it was essential for her to know that she was going to be able to defend herself if attacked again, which is why she undertook self-defense training. Brison writes:

> I also learned, after martial arts training, that I was capable, morally as well as physically, of killing in self-defense—an option that made the possibility of another life-threatening attack one I could live with. Some rape survivors have remarked on the sense of moral loss they experienced when they realized that they could kill their assailants (and even wanted to!) but I think that this thought can be seen as a salutary character change in those whom society does not encourage to value their own lives enough. (p. 65)

I wonder what Butler would do with this passage. While I doubt that even Butler would tell Brison to cultivate patience, forbearance, and forgiveness in relation to her assailant, it is also the case that her Levinasian approach implies that there is something inherently unethical about Brison's stance. Butler writes: "Given over from the start to the world of others, [the body] bears their imprint, is formed within the crucible of social life; only later, and with some uncertainty, do I lay claim to my body as my own, if, in fact, I ever do. Indeed, if I deny that prior to the formation of my 'will,' my body related me to others whom I did not choose to have in proximity to myself, if I build a notion of 'autonomy' on the basis of the denial of this sphere of a primary and unwilled physical proximity with others, then am I denying the social conditions of my embodiment in the name of autonomy?" (2004, p. 26). Physical vulnerability here is what "saves" me from the demon of autonomy. Does this mean that my attempts to protect myself physically render me unethical? It seems to me that if I am always responsible for the other regardless of what the other has done, and if this responsibility demands that I resist the temptation to injure even those who persecute and outrage me, then obviously I should not be relishing my realization that I could—and even might *want* to—kill my assailant (or any future assailant). If Butler raises the self's reverence for the other to an ethical virtue, Brison sees the virtue in being able to recognize one's own self as worth fighting for, particularly if that self is one that has been socially denigrated. From a Levinasian perspective, the quest for self-preservation is the antithesis of ethics; but from an alternative ethical perspective—in this case, a more straightforwardly feminist one—it is one of the pillars of an ethical world.

BEYOND BAD AUTONOMY VS. GOOD RELATIONALITY

More generally speaking, the problem with Butlerian ethics is that it consistently sets up a rigid dichotomy between bad autonomy and good relationality. Indeed, one could say that this is an instance where a vehemently anti-essentialist thinker, paradoxically enough, falls into the kind of poststructuralist "essentialism" where some possibilities—such as the idea that autonomy might sometimes be an important component of human life—become unthinkable. Butler often talks as if the fact that we are not fully autonomous creatures means that we have no capacity for autonomy whatsoever. Yet in the same way that having an unconscious does not erase the conscious mind but merely complicates its functioning, our lack of seamless autonomy does not render us completely devoid of it. Nor is autonomy always the antithesis of relationality, as Butler implies. Indeed, Butler portrays autonomy—any attempt at recentering the self—not merely as repugnant but as intrinsically *evil.* As she asserts, there is "no recentering of the subject without unleashing unacceptable sadism and cruelty": "To remain decentered, interestingly, means to remain implicated in the death of the other and so at a distance from the unbridled cruelty . . . in which the self seeks to separate from its constitutive sociality and annihilate the other" (2005, p. 77). I agree that self-assertion can take place at the expense of others. And I agree that the fantasy of sovereignty can promote contempt not only for others but also for alternative, more relational modalities of being. But I am not convinced that the subject who seeks to recenter itself is automatically sadistic and cruel, driven to annihilate the other.

What I particularly like about Brison's narrative of her (always incomplete) recovery is that, rather than establishing a firm binary between bad autonomy and good relationality, she—like Jessica Benjamin (1995, 1998)—sees autonomy and relationality as equally necessary and in no way mutually exclusive. Autonomy, Brison maintains, is not a matter of putting up walls around oneself—of claiming complete self-reliance—but can rather serve as the foundation for respectful relationships with others. Conversely, relationality may be a way to cultivate autonomy. Indeed, Brison uses much of her narrative to highlight the relational nature of autonomy, the fact that we often arrive at autonomy *through* relationality. For instance, she explains that one of the most devastating effects of trauma is that it shatters the survivor's trust in others so that relationality may—for the time being at least—seem impossible: if even *some* men rape and murder (or try to murder) women, then what does this say about men in general? How can I ever be sure that the man I interact with is not going to attempt the same? The effect of this type of questioning, in Brison's words, is that "one can no longer *be oneself* even to oneself, since the self exists fundamentally in relation to others" (p. 40). Brison further notes that "the main reason all of us, especially women, have to fear violent intrusions by others is that they severely impair our ability to be connected to humanity in ways we value" (p. 61). The implication of this is that the infringement of autonomy that violence represents wounds us in part because it destroys our capacity for relationality. The antidote to trauma, then, cannot be a retreat into the shell of a self-contained subjectivity but consists of rebuilding one's capacity for relationality. Yet this rebuilding only becomes possible once the survivor feels that she is able to protect the boundaries of her self against intrusions by others—that is, once she has recuperated a degree of autonomy. In this manner, the autonomous self and the relational self, Brison posits, are "shown to be interdependent, even constitutive of one another" (p. 61).

Butler's enthusiasm for relationality as a substitute for autonomy, rather than as its complement, causes her to cut off a considerable part of human experience, including the fact that we *do* usually have a sense of ourselves as quasi-bounded individuals who possess a degree of agency, and who are consequently not indiscriminately subjected to the will and actions of others. An experience such as Brison's is traumatic in part precisely because it pierces the personal boundaries that typically protect us against being impinged upon by others. Moreover, Butler's model overlooks the fact that the individuals who facilitated our formative coming-into-being are not necessarily the same as those we interact with as adults. We may have started our lives in a state of interpersonal vulnerability that made it impossible for us to dissociate ourselves from those who chose to wound us, but what keeps us from doing so now? Surely there is a distinction between the idea that we are inhabited by an ontological otherness that we cannot denounce—that we only have a self to the extent that we partake in structures of sociality—and the idea that we cannot sever our connection to *specific* others who injure us. Although it is true that our infantile experiences will always exert an influence over our lives, it is inaccurate to assert that, as adult subjects, our relationship to the world of others is always (or primarily) one of being persecuted and outraged. Butler consistently downplays the difference between the constitutive vulnerability of the child and the psychic realities of adult subjectivity, failing to consider the possibility that our infantile defenselessness does not necessarily translate into life-long helplessness. We undoubtedly carry the imprint of our formative vulnerability to our graves. But surely this is not the whole story, or even the main story; surely we are also deeply enabled by others, which is precisely why traumatic incidents, such as Brison's, fall outside the "normal" flow of life.

THE NEED FOR NORMATIVE LIMITS

It is Butler's resistance to the idea that autonomy is an important feature of human life—a resistance which amounts to an antipathy toward anything that even vaguely reminds us of the humanist subject—that in part explains her hostility to a priori principles of right and wrong. This hostility is of course endemic in posthumanist theory because this theory views ethics primarily as a matter of questioning hegemonic normative paradigms. From the Frankfurt School to Lacan, Foucault, Barthes, Derrida, and Butler, among others, there has been an attempt to unearth the violence intrinsic to our dominant ethical models: the fact that their claim to objectivity rests on a number of constitutive exclusions (say, the exclusion of women, or the exclusion of racialized others). One could indeed say that this is what critical theory—my own field—consists of: it reveals the oppressive underbelly of the norms that we have been taught to take for granted. I have always been—and continue to be—a huge supporter of this type of theorizing. But I have also come to see that sometimes the vehement critique of norms obscures the fact that we still need them. Butler often remarks that moral norms of behavior are not self-evident. This is true. But, then again, sometimes they *are* self-evident. It seems to me that dragging a woman into a ravine, raping her, and beating and strangling her unconscious is not a morally ambiguous act. And it does not bother me that my condemnation of this act arises from a priori principles I have inherited from my culture. I say this because I want to emphasize that there is no reason to think that a priori norms transcend our social world. Critical theorists, such as Butler, tend to be hostile to a priori norms in part because they associate such norms with the Enlightenment, which means that they view them as inherently metaphysical. But, as feminist philosopher Amy Allen (2008) has argued persuasively, a priori principles are always historically specific in the sense that they arise in particular social contexts. This, however, does not mean that they are invariably worthless; that is, while the loss of metaphysical foundations for our normative systems undermines their claim to universality, it does not automatically invalidate them. As Allen claims, rejecting "our historical a priori" would mean "surrendering intelligibility" (p. 35). As a result, as is the case with autonomy, the attempt to pretend that normative limits mean nothing gets us nowhere—except, perhaps, into a swamp of theoretical incoherence.

This swamp is where the Butlerian approach lands when it leaps from the recognition of my relational ontology to the conclusion that I am responsible for each and every other I encounter regardless of any normative considerations; this swamp is where this approach lands when it translates the fact that I was once a helpless child mishandled by my caretakers to the idea that I am ethically accountable for the man who tries to kill me after he has forced me to suck his dirty dick. Butler flees from ethical condemnation because it supposedly props up the condemning subject's righteousness by disavowing commonality with the one who is being condemned. As she argues, "condemnation is very often an act that not only 'gives up on' the one condemned but seeks to inflict a violence upon the condemned in the name of 'ethics'"

(2005, p. 46). Butler here—awkwardly enough—judges the violence of judgment to be more violent than the violence of the act that is being judged. I concede that there are situations where the normative moral order inflicts violence by its judgments—and even misjudges—but it seems like an overstatement to suggest that, in condemning those who commit acts of violence, I "lose the chance to be ethically educated or 'addressed' by a consideration of who they are and what their personhood says about the range of human possibility" (2005, p. 45). Butler maintains that condemnation "takes aim at the life of the condemned," among other things because "punishment works to further destroy the conditions for autonomy, eroding if not eviscerating the capacity of the subject addressed for both self-reflection and social recognition, two practices that are, I would argue, essential to any substantive account of ethical life. It also, of course, turns the moralist into a murderer" (2005, p. 49). It is difficult to escape the irony of the fact that this is one of the few places where Butler seems to appreciate autonomy and the capacity for self-reflection. The one who condemns becomes a murderer because she destroys the autonomy of the perpetrator whereas the perpetrator—even the murderer—becomes a victim by virtue of being condemned. Pushed to an extreme, Butler's vision could be argued to imply that those who murder cannot quite help themselves but those who condemn them are culpable of (soul)-murder; pushed to an extreme, it suggests that Brison's assailant—who tried to plead temporary insanity[3]—is less guilty than Brison herself is for daring to entertain the thought of being able to kill any future assailant.

The lack of normative limits—of a priori ethical principles—in Butlerian theory leads to places that are hard to defend: I am supposed to actively sustain those who hurt me, and this is the case regardless of whether they are sexists, racists, neo-Nazis, or homophobic religious fundamentalists. The lengths to which Butler is willing to go to defend the Levinasian notion that even the executioner has a face is revealed in *Parting Ways*, where she discusses Hannah Arendt's condemnation of Eichmann at the end of her book *Eichmann in Jerusalem* (1994). In her book, Arendt is critical of the ways in which Israel uses the Eichmann trial for its political ends, yet she also holds Eichmann responsible for his crimes, stating in closing that he deserves to die for these crimes. Butler proposes that at the moment that Arendt judges Eichmann, "some disposition of language binds them both together; she is part of a human plurality with him—indeed, with the likes of him. And yet the effect of her address to him is to exclude him from that very domain of plurality" (2012, p. 171). The implication is that Arendt, in judging Eichmann, fails to live up to her own ideal of plurality. In a strictly abstract sense this may be true. But the charge also illustrates the problematic nature of an ethics that operates wholly without norms, where literally nothing a person does renders him worthy of ethical censure. Yes, we need to revere plurality.

But we also need some way to decide what types of actions are acceptable. Eichmann emphatically did not respect plurality. I am consequently not sure it was Arendt's responsibility to extend to him the courtesy of respecting his. Butler has so much trouble with notions of sovereignty, autonomy, and agency—notions that imply the capacity for ethical accountability—that she comes close to defending Eichmann against Arendt's insensitivity; though she is not saying that Eichmann is not guilty, she implies that Arendt is *also* guilty for not including him in the plurality of humanity. This is why I find myself in a rare agreement with Slavoj Žižek and colleagues (2005), who observes that Butler's ethics is "an ethics of finitude, of making a virtue out of our very weakness, in other words, of elevating into the highest ethical value the respect for our very inability to act with full responsibility" (p. 137).

Interestingly, Butler's resistance to a priori principles dissipates in the context of her critique of Israeli state violence against Palestinians, for she argues that Palestinians have the right to have basic rights, such as the right not to be dispossessed of land, due to their membership in a global human community. Regarding Palestine's claim "to the lands that rightfully are its own," Butler writes: "One could formulate the right in light of international law or on the basis of moral and political arguments that may or may not be framed within a specific version of the nation-state" (2012, p. 205). I agree with this stance: I also think that Palestinians should have basic human rights regardless of whether or not they belong to a nation-state. But there is nothing about Butler's Levinasian ethical vision that supports her sudden turn to the kind of liberal rights-based cosmopolitanism that can be traced, through Arendt, all the way back to Kant. If Butler stayed faithful to her Levinasian approach, she would not be calling for equal rights for Palestinians but rather saying that self-preservation should not be a priority for them, that, indeed, there might be something profoundly unethical about their quest for sovereignty and self-determination. Butler makes a valiant effort to show that her cosmopolitanism is not the same as that of Kant by arguing that it is precarity rather than the integrity of the autonomous self that is the foundation for equal rights. But this does not change the fact that, in this instance, she falls back on the very system of Enlightenment morality that she has spent much of her career criticizing, so that all of a sudden equal rights are all the rage (Butler 2012, pp. 205–16). It would of course be possible to argue that the Enlightenment does not own the ideal of equal rights, that it is possible to think about equal rights beyond their humanistic context, as Derrida (2006) does when he claims that "what remains irreducible to any deconstruction" is "an idea of justice—which we distinguish from law or right and even from human rights—and an idea of democracy—which we distinguish from its current concept and from its determined predicates today" (p. 74). But Derrida's elusive definition of justice and democracy is not what Butler is working with when she, in a Kantian vein, calls for international laws that recognize the rights of individuals not on the basis of their attachment to nation-states but rather on the basis of their humanity.

THE POLITICS OF MEMORY

It seems to me that Butler cannot have it both ways. If she is going to recoil from any mention of the Enlightenment, as she consistently does, then she cannot use its values whenever these happen to suit her political purposes. Furthermore, because Butler's disdain for the Enlightenment subject causes her to strip the posthumanist subject of all autonomy, her theory does not offer much insight into what it might mean to try to rebuild the autonomy of those who have been forcefully deprived of it. Here Brison's commentary on the ways in which self-narrativization can buttress the trauma survivor's sense of self is more helpful. Brison does not pretend that narrativization erases the experience of trauma, or even that it offers a fully satisfactory (let alone accurate) account of it, but merely stresses what I already alluded to above, namely that self-narratives translate devastating traumatic memories into narrative memories that are actively constructed and therefore conducive to a degree of agency. As Brison explains, narrativization "defuses traumatic memory, giving shape and a temporal order to the events recalled, establishing more control over their recalling, and helping the survivor to remake a self" (p. 71). If traumatic memories are repeated involuntarily, narrativization allows the survivor to gain some much needed distance from them. "It does this not by reestablishing the illusions of coherence of the past, control over the present, and predictability of the future," Brison specifies, "but by making it possible to carry on without these illusions" (p. 104).

Brison acknowledges the possibility that excessive narrativization might retraumatize the survivor. And she also admits that listeners might be traumatized by hearing stories of violence, so that, for instance, women who have not been assaulted might grow excessively fearful from having heard countless rape narratives. Recalling her own experience, Brison states, "Given the stories of rape I'd grown up with and the ones I'd heard and read about again and again in adulthood, one might say I remembered the rape even before it happened, as a kind of postmemory . . . informing the way I lived in my body and moved about in the world" (p. 86). Yet she also notes that we are arguably even more traumatized by silence, for silence often transmits trauma enigmatically, making it all the more difficult for us to process its impact; after all, as Freud already understood, it is hard to process—work through—what we cannot name. Equally problematically, silence isolates us from others, depoliticizing traumas, such as rape, that are intensely political.

Brison reports that hearing other women's rape narratives in her survivors' support group was what allowed her to get angry at her assailant. Like many rape survivors, Brison was initially unable to feel anger toward her rapist. But listening to the stories of other women—women who had also been brutalized and who had, like she, thought they would die—made her so angry at *their* assailants that she was eventually able to see that she, also, had the right to feel rage at her own. In this sense, the memories of other women were essential for her own recovery. Yet the pressure on rape survivors to forget about their experiences is strong, not just because of the stigma attached to rape, but because benevolent onlookers assume that dwelling on what has happened is counterproductive. Brison recalls that her French lawyer said to her: "When the trial is over, you must forget that this ever happened" (p. 86). When she protested that she probably would not be able to, he insisted, "But, *Madame*, you must make an effort" (p. 86). Likewise, after Brison published an article on sexual violence three years after the assault, a well-meaning colleague said to her: "Now you can put this behind you" (p. 35). Brison remarks that not only can she (obviously) not put the assault behind herself but that doing so would turn it into "an isolated event, of concern only to me" (p. 86). That is, forgetting would depoliticize the event, translating it into a "mere" individual trauma: a matter of bad luck rather than a symptom of systematic heteropatriarchal violence against women. Against this backdrop, Brison concludes that countering the injunction "to forget is the political necessity to bear witness to the injustice of sexual violence" (p. 97).

We are familiar with the notion that remembering traumatic experiences is a political act, particularly in the context of collective traumas, such as slavery, the Holocaust, and more recent genocides. Though Nietzsche (1995) may be right in suggesting that an excess of memory can sometimes be paralyzing, impeding the emergence of new modalities of life, of new passions, possibilities, and preoccupations,[4] there is also a great deal to be said for the idea that the commemoration of collective traumas—through public acts of grieving, official apologies and attempts at restoration, museums, monuments, and various artistic interventions, and so on—is both ethically necessary and socially curative. After all, the impulse to let sociopolitical atrocities fall into oblivion, or even to deliberately hide them, can be strong, particularly among those who are responsible for them. Furthermore, acts of remembrance are a means of honoring those who have suffered, of transmitting traumatic memory from one generation to the next, of building community and solidarity, and of making political statements about history, power, and oppression. In such contexts, forgetting would be ethically compromising, even indecent.

Brison emphasizes that, from the perspective of the survivor, the sharing of memories is important because it reintegrates the survivor into a community, thereby allowing her to "be reconnected with humanity" (p. 71). This is a powerful reminder that Butler's tendency to see the other as inherently persecuting can be misleading, limiting our capacity to see the other as a potential source of support. Furthermore, Butler's view of the other as persecuting is directly related to her resistance to normative limits: if the other is intrinsically persecuting, if there is no other who inhabits the world in nonpersecuting ways, then I cannot condemn the other for being that way. That is, admitting that others are not invariably persecuting would force Butler to acknowledge that there are times when *some* others deserve our condemnation. This would, in turn, require the further admission that human beings have agency, and this is Butler's biggest stumbling block, the one thing she does not seem to be willing to grant because this would, in her opinion, lead her back to the sovereign Enlightenment subject, or at the very least to this subject's contemporary avatar: the narcissistic neoliberal subject. Yet it may well be that Butler's flight from a priori norms does not actually allow her to escape the latter, for the rejection of such norms could be argued to be a symptom of the very neoliberal capitalism that she denounces. After all, the narcissistic neoliberal subject, who is used to an endless array of existential possibilities, does not like limitations on its freedom, including its freedom to buy everything that a decent department store makes available. As a consequence, one could say that a priori norms "decenter"—interrupt—this subject to the same extent as the Levinasian-Butlerian other does by introducing within its being "alien" elements that it experiences as constraining. In this sense, a priori norms may war *against* the neoliberal capitalist ethos of unmitigated choice. This is one reason I believe that they are not a completely unreasonable alternative to the "anything goes" relativism that nibbles at the edges of Butlerian ethics and that, paradoxically enough, carries its own violence.

At a key point in *Giving an Account of Oneself* (2005), Butler asks: "According to the kind of theory I have been pursuing, what will responsibility look like? Haven't we, by insisting on something non-narrativizable, limited the degree to which we might hold ourselves or others accountable for their actions? . . . Have we perhaps unwittingly destroyed the possibility of agency with all this talk about being given over, being structured, being addressed?" (pp. 83, 99). My response to this is, "Yes, we have." Or, more precisely, *you*—Judith Butler—have. *I* am still doing my best to hold onto some agency. This does not mean that I am about to dust off the skeleton of the Enlightenment subject. I understand the problems—the ethical violence—that this subject represents. But I also think that, for many of us, the lived realities of subjectivity tend to be quite far from the hubris of this subject. Butler sometimes sounds as if she were conducting a witch hunt against enormous egos. But where exactly are these king-sized egos? My sense is that many of us are trying quite hard to scrape together a modicum of ego strength, a modicum of autonomy, a modicum of self-determination. And those of us—like

Susan Brison—who have been severely traumatized are working overtime at this for the simple reason that our egos, autonomy, and self-determination have been violently stomped on. I do not think that an ethics of masochism would help them—would help any of us—lead more manageable lives. And it certainly does not do anything for our capacity to take responsibility for the pain that we may, often inadvertently, inflict on others.

NOTES

1. I discuss the matter in my latest book, *Between Levinas and Lacan: Self, Other, Ethics* (2015). New York: Bloomsbury Press.
2. I develop this argument in greater detail in my 2013 book *The Call of Character.*
3. The possibility of a psychotic break of course cannot be dismissed, but this was not Brison's impression of what happened, nor did the jury buy the "temporary insanity" plea.
4. See also Zupančič's analysis of Nietzsche in chapter 1 of *The Shortest Shadow* (2003).

REFERENCES

Allen, A. (2008). *The politics of ourselves: Power, autonomy, and gender in contemporary critical theory.* New York: Columbia University Press.

Arendt, H. (1994). *Eichmann in Jerusalem: A report on the banality of evil.* New York: Penguin.

Benjamin, J. (1995). *Like subjects, love objects: Essays on recognition and sexual difference.* New Haven, CT: Yale University Press.

Benjamin, J. (1998). *The shadow of the other: Intersubjectivity and gender in psychoanalysis.* New York: Routledge.

Brison, S. J. (2002). *Aftermath: Violence and the remaking of a self.* Princeton, NJ: Princeton University Press.

Butler, J. (1997). *The psychic life of power: Theories in subjection.* Stanford, CT: Stanford University Press.

Butler, J. (2004). *Precarious life: The powers of mourning and violence.* New York: Verso.

Butler, J. (2005). *Giving an account of oneself.* New York: Fordham University Press.

Butler, J. (2010). *Frames of war: When is life grievable?* New York: Verso.

Butler, J. (2012). *Parting ways: Jewishness and the critique of Zionism.* New York: Columbia University Press.

Derrida, J. (2006). *Specters of Marx* (P. Kamuf, Trans.). New York: Routledge.

Fanon, F. (1961). *The wretched of the earth.* (C. Farrington, Trans.). London: Penguin.

Levinas, E. (1998). *Entre nous: On thinking-of-the-other.* (M. B. Smith & B. Harshav, Trans.). New York: Columbia University Press.

Nietzsche, F. (1995). *Unfashionable observations*. (R. T. Gray, Trans.). Stanford, CA: Stanford University Press.

Ruti, M. (2013). *The call of character: Living a life worth living*. New York: Columbia University Press.

Žižek, S., Santner, E. L., & Reinhard, K. (2005). Neighbors and Other Monsters: A Plea for Ethical Violence. In *The neighbor: Three inquiries in political theology*. Chicago, IL: University of Chicago Press.

Zupančič, A. (2003). *The shortest shadow: Nietzsche's philosophy of the two*. Cambridge, MA: MIT Press.

Chapter 2

Troubling Naturalized Trauma, Essentialized Therapy, and the Asphyxiation of Dangerous Memory

Michael O'Loughlin

I am heavily implicated in the "business" of trauma. I teach courses in trauma to candidates in clinical psychology (O'Loughlin & McLeod, 2014); I write about trauma as a psychological construct, and I use clinical psychoanalysis to "explain" intergenerational and sociohistorical suffering (O'Loughlin, 2007a, b, 2008, 2009a, b, 2010, 2012, 2013). I have also written more than fifty affidavits, documenting diagnostic claims to post-traumatic stress disorder (PTSD), and assorted co-morbid diagnoses, on behalf of asylum applicants in U.S. federal immigration proceedings. I train and mentor others to do the same, and I have offered testimony in immigration proceedings. I engage in all of these activities, however, with an increasing sense of unease.

Take the asylum work, for example, an activity that I undertake on a volunteer basis. Every eight weeks or so I sit with an asylum applicant in my consulting office and listen for two hours to that person's life story, often in the presence of an interpreter—except, of course, that I am not actually interested in the applicant's story, nor is the applicant interested in sharing that story with me. We both understand that the stakes are much higher. I am charged with collecting "evidence" that will withstand the scrutiny of federal attorneys who approach the proceedings in a prosecutorial and adversarial manner. Thus, the applicant struggles to articulate a narrative that will fit an imagined or carefully tutored expectation as to what kind of "trauma" will count as grievous enough to make their case. It is not sufficient that they demonstrate exposure to catastrophic events, but the applicant and I share the burden of extracting "evidence" that this event has left a lasting imprint on the psyche—a psychic "scar" of which I will have more to say below. As Fassin and Rechtman (2009) note, the balance has shifted away from the validity and worth of the individual's experience of the traumatic event, toward the imprimatur of a professional who can rule out malingering and quantify suffering on the kind of positivist symptom scale that is at the heart of the *Diagnostic and Statistical Manual of Mental Disorders* [DSM][1] (American Psychiatric Association, 2013). To be clear, I do not have qualms about performing the asylum evaluations. It is indisputably valuable humanitarian work. My concern is that reductionist discourses such as the DSM, while hard-fought for as a policy tool by advocacy groups such as U.S. Vietnam War veterans agitating for benefits (Fassin & Rechtman, 2009), have distorted the discourse of trauma to the extent that our understanding of traumatic experience has become interpellated with utilitarian, positivist, biologized, and often medicalized language that undoubtedly takes us away from an existential understanding of the experience of, and the social and political production of, human suffering. Such reductionism risks not only diminishing human suffering, but, by eliding complexity, it also blunts arguments about reclaiming historical memory and redressing historical injustices.

An antidote to this reductionism, in the case of PTSD, is to be found in *Wartorn 1861–2010* (Alpert, 2011), Jon Alpert and James Gandolfini's nuanced portrayal of the complexities of post-traumatic combat stress. In this documentary, the bureaucratized military response to PTSD is brought face to face with the incredibly complex and tragic existential burden of war trauma shouldered by those who witnessed horror and by those who participated in the production of death and suffering. As one grieving parent of a soldier remarked, the army taught soldiers how to kill and then forgot to teach them how not to kill once they returned from combat. Neither did the U.S. Army provide war veterans with the kind of substantive therapeutic support that would allow them to work through their pain. The U.S. Army has now conjoined its reductionist understanding of PTSD with Martin Seligman's articulation of "positive psychology" (Seligman, 2002, 2011a) to develop Master Resiliency Training as part of its Comprehensive Soldier Fitness Program.[2] The belief, apparently, is that soldiers can be inoculated with positive thought as a defense against the symptoms of PTSD. So much for the power of positive thinking! In a worldview of manualized and putatively "evidence-based" therapeutic responses, the potential for acknowledging deep human suffering and how to address it, is completely negated, often with the kind of tragic consequences that *Wartorn* illustrates.

In this chapter I will first critique reductionist notions of trauma, and concomitant notions of bourgeois psychoanalytic therapy that are exclusively intrapsychic, blind to sociohistorical circumstance, and apolitical. Then, combining the liberation theory of Ignacio Martín Baró, with its argument for recovery of dangerous memory, with Françoise Davoine and Jean-Max Gaudillière's radical notion of analyst as *annalist* of unspoken history, I offer a more politically grounded approach to memory. Finally, critiquing the moral economy of conventional trauma theory, I conclude with the notion of therapist as moral witness, in the manner advocated by Avishai Margalit (2002).

CONUNDRUM OF "TRAUMA" AS TROPE FOR SUFFERING

In *Trauma: A Genealogy*, Ruth Leys (2000) explores a basic contradiction in the field—a contradiction that I know from experience puzzles clinical students of trauma: Is the fundamental goal of trauma treatment to engage trauma sufferers in forgetting or to engage them in remembering? To put it another way, is traumatic memory about the recovery, narration, and symbolization of traumatic experiences, or is it trauma best described as "'implicit' or 'nondeclarative' memory, involving bodily memories of skills, habits, reflex actions, and classically conditioned responses that lie outside verbal-semantic-linguistic representation"? (2000, p. 7). Leys points to the increased centrality of the concept of embodied memory in discourses of trauma since trauma neurobiologists, such as Bessel van der Kolk and associates (van der Kolk, 2014; van der Kolk, McFarlane & Weisaeth, 2009; van der Kolk et al., 1985), have claimed to identify epigenetic changes in the neurobiological substrate correlated with trauma impingements. As Leys notes, drawing on Hacking (1996), "by eliminating the question of autobiographical-symbolic meaning, it makes manifest the mechanical-causal basis of much recent theorizing about trauma" (2000, p. 7). Thus, just as a physical insult to the body leaves a scar, participation in a traumatic experience leaves both epigenetic and psychic scars, which then manifest in the symptoms that we cluster together in contemporary definitions of PTSD. In health care arenas, in which there is an increasing emphasis on "evidence-based practices," and in legal and advocacy arenas such as asylum evaluation and advocacy or litigation for benefits due to PTSD caused by war trauma, the attraction of such an apparently objective or externalizing approach is clear. A simple cause-and-effect relation between the traumatic event and ensuing symptoms offers a beguiling clarity—the kind of putative clarity that is especially valuable in litigation or in lobbying for legislation. Accompanying this simplistic operationalization, as Leys notes, is a corollary debasing of trauma due to the invocation of PTSD as a basis for damage claims in events that stretch the limits of the category to the bursting point. Leys cites, for example, the lawsuit brought by Paula Jones, claiming sexual harassment by U.S. president Clinton, and alleging that she experienced PTSD symptoms as a result of her allegedly harrowing experience (2000, p. 2). Simplistic definitions of trauma, such as those embodied in definitions of PTSD, and even the kind of mechanistic cause-and-effect descriptions of the workings of trauma in Judith Herman's influential *Trauma and Recovery* (1997)—where, without a trace of irony, she postulates "complex PTSD" as an improvement over conventional PTSD—have not only shaped psychiatric, legal, and historical discourses about trauma, but, no doubt, are also shaping the self-understanding of persons with symptoms of psychic distress that they believe are attributable to trauma.

THE MISSING UNCONSCIOUS

As I circulate through the classroom listening to students in my masters-level class on Trauma grapple with the key trauma concepts of hyperarousal, intrusion, dissociation, numbing, etc., as articulated by Herman in *Trauma and Recovery* (1997), I realize that the students are discussing the concepts as if defenses against suffering are conscious stratagems for dealing with painful material. There is no unconscious. This does not happen with our Ph.D. candidates, who—trained in one of a dwindling number of psychoanalytically oriented Ph.D. programs in the United States—are well-versed in psychodynamic thinking. This unremarked absence of unconscious process in the discourse of trauma can impose severe limitations on the interpretations of historians, anthropologists, and even psychiatrists, who may come to lean on mechanistic, neurobiological, or symptom-based understandings of how external events impact on the psyche. It is no coincidence that Cognitive Behavior Therapy (CBT) has become the dominant therapeutic paradigm in the Western world for treating psychic distress. CBT attempts to reverse symptoms of trauma that have been naturalized as a mechanistic response to an event. Primo Levi complained in *The Drowned and the Saved* that psychoanalysis missed the complexity of the human experience of suffering, because psychoanalysts could never fully understand the experience of the concentration camp inmate, despite their eagerness to co-opt that experience:

> I could not say whether we did or do so out of a kind of moral obligation toward those who were silenced or in order to free ourselves of their memory; certainly we do it because of a strong and durable impulse. I do not believe that psychoanalysts (who have pounced on our tangles with professional avidity) are competent to explain this impulse. Their knowledge has been built up and tested "outside" in the world that, for the sake of simplicity, we call civilian; psychoanalysis traces its phenomenology and tries to explain it; studies its deviations and tries to heal them. Their interpretations, even those of Bruno Bettelheim, who went through the trials of the lager, seem to me approximate and simplified, as if someone wished to apply the theorems of plane geometry to the solution of spheric triangles. (1988, pp. 84–85)

How much greater must the task of explaining trauma be, then, for theorists who depend on far more reductionist contemporary operationalized understandings of human experience—understandings that do not allow for an examination of the origins and depth of human suffering?

Leys addresses the tension between notions of trauma as external to the individual and exclusively intrapsychic notions that posit the response to trauma as an unconscious reaction to external events. Freud had postulated annihilation anxiety as the most central of these unconscious processes that are triggered by traumatic events. Ultimately, the tension between the internal and the external can be traced back, Leys notes, to the early French trauma theorists J. M. Charcot (1825–1893) and Charcot's student, Pierre Janet (1859–1947). Initially, Charcot's view, "attributing traumatic hysteria to psychological rather than anatomicopsychological changes" (Leys, 2000, p. 19)—which became the underpinning of Freudian psychoanalytic doctrine—was dominant. Since 1980, with the emergence of a reductionist DSM definition of trauma, as discussed earlier, as well as research into the neurobiological traces of trauma, the Janet perspective—with which Freud certainly quarreled—has gained prominence, and perhaps even hegemony in the field of trauma studies. Crucial to understanding Freud's view, Leys reminds us, is the concept of *nachträglichkeit* (in French: *après coup*), emphasizing that it is not the objective impact of the supposedly traumatic event that causes injury, but the delayed memory of that event that is reactivated at a later time. Hence, as Leys notes, "traumatic memory is inherently unstable or mutable owing to the role of the unconscious motives that confer meaning on it" (2000, p. 20). While Freud's own work, prior to his encounter with war trauma generated by the First World War, primarily focused on an interiorized view of trauma, he was forced by his encounter with shell shock victims to expand the parameters of his account. Faced with combat stress, Freud (1955/1920) posited the death instinct, and, as Leys notes, he was also forced to develop a whole new set of defense mechanisms, such as disavowal, negation, foreclosure, splitting, and primal repression (Leys, 2000, p. 24) as key defense mechanisms against catastrophic anxiety, an anxiety that, Freud believed, was ultimately grounded in a fundamental annihilation anxiety—fear of dying—in the soldier. Leys says that *nachträglichkeit* actually lends itself to a view of trauma that resists binaries, such as internal-external, and instead calls for a more fluid understanding of the dialogue between the psyche of the individual and the external sources of difficulty. I will expand this insight momentarily to explore the implications of context and collectivity in the human response to traumatic events.

Perhaps the most vexed question in addressing trauma is the role of memory. Leys addresses this by excavating the roots of psychoanalytic theory in the early theories of hypnosis articulated by Charcot, Janet, and others. The tension arises in seeking to articulate the psychodynamic effects of trauma as resulting in an unconscious hypnotic—or *mimetic* (Leys, 2000,

p. 8)—identification with the trauma, and the possibility for recollection and narration of the trauma in words. Concern about the latter, Leys suggests, provides the impetus for externalizing theories of trauma:

> Equally crucial, the antimimetic turn within the mimetic paradigm—the therapists' demand that the patient *be a subject* capable of distancing herself from the traumatic scene—is simultaneously the moment when emphasis tends to shift from the notion of trauma as involving a mimetic yielding of identification to a notion of trauma as a purely external cause or event that comes to an already constituted ego to shatter its autonomy and integrity. . . . The result is a rigid dichotomy between internal and external such that violence is imagined as coming to the subject entirely from outside. (2000, p. 37)

The external view carries some positive political valence, as Leys notes, in that it frees the trauma sufferer from any suggestion of collusion in her or his own suffering. It is probably, in part, this simplification, with its redemptive connotations, that irked Primo Levi, who understood all too well the ethical conundrums of life in the *lager* and the complexities of trauma narrative.[3] A particular difficulty with the mimetic approach, which recognizes the implication of the unconscious in "creating" trauma in an individual, Leys points out, is that it denies the veridicality of memory and leaves open the possibility that the actual trauma, as experienced, is potentially a confabulation: "The hypnotic suggestibility of the victim of dissociation or PTSD makes the patient's testimony about the historical truth of the traumatic origins inherently suspect owing to the potential for hypnotic confabulation and 'false memories'" (2000, p. 38). As Leys explains, and my experience preparing affidavits for U.S. immigration proceedings bears this out, the presence of a potentially fictive or subjective—or, God forbid, unconscious—dimension to traumatic experience defies the rigid polarity between internal and external on which the positivist medical and legal foundations of contemporary trauma discourses are constructed. In addition, Leys notes that any potentiality to explain such well-recognized phenomena as *identification with the aggressor* is lost, because the active working of the unconscious cannot be named:

> The mimetic theory makes it possible to sympathetically acknowledge the hideous ways in which the victim can come to psychically collude in the scene of violence through fantasmic identifications with the scene of aggression. Whereas the complete rejection of any idea of the mimetic renders the source of such identifications mysterious. (2000, p. 38)

Leys raises important questions that have deep import for how we understand the therapeutic process of trauma "treatment"; the nature of trauma "testimony" as collected by historians and documentarians; and the legal basis of what constitutes the "evidence" that is proffered either in individual cases of traumatized persons seeking redress, or in the case of judicial proceedings or truth commissions seeking to document mass traumas, such as genocides, mass rape, use of children as soldiers and so on.

AN ESSENTIAL PSYCHOANALYSIS

Psychoanalysis had radical origins and intentions, but, sadly contemporary psychoanalysis in North America—particularly psychoanalysis as clinical practice—suffers from what Russell Jaccoby (1975) terms *social amnesia.* Elizabeth Danto's (2005) book, *Freud's Free Clinics* documents the early aspirations of psychoanalysis to develop a praxis of social justice. As Watkins and Shulman (2008) note in *Towards Psychologies of Liberation,*

> prominent members of the early psychoanalytic movement who were Marxists included Erich Fromm, Otto Fenichel, Gustave Landauer, Annie Reich; socialists included Bruno Bettelheim, Greta Bibring, Helene Deutsche, Ernst Simmel, and Siegfried Bernfeld; communists included Edith Jacobson, Marie Langer, and Wilhem Reich; and social democrats included Karen Horney, Paul Federn, and Sigmund Freud. (p. 58)

With its emphasis on symptoms only as surface manifestations, and with an acknowledgement that all actions are embedded in contexts, Watkins and Shulman are correct in noting that depth psychology is ideally suited for developing rich conceptualizations of the embeddedness of human subjectivity and human action in cultural, historical, and institutional contexts. Early psychoanalysis also had a strong focus on *praxis*, on the carrying over of these analytic ideas into analysis of and intervention in the problems of everyday life. Watkins and Shulman note:

> In the early period of psychoanalysis forged in Red Vienna, psychoanalysts were personally involved in initiatives for free clinics for psychoanalytic treatment, free clinics for reproductive health care and education for women, experimental schools for children of the poor, the kindergarten movement, school-based treatment centers for children traumatized by war and poverty, settlement house psychology classes for workers, the first child guidance clinics, and suicide prevention centers. They paid attention to building conditions for peace and stability in Austria and Europe, put forward initiatives to help women struggle against various forms of domination and control, and suggested architectural changes for public housing that would help build urban families' sense of community, understood to undergird psychological health. (p. 56)

Freud, himself, of course, tackled larger societal issues in works such as *Civilization and Its Discontents* (1930) and *The future of an illusion* (1927), and he was chagrined at the coup by which American psychiatrists gained exclusive control of psychoanalytic training in the United States and used it to exclude lay analysts. With the exodus of Jewish analysts from Austria and Germany during World War II, many sought refuge in the United States, and, as Neil Altman (1995) shows in *The Analyst in the Inner City*, anxious about their outsider status as Jews, many émigré analysts worked hard to earn a place in the mainstream, white profession of American psychoanalysis. The price they paid for this assimilation, Altman notes, was to turn a blind eye to racism and inequality in the profession and to abandon any interest in social justice or praxis. Shibboleths such as the notion that certain classes of marginal people—notably persons of limited means and those with certain psychotic disorders or complex social suffering—were *unanalyzable*, and mendacious and self-serving arguments about the need for rigidity in schedules, fees, etc., served to further perpetuate the image of psychoanalysis as elite, out-of-touch, racist, classist, etc. In his (1953) *History of Psychoanalysis in America,* Obendorf noted: "Psychoanalysis has finally become legitimate and respectable, perhaps paying the price in becoming sluggish and smug, hence attractive to an increasing number of minds which find security in conformity and prosperity" (p. 207, quoted in Moskowitz, 1996, p. 29). Paul Stepansky (2009) recently noted in *Psychoanalysis at the Margins,* that American psychoanalysis has been profoundly myopic about the long-term consequences of its blinkered self-interested goal of creating an exclusive privileged white club of well-remunerated analysts working for the power elite. Shulman and Watkins pull no punches in describing how much of an enforcer of orthodoxy the psychoanalytic establishment in the United States was:

> Psychoanalyst Harry Stack Sullivan courageously tried to address the racism and militarism of America, and found himself ostracized by his own colleagues and plagued by financial worries during the final decades of his life. Other analysts in the cultural school of psychoanalysis, such as Fromm and Horney, worked with psychoanalytic insights, reading from them not universal truths but situated conflicts, descriptive of the impact of culture on psyche. The heart of the psychoanalytic movement in the United States ostracized both Fromm and Horney. Wilhelm Reich, radical advocate for women's reproductive rights and to whom we are indebted for inspiring many approaches to psyche/soma healing, was arrested and imprisoned toward the end of his life on charges of violating interstate commerce laws. He died in an American penitentiary. (p. 58)

From a pragmatic perspective, American psychoanalysis ultimately made a grievous miscalculation by hitching its wagon exclusively to psychiatry in the early days. While psychoanalysis had unprecedented influence in psychiatry through the 1950s, the invention of psychopharmacological treatments for psychosis and schizophrenia, and later for depression, anxiety, and other supposed disorders, eventually brought American psychoanalysis to the brink of extinction. Robert Whitaker's (2001, 2010) history of the opportunistic shift of psychiatry away from psychoanalysis and toward psychopharmacology documents how institutional psychiatry has virtually abandoned psychoanalysis in favor of more profitable, brief medical consultation and a decidedly deterministic and biologized view of mental disturbance as neurochemical in origin. Ethan Watters' (2010) recent book, *Crazy Like Us: The Globalization of the American Psyche* underlines how this "victory" is leading to a worldwide colonization of mental health by reductionist biological and psychopharmacological discursive practices.

Psychoanalysis, History, and the Recovery of Memory

Ignacio Martín Baró, a Jesuit priest and psychologist in El Salvador was gunned down by government soldiers with some colleagues, his housekeeper, and his housekeeper's daughter, in 1989. Martín Baró was a thorn in the side of the military junta because he chose to speak truth to power. His work fused his skills as a psychologist, his humanitarian impulses, his belief in the social justice principles of Liberation Theology, and a commitment to praxis and to conscientización as advocated by Paulo Freire. Conscientización, in Freire's thinking (e.g., 1969, 1970), refers to the capacity of a facilitator to assist people in coming to new capacities to read their worlds critically so that they then have the capacity to act to change their living conditions. While the modernism of Freire's model has been superseded by postcolonial theories that reject the simplistic binaries of oppressor and oppressed, black and white, and so on, Martín Baró's (1994) work makes a strong moral claim in that he actually spoke truth to power in a way that mattered, and because he focuses significantly on what is perhaps the greatest weapon that can be turned against totalitarian regimes, the recovery of dangerous memory. Martín Baró (1994) recognizes ahistoricism and individualism as significant faults in contemporary psychology (pp. 22–23) and he argues for a psychology that focuses on the recovery of memory: "Thus, the recovery of a historical memory supposes the reconstruction of models of identification that, instead of chaining and caging the people, open up the horizon for them, toward their liberation and fulfillment" (p. 30). He speaks of ways in which mass media and the state apparatus obfuscate the working of ideology, and he points to the need for facilitators who can de-ideologize everyday experience so that it can be exposed to scrutiny. He says each person needs "to say the word of one's own existence" (p. 40) and, following Freire, he suggests that "[t]hrough the gradual decoding of their world, people grasp the mechanisms of oppression and dehumanization." "This," Martín Baró says, "crumbles the consciousness that mythifies the situation as natural, and opens up the horizon to new possibilities for action" (p. 40). What is crucial here, and this is most relevant to any discussion of the possibilities of liberatory psychoanalysis as Erich Fromm and others understood, is that the intrapsychic feelings of the individual are understood within the context of sociohistorical circumstance, as opposed to in isolation from the social. Martín Baró puts it this way:

> Taking conscientización as the horizon for psychology's work preserves the focus on the personal that psychology finds necessary, but not the person as opposed to or foreign to the social. The personal here is the dialectical correlate of the social, and, as such, incomprehensible if its constitutive referent is omitted. There is no person without family, no learning without culture, no madness without social order, and therefore neither can there be an I without a We, a knowing without a symbolic system, a disorder that does not have reference to moral and social norms. (p. 41)

If indeed the subjectivity of individuals and groups is constituted ancestrally and historically, the recovery of memory ought to be a key tenet of any approach to liberatory cultural work. Unfortunately, as Martín Baró learned to his cost, recovery of memory requires the return of the shadow side of history and being, a narrative that counters the master-narrative, a narrative that counters the official story, the party line, the received ideology. Hence recuperation of memory is extremely dangerous work to undertake because of its revolutionary potential. The Tian'anmen Square massacres in China and the protests of the Mothers of Plaza de Mayo in Argentina illustrate the courage, conviction, and danger involved. Not surprisingly, Martín Baró suggests that war and violence are most susceptible to "a rationalizing ideologization" (p. 112). It is important to note, however, as the anthropological inquiries of João Biehl (2005) and Nancy Scheper-Hughes (1992) illustrate, that rationalization applies not only to military and physical violence but also to institutional and social forms of violence, such as endemic poverty, bigoted and inequitable schooling, inequitable and dehumanizing health care, and institutional welfare services for those who are marginal in capitalist economies. Since capitalist societies benefit from not only obfuscating the mechanisms that produce inequality but also from a flight to consumption, those who would either question the promotion of consumption or interrogate the ancestral and historical underpinnings of contemporary subject formation (e.g., as Foucault, Bourdieu, Deleuze, Guattari, and others have done) are challenging the most powerful hegemonic forces in any society. The starkly political implications of this stand—and no doubt the reason it might be anathema to bourgeois psychoanalysts and psychologists—is apparent in Martín Baró's words:

> Latin American peoples need a clear historical memory in order to trace the workings of their history, and to know where to seek the causes of their long-standing oppression and their present situation . . . memory is especially important in the present situation when the ruling groups are carrying out a vast propaganda effort to blame the problems of Latin America on East-West conflict and more specifically on "communist subversion" as though the ills of Latin America derived from Soviet expansionism or first began when Fidel Castro rose to power. If they attain a clearsighted historical consciousness, Latin Americans will be able to use events and facts to evaluate the ideological proposals now being put forward, and in so doing they will also be able to unmask the Orwellian quality of the dominant language. (pp. 218–19)

The Analyst as "Annalist" of Inaudible Histories

I borrowed the title of this section from a section heading in Françoise Davoine and Jean-Max Gaudillière's (2004) *History beyond Trauma*. Rather than focus on all of the areas of theory and praxis in which psychoanalysis can contribute to the reclamation of suppressed memory, I decided to just develop one core idea from what is a surprisingly radical treatise on psychoanalytic work. Davoine and Gaudillière, drawing on Lynn Hunt's (2002) work on the French Revolution, point out the appalling reductionism involved in articulating an intrapsychic notion of clinical practice that takes no account of historical context. Instead of seeing difficulties of the individual as embodying individual disorder or lack, Davoine and Gaudillière argue that we must pay attention to the gaps and ruptures of individual experience because they are symptoms pointing us precisely to the moments of history that have been erased: "[T]heir absence of boundaries is the source of their ability to bear witness to the stories that have been erased from history, the history of breakdowns in the social order" (p. xxi). Persons suffering severe symptoms such as psychosis and major depression, therefore, may need our assistance to bring "into existence zones of nonexistence wiped out by a powerful blow that actually took place" (p. xxvii). In referring here to actual traumatic events, Davoine and Gaudillière are well aware, of course, that while such events may have occurred in real time, such as, for example, in battlefield trauma, they could reflect the spectral presences of restless ghosts and unsymbolized archaic and ancestral experiences. My own work (O'Loughlin, 2012) on the catastrophic consequence of The Great Hunger in Ireland in the 1840s, a catastrophe in which a million died, and a further 3 million destitute fled Ireland in coffin ships, is built entirely on this premise and is supported by important theoretical and clinical work from psychoanalytic theorists, Holocaust scholars and other trauma scholars.[4] For Davoine and Gaudillière, therefore, a manifestation such as psychosis is a welcome messenger, a signifier, pointing us to untold and sometimes untellable stories.

History is spoken through the symptom: "Sometimes a fit of madness tells us more than all the news dispatches about the leftover facts that have no right to existence" (p. xxvii).

The role of the analyst as *annalist*, therefore, refers to the role of the analyst as recuperator of memory and history, "the chronicler who keeps the records of a gesture that has been silenced" (p. 28). Madness, in this scheme, can best be conceptualized as severance of social linkages between individuals and ancestral epistemologies, spiritual practices, and ways of being. As Jonathan Lear (2006) noted in *Radical Hope*, the consequence of the Westward expansion in the United States meant cultural devastation for the indigenous peoples of what became North America. Kai Erikson (1976) speaks similarly of the cultural devastation experienced by residents of the mining community of Buffalo Creek when pollution from the local mining industry caused a community to be broken up and located to disparate places. I have applied similar arguments to the analysis of the plight of Aboriginal Australians (O'Loughlin, 2008, 2009a, b). In all such cases, a conventional medicalized, individualized, intrapsychic approach would locate so-called pathologies, including addictions, domestic violence, depression, failure to engage in gainful employment, and failure to participate as a functionary in a late-capitalist economy, as symptoms of deviance, pathology, or even madness. Nancy Scheper-Hughes (2003) refers to this syndrome of institutional violence, neglect, dehumanization, and commodification as *invisible genocide*. Lest we sit back and breathe easy because of our bourgeois accoutrements, Scheper-Hughes tells an appalling, cautionary tale of her frail parents' final days in geriatric care. It seems that even the privileged rapidly lose respect when they become either physically diseased like her dad, or suffer dementia like her mom. Mechanisms of pathologization and condemnation—invisible genocide—are occupational hazards for all of us when we can no longer play the game as apparatchiks of the system.

A key concept in Lacanian theory, of course is the *question*. Davoine and Gaudillière speak to how easily an analyst can open or close the field of *logos*:

> A disingenuous reply or an embarrassed silence, when adamantly repeated, sends the subject into nonexistence on this point. He exiles himself, falls silent, goes crazy. Instead of speaking to him, people speak of him as an aberration . . . he is made into a fool, a madman, an innocent—until he manages to find someone else who accepts the challenge of reopening the question. (p. 70)

Ignacio Martín Baró devoted himself to just such a pursuit.

With respect to method, Davoine and Gaudillière have little patience with analysts who put fancy theories or portentous pronouncements between themselves and their patients.

> Today, as well, pseudo-science and psychodiafoiresque theories, and especially the newspeak for internal use, impeded access to madness and traumas. With a bit of kitchen Latin, seasoned with a few obscurities borrowed from more firmly grounded discourses, it will always be easy to make an appointment with the chorus of the learned so as to conclude after some gibberish that has no bearing on the case, that "this is exactly why your daughter is mute." . . . "It isn't so simple," said Gilda, "simply to meet someone." (p. 249)

This "meeting" in the presence of a sensitive analyst, attuned to "fossil messages" in the being of the patient, eventually leads to the possibility of finding tattered remnants of those severed social links and stitching together a patch in the ruptured narrative of a person or community of people, much, as I noted elsewhere (O'Loughlin, 2009b) my mother used thread to darn holes in our socks and the elbows of our sweaters.

Davoine and Gaudillière conclude their final paragraph, with a fitting epigraph to the possibility of a liberatory psychoanalysis:

> This is the only membership we want to boast of, here at the end of this book. At the moment of conclusion, Rabelais invites us to not let ourselves be fascinated by the horrible beauty of recorded catastrophes. "Whereof one cannot speak . . .": the putting in the story/history of this impossibility bears witness to the path we had to travel in order to pass from mouth to mouth and inscribe it. In reality, this "bloody rough way," as Wittgenstein calls it, goes through traumas and madness to secure the production of freedom among men. (p. 256)

TROUBLING TRAUMA: MORAL GENEALOGY AND MORAL WITNESS

In *The Empire of Trauma* (2009), Fassin and Rechtman offer a critique of the psychologization of trauma and the extrapolation from individual suffering to the effects of collective trauma on whole societies. They suggest that over the twentieth century, the shift from trauma neurosis to PTSD has led to "a narrowing of the gap between the climate of public opinion and the preoccupations of mental health professionals, between the moral economy and medical theory" (2009, p. 22). They show how, through the utilitarian and financial imperatives of personal injury litigation and veteran advocacy for benefits, the medical model has "infiltrated social discourse" (p. 22), shifting Western societies from "[a] realm in which trauma was regarded with suspicion to a realm in which it carries the stamp of authenticity" (p. 23). This has led to the normalization of narrow, psychologized trauma discourses, of which the definition of PTSD in the DSM is the apotheosis. Fassin and Rechtman seek to articulate a moral genealogy of trauma: What is it that thinking of certain human experiences through the lens of trauma and victimhood produces? They suggest that our modern, reified concept of trauma has produced "a new relationship to time and memory, to mourning and obligations, to misfortune and the misfortunate" (p. 276). We are creating a new trauma culture in which there is "unprecedented ability to talk about—and hence experience—the violence of the world" (p. 277). From the point of view of an anthropology of subjectivity, Fassin and Rechtman suggest that this "new language of the event" (p. 6) shapes the subjectivity of victimhood and the ways in which victims characterize their experience of suffering. As happens quite literally in the case of judicial asylum proceedings, sufferers must master the only narrative that matters—the master-narrative of trauma— however oppressive and erasing that may be (cf. Summerfield, 2001) in the service of survival or achievement of a utilitarian goal, such as acquiring a residence permit, an award of compensation, or access to military veteran health care. This of course begs the question:

> what does this process not allow to be said, and who are those whom it makes possible to leave out? In other words, while trauma is a language that appears both neutral and universal in its account of victims, it significantly fails to throw light on certain signifieds and certain agents. Identifying the gaps gives us the means to grasp the figure of the victim delineated by trauma. (p. 281)

At its most reductionist, Fassin and Rechtman argue, with an exclusive focus on symptomatology, trauma erases both victim, perpetrator, context, and history, instead focusing exclusively on the mark left on the perpetrator. As they note, in discussing the psychotraumatology of asylum evaluation, "When more credence is given to a medical certificate attesting to post-traumatic stress than to the word of the asylum seeker, what conception of the law and of the subject is operating?" (p. 8).

What seems to be called for then, as Giorgio Agamben notes in *Remnants of Auschwitz* (1999), is some means of bringing the unspeakable back into discourses of trauma. He argues that it is the very incommensurability of traumatic experience—of which indeed Holocaust extermination is the archetype—that provides an opportunity for witness. It is from this *nonplace* that testimony can emerge:

> *Testimony takes place in the non-place of articulation.* In the non-place of the Voice stands not writing but the witness. And it's precisely because the relation (or rather non-relation) between the living and the speaking being has the form of shame, of being reciprocally consigned to something that cannot be assumed by a subject, that the ēthos of this disjunction can only be testimony—that is, something that cannot be assigned to a subject but that nevertheless constitutes the subject's only dwelling place, its only possible consistency. (1999, p. 130)

In Agamben's terms, then, it appears that attention to the *remnants* (e.g., of Auschwitz) is what is needed: ". . . so the remnants of Auschwitz—the witnesses—are neither the dead nor the survivors, neither the drowned nor the saved. They are what remains between them" (1999, p. 164). A possible solution, therefore, to addressing trauma and recuperating dangerous memory would appear to lie in the acutely attuned listening gained by combining the sociopolitical sensibility suggested by Martín Baró's work and attunement to fossil memories and historical silences suggested by Davoine and Gaudillière, with the ethical sensibility suggested by Agamben. This sensibility is articulated further by Avishai Margalit in *The Ethics of Memory* (2002). In noting that memory is "*knowledge from the past*, it is not necessarily knowledge about the past" (2002, p. 14), Margalit also underlines that recuperation of memory is more about recuperating sensibility than about establishing veridicality or resurrecting factual or chronological narrative. While recognizing all of the dangers of recuperated memory—with its attendant risk of recuperating old hatreds and humiliations, and hence stoking an impulse for vengeance—Margalit's hope is that our capacity to bear moral witness can lead to the creation of ethical communities of caring that serve as a bulwark against the repetitions of tyranny:

> why cannot humanity be shaped into a community of memory and why cannot it be formed into an ethical community based on the thick relation of caring? . . . Ought not this moral community to have some minimal sense of memory for, say, the Gulags, the Kulaks, Majdanek and Treblinka, Hiroshima and Nanking, as warning signposts in human moral history? (2002, p. 71)

Margalit offers a utopian view, but living in a dystopian world where conflict is perpetual and dissent or even remembering can be dangerous, his view provides an important compass bearing for those of us who harbor visions of healing and social justice

NOTES

1. For critiques of DSM and the globalization of American psychiatric concepts, in addition to Fassin and Rechtman (2009), see Bracken (1998), Summerfield (2001), Watters (2010), and Young (1995).

2. See claims for the effectiveness of this program at: http://www.army.mil/article/72431/Study_concludes_Master_Resilience_Training_effective/ [Retrieved on 3/2/14], and for an overview see Rendon (2012). For discussion of the supposed psychological underpinnings of the training, see for example Casey (2011), Peterson, Park and Castro (2011), Reivich, Seligman, and McBride (2011), and Seligman (2011b).

3. See Langer (1991) and Lanzmann (1995) for discussion of the problematics of reducing trauma testimony to comprehensible narrative truths.

4. For review of relevant literature see, e.g., O'Loughlin, 2008, 2009a, 2010, 2012, 2013.

REFERENCES

Agamben, G. (1999). *Remnants of Auschwitz: The witness and the archive*. New York: Zone Books.

Alpert, J. [Director]. (2011). *Wartorn 1861–2010* [DVD]. HBO Studios.

Altman, N. (1995). *The analyst in the inner city: Race, class and color through a psychoanalytic lens*. Hillsdale, NJ: Analytic Press.

American Psychiatric Association. (2013). *Diagnostic and statistical manual of mental disorders*, 5th Edition: DSM-5. Washington, DC: American Psychiatric Publishing.

Biehl, J. (2005). *Vita: Life in a zone of social abandonment*. Berkeley: University of California Press.

Bracken, P. (1998). Hidden agendas: Deconstructing posttraumatic stress disorder, In P. Bracken & C. Petty (Eds.). *Rethinking the trauma of war*. London: Free Association Books.

Casey, Jr., G. W. (2011). Comprehensive soldier fitness: A vision for psychological resilience in the U.S. Army. *American Psychologist*, *66*, 1, 1–3.

Danto, E. (2005). *Freud's free clinics: Psychoanalysis and social justice, 1918–1938.* New York: Columbia University Press.

Davoine, F. & Gaudillière, J. (2004). *History beyond trauma*. New York: Other Press.

Erikson, K. (1976). Loss of community at Buffalo Creek. *American Journal of Psychiatry, 133,* 302–5.

Fassin, D. & Rechtman, R. (2009). *The empire of trauma: An inquiry into the conditions of victimhood*. Princeton, NJ: Princeton University Press.

Freire, P. (1970). *Pedagogy of the oppressed*. New York: Continuum.

Freire, P. (1969). *Education for critical consciousness*. New York: Continuum.

Freud, S. (1930). *Civilization and its discontents*. SE, 21, 59–145.

Freud, S. (1927). *The future of an illusion*. SE, 21, 3–56.

Freud, S. (1955/1920). Beyond the pleasure principle. In *Beyond the pleasure principle: Group psychology and other works*. Trans. J. Strachey. London: Hogarth.

Garland, C. (1998). Thinking about trauma. In C. Garland (Ed.). *Understanding trauma: A psychoanalytical approach*. London: Karnac.

Hacking, I. (1996). Memory sciences, memory politics. In P. Antze & M. Lambek (Eds.). *Tense past: Cultural essays in trauma and memory*. New York: Routledge (pp. 67–87).

Herman, J. (1997). *Trauma and recovery*. New York: Basic Books

Hunt, L. (1992). *The family romance of the French Revolution*. Berkeley, CA: University of Califronia Press.

Jaccoby, R. (1975). *Social amnesia: A critique of contemporary psychology from Adler to Laing*. Boston: Beacon Press.

Langer, L. (1991). *Holocaust testimonies: The ruins of memory*. New Haven: Yale University Press.

Lanzmann, C. (1995). The obscenity of understanding: An evening with Claude Lanzmann. In C. Caruth, *Trauma: Explorations in memory*. Baltimore: Johns Hopkins University Press.

Lear, J. (2006). *Radical hope: Ethics in the face of cultural devastation*. Cambridge, MA: Harvard University Press.

Levi, P. (1988). *The drowned and the saved*. New York: Viking.

Leys, R. (2000). *Trauma: A genealogy*. Chicago: University of Chicago Press.

Margalit, A. (2002). *The ethics of memory*. Cambridge, MA: Harvard University Press.

Martín Baró, I. (1994). *Writings for a liberation psychology*. In A. Aron & S. Corne (Eds.). Cambridge, MA: Harvard University Press.

Moskowitz, M. (1996). The social conscience of psychoanalysis. In R. Perez Foster, M. Moskowitz, & R. Javier (Eds.). *Reaching across boundaries of culture and class: Widening the script of psychoanalysis*. New Jersey: Jason Aronson.

Obendorf, C. P. (1953). *History of psychoanalysis in America*. New York: Harper & Row.

O'Loughlin, M. & McLeod, B. (2014). "Thinking beyond our means": Engendering a depth understanding of trauma. In M. O'Loughlin & M. Charles (Eds.), *Fragments of trauma and the social production of suffering: Trauma, history, and memory*. Lanham, MD: Rowman & Littlefield.

O'Loughlin, M. (2013). Reclaiming genealogy, memory and history: The psychodynamic potential for reparative therapy in contemporary South Africa. In C. Smith, G. Lobban, & M. O'Loughlin (Eds.). *Psychodynamic psychotherapy in contemporary South Africa: Contexts, theories, practices*. Johannesburg, SA: Wits University Press.

O'Loughlin, M. (2012). Trauma trails from Ireland's Great Hunger: A psychoanalytic inquiry. In B. Willock, R. Curtis, & L. Bohm (Eds.). *Loneliness and longing: Conscious and unconscious aspects*. New York: Routledge.

O'Loughlin, M. (2010). Ghostly presences in children's lives: Toward a psychoanalysis of the social. In M. O'Loughlin & R. Johnson (Eds.). *Imagining children otherwise: Theoretical and critical perspectives on childhood subjectivity*. New York: Peter Lang Publishing. [Reprinted in M. O'Loughlin (Ed.). *Psychodynamic perspectives on working with children, families and schools*. (2013). Lanham, MD: Jason Aronson.]

O'Loughlin, M. (2009a). An analysis of collective trauma among indigenous Australians and a suggestion for intervention. *Australasian Psychiatry, 17*, 33–36.

O'Loughlin, M. (2009b). *The subject of childhood*. New York: Peter Lang.

O'Loughlin, M. (2008). Radical hope or death by a thousand cuts? The future for indigenous Australians. *Arena Journal, 29/30*, 175–202.

O'Loughlin, M. (2007a). Bearing witness to troubled memory. *Psychoanalytic Review, 94*, 2, 191–212.

O'Loughlin, M. (2007b). On losses that are not easily mourned. In L. Bohm, R. Curtis, & B. Willock (Eds.). *Psychoanalysts' reflections on deaths and endings: Finality, transformations, new beginnings*. New York: Routledge.

Peterson, C., Park, N., & Castro, C. A. (2011). Assessment for the U.S. Army comprehensive soldier fitness program: Global assessment tool. *American Psychologist, 66*, 1, 10–18.

Reivich, K. J., Seligman, M. E. P., & McBride, S. (2011). Master resilience training in the U.S. Army. *American Psychologist, 66*, 1, 25–34.

Rendon, J. (2012, March 22). Post-traumatic stress's surprisingly positive flip side. *New York Times Magazine.* Retrieved from http://www.nytimes.com/2012/03/25/magazine/post-traumatic-stresss-surprisingly-positive-flip-side.html?pagewanted=all. Retrieved 3.2.2014.

Scheper-Hughes, N. (2003). A genealogy of genocide. *Modern Psychoanalysis, 28,* 167–97.

Scheper-Hughes, N. (1992). *Death without weeping: The violence of everyday life in Brazil.* Berkeley: University of California Press.

Seligman, M. E. P. (2011a). *Flourish: A visionary new understanding of happiness and well-being.* New York: Atria Books.

Seligman, M. E. P. (2011b). Building resilience. *Harvard Business Review, 89*, 4, 100–106.

Seligman, M. E. P. (2002). *Authentic happiness: Using the new positive psychology to realize your potential for lasting fulfillment.* New York: Free Press.

Stepansky, P. (2009). *Psychoanalysis at the margins.* New York: Other Press.

Summerfield, D. (2001). The invention of post-traumatic stress disorder and the social usefulness of a psychiatric category. *British Medical Journal, 322,* 95–98.

Van der Kolk, B. (2014). *The body keeps the score: Brain, mind and body in the healing of trauma.* New York: Viking.

Van der Kolk, B., McFarlane, V., & Weisaeth, L. (Eds.). (2009). *Traumatic stress: The effects of overwhelming experience on mind, body, society.* New York: The Guilford Press.

Van der Kolk, B., Greenberg, M., Boyd H., & Krystal, J. (1985). Inescapable shock, neurotransmitters in trauma: Toward a psychobiology of post-traumatic stress. *Biological Psychiatry, 20*, 3, 18, 365–70.

Watkins, M. & Shulman, H. (2008). *Toward psychologies of liberation.* New York: Palgrave Macmillan.

Watters, E. (2010). *Crazy like us: The globalization of the American psyche.* New York: Free Press.

Whitaker, R. (2010). *Anatomy of an epidemic.* New York: Crown.

Whitaker, R. (2001). *Mad in America.* New York: Basic Books.

Young, A. (1995). *The harmony of illusions: Inventing post-traumatic stress disorder.* Princeton, NJ: Princeton University Press.

Part II

BIOGRAPHICAL REMNANTS

Chapter 3

Wit(h)nessing the Other's Trauma

An Exploration of Barbara Loftus's Painting through the Work of Bracha Ettinger

Angie Voela

A recollection: I am holding in my hands Barbara Loftus's (2011) exhibition catalogue: *Sigismund's Watch: A Tiny Catastrophe*. A colleague has asked me to look at Barbara's work. My colleague is an art historian but does not use psychoanalysis very much. She would like my help with some "fiddly concepts." I do not know much about the artist, apart from the fact that her work deals with memories of the Holocaust. As I open the book at random, I come across *Hildegard under the Table*, a painting of a young girl playing with her dolls under a dinner table, half concealed and shaded by a heavy, dark tablecloth.

What a beautiful painting, I think to myself, admiring the colors, the brushwork, and the composition. I used to like hiding under the big dinner table when I was a child, arranging little toys on a recess formed by the wooden frame and a missing drawer. The girl's bow reminds me of an old school photograph of my aunt: three rows of girls, all with similar bows. It must have been the fashion before the war. Sweet woman my aunt—meek, vulnerable. She never stopped talking about her dad's bankruptcy and how they lost everything. Hildegard's body retains a hint of chubbiness, the kind of roundness children lose as they get older; how old is she? My son is not a baby anymore. What is she looking at? Suddenly, I am seized by a feeling of anxiety, and shame: how can I *enjoy* this picture when it refers to the Holocaust? How ridiculous of me to think of myself, my aunt, my son! I cannot help my friend. I don't know enough about the Holocaust.

The present paper, which is entitled "Wit(h)nessing the other's trauma," is a theoretical response to my encounter with Barbara Loftus's painting. It draws on Lacanian psychoanalysis and the work of painter, philosopher, and psychoanalyst Bracha Ettinger. Ettinger's work is in dialogue with both the cultural studies of trauma and the theory of psychoanalysis. Unlike many theorists who insist on the incommunicability of an historical trauma like the Holocaust, Ettinger proposes that the disposition to sharing trauma is inherent to subjectivity and humanity, harking back to the coexistence of the mother and the child. Critiquing Lacan's version of the mother-child relationship as one of unavoidable separation which is subsequently banished to an inaccessible Real and permanently superceded by the phallic signifier in the symbolic order, Ettinger (2006) develops the notion of the Matrix as a signifier of copresence and coproduction (copoiesis) which complements the phallus. Both her artistic work and her theoretical contributions are therefore developed in two contexts: the revision of subjectivity, especially feminine subjectivity, as copoiesis and witnessing, and the revision of trauma as the inherently common basis for remembering events like the Holocaust, especially today, at a time of pervasive cultural amnesia. Artwork is central to this endeavor. It is the locus in which the witnessing takes place and the domain in which we become, what she calls, *partial subjects*, deliberately echoing and challenging the Lacanian key notion of the *partial object*, the elusive source of enjoyment hailing from the Real. There is an inherent ethical dimension to witnessing the other's trauma and to becoming partial subjects. Ettinger locates it in the unconscious affective qualities of the experience. Yet, it might be prudent to ask what happens to this ethical dimension when the effects of the encounter arise into consciousness and into the contemporary culture of amnesia.

Below, I discuss the ideas of witnessing the other's trauma and becoming a partial subject in the realm of the artwork. I explore this composite locus which encompasses the artwork, the act of witnessing, the trauma, the painter's perceived and unrecognised intentions, me as subject, and the several "others" who, as we shall see below, are invited and implied in this encounter. My intention is not to develop an exhaustive list of participants but to highlight some synergies between Ettinger's work and current work in cultural and trauma studies.

LACANIAN PSYCHOANALYSIS AND THE EXAMINATION OF EXPERIENCE

The paper is written in three parts. In the first part below, I offer a brief account of contemporary debates on trauma in cultural studies and art history, in order to indicate how Ettinger's perspective differs from but also complements existing approaches. The discussion in this section draws on a central and increasingly important concern, namely that direct representations of the Holocaust could be fainting from collective memory. In the second part of the chapter I give a detailed account of Ettinger's notion of the Matrix as alternative to the phallic economy, as well as of her theorization of witnessing and sharing, and of the fragilized subject, the latter being proposed as a viable and necessary contemporary alternative to the traumatized subject. In this section, I attempt to convey not only Ettinger's distinctive approach, but also the way in which cultural memory, in this case of the Holocaust, is rethought and revitalized via psychoanalytic theory. In the third part, I return to the work of art as a composite scene with a view to comparing Ettinger with Lacan. A critique often extended to Lacanian psychoanalysis is that the emphasis on the economy of the phallus obscures other routes of making sense of experience. Ettinger often refers to the immaterial locus between the artwork, the artist, and the viewer as a *nonplace* which reverberates with the affective potentiality of their encounter: a non-place of transgression at the margins of language (Ettinger, 2006, p. 140). Such a transgressive nonplace is not unknown to Lacanian psychoanalysis (Bosteels, 2003). It is not perhaps copoetic but arises with interpretation, an event which is significant for the radical revision of subjectivity. In this section, I argue that by aligning the event and nonplace of interpretation to the complexity of the encounter between partial subjects we may get a better idea of the ethical imperative involved in remembering-witnessing today. In that sense, my main concern is not to privilege one theoretical framework over another but to consider the interpretative possibilities arising in their juncture.

CONTEMPORARY CONCERNS

It was not until Barbara Loftus was a grown woman that she learned about her mother, Hildegard's, childhood memories of prewar Nazi Berlin. Hildegard had never wanted to talk about the past, but she broke her silence shortly before her death. She described the interior of the house in Keithstrasse, her mother and father, and various memories, among them a bitter row between her mother and father caused by the latter's bankruptcy due to hyperinflation: the mother tears her husband's gold watch from his waistcoat pocket, throws it on the floor, stamps and smashes it with her heel. Barbara Loftus's collection *Sigismund's Watch: A Tiny Catastrophe* was exhibited at the Freud Museum, London, in 2011. It included two versions of *Hildegard under the Table*, a photographic representation of the smashing of the watch with actors playing the role of the parents, and a series of three paintings on the same subject: a close-up of a smashed watch; a close-up of a hand grabbing a watch; a close-up of a shoe about to smash it. The collection also includes: *The Bridge Party*, depicting four women playing bridge; *The Staircase*, a typical bourgeois house interior staircase with a female figure descending and holding a letter; *Window: The Letter*, a painting of a woman standing by the window reading a letter; *Passing*, a close-up of a statuette passing from one pair of hands to another; *Staircase: Confiscation*, the same staircase with a laborer carrying a cardboard box; and *Empty Wardrobe*, a close-up of a bare piece of furniture. Barbara usually supplements her artistic work with documents and photographs of the time, trying, as she says, to understand the context of her mother's early life. An encounter with Hildegard's childhood brings up a host of theoretical concerns regarding memory, truth, subjectivity and spectatorship. For instance, how does a narration of events turn into a visualization of spaces? What is the value of that product? Whose truth does it speak? If it is not a "real" piece of the past, and, therefore, of historical-archival interest, how does it operate as a commemoration of an event like the Holocaust? In this section, I address some of these concerns, showing how they are accommodated in Ettinger's work. My account is by no means exhaustive. It does, however, attempt to encompass concerns in three fields relevant to Ettinger's work: art history, psychoanalysis, and cultural studies/trauma studies.

In his article on landscape photography and its relations to the representation of the Holocaust, Baer discusses Dirk Reinhartz's photograph "*Sobibor: Extermination Camp Grounds*" (Baer, 2000, p. 39). The photograph depicts a nondescript wood, which at first sight appears unrelated to the specific historical event. Yet, by referring to the Holocaust only in the title, the photograph creates *a site of memory*, or what Pierre Nora calls a *lieux de mémoire* (1989, p. 7). Such sites of memory, Baer argues, are now emerging more often than documentary photography, marking a clear shift in the way we remember this historical event as fewer and fewer survivors remain.

The operation of *sites of memory* is relevant to my argument and I discuss it in some detail. Looking at Reinhartz's photograph, Baer argues, creates a sense of having arrived too late (*après coup*) and a feeling of exclusion (Baer, 2000, p. 40). At the same time, the appreciation of the artistic merit of the photograph compels us to consider whether it is possible to enjoy art on aesthetic criteria alone, ignoring the historical context (Baer, 2000, p. 42). The image also invites us to consider our position as viewers. Representational art usually creates a feeling of being addressed by the work of art. Looking at "Sobibor," however, is difficult, as the viewer's eye has nowhere to go but remains fixed on a place that is absorbing yet unstable (Baer, 2006, p. 47). Thus, prior to any effort at commemoration, explanation, or understanding, we must come to terms with the belated witnessing itself. We must also "find a place and a position from which we may gain access to the event" (Baer, 2000, p. 43).

At the same time, the ordinariness of the landscape and its flatness, accentuated by darkroom processing, force all viewers to the same position, a collective *we* before the site of an event that all but completely shattered the most basic human bonds (Baer, 2000, p. 47). "Sobibor" further reverberates with the untold stories of those who vanished in the Holocaust. Even when we resort to knowledge gleaned from archives, a sense of ungroundedness persists, as we realize that the possibility of knowledge and comprehension was itself destroyed with the Holocaust (Baer, 2000, p. 46). Thus, concludes Baer, such images reference the (unrepresentable) Real: the *here and now* against the *there and then*, the having arrived too late and an uncanny sense of nonbelonging. They challenge knowledge with their very uselessness to historians and professional truth seekers (Baer, 2006, p. 50) through the *nothing* that refuses to be transformed and the sense of placelessness which comes across with their visual reference to this no man's land (Baer, 2000, p. 46).

Barbara Loftus's interiors are a *lieux de mémoire.* But in the case of *Hildegard under the Table* at least, I am not so sure about my exclusion from the picture. I find myself having already gained *an* access to it by way of an "excessive" inclusion, rather than by searching for a viewing position from the start. Thus, my unquestionable *belated arrival* at the site is momentarily preceded by an all too early and misplaced "false recognition" which, following Ettinger, we may take into consideration rather than discard as irrelevant. My sense of the Real therefore comes not from immediate exclusion but from the spatial coincidence of two incompatible emplacements: being "in" and "out," arriving both early and late. The same applies to the artist's treatment of time and place: the interiors Loftus envisages as *too late* are situated at a time *before* the big historical event and form an imaginary past of a past, useless to the historian but no less true and traumatic. The interiors are hers and her mother's; witnessing scenes that might not have been witnessed by Hildegard; events related to them—the confiscation of valuables—have been narrated, but that is the only fact we can verify; the paintings announce an event yet to come, too early too late, leaving the house, the latter to become a site of loss, of property, and then of life. These simultaneities of places and times suggest that between the viewer, the artist and the work, we may need to situate a revised and much more "generous" and "inclusive" conceptualisation of the Real.

The nature of memory and truth are also implicated in the encounter with Hildegard's childhood. Testimonies of historical traumatic events are normally accepted as truth-bearing documentary material, but whose memory and truth does a *lieux de mémoire* concern? Are the scenes of Hildegard's childhood home merely nonplaces of the adult daughter's imagination? Antze (2003) draws attention to the metaphorical relationship between infantile and adult memory in Freud's work. Freud, he argues, singled out a very small number of scenes from early childhood but was not interested in their declarative content. He was interested in re-collecting and joining them together *differently* during analysis, so that they took on new meanings and came to depict previously unsuspected situations and relationships for the patient

(Antze, 2003, p. 106). The historical reality of such early scenes was of secondary importance. Freud was therefore more interested in finding scenes with a *figurative power* to capture something central about the patient's life that had previously been obscure, and the grounding was *poetic* rather than historical. Such scenes can "open an imaginative space where something *other than me*, something I am not, can be used to reimagine me" (Antze, 2003, p. 109, emphasis added).

Can the *other than me* reconfigured in the locus of the artwork be not the individual child but another person? Can the figurative power of an artistic representation of childhood spaces capture something central to collective trauma? Can the ability to join the pieces of a childhood scene *differently* permanently sustain a poetic, metaphorical reworking of trauma? The scenes that interest Ettinger are not strictly individual and provisionally allow for such playful permutations. For Ettinger, a painting is not just a tableau or a world in itself, but "a transport-station of trauma that allows for passage between subjectivities" (Pollock, 2009, p. 52). Art, therefore, communicates, transforms, and shares the meanings of infantile scenes and traumas without dislodging them from their historical groundedness or tampering with their origin. At the same time, it invites rather than excludes others.

This invitation to others relates directly to ways of sharing and remembering historical traumas. In the almost canonical *Unclaimed Experience* (1996), Caruth's central argument pertains to the impossibility of perceiving the present in any other way than through an explication of the past. However, in her analysis, the witnessing of the other's wound always involves an act of separation, as is shown in the discussion of Clorinda's disembodied voice which must be separated from speech in order to be heard (1996, p. 8), or by the dream of the burning child, which conveys for the father the traumatic Real of the son's death beyond the realm of language. Again, in Caruth's reading of *Hiroshima Mon Amour*, the sharing of the trauma at Hiroshima, the site of catastrophe, "resonates beyond what we can know and understand" (1996, p. 56). It is, therefore, she concludes, "in the event of this incomprehension and in our departure from sense and understanding that our own witnessing may indeed begin to take place" (Caruth, 1996, p. 56).

Ettinger adopts a different perspective to sharing the trauma. She begins from a similar acceptance of the trauma's centrality in contemporary art and culture and of history as nonlinear and determined by the past. However, she does not approach the encounter with the traumatic Real in terms of separation. Considering Caruth's work from Ettinger's perspective, I would argue that the former appears to be pursuing trauma as an impossible *object a*[1] arising for successive acts of separation: of the voice from the text, the rhetorical trope from language and the material site from the witnessing of loss. Ettinger, on the other hand, posits a witness who will receive the other's trauma as *difference* but not strictly separated from the other, since the mental landscape in which the encounter takes place belongs to both. At that point, it seems to me that Ettinger also deliberately turns away from a rigorous differentiation between the structural trauma of birth and entry into language and historical traumas like the Holocaust (see La Capra, 1999). As a matter of fact, she proposes the former as the necessary human condition for the successful reception of the latter (Pollock, 2004, p. 19).

Ettinger's approach to trauma and art opens interesting pathways for sharing and commemorating historical events. By looking beyond immediate witnessing and the experiences of survivors, she attempts to create a robust theoretical and empirical basis for the experiences of those that come afterwards, après coup and always too late. At the same time, Ettinger's theoretical formulations chime with calls for the revision of psychoanalysis as well as with current concerns about the cultural shifts in the representation of trauma.

The reconfiguration of Lacanian theory by Ettinger is therefore to be understood in the wider context of how psychoanalysis understands the contemporary psyche. Olkowski (2007), for instance, critiques psychoanalysis for lack of openess to human pain and the sharing of pain, finding it a rather "closed" field mostly interested in theorizing the avoidance of unpleasure and the need for sublimation. But, notes Olkowski,

> If the psyche, the world, and the cosmos are not closed systems, if there is the possibility that they are open to vast material and energy flows, then something else may be conceived. Trauma itself would demand "reconceptualization" (2007, p. 63). This reconceptualization would also take into account the historical repression of women's difference, and will acknowledge "how few words, images and ideas we currently possess for describing the myriads of sensibilities we usually lump together as 'sexual.'" (Olkowski, 2007, p. 64)

As we shall see in the next section, Ettinger offers credible suggestions in both directions.

At the same time, various concerns are raised in the field of cultural studies: about the transcendentalization of trauma and the loss of its historical specificity when turned into "trauma for all" (Mowitt, 2007); about the contemporary glut of information surrounding the Holocaust which triggers a surge of derivate mental images (Baer, 2000, p. 44); about the sensualization of the other's pain which preys on the conflation of testimony and confession (Modlinger & Sonntag, 2011); about the dark glamor of trauma, the limits of empathy and the disavowal of the victim in the act of identification or in the language of sympathy (Modlinger & Sonntag, 2011); about the near-impossibility of giving an account of oneself, let alone telling the other's story (Davis, 2011). Radstone highlights the oxymoronic popularity of trauma today and critiques the Manichean binaries of "inside" and "outside," "trauma" and "normality," "victims" and "perpetrators" (2007, p. 19) currently favored in the field of Trauma Studies. She finds that the topological "flattening out" of the psyche blunts the distinction between intrapsychic and intersubjective processes (2007, p. 20). Radstone emphasizes the unconscious processes in the production of the mind's scenes and meaning, drawing attention to the activities of condensation, displacement, and symbolization fundamental to the Freudian model (2007, p. 18). She also recommends admitting into the reckoning "the darker side of the mind," such as sexual fantasies, that trauma theory usually sees only as coming from outside (2007, p. 19). Thus, she proposes moving beyond modernity's autonomous and knowing subject to "a model of subjectivity grounded in the space between witness and testifier within which that which cannot be known can begin to be witnessed" (2007, p. 20).

I cannot claim that Ettinger directly responds to Radstone's concerns, but she certainly seems to suggest an expansion of the intersubjective relation in order to accommodate various psychoanalytic functions: jouissance, traumas, pictograms, fantasies, affects and channels death-drive oscillations, libidinal-erotic flow, and the imprints of affective traces differently (2000, p. 195). Ettinger constructs a realm which is not marked by incommunicability and separation but by communicability and commonality. The art-scene, in which the trauma emerges, is therefore like a Deleuzian assemblage of affects, trajectories, forces, memory traces, multiple, and copoietic gestures, which both enrich and frustrate sovereign subjectivity and autonomy. At the same time, this process creates a welcoming space for anyone who has the desire, the ethical capacity, or merely the curiosity to remember someone else's pain. Below I flesh out Ettinger's main theoretical construction, the *Matrix*. I also introduce the operation of "*metramorphosis*"[2] which is taking place in its space, and the notion of becoming a partial subject while witnessing the other's trauma.

THE MATRIX, METRAMORPHOSIS, AND THE EXPERIENCE OF SHARING THE OTHER'S TRAUMA

The experience of witnessing the other's trauma and becoming a partial subject can be discussed in two ways: in terms of a universal human disposition, for which the symbol Matrix is proposed, and as a process which involves the transformation of time and place within the space of the artwork. With both of them, Ettinger questions the phallic economy as the only outcome of the infant's separation from the mother. In order to construct a different economy, she challenges the Lacanian myth of lack at the center of being—as well as the pronouncement of femininity as "not-all"—not fully encompassed under the (phallic) signifier and language. Ettinger claims that even if we agree with Lacan that woman as "not-all" cannot be captured by the symbolic signifier, there is no reason to exclude the capacity to link to the Other from the symbolic domain or from a theorization of subjectivity. The Other in Ettinger's formulation is initially the mother, but the latter is not as an indistinct and unitary presence as in Lacanian theory. Even the most primordial experience of the mother, Ettinger states, is characterized by *togetherness in difference*. Even in the womb, there is togetherness in separation.

Upon this revision, Ettinger develops the notion of the *matrixial borderlinking* as an ability to link with the Other just as universal as separation and castration. She proposes the Matrix as a symbol (2000, p. 197) and a paradigm supplementary to the phallus (Pollock, 2004, p. 11). The Matrix, therefore, is not based on lack and the phantasmatic appearance of the *object a*. It is rather defined as a symbol for a nonphallic sphere of a not-one-ness (more-than-one but not everything and/or less-than-one but not nothing), which includes a recognized unknown. [It] is composed of the known and the unknown; it is a meeting place for the coemerging I and the not-I(s) which neither assimilated nor rejected (Ettinger, 2000, p. 197).

The Matrix harks back and gives a new meaning to the Real. Ettinger's Real is not Kristeva's (1992) *chora* but a locus in which elements of subjects exist and subjectivities are constituted via recognition, even without knowing one another (Ettinger, 1992, p. 199). The emphasis on "elements" rather than on fully constituted subjects indicates that the Matrix contains the possibility of recognizing the other in their difference and unknownness—the terms being understood as both in a psychic and a sociopolitical sense (1992, p. 200). Thus, adds Ettginer, the Matrix does not operate on metonymy and metaphor like the phallic/symbolic order, but at the edges of both.

Ettinger is therefore keen to situate this new symbol, the Matrix, at the margins of language and on the side of Real as affect, allowing it to become a field of possibilities rather than a cutting off point. For that reason, she claims that the Matrix enables the process of *metramorphosis*, which is a process of change in borderlines and thresholds, taking place between being and absence, memory and oblivion, I and not-I (1992, p. 201). Significantly, consciousness is not excluded from the process. But metramorphic consciousness has no center and does not attempt to hold a fixed gaze. It resides in or slides in and out of the realm of borderlines, margins, and thresholds, transgressing the old and creating new ones (Ettinger, 1992, p. 201). It forms part of the copoietic activity (Ettinger, 2006, p. 144).

This copoietic activity is important for the sharing of traumas. Ettinger locates the experience in the circulation of traces, affects, and unconscious threads that communicate, or, in her words, disperse aspects of the trauma between the I and the non-I (2006, p. 141). Trauma is ontogenetic, its sharing inherent. This is how Ettinger describes the experience of sharing traumas:

> Since I cannot fully handle events that profoundly concern me, they fade-in-transformation while my non-I becomes wit(h)ness to them. . . . In the matrixial psychic sphere, my imprints will be transcribed in the other, and to begin with in the m/Other. Thus my others will process traumatic events for me, like my m/Other processed archaic events for my premature and fragile subjectivity. (2006, p. 141)

The matrixial metramorphosis therefore draws upon a fundamental inclination to coemegrence and cofading of memory and oblivion. It transfers the knowledge of these events with-in-to the matrixial psychic sphere. Knowledge here is understood as *conaissance*—being-born-together—which is not necessarily cognitive and may not enter direct representation. This formulation introduces the possibility of conscious knowledge, not rigorous reflection perhaps, but as an experience of *transsubjectivity*. Ettinger adds that we may begin to reflect on it by starting from the errors introduced by symbolic language (2006, p. 144).

I am thinking, at this point, about my "error" of approaching Barbara Loftus's painting via the traces and snippets of my own family stories—being unable to pursue them further, stopped short both because I do not know more about these histories and because the other's trauma takes over; wondering about traumatic events I cannot or have not possibly attempted to address; of Barbara's continuous commemoration of the maternal trauma; the proliferation of images; how these images have a life of their own beyond the mother's experience; how Hildegard might have responded to them. Would she recognize the scene of her childhood? Would that matter, as they are transformed by all of us viewers?

As a response to these questions, I quote Griselda Pollock's emotive reflection on Ettinger's work. Pollock, an art historian, draws attention to the almost self-evident nature of sharing traumas. She also suggests that as part of the experience, maternal desires surface and are communicated with or beyond language, as well as fragments and memories of pasts handed down to us by mothers and others. These delicate operations place the transmission of cultural memories in wider human-subjective context. Several of these aspects eventually find their way in the scene of the artwork and compose a transsubjective experience:

> If I am affected, after the event of the making, by the encounter with the artwork of another, itself "born" from its own transsubjective borderlinking with its own known and unknown others, its own and other's histories, its own sensitivities to the world, am I not sharing and processing transsubjectively, rather than engaging intersubjectively, and doing so, engaging not with communicated meanings or clear narrations (including the structuring discourse of the Other I discussed above), but with traces, elements, remnants of an encounter-event at and from

> another time and space transported to and by me into other spaces and times in an equally affecting way which can only resonate in me because of specificities within me of which I, in turn am not aware, lending, unconsciously perhaps, the un-cognised affectivity to the event of the other in such a way that my response animates, rather that resurrects, the work while the work animates something until now unknown to me? (Pollock, 2009, p. 48)

With the development of the notion of the Matrix and the process of metramorphosis, Ettinger challenges the foreclosure of the trauma in psychoanalytic theory and highlights the process of becoming a partial subject via a transformation in time and space rather than via an experience of the return of the Real. In that context, trauma is not the messenger of the death drive but defies the fear of death through a yearning for sharing with an unknown other. This is Ettinger's psychocultural alternative to the lure of the death drive. Trauma, therefore, both prenatal and historical, produces "fragilized-conaissance" (Pollock, 2009, p. 46), or a *becoming vulnerable* in the Levinasian sense, further described as "a partial disappearing to allow jointness" (Ettinger, 2006, p. 145). On the psychoanalytic plane, this allows Ettinger to envisage subjectivity as lingering in its partial dimension at the risk of regression, fragmentation, and dispersal. It also risks the pain of wit(h)nessing and being made fragile but not necessarily being traumatized. In that sense, becoming a partial subject involves giving oneself over to an encounter with the Other, but not as a subject in search for an object (Ettinger, 2006, p. 146).

This expanded, fragilized understanding of humanity-subjectivity now becomes the basis for remembering events like the Holocaust as traumas of the humanity. Artwork that arises as a response to them reminds us of the horror and the historical rupture of humanity. Pollock notes: "but thus traumatized we are also *solaced at a deep level* by the potential contact with what formed our humanity, with what humanized us as a dimension able to share or rather unable not to share" (Pollock, 2009, p. 52, emphasis added).

What does it mean to become partial subject? What does it mean to go beyond the phallic order and into the matrixial borderlinking? My "inadequate" historical knowledge leads me into that realm. There, I am becoming an "ignorant" subject, but no longer ignorant of my own processes and the (phallic) desire for mastery and knowledge. I begin to realize that I do not want to know everything. I am staying within the (feminine) not-all of knowledge which tells me that both the painter and I are lost in the infinity of overlapping circles of half-told and untold stories. In that sense, my stock of mental representations of the Holocaust or other historical atrocities will never be enough and will never be exhausted, and neither will Barbara Loftus's. At that point, the desire to know-all, an epistemophilic desire to know and to speak from the point of view of certainty, becomes rather peripheral.

I am also beginning to discern how the notion "partial subject" relates to the difference between seeking and finding or between searching and simply encountering the world around me. Copjec quotes the example of the American artist Jasper Johns interviewed by the critic Leo Steinberg. When Johns is asked how he selects objects for his work, he replies that they more or less appear to him in their simplicity and usually lack "deeper" meaning. Steinberg observes: "[Johns] so wills what occurs that what comes from without becomes indistinguishable from what he chooses" (2002, p. 39). Copjec remarks that there could be no better description of the Lacanian "headless subject" as the absence of that egoistic self-consciousness, which often causes us to succumb to the force of events and to the wills and desires of others, or, more poignantly perhaps, to be moved to superficial and short-lived pity (Copjec, 2002, p. 40). Although Copjec's discussion retains the notion of the *object a* and focuses on how the death drive is sublimated in life, I find the Lacanian "headless subject" pertinent to Ettinger's paradigm. In both cases, with or without the theoretical support of the drive, it concerns the fundamental disposition to approach—or rather to being approached—by the world *differently*, beyond desire, knowledge, and preconceived ideas. Such an encounter, which may be traumatic, may also convey jouissance. The enjoyment of art certainly conveys something along these lines.

ARTWORK AS A NONPLACE AND THE ETHICS OF WIT(H)NESSING

So far, I have focused on how Ettinger's work departs from Lacanian psychoanalysis and explored the sharing the other's trauma from her perspective only. In this section, I wish to highlight some convergences between Ettinger and Lacan, which may further enrich our understanding of wit(h)essing. These convergences concern the work of art as a unique material locus, a place or space in which we are both traumatized and solaced. As I pointed out in the introduction, such places are not unknown to Lacanian psychoanalysis or to French philosophical thought but are assigned functions which, at first sight, might not appear pertinent to Ettinger's work. A more careful examination, however, shows that they actually enhance our understanding of the latter's work and provide a better perspective for appreciating the space in which the ethical imperative to share and remember arises into consciousness.

The notion of the nonplace is important in French philosophy and occurs in the works of Foucault, Derrida, the Lacanian theorist Jacques Alain-Miller, Badiou, Ranciere, Levinas, de Certeau, and others (see Bosteels, 2003). It concerns both real places of otherness or resistance, like the roadblocks of May 1968, and linguistic departures from or transgressions of conventional symbolic meaning. Here, I wish to point out some commonalities between

Ettinger's artwork as nonplace as locus of traumatization and solacing and the nonplace in Foucauldian and Lacanian thought.

First, I want to point out that the coexistence of horror and solace at the same locus agrees with Foucault's definition of a nonplace or heterotopia (Bosteels, 2003), as a site in which incompatible emplacements can coexist side by side. That such a place exists in Ettinger's work is indicated by the definition of the artwork as a site of encounter, not fusion, where various elements can converge, conjointly but differently (2000, p. 195). The foucauldian nonplace can be both linguistic and material. It is further perceived as adjacent to ordinary, everyday spaces, and set aside with specific but permeable borders. Foucauldian scholars note that nonplaces often appear in history as sites of passage rather than permanent abodes (Hetherington, 2001). Among them, we find the French Palais de Royale, in which people from all walks of life mingled on the eve of the French Revolution. A similar transitoriness permeates the work of art in Ettinger's writings, seen as a transport-station of trauma that allows for *passage* between subjectivities that desire coaffection or coemergence (Pollock, 2009, p. 52) or as *passage-lane* for affected events, materials, and modes of becoming. We could therefore consider Ettinger's artwork as a contemporary nonplace which chimes with a permanent philosophical demand for a locus outside the regulation of logos and power, for a subversive space beyond dominant culture. In that sense, the representation of historical traumas, and indeed of the Holocaust, shifts from the realm of History or Art and is further aligned to the revolutionary-radical potential of a permanent nonplace. Yet memory and remembering in a nonplace should not be understood as products of monumentalization; they are processes of maintaining a space of perpetual interaction and sharing, alive and capable of sustaining more than one (partial) subjects.

Ettinger (2006) also sees the work of art as a space that "captures outside something encapsulated inside" (as cited in Pollock, 2009, p. 40). In that capacity, it chimes with the Lacanian Real as extimate space. I explain this convergence below. The Lacanian Real is usually designated as the domain that resists symbolization and remains repressed or unassimilable (Evans, 1996, p. 160). However, it is also the simple, naked materiality of the external world (Evans, 1996, pp. 159–60). Lacan designates the dual status of the Real with the neologism *extimacy* (extimité), joining "exteriority" and "intimacy," also pointing at how psychoanalysis problematizes the opposition between the inside and the outside (Evans, 1996, pp. 58–59). The preservation of the trauma in space, therefore, involves learning to speak in terms of extimacy and recognizing that material spaces can do things for subjects, rather than only operating as background for actors' initiatives. In that sense, Lacan and Ettinger converge on a more "positive" and materialistic articulation of the Real in terms of space.

There is, finally, another quality of the nonplace relevant to this convergence. It involves the disruption of conventional time, which Foucault designates as a "heterochronia" and Jacques Alain Miller as the event of interpretation. An *event* is a rupture with the past which does not fail to take into account its structural overdetermination (Bosteel, 2003, p. 120). It creates a nonplace of break and continuity with the past, a new beginning, and, more importantly, a traversal/transgression of the past (Voela, 2011). In that sense, the interpretation-event happens or, better, constitutes a *right time*, the "neither too early not too late" but the "*on* time." Although Ettinger takes great care to differentiate the historical trauma as an event from coming across an artwork as an encounter, she does speak of the latter as a timely encounter: "Art links the too-early to the too-late, and plants them in the world's time as matrixial time. To metramorphose a traumatic Thing-encounter and Thing-event is to extract the too-early and too-late from the indifference toward with-in-visibility with-in-difference" (2006, p. 150). I suggest, therefore, that, at least for the spectator, the metramorphosis taking place at that point is both an act of interpretation and a transsubjective witnessing. Just as the interpretation-event upsets, challenges, and reconfigures subjectivity, so the encounter with the artwork *is the timely encounter* which both dissolves and holds together the too-early and too-late of the trauma. However, the demand that the ethical nature of the event be recognized, cannot, in my view, reside solely in the transsubjective encounter. It must arise into consciousness as transgression and break, as interpretation and recognition of an ethical obligation against indifference. This is how I understand the ethical implication of Ettinger's suggestion that the other fragilizes me in this encounter: it is intimated in the transsubjective realm of a fortuitous encounter as jouissance or anxiety but must nevertheless be transformed into a conscious decision to uphold the meaning of the other's trauma as a permanent nonplace of cultural and personal significance. The topological simultaneity of elements in the matrixial must not exclude interpretation as one of the possible transgressive effects with-in-to the feminine (see Ettinger, 2006, p. 140).

As I return to Hildegard's painting, I appreciate the Matrix as registering events without witnesses and passing them on to wit(h)nesses without events (Ettinger, 2006, p. 151). At the same time, I realize that I cannot fail to arrive at the same end and conclusion foretold, the pleasure and anxiety of the first encounter with the image. My exploration of meaning and matrixial non-meaning, this very chapter, is after all a long detour, like the Lacanian drive, around an elusive object which brings me back to an image of childhood, Hildegard's painting, a *lieux de mémoire*. I am also reminded, at this point, of another aspect of childhood and Deleuze and Guattari's invitation to refuse sovereign knowledge and to succumb to becoming a child[3] (1988, p. 306). This is perhaps the level at which the *lieux de mémoire* operates as an open invitation to always encounter the visible world as new and seeking meaning, as a child. Then I notice that yet another meaning of childhood inhabits the painting: Hildegard's toys at the foreground remind me that children spend hours rearranging their toys, regrouping and ordering them differently, never tiring of the process. Adults do the same when processing infantile memories (Antze, 2003). It is perhaps upon these grounds that we now need to proceed: trying to establish the durability of images and scenes of trauma which we can rearrange in copoiesis and wit(h)nessing but without reducing them to banality.

As I linger on Hildegard's painting, I trace her gaze. I realize that, after all, she might be looking at the confiscation of valuables or the mother crushing the father's watch under her heel. This obvious meaning strikes me as so restrictive that I withdraw my gaze from the painting.

NOTES

1. The *object a* is the key theoretical notion in Lacanian psychoanalysis. It emerges with the child's separation from the mother and simultaneous entry into the symbolic-language which gives rise to Desire but signals the loss of jouissance. The notion of the *object a* is constructed with reference to another key notion, lack, and the idea Desire can never be properly addressed since it is constituted around a lacking, absent core. In that sense, the pursuit of objects (sexual or culturally validated) which mostly satisfies ordinary desires constitutes the metonymic chain of signifiers harking back to the elusive *object a*. Yet a modicum of the *object a* is attained through ordinary objects. Lacan lists the *voice* and the *gaze* among the manifestations of the *object a*. These objects "resist analytic action—which involves speech, putting things into words, trying to say what the problem is—and are related to a *jouissance (enjoyment)* that defines the subject's very being" (Fink, 1997, p. 92).

2. The term "metramorphosis"—the word "metamorphosis" with an inserted "r"—suggests transformation and nonphallic becoming but also the fear of transgression which subjects must overcome. This also marks Ettinger's departure from Kristeva's claim that "matricide" is seen as essential (Ettinger, 2006, p. 34). Ettinger further notes that she uses the term metramorphosis to mean routes of passability, transmissibility, transitivity, and temporary conductivity between psychic strata as well as subjects (Ettinger, 2006, p. 94).

3. Becoming in Deleuze and Guattari (1988) regards the continual production of difference. The emphasis is on process rather than outcome. Becoming-woman and becoming-child are seen as subcategories of becoming-minoritarian, that is, pursuing transformation in a nonaggressive, nonmasculine, and nonauthoritarian manner, but without envisaging a particular goal or end state.

REFERENCES

Antze, P. (2003). The other side: Memory as metaphor in psychoanalysis. In S. Radstone & K. Hodgkin (Eds.), *Regimes of memory* (pp. 96–113). London, UK: Routledge.

Baer, U. (2000). To give memory a place: Holocaust photography and the landscape tradition. *Representations, 69*, 38–62.

Bosteels, B. (2003). Nonplaces: An anecdoted topography of contemporary French theory. *Diacritics, 33*(3), 117–39.

Caruth, C. (1996). *Unclaimed experience: Trauma, narrative and history.* Baltimore: John Hopkins University Press.

Copjec, J. (2002). *Imagine there is no woman: Ethics and sublimation.* Cambridge, MA: MIT Press.

Davis, C. (2011). Trauma and ethics: Telling the other's story. In M. Modlinger & P. Sonntag (Eds.), *Other people's pain: Narratives of trauma and the question of ethics* (pp. 19–24). Switzerland: Peter Lang.

Deleuze, G., & Guattari, F. ([1988] 2008). *A thousand plateaus: Capitalism and schizophrenia.* London, UK: Continuum Press.

Ettinger, B. (2006). *The matrixial borderspace.* Minneapolis, MN: Minnesota University Press.

Ettinger, B. (2000). Transgressing with-in-to the feminine. In P. Florence & N. Foster (Eds.), *Differential aesthetics* (pp. 185–209). London, UK: Ashgate.

Ettinger, B. (1992). Matrix and metamorphosis. *Differences, A journal of feminist cultural studies, 4*(3), 176–208.

Evans, D. (1996). *An introductory dictionary of Lacanian psychoanalysis.* London, UK: Routledge.

Fink, B. (1997). *The Lacanian subject: Between language and jouissance.* Princeton, NJ: Princeton University Press.

Hetherington, K. (2001). Moderns as ancients: Time, space and the discourse of improvement. In J. May & N. Thrift (Eds.), *Timespace* (pp. 49–72). London, UK: Routledge.

La Capra, D. (1999). Trauma, absence, loss. *Critical Inquiry, 25*(4), 696–713.

Loftus, B. (2011). *Sigismund's watch: A tiny catastrophe.* London, UK: Philip Wilson Publishers.

Modlinger, M., & Sonntag, P. (Eds.). (2011). *Other people's pain: Narratives of trauma and the question of ethics.* Switzerland: Peter Lang.

Mowitt, J. (2007). Trauma envy. In K. Ball (Ed.), *Traumatizing theory: The cultural politics of affect in and beyond psychoanalysis* (pp. 349–76). New York, NY: Other Press.

Nora, P. (1989). Between memory and history: Les lieux de mémoire. *Representations*, 26, 7–24.

Olkowski, D. (2007). Catastrophe. In K. Ball (Ed.), *Traumatizing theory: The cultural politics of affect in and beyond psychoanalysis* (pp. 41–66). New York, NY: Other Press.

Pollock, G. (2004). Thinking the feminine: Aesthetic practice as introduction to Bracha Ettinger and the concepts of matrix and metramorphosis. *Theory, Culture and Society, 21*(1), 5–65.

Pollock, G. (2009). Art/Trauma/Representation. *Parallax, 15*(1), 40–54.

Radstone, S. (2007). Trauma theory: Contexts, politics, ethics. *Paragraph, 30*(1), 9–29.

Voela, A. (2011). Heterotopia revisited: Foucault and Lacan on feminine subjectivity, *Subjectivity, 4*(2), 168–82.

Chapter 4

In Search of Forgotten Memories after Thirty-Three Years

A Journey Home

Minh Truong-George

This chapter will describe the processes I went through when I decided to return home to Vietnam, thirty years after fleeing from there with my family as an eight-year-old girl. Revisiting the places we had lived in Vietnam, meeting relatives we had left behind, and retracing the journey of our original escape to Malaysia, together with over six hundred other people on a twenty-four meter fishing boat, set me off on a deeper, even more tumultuous, adult journey of painful rediscovery, remembering, and feeling.

This journey is not yet complete. Writing about it here, and working on a short documentary film about it, is an important part of my attempt to integrate what happened and to fill in some of the blanks in my psyche that, until recently, I did not even know existed.

In the mid-1970s the Communists accused my parents, an ethnically Chinese couple, of being "Capitalists," and we were stripped of our home and belongings. To avoid being put into "labor camp" my father fled and went into hiding until we were able to reunite as a family and eventually escape. After spending a year in a refugee camp in Malaysia we found ourselves part of the first wave of "boat people" to arrive in New Zealand in February 1980, when I was nearly ten years old.

As I grew up, if I were asked about our escape from Vietnam, it seemed like something far away—an adventure that involved my tears at leaving my dog and grandmother behind, a struggle with Thai pirates, blacking out due to thirst, and hearing whispers that someone had died on the boat. In my mind, it had become an old tale that was not "real" anymore. I grew up knowing the words of my story, but there were no feelings attached to those words, just numbness.

Despite my training as a psychotherapist and many years as a client in my own therapy, I am still surprised at how deeply my own psyche, and those of others around me, resisted the resurfacing of traumatic experiences. I will describe how I have found the metaphor of "mummification" useful in understanding the many complex protective intra- and interpsychic processes, which my family and I developed in order to survive the traumatic loss of our home and community. I will also discuss trauma from a Buddhist perspective, and show how that has helped me to understand that some of the ways our psyches try to stay fixed, to resist "reality," actually cause further alienation, suffering, and retraumatization.

In July 2010, more than thirty years after leaving Vietnam, I was on a Buddhist retreat when I realized that I needed to go back to Vietnam—to remember and be remembered, and to do this before my elderly aunts passed away.

THE JOURNEY

After planning my return to Vietnam, with my brother joining me for part of the trip, I began working with friends to raise enough funds to make a documentary of the journey home. Despite stern and anxious resistance from some family members, I set out for Vietnam in late 2010, with a friend and a cameraman. We first traveled to Malaysia to look for the village where our refugee boat had landed, and to find the refugee camp, where we spent almost a year, before being sponsored to New Zealand. The predominant experience I had in Malaysia was of overwhelming frustration at not being able to (re) locate certain aspects of my memory in order to "unite" the present with the past.

I recall a sense of heightened awareness as we arrived at the village where I hoped to find the remnants of our abandoned boat. I noticed that I was holding my breath as tremors coursed through my body, while hearing a calm voice in my mind telling me to breathe. I walked around the village with my eyes, ears, and nose alert to any signs of familiarity, as if my life depended on it. My heart lunged forward each time I recognized a familiar sight or smell while I was seeking evidence that my memories were grounded in reality. Conversely, I also felt rising tension, fear, and even anger in my chest as my eyes more often than not encountered a changed environment from the one I remembered. Instead of the bare stretch of sandy beach that I had walked on as an eight-year-old, the village was now lined with little colorful cabins for tourists. This caused me to feel strangely anxious, and I felt an overwhelming desperation to search for a place, any place, where I could experience a "true" memory of my eight-year-old self.

As we were guided deeper into the quiet of the jungle, weaving our way through the coconut plantations, I recall attempting to still my inner experiences by slowing down my breathing, quieting my thoughts, and tuning in for any resonance I could feel that belonged to my eight-year-old self. I was not aware that I had (dis)placed this young part of myself until I reconnected with "her" at the end of a banana grove. It was a surreal experience when suddenly the smell of the jungle dampness, together with the constant chirping of insects and the stillness of the air, matched my memory of the past and I began to sense my eight-year-old self reappearing. It was a palpable moment as my guide and friend fell into silence with me, and, almost ghostlike, I felt with relief the child and her sadness melding into me.

As part of the documentary, I wanted to interview the villagers to hear their memories of the past. But as we interviewed each person, I became more despondent as each recalled the past very differently. They offered discrepant versions of what had happened the afternoon our boat arrived on their shore, and what had subsequently happened to our boat after we left the island. Some people said the boat just rotted away, some said they torched it to the ground, while others said we had never arrived! I felt incredulous, and noticed rising rage in my solar plexus that these people could get their memories so mixed up, especially as my eight-year-old memory was dependent on their memory to collectively make sense of what really happened.

I was determined to find something that linked us to the boat that took me away from Vietnam, my numerous searches along the beach were finally rewarded with the discovery of an embedded piece of barnacle-covered timber, jutting out of the sand. I began digging furiously, hoping to uncover more evidence of my journey. To my amazement, I grabbed hold of a thick rope buried in the sand. I pulled hard at the rope, as I felt sure that this was the anchor of our boat. But after many vigorous attempts at digging it out, I was forced to let go of my hope and surrender to the incoming tides, which kept sweeping aside my efforts. In the end, I had to accept that this island and its surrounding ocean would forever hold parts of my childhood. Along with the changing tide, I too began experiencing a changing tide of gentle gratitude toward the sea for its safekeeping of a crucial part of my life.

REENTERING VIETNAM

I had not known that I carried the same anxiety or fears that my parents and the people of their generation exhibited whenever they spoke about Vietnam and the things "the Communists" could do to a person, until the moment the plane landed in Ho Chi Minh City. I attributed their fears and irrationality to unprocessed trauma or an overdramatization of how things were. Because I had spent a reasonable amount of time engaging in psychotherapy, I was sure that I had dealt with whatever trauma I carried due to my exposure to war and displacement. I was wrong. When I walked out of the plane, I understood for the first time what it must be like to exist in my parents' bodies; the tremors that shuddered throughout my body and the tightening grip that I could feel clamping my pounding heart were what I later came to identify as symptoms of past trauma and anxiety attacks. I told myself to breathe deeply, to not worry, and to be rational: "You've got a visa. You're not doing anything wrong. Don't look so nervous. Smile. Make eye contact with the Customs officials. No, don't make eye contact . . ." I felt terrified.

REMEMBERING

I have spent many, many hours since my trip reflecting on the intricacies and complexity of how my psyche works, the way memories overlap one another, either totally covering up some cracks underneath, or cleverly inserting a piece of jigsaw into the picture so skillfully that I would become oblivious to the missing piece or blank. I only came to notice these blanks once the jigsaw pieces slotted in smoothly and I experienced a feeling of ease in my body. For example, I had not known that my somewhat eclectic sense of aesthetics came from being exposed as a child to both Chinese and French architecture. Glimpsing the expanse of peeling duck-egg blue walls, wrought iron furniture, and framed Chinese portraits of my ancestors, in my grandmother's attic made me feel such delight and awe. In recognizing this eclectic interplay of French, Chinese, and Vietnamese aesthetics, I felt strangely and deeply soothed.

This "fitting in right" experience went further than being able to understand my aesthetics. Who I inherently am as a person made more sense when I was physically in Vietnam. My Western friends had always told me that I was too busy, too intense, and that I worked too hard. I grew up feeling uncomfortable in my own skin, forever trying to be less of these things that I was accused of being. This changed while I was walking the streets of Ho Chi Minh City one afternoon, struck by the realization that there were at least a million others just like me. I experienced such ease in my own skin for the first time, and relished knowing how very poised, contained, and aware my people are. They reminded me of a watercolor painting of schools of golden fish gracefully flowing in the pond of life. I became one of them.

Part of the journey home was built around visiting places and people that were a part of my past. I did not know then, but, as I visited these places, I realized I had a deep longing to know whether the life I remembered was "real," and whether there were still visible links that would indicate to me that it was indeed real. Everywhere I went, I was aware of scanning the environment, both searching for familiarity and being vigilant for danger. I noticed strong responses of panic and heavy-hearted disappointments whenever I did not find things that resembled my previous life, or elation and vitality whenever I recognized something.

These two extremes of elation and deep disappointment, and the desperate need to connect the past with the present, would constantly wrestle inside me. I remember such excitement the day I laid eyes on my old primary school, and then the deep sadness when we were not allowed to enter the school grounds until all the students had left for the day. It was a long wait for the end-of-school bell and the chance to walk onto the empty asphalt playground. With longing, I imagined seeing the ghostlike eight-year-old "me" wandering outside a classroom, hearing the sounds of classroom noises and smelling that pungent damp smell arising from the heated playground whenever it rained.

Perhaps one of the most important events for me was returning to Phan Thiet, the town where I was born, and standing outside our old house where we lived until it was confiscated in 1975, when the Communists took over South Vietnam. I felt very torn between a deep longing to go in and find out whether the inside was like I remembered, and my father's command not to let people know that I had once lived there in case I got into trouble. This feeling stayed with me until I decided on the last day to venture out onto the streets of my hometown alone. I found myself walking back and forth past our old house, trying to figure out whether I should try to get inside. I could feel the tension inside me, hearing my father's pragmatic voice anxiously warning me not to get into trouble, versus my more idealistic voice clearly saying that if I let fear win and let it coerce me into distrust, then life would no longer be worth living. As I was wrestling in my body and mind with what to do, a woman confronted me, asking what I was doing walking back and forth.

I did not know at that moment which voice I would follow; my father's voice and all of the trauma that sat within him—to not trust and thus lose out on the chance to see the inside of my abandoned home—or my own voice, to trust and risk being harassed or thrown into jail. But I knew that it was more than the physical risk involved, it was an opportunity to engender a change toward peace and trust. I chose to trust by asking the woman to help me get inside.

At first she tried to talk me out of it, but eventually she found a key, and with terror pounding in my ears, I was able to step inside my childhood home for the first time in thirty-five years. I had an out of body experience in which I was aware of my voice telling me to breathe deeply and to stay open to the experience. Everything seemed so much smaller, and the house was narrower than I had remembered. As I walked toward the back, I recognized the kitchen, and with it the water-well making gentle lapping noises. My tears flowed as I was reminded of the nightly sounds the water-well used to make. I remembered instantly how it used to soothe my sadness and fear of not knowing where my father was, and how it used to lull me to sleep. Seeing my tears, the woman who had let me in asked whether I was feeling sad, not realizing the indebtedness I felt to her for the opportunity to know whether what I remembered was real. It felt as if I had entered a forgotten place inside my heart and body that I had not known existed, and drank deeply from its well. Reentering the physical space of my childhood has also enabled the unlocking of a forbidden space in the psyche of my family.

BEING REMEMBERED

I have expressed above how important it has been for me to be able to recognize and remember aspects of my life in order to integrate past and present. It is something that happens intrapsychically, the sifting of old and existing data without necessarily engaging with other people. However, I have come to realize that being remembered by others, and being validated and welcomed back by the people that made up the structures of my formative years, was also crucial in my healing process.

It was the experience of being remembered by my frail eighty-five-year-old aunt, who was bedridden and fast approaching senility, that made me truly understand the potency of family connections and the importance of experiencing a place of belonging. Initially, I could not understand her incoherent speech due to the effects of a stroke, but when she finally looked into my eyes, and with tears in her eyes said she remembered me, I realized it is never too late to be recognized as kin, to be taken into the fold of family, and to feel within one's body what being part of a family system feels like.

Reconnecting to my aunt and ancestors touched me profoundly, and seeing my brother similarly affected also helped me think about him in a different way. Until then, I had largely seen him as just another of the unimaginative moneymaking individuals who had no time for anything beyond work. In contrast, to my family, I was an "idealistic hippie," going on retreats and wanting to trust and help people less fortunate than ourselves.

The split was wide; neither of us was able to recognize that each was fulfilling a need for the family's survival. My ancestors have a history of surviving numerous wars, first fleeing from China to Vietnam, then my generation fleeing from Vietnam to New Zealand. We survived on the basis of extreme hard work, tenacity, pragmatism, and a good dose of mistrust. Pragmatism and mistrust became the overt cultural and familial code of conduct under which all members of my family operated.

Hellinger, Weber, and Beaumont (1998) suggest that healing the family split involves the need to address and reorder "disruptions" and "disturbances" within the family system. This "Order of Love" describes how each member of the family, whether young or old, dead or alive, takes up an order or a space within the family constellation, which needs to be remembered and acknowledged. When there is exclusion or disruption to this order, members of the following generations will be affected and will unconsciously be called into fulfilling the family's need for healing in, perhaps, unhelpful ways, until reordering is complete.

By going back to Vietnam and fulfilling the role I played within the "family constellation," I was able to see our different perspectives and functions as complementary rather than as a polarization between pragmatism and idealism. We needed each other to fulfill complementary functions (albeit in very unconscious ways) to enable wholeness in the family system. Rather than being locked-in to the experience of the misfit and of not being understood, I began to understand my role as my family's "heart keeper," whose role was to protect the heart and integrity of the family, which has provided an important balance to our family.

REMEMBERING THE NOT FORGOTTEN

As well as the insights gained about my family system, it became apparent how leaving Vietnam as a young child now impaired my ability to interact with others in a culturally sensitive and age-appropriate manner. I noticed that while other members of my family were conversing, I remained very quiet and "well mannered," as if I were still a young child amongst her elders, who had to be seen and not heard. I realized that I did not contribute to the conversation unless I was spoken to, and this was not because I was tired or lacked the language. The gaps in my communication were due to missing the opportunity to grow up into a woman within my Vietnamese culture. By returning to Vietnam, I had physically and psychically reentered my eight-year-old's body, thoughts, feelings, and behaviors, which at times felt more real than the experience of the grown adult that I was.

Along with these in-and-out-of-body distortions, I noticed a deep anxiety in my solar plexus and heart as I got closer to my birthplace. I felt as if I were running out of air, and needed to do whatever I could to stop this escalating anxiety. As we walked, I noticed myself falling further behind my traveling companions, struggling to keep up, feeling insignificant and just going along with what others wanted, without knowing what was best for me. When I realized that my anxiety was about being abandoned by the group, I became scared to ask for support, despite being conscious that the whole purpose of my journey home was to gain a different experience with the support of my friend. The pounding in my chest and ringing in my ears when I tried to speak to my friend about my anxiety showed me the terror I must have felt as a child, trying to make sense of the chaos that surrounded me.

In trying to speak of this mounting terror while on the trip, I discovered that my listeners needed significant robustness to be with my overwhelmingly chaotic and terrifying experience of trauma. Unfortunately, my attempt to stay aware of my healing process by trying to articulate the swelling trauma inside resulted in the early departure of my friend from the journey and the reenactment of my feelings of rejection and abandonment by the collective unconscious.

POSTJOURNEY

After nearly four weeks of traveling in Vietnam, I returned to New Zealand very full. On one hand, I felt elated that many blanks deep inside me were filled in, especially the insights and joy I felt about why I am the way I am. It felt wonderful to be "normal" amongst several million countrymen. On the other hand, I lost a friend and my anxiety was increasing. This was greatly exacerbated when my efforts to reconcile with my friend were rebuffed. Ironically, what began as an attempt to heal past trauma, specifically to gain the support I did not get as a child on the refugee boat, ended with the reenactment of a similar experience of being shut down when I attempted to stay congruent and visible with my fears, sadness, and tears. This powerful muddle of "real-unreal," "conscious-unconscious" terror was the beginning of a very dark journey into understanding and healing my terrifying experiences of early trauma.

POST-TRAUMATIC STRESS DISORDER (PTSD)

The trauma symptoms returned when my friend told me that she did not wish to work through the rift between us and withdrew all her support from the documentary project that we had set out to do together. I could not stop the tremors which began in my stomach and spread throughout my whole body. My chest felt as if it were being squeezed tightly. I heard myself gasping for air until the gasping became deep sobs, alternating with what sounded like a large animal's cries of pain and terror. I could not believe I was alone in this place again. I could not stop crying. It went on for hours that day, and then sporadically throughout the next twelve months. I remember being surprised at first by the sounds that were coming out of me. And when the sobbing died down, I heard my own adult voice trying to soothe myself: "It's okay, Minh. This is how much you hurt inside. This is how terrified you were when you had no one else to hold you. . . ." And then the crying would start all over again.

That initial onset of distress changed over time. It later turned into black grief which left me feeling like I was being hemmed in by a heavy, smoky, oppressive, pungent cloak. It went everywhere I went. Some nights (and mornings), I would wake up with the strangest feeling in my heart, as if acid were being dripped onto it, releasing adrenalin, which would keep me in a prolonged state of vigilance.

As time went on, the ongoing grief turned into episodes of terror, which saw me either struggling to go to sleep or waking up in a state of fear and anxiety, gasping for air, with my heart pumping, solar plexus burning, blood coursing, and head heavy and numb. When this happened, there did not seem to be any boundary between others and myself. In fact, I became so sensitive to any form of trauma that I began waking up in a panic each time there was an earthquake in other parts of New Zealand. Even though I knew my symptoms were psychosomatic, the immediate thought whenever it happened was "Oh, no! Please stop!" This automatic reaction of panic and terror was so gripping that each time it happened, I forgot that the more I panicked the worse it got.

The other insight was seeing how quickly my mind forgot how terrifying it felt when triggered; it felt like a new experience every time. No matter how familiar these deeply distressing symptoms were, my psyche never got used to it. It always felt like a massive jolt to my system, and I always reacted by feeling a desperate need for it to stop. And when the symptoms abated, to my surprise and utter frustration, I always quickly forgot the felt experience, so that each experience of shockwaves was felt as if for the first time.

Levine and Frederick (1997) write of the need for humans, like animals, to be allowed to release trauma when they encounter it through the naturally-occurring shaking of the body. They believe that, like animals, we possess our reptilian brain's capacity to deal with trauma effectively. However, we have become overdominated by our cognitive brain's tendency to think through problems, and to halt, rather than support, the necessary psychophysiological workings of the body via trembling and shaking in order to rid itself of adrenalin and trauma.

Despite the need for release of trauma to occur, staying with this kind of experience is terrifying without proper understanding and support. Trauma sufferers find it difficult to articulate what is happening, and it is incredibly difficult for friends and family to help or stay with their loved one's experience of trauma.

EXTERNAL VOICES: INTERPSYCHIC TENSIONS

Suffering from traumatic flashbacks was hard enough, but it was even worse when I experienced what felt like judgment and rejection from others. I became defensive and hypervigilant, and distanced myself from possible triggers such as the pain I felt when I came into contact with other people's avoidance or awkwardness. Comments such as "But you were never shot at, so how can you have PTSD?" or "But it was so long ago, and you were so young, shouldn't you let it all go now?" were common, and very prone to trigger my symptoms. These comments usually came from people who had not personally experienced such trauma; they included some old friends, some colleagues, and some spiritual friends, who I had presumed would tolerate being with me in my distress. I felt a terrible sense of bewilderment and grief when I realized that they could only perceive me as a well-functioning psychotherapist, and consciously or unconsciously stayed remote from me during those twelve months.

Conversely, with friends who had experienced trauma I experienced their anxiety, and even an angry desperation for me to be healed quickly. Comments such as "Don't you think you should be medicated?" or "You shouldn't have gone back to Vietnam and stirred all of that up" or "They went back last year and they didn't suffer from PTSD" or even "I thought all of your training as a psychotherapist would have helped you instead of making you worse." I felt there was very little awareness or opportunity within my community of friends and family to provide a safe container for me to release and heal trauma.

INTERNAL VOICES: INTRAPSYCHIC ASSAULTS

As the months went on, the trauma symptoms wore me down, leaving me raw and without a skin to hold my experiences together. Apart from trying to protect myself from the interpsychic reenactment of abandonment when I was most vulnerable, I was also aware of the tension I felt when dealing with my own inner voice. Sometimes it showed up and exacerbated an unconscious and destructive belief that I must have been such a bad baby or such a bad friend that I drove others away. These voices of self-condemnation, shame, and guilt were just as brutal as those external voices.

It was a hard battle to not believe those voices. Sometimes, I became angry with myself for going back to Vietnam and wished I had never gone. After years of involvement with psychotherapy, both as client and as therapist, I was fearful of losing faith in psychotherapy as my vocation, for I felt little relief from my traumatic symptoms.

I was also scared of losing faith in my Buddhist practice—nothing held purpose and meaning if I could not rid myself of the agony I was in. I felt that there was overwhelming motivation for everyone, including myself, to just put the trauma back into the dark unconscious corner of our minds and get on with life. My conscious mind knew that entombing trauma was not a viable option, but I still needed relief; and this struggle for relief came one day when a spiritual friend took my symptoms seriously and patiently listened as I described my experience, rather than belittling the pain or wanting me to feel better. After our hour-long walk and talk, she said to me "Wow, Minh, it sounds like you're really enduring the terrible suffering that the Buddha spoke about, which we all want to avoid. . . ."

Those few quietly spoken words seemed so simple, yet they woke in me the reality of my situation and offered relief whenever I could remind myself of this truth. Of course I had been aware of this truth many times before, but then it was just a thought occupying my headspace. Now the truth reverberated in my whole being. I began to understand the psyche's absolute need to make the trauma "go away" and the wish to not see that there is suffering in the world. Grateful for this reminder of the truth, I took solace in the reality that I was suffering like so many people all over the world and that, like them, I suffered more because I tried to deny this truth, and had become isolated in the belief that we are alone in this experience.

Despite understanding this need to stay with the experience of terror and to soothe and soften toward it by breathing and telling myself I would be OK, my instinct, whenever triggered, was to recoil and take flight. It took many episodes of being triggered before I could alter this reaction, and remember that fighting it did not help. With practice, I got quicker at remembering this truth, and learned to feel the poignancy of the human condition and to turn kindly toward my terror, rather than panicking and running. Paradoxically, once I stopped flailing against the fear of falling into a bottomless dark pit, I began to find comfort in nestling into the quiet darkness of this experience and I felt myself gently soothed and cradled by what I began to identify as "the lap of humanity."

With this insight came more forgiveness toward others and myself for wanting to avoid knowing of this terrible experience of war, trauma, and displacement. I realized that people's awkwardness was not because they did not care, but because they lacked the capacity to bear the experience of fragmentation in the face of such trauma. I also realized that it is usually unbearable for family and friends to see someone in such a state of pain. Thus, pushing for quick resolution was the only way they could keep themselves safe from the experience of PTSD.

REMEMBERING, WITNESSING, AND CREATIVE EXPRESSION

A year after my return, and some time after gaining a better understanding of surrender as a tool toward healing trauma, I was able to begin looking at the sixty hours of documentary footage that were shot in Vietnam. At that time, only two friends could tolerate being with my trauma; one listened and gave osteopathic treatments, the other offered to watch the footage with me. After hundreds of hours of watching and editing my documentary, I realized the healing power of being allowed to safely remember and re-remember with another, to have my memories witnessed by another, and the healing powers of creative expression. Making my documentary *Journey Home* (2012), which was premiered at a psychoanalytic conference, became a strong healing channel in the integration of my trauma. It enabled a greater understanding of trauma, including the necessity to break the silencing of trauma, which played such a crucial role in my experience of PTSD.

MUMMIFICATION AS A METAPHOR

When I reflect on the terror that I experienced and the lack of awareness from others of my inner hell, and the conundrum of how one makes visible what is taboo and unseen, I started to feel that I was wrapped in many layers of cloth, which were starting to unravel. The cloth felt like it was protecting me from the harshness and rawness of skin making contact with air after years of being kept from the light, but the cloth also kept me bound up in my own trauma and fears without the possibility of release. Similarly, the cloth also acted as a protection for others from having to bear witness to what my suffering actually looked like underneath its layers.

In their seminal work on intergenerational trauma, Abraham and Torok (1994) provided further understanding and described a process of "entombment" whereby "trauma is encapsulated so its effects cannot be felt [and] it becomes an unconscious secret the sufferer must bear" (p. 130). As I began to heal, I found myself more and more fascinated with the idea of mummification as a metaphor for understanding what was happening to me.

Through mummification, the ancient Egyptians attempted to preserve the dead body so that it would be recognizable and available to the soul in the afterlife. Paradoxically, unlike ancient mummification, where the dead parts are kept preserved for the afterlife, in "psychic mummification," which involves the disavowing and silencing of trauma, we individually and collectively try to make dead those painful aspects of ourselves that are in fact alive. Ironically, by trying to wrap up trauma and lock it away, we unwittingly ensure its preservation and continuing existence.

TRAUMA FROM A BUDDHIST PERSPECTIVE

Buddhism did not begin as a thought or a concept. It began after the Buddha discovered the cure to the human predicament of being endowed with the preciousness of life while burdened by the experience of unsatisfactoriness and suffering.

In his first teaching after gaining enlightenment, the Buddha addressed this predicament in his teaching of "The Four Noble Truths." The First Noble Truth is that feelings of unsatisfactoriness and suffering are inevitably part of human life. The Second Noble Truth is that our instinctual, unconscious and automatic denial and avoidance of pain, and our craving for pleasure, are the cause of suffering. The Third Noble Truth states that there is a way leading from suffering, and the Fourth Noble Truth describes in detail the path toward peace and Enlightenment. Despite such a blunt statement of the human predicament and the inevitability of human suffering, the Four Noble Truths teaching is actually a message of hope, because there is a cure if we are prepared to take the remedy.

But, in our unenlightened state, we invest our energy in trying to create pleasurable experiences, usually unconscious to the reality of the impermanence of every worldly phenomenon and refuge. No matter how pleasant we make our lives, pleasure does not last, and nothing makes us permanently secure. We can end up shocked, battered, or traumatized by what life serves up.

The Buddha likened our experience of pain to the piercing of a dart. Rather than tenderly attending to the immediate experience of pain caused by this dart, we become shocked by it, resist, and resent it. And as result of this resistance, we become "pierced" by "second darts" which deliver their own emotional and mental pain. As taught in the Buddha's *Sallatha Sutta:*

> When an untaught worldling is touched by a painful (bodily) feeling, he worries and grieves, he laments, beats his breast, weeps and is distraught. He thus experiences two kinds of feelings, a bodily and a mental feeling. It is as if a man were pierced by a dart and, following the first piercing, he is hit by a second dart. So that person will experience feelings caused by two darts. . . . (*The Dart*, Samyutta Nikaya 36.6)

This first dart can be a general underlying unsatisfactoriness of life (such as a broken computer), or a more painful and traumatizing experience (such as war or displacement). While we cannot escape the first dart, we can avoid the second dart by learning to openly and honestly be with the way things are, rather than trying to avoid or distort what is actually happening. In other words, the way leading to peace and contentment is to attend to the raw felt experience of the wound made by the first dart, rather than resisting it or making up stories about it.

This seems like such a simple thing to do. And yet, even when I was aware of the Third and Fourth Noble Truths, I had to endure the anguish and terror of the second dart before I could learn to stay with the bare experience of the first dart. In hindsight, I can see how this refusal to stay with the first dart compounded my reexperience of trauma. What was initially an impersonal and circumstantial first dart (being born into a war-torn country) became much more painful as my family and community collectively attempted to avoid the reality of this pain. My attempt to return to the first dart, to remember that raw terror of being birthed while bombs dropped nearby, was met with strong resistance in others against the remembering and exposing of this trauma. Not only was it difficult for me to see and experience my own trauma, others did not want to come into contact with it. Rather than coming into contact with the rawness of my pain, people's defense against my trauma met my feelings of resentment and terror instead. Either way, the all-round avoidance of the first dart meant that people did not have the capacity to deal with the magnitude of my actual trauma, or to help me with the second darts of my resentment and terror.

Not being able to stay with the first dart, and the instinctual pull to mummify pain and trauma by individuals and societies, is a continuing cause of suffering. Throughout human history, in the necessary process of reconciliation, victims of injustice, abuse, war, and oppression have needed the perpetrators to witness, understand, and respond with empathy and remorse to the victims' experience of pain and terror. However because of the instinctual processes involved in the avoidance of the first dart, everyone inevitably ends up experiencing and expressing the second darts of anger and outrage rather than raw pain, which is then reactively met by more resistance and defense. This constant struggle of not being able to be with the way things are is itself traumatizing because we persistently fail in our attempts to get rid of pain by placing it elsewhere. As seen in my own experience, no matter how often my body experienced the debilitating symptoms of trauma, I never got used to it; I just wanted it to stop, and I very quickly forgot what that experience felt like until I was once again jolted with shock, disbelief, and despair. Thus I was forever caught in the cycle of wanting things to be different than how they were.

CONCLUSION

The journey home and the act of remembering were absolutely necessary to enable me to make a fuller connection to my culture, my family, and myself. In hindsight, and from a relatively more peaceful place, it terrifies me to think what my life would be like had I not tried to remember my past and the effect which my mummified trauma would have on me and my children. I also worry about the millions of other children continually being born into the continuing trauma of famine and war. I worry for them that they might carry what I carried inside; and I worry for them should they embark on the terrifying journey of remembering. Indeed, the possible consequences of forgetting and remembering are very real, as can be seen from my experience. Remembering trauma is just the beginning; how we bear what we remember, and the psycho-spiritual journey involved, is paramount in the process of healing.

It was very clear to me that my terror abated when I stopped focusing on the second darts, and instead coaxed myself to experience the raw pain. In that experience of being with bare experience, I saw that I was no different from those struggling to survive in war-torn countries. In those moments, my personal identity, my gender, my ethnicity, my nationality, my rights, my political stance, and all that I had displaced and reclaimed in my journey home to Vietnam, became suspended momentarily. The only feeling I was aware of was a compassion for myself and all those who are suffering because of war, loss, and displacement. I glimpsed the possibility that when we each commit ourselves to staying with the first dart—the present raw felt experience, to learning to bear the pain and opening the heart to see the pain in ourselves and in our perceived enemies, the cycles of retaliation or lamenting may pause, and reparation and peace may come.

This staying with the first dart is an important issue for the psychotherapeutic profession. It is vital to the healing of trauma for individuals, as well as cultures and societies in conflict. How many of us in the helping professions can accept the perhaps unpalatable reality that the whole of our existence is underpinned by our desire to eliminate pain and to gain pleasure? How aware are we of our own tendency to avoid pain? Have we, through our own remembering and healing, come into contact with our first dart? Can we stay with the immediacy of that feeling? Can we bear to sit alongside our clients and tolerate their psychosomatic symptoms of pain, rather than quickly moving into exploration of the second darts of emotional and mental pain? Do we instinctively recoil from trauma and suffering and attempt to help clients rid themselves of it, or do we help clients to embrace the experience of human suffering as a gateway toward deeper healing and compassion?

Until we can deeply understand, accept, and normalize our basic human strategy to mummify pain and deny suffering, we cannot individually and collectively move beyond our reactions of shock, anger, outrage, and retaliation whenever we come into contact with it. By understanding how deeply entrenched this condition is, we may be able to respond with wisdom and compassion rather than distress and outrage.

REFERENCES

Abraham, N., & Torok, M. (1994). *The shell and the kernel.* Chicago, IL: University of Chicago Press.

Hellinger, B., Weber, G., & Beamont, H. (1998). *Love's hidden symmetry: What makes love work in relationships*. Phoenix, AZ: Zeig, Tucker & Co.

Levine, P. A., & Frederick, A. (1987). *Waking the tiger: Healing trauma—The innate capacity to transform overwhelming experiences.* Berkeley, CA: North Atlantic Books.

Sallatha Sutta: *The dart.* (1998). (Samyutta Nikaya 36.6). (Nyanaponika Thera, Trans.). Retrieved December 15, 2013 from http://www.accesstoinsight.org/tipitaka/sn/sn36/sn36.006.nypo.html.

Truong-George, M. (Producer/Director). (2010). *Journey home* [Motion Picture]. New Zealand. [Unreleased].

Chapter 5

The Sense of Loss and the Search for Meaning

Norma Tracey and Graham Toomey

THE SEARCH FOR IDENTITY

This is about an Aboriginal man's search for his identity, his attempts to psychically find his internalized good father, and in so doing, his own cultural Aboriginal roots. He is not a patient. His story is as told to me. The creative myths of his ancestors permeate his art. He had no fear of the madness in which his and indeed all creativity resides. I propose that it is in finding expression of this symbolization in concrete artistic form, be it art or writing or drama, that the human psyche recovers from trauma. Graham:

> When I do a painting, I know it is my ancestors' spirit not me—their spirit, my hand painting their stories. Up country, where my people came from, as I paint, I hear the children laughing and playing in the stillness near the creek as the water washes down on the rocks. This is not a made-up thing. I can hear them. I think too of how this changed from a happy place to a place of blood and death. We black people all have shame in us, but when I do this painting work, I have pride in who I am. I write our stories in paintings—better than in words. The spirits of the children, and the spirits of my ancestors are alive in me when I paint.

I use this chapter to study what processes work to effect the healing of trauma, the finding of the loved internal person from the psychic processes of childhood, an experiencing of the sweet sadness of loss for those who are never lost and never found. In his search to make links to his historic continuity, Graham reaches a spiritual core of a forgiving father, with many forgiving ancestors and so becomes able to live with himself. His art is the link. "I couldn't make sense of anything. It was just this one morning, I woke up thinking, 'I am not a white man with some Aboriginal blood. My father was an Aboriginal. I am a black man with some white blood.' At that point my life began." At that point he began to paint.

BACKGROUND: TRANSGENERATIONAL TRAUMA AMONG ABORIGINAL AUSTRALIANS

With the new colonial settlement of Australia came not only physical disease but also a serious uprooting of all that was familiar for the Aboriginal people. It was a violent, annihilating situation ending in total subjugation of a proud nomadic people with their spirituality, their intrinsic connection to earth and nature, and their survival of forty thousand to eighty thousand years. With the coming of early "whites," Aboriginal people were moved off their sacred land, dispersed from their normal communal life, robbed of their hunting grounds, and left dependent on the white man for their daily subsistence. Through the claims of a law, called *Terra Nullius*, or land belonging to no one, they were denied existence as a people. Then they had their children born of white men taken from them and given to white families as a matter of law. The damage caused by this flowed down through the generations. A devastated people left in a state of failure and shame reaps the awful results of such abuse even today. A growing body of literature over many years has highlighted the causes and extent of the domestic violence and sexual abuse, suicide, poverty, unemployment, physical illness, lack of education, racism-induced stress, single-parent families, substance and drug abuse (e.g., alcohol, sniffing petrol) that continues to devastate indigenous families and communities. These have contributed to social isolation, loss of identity, and self-esteem.

The transgenerational trauma carried by a race dislocated from its culture, its tribal basis in communal living, its spiritual values attached to the earth and the land, often brings shame and a sense of deadness.

In this chapter, we hope to show that these effects are not the only outcome. For the survivor of trauma, there is the possibility of a special creativity. Within the healing an internal narrative, expressive of the power and resilience of the psyche integral to the human condition, is discovered. Born out of trauma, there can be a belief in one's capacity to overcome the truly terrible, a new birth of faith from within the faithless, meaningless, autistic space, real hope born from despair and love in a loveless context, that can together triumph over hate and rage. The terrible sense of loss, when all one takes for granted is destroyed, can be overcome. The recovery of identity for the Aboriginal people takes place in the process of finding their spiritual roots through the aesthetic, not as an expression of the old world but as part of finding a new way of being that has their "old" soul in it. The sounds through music, the sight through art, the experience through drama and literature, all resonate with the pain of others to create a universally shared empathic witnessing, not only for this ancient race, but also as a template of what can happen to any traumatized people. Through art, our unconscious communicates to our conscious mind; art and literature also use this bridge to communicate with the conscious and unconscious minds of others.

I met Graham when he was seeking part-time work as a bus driver with our organization, Gunawirra.[1] He told me he was a mature-age student, father of two children and that he was studying culture and art at the local Technical and Further Education (TAFE) college special to Aboriginal people called EORA. There was an exhibition of artwork at this technical college not long after this and Graham asked if I would like to see it. His art immediately stood out for me without my knowing it was his. I bought a painting. His paintings now cover the walls of Gunawirra. Graham now works for Gunawirra as our resident artist, our teacher of Aboriginal culture for our young mothers. He also teaches pottery and art to our preschool children in regional and country New South Wales. He is particularly known for his stories of *The Dreaming* (earliest myths of the Aboriginal elders having to do with the spirits and the creation of the world). Graham has a book in process on the dreaming stories at this time. This is his story as he told it to me.

GRAHAM'S NARRATIVE

Graham's art is integral to his story, and the reader will find it useful to consult Graham's website to get a sense of the visual and spiritual scope of his artwork;[2] Graham experiences himself as a seeker in a spiritual sense. He sees his life journey as a journey transgenerationally transmitted from his great-great grandfather. In his past family and culture and community, he seeks his own roots and the mythology of his own history and his race's history. He finds expression of these in his own paintings created by "those inside me, the spirits of my ancestors who live and dwell within me." We are thinking here of transgenerational continuity. We are asking in this chapter why one person might become an artist and why another may well lose their way completely and wander through a life that is confused and meaningless. The role of an illusion is a developmental process that allows for symbol formation.

Milner (1952/1987), in her seminal paper "The role of an illusion in symbol formation," offers a clear understanding of the way people use objects from the world around them to give meaning to their emotional internal world. This needs a special step in the imagination. It is a step every artist and writer must dare to take—a saltshaker might become a train; a box might become a cave. This capacity to dream the world around us and its objects into a place having internal meaning for us is central to all I write about here. In that magic moment, we imbue external objects with our own internal meaning. Then, as a group, we add further meaning to objects, giving them the status of symbols. These symbols are so meaningful to our internal world that many have died for their preservation—the Christian cross, the Star of David, and the crescent moon are such symbols. Why that capacity is present for some and not for others is certainly linked to early mothering in ways we are just beginning to understand. It is also linked to a psychic space within for imagining. It is part of the "mentalizing" process of every artist and creative writer.

Yet why for some can this level of development not be reached, and how did Graham arrive at it? What is important to our thinking here is why one person might abuse drugs or alcohol, while another is seeking resolution of their identity by identifying with their culture, their history, and their ancestors. It is important in the discussions with Graham to seek an understanding of how much the tradition of reaching back in his culture helped to support his identity and give meaning to his art and his life.

So I (Norma) asked many questions: "Graham how did you become aware that you had an Aboriginal background? Was it something that grew gradually in your mind as you were growing up? Did you suddenly discover you were Aboriginal? What kind of meaning did it have for you?"

Graham

I am Graham. I was born in a little country town called Narromine. I belong to the Wiradjuri people and the Wongaibon people who come from Nyngan, so I regard myself as belonging to both those tribes. I feel my blood belongs to both those people. I think as a child I was aware of my Aboriginal father. My mother and father broke up when I was five—I used to visit my father and his family every weekend up to the age of ten. I found it very difficult when I was young to understand who I was and where I belonged and who was right and who was wrong. All week, I stayed with my mother and my white grandmother and all non-Aboriginal people. On the weekend, I went back to my father who was Aboriginal, so I found it extremely difficult to understand who I was. I questioned, even in my very young mind, a lot of what my mother was saying. "How could Aboriginal people be so bad and yet when I went back there was so much caring and they so loved me?" My mother and her family had no idea of the degree of community and love and warmth that created in me when I went back to my father's people. They were always hugging me and saying, "Be proud son!" It's amazing now when I think back about it and it's only in the last three or four years that I started to do that.

It is not until I have got older that I have regarded myself as an Aboriginal person. Sure I felt within me that I was part Aboriginal, but because I spent so much of my time away from my dad, relatives, and "country" it was hard to feel that I appreciated my heritage. But the biggest connection and memory I had with my father and his people was a sense of overwhelming love. It was a feeling of being special. I would walk into the house and my grandmother would say, "Here is big Graham!" and she would constantly say, "Be proud of who you are, son!" My grandmother's family made Aboriginal people out to be truly special and they always were able to tell me, "You are going to face difficulties in your life because you are Aboriginal and because of your colour and your background." I have experienced that all my life, but I think now I am fortunate to have both cultures. Now that I am older, I can look back and make up my own mind. I now regard myself as an Aboriginal person with non-Aboriginal blood. For thirty years of my life, it was the complete opposite, I was a non-Aboriginal person with Aboriginal blood. About three years ago I wanted to know what Aboriginal culture really was about, and I realized I knew almost nothing. So I went to EORA TAFE in the hope that I would learn something there. That was the door that opened so many other doors for me and I was so lucky to have gone there.

I try now to tell my children to feel proud that they are part of the oldest living culture in the whole world. "Tell people where you come from. Let them know what Aboriginal culture is about!" I had learned from white men and school about how the white man had come here to try and make this country better. I got such a shock when I heard of all the terrible things they did to our people. Now I am on a little adventure where I am trying to teach people about culture. I always enjoyed drawing and it has really blown me away when I kind of discover I can paint things. I am a really spiritual person and I really feel right now my ancestor spirits are in me and with me and that they guide me, and they always have, but I just haven't thought about it or experienced that it is really there as I do now. That is why I am so spiritual. That is why I regard myself as more Aboriginal than non-Aboriginal. My loving the moon, the stars, loving nature, being aware of it, being aware of the trees, I tell myself, is part of my being Aboriginal. Through my art I love to tell stories about culture, about ceremony, about spirituality. I can't say much or speak to people, but if I have a painting it can tell the story. I am just so lucky in that I can travel on this journey even though I do not know where this journey is going.

THE PSYCHIC PAIN IN TRAUMA

Loss and suffering function as powerful forces that draw us to work through our pain to give it shape, and to release it, expressing it to others to make sense of it and to find meaning. This is art. This is also the stories, the spiritual essence of *The Dreaming*. It is also the basis of the *Dadirri* circle of the Aboriginal communities throughout Australia. Elders and other men of the village are called by the one in pain through loss or death or trouble with the law. A circle is formed by the men, a witness circle where the sufferer is heard in the deepest recesses of each hearer's "soul." No one speaks a word but the one in trouble. The pain goes on in myriad conscious and unconscious ways until the sufferer comes to terms with despair and reaches a state of mind that we might call acceptance. Through Graham's art he invites others to become witnesses to his peoples' suffering. These witnesses allow him and those who witness it to be known and to feel less abandoned, to find pride in history. Repair through connection and integration is what the Dadirri witnessing achieves in the unconscious.

PERSONAL HISTORY NARRATIVE

Graham's narrative expresses how trauma experienced in childhood can become a dominant theme in adulthood, influencing one's identity, crying out for expression, and determining preoccupations. Graham felt driven to find release through expression of his art. Through the symbolic or direct expression of trauma experience, the survivor can bring some order into the emotional chaos and so find meaning and thereby regain some sense of continuity and connection. The historic narrative within is what gives our life continuity and meaning. The severing of this narrative history is the serious event that occurs in trauma. In trauma, the primary empathic bond is ruptured and, in its absence, internal representation of the relationship between self and other is destroyed. At the core is the sense of abandonment, because at the center of the traumatic experience is the fear, the dread of the terror of death.

This is what Graham helped us understand. His art repaired that historic narrative. When the artist has a special talent and the world recognizes it, the public recognition becomes a source of self-esteem as well. Graham's art was chosen, and he was selected as a finalist in the New South Wales Aboriginal parliamentary awards. He kept saying, "Do you think they got the name wrong and it is someone else?" He literally lay awake for two nights unable to sleep. What preoccupied him was that he was accepted as an Aboriginal artist among other male Aboriginal artists. He was "one of the men." Bose (2005) writes that

> The function of the work of art, in a reciprocal process between the art object and its maker, in the making and in the performing of it, can then be seen as being able to reassert the ability to find meaning and symbolic form and to therewith communicate to another, to have a witness, and to also communicate with oneself and with dissociated aspects of self-experience. (p. 69)

What exists inside as unformulated chaos can be formulated, given shape and meaning, and be witnessed by the self through another. Through the creative process, painful disorganizing elements are shaped into images or ideas that have substance and reality. This process counteracts the tendency toward dissociation, the common legacy of trauma.

I asked Graham, "What happens inside you when you paint? You seem amazed that you have this wonderful gift as an artist."

Graham

I feel that I was in a deep sleep, my mind was clogged, my vision was blurred and then one day, about three years, ago my ancestors awakened me. They woke me up to reattach themselves to the world that they left physically long ago. They speak to me spiritually via visions, feelings, ideas, and emotions that they give me, which I then transform into creative works. I'm the voice of my ancestors, telling and showing people of today about their visions, thoughts, and feelings from a time and place long ago. We communicate daily, but it's at night that I really feel and hear them. When the noise has gone, when the light is dim, this is the time I feel we become connected. I like to think they are in the spirit world sitting around a fire talking to me, without the distractions that can block the messages they are sending me. Many a time I have laid in bed and can't sleep or have awakened with thoughts; it's then I go to work creating the message that has been sent to me. I feel I'm blessed to have this connection and will continue to share these messages through my creative works until it's my time to travel spiritually back to my ancestors and homelands.

I did one particular painting, and I could see an emu, and I could see this vision, and without knowing this connection—except to be aware that emus were part of the country my ancestors came from—this Aboriginal thing I was painting, like the spirituality, consumes me and takes over. I went to college to learn about the culture, but I know now these are my own thoughts and I can translate the culture from inside myself and from my own thoughts.

Now, I look back and I see all the little things I did as a kid and how good I was at art. I remember I did something at school when I was about twelve and it was that good they got me up in front of the school and said, "Look what Graham has done!" It was about diamonds and I draw diamonds an awful lot; it's kind of like doodling, but diamonds are a really big part of where I am from because we have scarred trees that are kind of burial places. My ancestors drew diamonds on trees, so there's this that I wasn't aware of until I started doing my own art. It's a strange feeling. I never feel scared. When I first started to do this, my mother couldn't understand. She would come over to get the grandkids and we'd start talking, and I'd share with her what the white people did to the black people when they first came here. She'd say the Aboriginal people weren't exactly that good to the white people either. We still talk and she sees me, but I don't talk about these things with her at all—they upset her and she simply does not understand them, and she was getting upset by me talking about this Aboriginal stuff. Somehow, she did not know or acknowledge it, as if she had done something shameful even. She is slowly understanding that it means a lot to me and so she allows it. She has the culture mixed up with her anger toward my father for leaving her and the children.

I would like to talk about that and about some of the mythology, and I am interested in how amazed I was at the degree of cruelty toward the Aboriginal people in early colonization, and I wanted to ask you about my shame because a lot of your Aboriginal patients seem to come from a special space inside themselves where they are ashamed of themselves.

I was like that for a long time. I would like to really talk about this myself. The only thing that gets things done sometimes is "people power" and it is not different from the conflict of the Aboriginal people because the shame does turn into anger eventually. We, Aboriginal people, believe in the power as that which will do most for our people. I get angry because they make out as if we are criminals because we are angry at being subjugated. I am identified with the injustice my people have suffered and this is how I want to use my art. I want my art to give people knowledge of what the art, *The Dreaming*, our stories, the things we are not ashamed of in our Aboriginal culture are that will empower us. It's a kind of magic that I want to give and share. There's so much to be learned, there's so much stereotyping that cuts across the truth of who and what we are, and I think art is such a powerful way of raising awareness. I can see and understand the non-Aboriginal side as well.

I grew up in a time where Aboriginal people were seen as rubbish, as vermin, as a nothing. I think we were so ashamed and afraid, terrified to speak up, to have a voice, that we accepted that we were nothing people. My grandmother was part of the *stolen generation*. We were instructed by our parents to be afraid—just don't say too much because they are fearful of the response. Things will get back to the welfare or the police. They were pretty mixed up themselves because it's been generation after generation where you are told not to speak up, not to be heard, because of the fear of reprisals. Well, my father didn't really come across much of that. When he was fourteen he went and started work, but his mother and father, they would have grown up with a sense of terror. They were moved on from place to place. They started in Nyngan and were forced down the Bogan River to different reserves until they reached a place called Albert. This was a really little place back in the 1920s. Albert was where my dad was born in a tin shack on the Bogan River. Some years later my people were forced to move to Dandaloo and then eventually into a house in Trangie, Narromine. It was where I was born because Trangie did not have the proper medical services to deliver children. They were moved on from place to place. They started in Nyngan and were shuffled down the river to different reserves until they reached a place called Albert. This was a really little place back in the 1920s: Dandaloo in Trangie, Narromine, really little places on the rivers in the reserves. My mother's family came from Pilliga Forest around Mudgee. They were a mixture of Irish and English families. They were very hard people and my mother doesn't talk very much about it, but they were very hard and that is how they had to grow up there. There was love there, but it was nothing like the Aboriginal side and it was very different. From when I was six or seven, I just didn't ever have a dad around, and now I look back and I see there was no encouragement, no guidance—those valuable things you look to from a father like "Good onya, son!" I was only able to go home to my dad on weekends once a fortnight. I kind of lost touch with my father's community in the end, and I was left to just make up my own mind. I could see them with my own eyes, walking around the street. I didn't see them as bad because of the fighting. Mostly, that was because they just were drinking all the time, not doing anything with their lives, just sitting around. I understand now that it was a bit of a statement, in a way, that they didn't belong. They had nowhere to go. Maybe some tried to get work, but the white people took one look, saw they were Aboriginal, and wouldn't give them any work. It was a terrible history. Actually people were scared to employ Aboriginal people because there was so much prejudice that they feared people wouldn't go to them because they employed Aboriginals.

My wife is white. I've known her since we were at school and although there was some degree of protectiveness and stereotyping when I first went out with her, once I approached her parents and told them, "I want to marry your daughter and I promise you to take care of her and to always guard and protect her," they were fine. I think they thought I showed a lot of care and that I would make a very good partner for her, and we have two children. one boy and one girl. My boy is fourteen; my daughter is seventeen. My daughter was born with the cord wrapped around her neck and we were in danger of losing her. The nurses had left and her heartbeat was going crazy and then slowing down. I was terrified! I went and got a nurse who came back in and straightaway they treated her, so, in a sense, I saved my own daughter and that makes her extraordinarily important to me. I love my son, but she is very special and that shock was immense. She was the first and they had to take her away and keep an eye on her for a few days. It was a very stressful time indeed. She is beautiful now. We waited a little bit longer then to have a boy because we were just so scared. His name is Jacob. I was just too frightened, I think, so I didn't give him an Aboriginal name like I would've liked to. I am a very proud man and proud of where I come from.

One weekend when I went home to see my dad, I wanted to go and see where my dad and my ancestors came from. I really wanted to feel and get an idea of what my background was, and the last time I'd been there I was three and could hardly walk. So I told my dad, "I'm going to go down the river and back to our own country." My brother said, "I'll come with you!" I could hear something in the wind and then I started to say to myself, "Are you making this up because you want to hear something, to believe that there is something magic about this place?" But I knew I wasn't making it up and I don't think it was a mind thing. There was a presence there, and, as I walked, I could hear all these voices. I walked up to the bank of the river and I climbed right up high then and I couldn't see anything, but I felt safe. There was an incredible calm. I wasn't frightened. I said, "Just please show me who you are?" and then I just thought, "I want to take something from this land to be mine, to be in touch with the land, to be in touch with my ancestors who were part of this land." I asked permission of them. I said, "I want to take something from here and I hope you don't mind." I spoke to my own spirits and I bent down and I picked up some rocks. You see, in our Aboriginal culture, by taking part of the land I was taking part of them. I put the rocks in the car and went back to Dad's place, and I sat my dad down and said to him, "Look what I picked up down off the river!" I showed them to my children and I want my children to know this is part of our ancestors who walked on these rocks: "I want you to keep these and give them to your children, and your children will give it to their children." When my dad heard, he became proud and happy knowing I understood the importance of respecting our ancestors and "country." "I feel this is very important. This is our past! The land is part of my past inside me." Like there's something outside, but it's inside me, my own ancestors walked on these very rocks. So I sat my kids down and I said, "See, these rocks I want you to respect them, I wanted to protect them."

A few months later, I took my children out there at their request, and I helped them understand what our background was, where we came from, where our people came from, how important it was that they respect our past. I wonder if the kids think it's a bit of a silly thing giving them this rock or if they will really understand the spiritual meaning in it. When I've got these rocks with me, I know my people are with me and I know nothing can be changed or taken away from me.

This Billabong on the river is a very sacred place where fathers and sons come to pay respect and to learn the value of their own people. There are hundreds and thousands of these little stones and every one of them represents a father and son, together, coming to learn respect for their people and their land, their place. I don't know if this happens anywhere else in the world, but I do know that it means something very deep to me. I do my paintings out of my thinking like that. It comes from the same place inside me. These are magical, special things in our culture and in our lives that I want to represent in my painting. They are spiritual in a way our people have known spiritual for thousands of years. Spirituality to me is this connection to my ancestors, to the earth, to my art. The first painting I did was of Biami—the moment of creation. In the *Homelands* painting, I am trying to say that the trees actually do have life, because they are alive. They have blood, the blood of life in them. I see this place I have told you about as a world I can go to at any time in my mind, not in reality but in my mind. When I do my art, what I am doing is giving the image of my country in my mind, the land that is part of me, my connection to my spirituality, to my dream time, to my totem. I could look at the stars every single night. That's what my people used to do. There was nothing else to do. They weren't watching television, they were looking at the stars, they were looking at the eastern sky, they were seeing the animals like an emu in the sky. When they saw the emu in the Milky Way, that meant the season was changing, the emu on earth had laid its eggs, and this was the time to go and collect them. I aim to keep that knowledge and give it to our Aboriginal children. I would have loved to have been here five hundred years ago walking through the bush, having my son next to me, teaching him about what is natural and good in the world around us, finding the emu eggs, knowing to only take one or two so that you leave some, so that life can go on, giving him this important message that there can be life for all if we are careful of the world we live in. I just think I am so extraordinarily lucky. I know that, somehow, someone guided me—and it's not just rolling up your sleeve with hard work, it's inspiration from inside you that comes from the spirit of your ancestors.

People say to me, "Aren't you scared of this?" We talk and I say, "No, it calms me. I am never afraid of it. I can name myself. I can have a name. I can be a person, and I can teach people about our culture in a way that makes them feel like a person, and that way I keep it alive in myself. It helps me reach the goals I want to reach in my life and with my children. I am so grateful, thank you." When I talk about our culture, stories, beliefs, and values, I feel very proud and honored to be teaching people of my amazing culture and others. This in my mind is how my people can deal and cope with trauma and be proud of who and where we come from.

FREEING THE IMMOBILITY OF TRAUMA

The Aboriginal people knew this about being a person and their Dadirri circle where the men of the community sat in silence listening to the pain of the speaker for as many hours as it took is the antecedent of modern psychotherapy. Modern psychotherapy supports the person going into madness and holds the person when she or he is in the hopeless, faithless, loveless place, until born from within are the big three foundational pillars that give meaning to life—faith, hope, and love.

I now want to use this chapter to discuss more precisely how the freeing of the immobility of trauma allows the deepest forms of aestheticism and creativity to emerge. One paints or sings or writes oneself into existence anew. One dares to "know" those parts of the self as characters that have the potential to be the fabric of one's future being. This space then can be likened to the womb, where a conception between the analytic therapist and the patient can take place, but even more significantly one between *the patient and his or her unknown self.* Words like forgiveness of self and others, the possibility of atonement, a depth of reverence, awe and spirituality come to mind. One moves from being mindless to being mindful of oneself and the other. All people do not need psychoanalysis to achieve this. A stage in maturing, an event in one's life, may awaken what has lain dormant, off stage, unable to be dreamt or experienced for many years, but I believe the action might be the same, and that is the movement between passion and the symbolic.

In therapy relating to trauma, there is a psychic space between a therapeutic couple, therapist and patient, where experience is not the "feeling" of pain but the "suffering" and tolerating of it (Bion, 1977, p. 20). Here, chaos resolves into order through the capacity to symbolize, and hence give meaning. Those symbols, whether through art, literature, or music, are the bridges. I use the model of a stage on which our life drama—our life narrative—has the potential to be enacted. However, with respect to trauma, I propose that it is an empty stage or an autistic space in which the psychic enactment does not dare to present itself, because it has presented itself before and been blown to bits by the trauma. In this autistic space, the possibility of becoming is absent, the terror of being is enormous. There, the confusion of becoming or moving toward life, and therefore dying, becomes unbearable.

The aesthetic experience, the work of art or music or literature, is a bridging, an interactive psychic event in the space between trauma and healing. To activate this internal autistic psychic space deadened as a result of the trauma, one needs to dare to experience the suffering in the suffering. In so doing, the unbearable aloneness of human suffering is eased, not only by oneself being witness to the pain, but also by the symbolizing of it as a universal theme shared by others, communicated through art or drama or literature. *The ceasing to exist in our internal psyche is the exact opposite of the capacity to find meaning through the aesthetic experience.* It never ceases to be relevant to my thinking that a people, denied a meaning as a people by law, should have as their main means of expression a depth of art and its symbols and a connection through *The Dreaming*, to the spiritual stories of their ancestors. It is as if they knew this was the road to cure for trauma: Retain your spiritual base, and express through art and experience the care of others through the deep listening circle of *Dadirri*.

SUFFERING THE PAIN IN THE SUFFERING: THE BEGINNING OF PSYCHIC LIFE

The stories of *The Dreaming* were a way of finding meaning, an expression of the deeply spiritual and imaginative through art and storytelling. This was integral to Aboriginal culture from its beginnings in Australia. There is nothing new in this. Since the beginning of time the human condition has been expressed in art, literature, opera, drama, dance, and music. The *witnessing and the capacity to imagine and use symbolically* are the two main ingredients for the healing of trauma. The empathic sharing created by the communicating arts eases the very center of all trauma, the terror of death and the fear of total loss and abandonment. Bion (1990) writes, "Many fear 'going mad,' some indescribable disaster, 'breakdown'" (p. 382). For "In Bion's view there is no pain without imagination, and, in the absence of pain, no mental life. There is instead 'nothingness' for which many types of activity may be a 'cover'" (Williams, 2010, p. 26, citing Bion, 1990, p. 610). Meg Harris Williams (2010) further elaborates on Bion: "His writings are imbued with a sense of danger regarding the very real possibility that mental life can be extinguished if imagination is not, at the very least, 'given an airing'" (p. 26). The traumatized dare not enter into chaos; they fear chaos means "death." To experience the nature of "catastrophe" feels like death. However, Bion, and later Williams (2010), emphasize how chaos is the beginning of life. It is "death to the existing state of mind" (Bion, 1970, p. 79). But in fact it is the truth, it is food for the mind, and the mind grows thereby. Mental growth is felt as "catastrophic and timeless" (Bion, 1970, p. 108). Yet this chaos is a beginning of life, and when directed and expressed in art, drama, literature, opera, and all forms of aesthetic expression, it makes the intolerable tolerable, the unbearable bearable.

NEUROBIOLOGY OF TRAUMA

There is an absolute parallel for this in the neurobiology of trauma. The mental, emotional, and physical are in accord. According to Rothschild (2003), the two areas of the limbic system central to the storage and retrieval of memory are the amygdala and the hippocampus. The amygdala is the area most clearly implicated in the evaluation of emotional meaning related "to highly charged emotional memories such as terror and horror, becoming active both during and while remembering a traumatic incident" (Rothschild,

2003, p. 12). The hippocampus creates the cognitive map of the experience, "putting our memories into their proper perspective and place in our life's time line" (Rothschild, 2003, p. 12). It functions by comparing the events of present experience with events from the past, and determining whether and how the events are associated. When placed in perspective, the event becomes an experience that fits into the channel of life-historical narrative experience. But when it is "walled off," the result is that the traumatic event is "prevented from occupying its proper position in the individual's life history" (Rothschild, 2003, p. 12). It then continues to invade the present, affecting the integration of the traumatic experiences and memory.

In "The Body Keeps the Score," van der Kolk (1994) sees this integration as all-important because it gives the experience a historical place and sequence. Without this grounding, it keeps interrupting the present with serious consequences that disturb the emotional world and life of the person. Memories walled-off due to trauma retain their power and freshness on an affective level even years after the event. Traumatized individuals are unable to modulate new, incoming stimulation, which interferes with the amygdala and hippocampal functions, thus bypassing the prefrontal cortex, which would normally assist with the cognitive evaluation of the experience. Studies have shown that trauma sufferers process their trauma from the bottom up—body to mind—and not top down—mind to body (van der Kolk, 1994). In order to treat trauma effectively and to integrate the cognitive, emotional, and affective memory, therapists must move beyond words and language.

IDENTITY AND SYMBOLIZATION IN ART

In *Icon and Idea*, Herbert Read writes that "art is finding (rather than seeking) new symbols to signify new areas of sensibility" (1955, p. 53). The artist establishes symbols by becoming conscious of new aspects of reality, and by representing his or her own consciousness of these new aspects of reality. The French Catholic philosopher Jacques Maritain's theme, in his 1944 article "Poetic experience" is that Western art has progressively laid stress on the artist's 'self,' and that it has plunged deeply into the incommunicable world of creative subjectivity. Painters are people who seek after themselves, and are carried along beyond the natural appearance of things in desperate search of a deeper reality. According to Maritain, at the root of the creative act there must be a quite peculiar mental process without parallel in logical reason, a process through which things and the self are held together by means of a kind of experience of knowledge which has no conceptual expression and is shown only in the artist's work. He calls this process creative or poetic intuition, and he goes on to say that in poetic intuition, objective reality and subjectivity, the world and the whole of the soul coexist inseparably. In poetry, we enter "a nocturnal empire," a primeval activity of the intellect which, far beyond concepts and logic, exercises itself in vital connections between imagination and emotion, which is very much how Jacques Maritain saw the creative arts. That "nocturnal empire" is the area of the stories of *The Dreaming* in Aboriginal culture. In the area of our own dreaming, during the night where our conscious mind surrenders and allows it, it is accessible and active to an audience of one. The dreaming of the night is a totally private film put on for just one person; the dreaming of the day, when it is taken to another level by the conscious self and expressed through art, becomes a means of healing our being. During our conscious waking time its narrative is able to be freely accessed and expressed by our conscious mind for the witness of others.

Our Dreaming—*The Dreaming*

So from where does *The Dreaming* come? Is that a natural process, nature's own gift to people so that they can live with their own unutterable pain and make it utterable? Is the very dream itself curative, and are we simply moving it to another level in art, literature, drama, music, and dance? Is that our own unconscious analyst doing the work of cure, and can it be the Aboriginal inside each of us, creating our own personal stories of *The Dreaming*? Is the problem of trauma one in which the dreamer can no longer dream and so cannot conceive of and develop their own cure? And when that happens is it that the "author within" can no longer develop a story to write or even find an audience to write for? Does trauma kill the capacity to imagine? Both the dream and these questions are at the core of our capacity to imagine and to make "images of"—not only in all art and storytelling and music but also at the core of all healing.

Both Sigmund Freud and Frances Tustin wrote of being one with the universe as an oceanic feeling, and both explained it as a regression to the early infantile state of consciousness, when a child's ego is not yet differentiated from the surrounding external world. Is art, music, poetry, literature taking place as a result of the ability to regress to our infantile states in the womb of the mother's body, in the womb of the mother's arms, in the womb of the mother's mind? This regression may be essential to the creative process.

INTERNAL OBJECTS AND TRAUMA

It may be that trauma destroys internal relationships and links, so that in trauma protective internal objects fail in their function to protect. What is left is an autistic space where relationships once were, where thought would be if it was not now too terrible to think. This would be a space where feeling would be—only it is now too terrible to feel. *The artist rebuilds both the destroyed self and the destroyed loved object through the aesthetic experience of art.* Through the practices of art, there may be a restoration of internal relationships through symbols, with these symbols including images, stories, and sounds that are now able to give meaning, and, in so doing, heal the sense of loss.

The basic tragedy of trauma is the loss of meaning it causes. The restoration of that meaning can only come into being as a result of suffering the loss, mourning it, and beginning the task of creation again. This process is essential to what this chapter is about. Herbert Read wrote that psychoanalysis had done an incalculable service to art by showing that art originates from the beginning in symbolization, and that the process of symbolic transformation, which is fundamental to the creative process in art, is also biologically fundamental, thus proving that the artist's feeling that what he was doing was real and not just escapism was correct. A new thing has been created. In this way, the original tremendous primary drive to physical union with another living being has been able to transform itself by means of the process of symbolization.

The healing mind emerges as a result of being its own witness in the dream, and in consciousness its own observing ego; in art forms, it reaches the universality of witnesses, attentive and receptive to what has happened. It is through a creative action from the unconscious that the analyst assists the patient to be able to build his or her own bridges from the unconscious to consciousness until the traumatized person can again or for the first time become a healer and do their own creative work.

The achieving of a symbol means the mourning of a loss, and the symbol is the substitute for that loss. The psychoanalytic therapist works then most seriously in the area of loss. We are the professional mourners, the chorus of the Greek tragedy. In their patients analysts find that this whole process of symbol formation has been interfered with, or perhaps never even properly established. The central movement in the process of finding the symbol requires the temporary merging of the idea of the original thing with the idea that the substitute becomes the symbol.

EXISTENCE AND NONEXISTENCE

I want to use this final part of the chapter to give further understanding to the dynamic of positive and negative, of existence and nonexistence. It is in the tolerance of this dynamic that art is born, and through it art becomes the bridge via symbolism. Bion writes about the value of psychoanalysis depending largely on its capacity to rehabilitate damaged internal objects through the "corrective emotional experience" aspect of the process. Meg Harris Williams says the goal of the psychoanalytic encounter is that of "restoring and shaping any points of thwarted or stunted growth" (Williams, 2010, p. xv). She writes eloquently of this quest to reconnect with the "inward sense" that makes our lives beautiful. Here, symbol-making refers to the "aesthetic qualities of transference-countertransference," and with that, its "quest for the meaning of emotional experiences" (Williams, 2010, p. xix).

Some patients may reach a state that Bion (1970) described as "non-existence" (p. 20). Such a person, living in an absence rather than a presence, creates a space that can be called nonexistence, but this nonexistence is not actually an accurate description. Rather, it is full of envy and rage toward anything that does exist. It is indeed a negative lifelessness and is full of hatred of life. Within it seems to be a terrifying superego, so cruel, so powerful, so destructive that it denudes the person of any right or will to live. I see this as the exact opposite of the creative symbolic action of art, which introduces the person to his own inner self. In that situation, when the love–hate tension can be fully experienced, it leads to truthful self-knowledge. Turbulence is a sign of the presence of both the human personality and fundamental reality—of "That beauty which, as Milton sings, / Hath terror in it" as Wordsworth wrote in "The Prelude" (1888, XIII, pp. 225–26).

Blake (1790/1966) describes human creativity in terms of the cleansing of the vision that takes place when the vitality of the passions is acknowledged in the marriage of "heaven and hell." To *see* Infinity is to *be* human in the Blakean sense. He adds, "Without Contraries Is No Progression. Attraction and Repulsion, Reason and Energy, Love and Hate, Are Necessary to Human Existence" (p. 149). Williams (2010) writes that Blake's view supersedes both the Christian doctrine of sin and repentance and rationalist empiricism, noting that "Non-entity rather than sin comprises the evil to which man is prone, and is only reversible through the spiritual dynamism of contrary passions, which regale him with a complex vision" (p. 37). Bion's formulation of the way a "no-emotion" comes to replace emotions is very similar: "the absent fulfilment is experienced as a no-thing . . . there is thus created a domain of the non-existent" (Bion, 1970, pp. 19, 20).

"Sooner murder an infant in its cradle than nurse unacted desires," Blake wrote provocatively (1790/1966, p. 152), meaning that desires or passions that achieve no aesthetic organization or fulfillment are, in effect, murdered infants in the world of the mind. "Conflict within, chaos, catastrophe, and the tolerance of it is what bring us to beauty and truth. It follows that the entire world of psychopathology can be seen in terms of retreat from the aesthetic conflict" (Meltzer, 1986, p. 208). The world of art, of literature, of opera, of drama, of poetry, of music, of dance, is a world where conflict of opposing emotions of love and hate, of existence and nonexistence, can be accepted as part—or indeed the very life force—of the human condition.

ACKNOWLEDGEMENT

I (Norma) want to acknowledge the generosity of Graham Toomey in sharing his narrative. For the countless ways his presence and work have brought the Aboriginal soul to Gunawirra, I thank him.

NOTES

1. See Gunawirra.org.au.
2. Graham's work can be seen at www.grahamtoomey.com.

REFERENCES

Bion, W. R. (1970). *Attention and interpretation*. London: Tavistock.

Bion, W. R. (1977). *Seven servants: Four works by Wilfred R. Bion* (*Elements of psycho-analysis, learning from experience, transformations, attention and interpretation*). New York: Jason Aronson.

Bion W. R. (1990). *A memoir of the future* (*The dream* [1975], *The past presented* [1977], *The dawn of oblivion* [1979]). London: Karnac.

Blake, W. (1790/1966). The marriage of heaven and hell. In G. Keynes (Ed.). *The complete writings of William Blake* (pp. 148–58). UK: Oxford University Press.

Bose, J. (2005, Spring). Images of trauma: Pain, recognition, and disavowal in the works of Frida Kahlo and Francis Bacon. *Journal of the American Academy of Psychoanalysis and Dynamic Psychiatry, 33*(1), 51–70.

Charny, I. W. (Ed.). (1999). Art and *trauma. International Journal of Psychoanalysis, 76*, 995–1005.

Harris, R. J. (1970). *Poems*. Strath Tay, Perthshire: Clunie Press.

Meltzer, D. (1986). *Studies in extended metapsychology: Clinical applications of Bion's ideas*. Strath Tay, Perthshire: Clunie Press.

Milner, M. (1952/1987). The role of illusion in symbol formation. I. *The suppressed madness of sane men: Forty-four years of exploring psychoanalysis.* London: Tavistock and the Institute of Psychoanalysis. *New Library of Psychoanalysis, 3.* Reprint: London: Brunner-Routledge, 2002.

Read, H. (1955). *Icon and idea*. London: Faber & Faber.

Rothschild, B. (2003). *The body remembers casebook: Unifying methods and models in the treatment of trauma and PTSD*. New York, NY: Norton.

van der Kolk, B. A. (1994). The body keeps the score: Memory and the evolving psychobiology of post-traumatic stress. *Harvard Review of Psychiatry, 1*(5), 253–65.

Williams, M. H. (2010). *The aesthetic development: The poetic spirit of psychoanalysis*. London: Karnac.

Chapter 6

Anglo-German Displacement and Diaspora in the Early Twentieth Century

An Intergenerational Haunting

Nigel Williams

In this chapter I look at a little-known episode in the history of migrant communities: the break-up and disappearance of the Anglo-German community in Britain as a consequence of the First World War. I draw partly on a "history from below" approach, but one that is further informed by a contemporary growth in the availability of family ancestry records. Theoretically I am interested in a psychosocially informed perspective that can help focus on the role of memory, its erasure, and the construction of posttraumatic narratives of identity. Professionally I draw on research into practitioner-based approaches to intergenerational memory and memory erasure. Personally I draw on research into my own Anglo-German family and my involvement with colleagues from family history societies in Britain and in Germany. There is a methodological autoethnographic element to this work in that I include some of the experiences I have had in doing this research while, at the same time being involved in interrogating my own and others' family histories.

The First World War destroyed the German communities that had thrived in Britain during the Victorian and Edwardian period. This destruction came about by a combination of huge popular hostility, driven by a xenophobic right-wing press, and actual wartime events (notably the sinking of the Lusitania in 1916). Government measures included mass internment and deportation. The combined factors of mob violence and government action led to the disappearance, by the early 1920s, of the extensive and complex German communities in Britain. As Panayi (1991) has noted, the May 15, 1915, edition of the patriotic journal, *John Bull,* provides a powerful insight into the anti-German mood of the times in the words of Horatio Bottomley, the journalist, financier, and former London member of Parliament:

> I call for a vendetta against every German in Britain, whether naturalised or not, you cannot naturalise an unnatural beast—a human abortion—a hellish freak. But you can exterminate it. (Panayi, 1991, p. 233)

How many Germans were affected? No one really knows as migration had been essentially unregulated since the start of the German royal lines in Britain, but estimates vary somewhere between thirty thousand and fifty thousand. Some, including my direct family, managed to hide. Most could not. This largely invisible and unacknowledged ethnic cleansing has had, and continues to have, consequences in our world today. I'm going to try to map my and my family's thread in the fabric of this social and cultural trauma, but first, I will set the scene by outlining the cultural context of the community it affected.

My father (Ray) wrote a memoir before he died. In it, amongst many other things, he wrote down what he knew of our German ancestors. None of the story I have just alluded to appeared in his carefully written account. Not a word. He would have been interested in the truth had he known it or had some way of knowing. He bemoans as he writes how "infuriatingly incomplete" his knowledge is, the only echo of the extreme affects of this period is in his word "infuriating." In 1917, he was one year old, an unwitting survivor of something he knew not.

HISTORICAL AND CULTURAL CONTEXT OF THE LONDON ANGLO-GERMAN COMMUNITY

By the time the nineteenth century closed, the German community in Britain was by far the largest migrant group. Germans were established at every level of the class structure, although the majority were bakers, sugar bakers, and pork butchers. My family were hairdressers, a triumvirate of three brothers and their German and English wives, making a living in the bustle and buzz of middle-class central London. They apprenticed, worked long hours, and gradually, over a decade from 1880, they became upwardly mobile, running their own salons, along with other business ventures and parallel professional services such as chiropody, manicure, and massage. They were representative of a new breed of service industry, trading in large part on the cultural prestige of being German in London. Hairdressers made a significant contribution to the shop-working-hours reform movement, a bill that took nearly thirty years to become law, such was the opposition to it. It was finally passed into law on May 1, 1912. Shop hours were long and arduous, with low pay, and typically apprenticeships lasted several years. Established fellow countrymen often exploited the incoming next wave of migrants, who would be younger and less resourced (Towey, 2004, p. 29).

All migrants are subject to push-pull factors in their motivation for migration. In the case of the Germans in London, poverty, political turmoil, and the unpopular and long military service (three years for Prussians) were important reasons to leave. A strong pull factor, however, was the unique position of the long-standing Royal family connections going back to George the First. This attracted those with skills or seeking to acquire skills of "being in service." From German housekeepers, teachers, to "royal hairdressers," hopeful migrants competed for the needs of London's new middle and upper classes. In working-class areas, hairdressers, pork butchers, and bakers serviced the needs of the industrial workers, supplying fast food and weekly high quality shaves and haircuts. The theme was the same, service and "civilizing" (Elias, 1994, p. 54). The German migrants' emphasis on hard work, tidiness, order, and physical culture also traded on the Prince Albert factor and the "modern family" that he and Queen Victoria had projected as an ideal. My ancestors traded on modernity. If you wanted to look and be modern then you needed at least one if not several of their services. Even the steel of their scissors and pork butchery tools were German made. The lotion and potions of the chiropodist, beautician, and manicurists were manufactured in Germany.

How had this situation of complex migration come about? In the last quarter of the nineteenth century, Britain was unusually unregulated. None of my ancestors had passports; they do not appear in passenger lists, they arrived possessing only the paperwork that they needed in order to leave their home principality. Those who paid to escape military service did not even have this. The longer and better-known journey to America was more costly. Many Germans, intending to travel to America, stopped in London, so the shorter journey represented a significant pull factor.

Other key push factors were political and economic. The museum of migration on Ellis Island, in New York Harbor, organizes the immigrant waves in years. The Forty-Eighters, as they were known, went to America as ambitious, politically disenfranchised reformers denied the hope of political emancipation in the failed revolutions of 1848 in Germany. Karl Marx, although he arrived later in London via Paris, was one of these. By contrast, Frederick Engels' name appears on a local passenger list from Antwerp to London in 1837. Engels was actually more typical of Anglo-Germans in that he went back and forth on business, including that of organizing international revolution. Others who did not have revolution in mind came for three months after the harvest to play in touring brass bands that frequented most English seaside resorts. Many pork butchers were "chain migrators" (Wustner, 2012), each family group training up a new set of skilled male and female workers who would then migrate and open a new outlet in a British industrial city.

The Marx family arrived from Paris in 1849. Marx, despite his dangerous reputation, traveled back and forth to Germany visiting friends and later in life convalescing. London was a key destination for revolutionary activists, and this had a strange and very personal bearing on a particularly important phase of the Anglo-German diaspora: the mass internment of enemy aliens that began in the autumn of 1914 and continued through the summer of 1916. During this period of time massive and extensive rioting against Anglo-German families and businesses took place. The internment was as much about managing the agent provocateur aspect of stirred up social unrest as it was about a clearly defined legal process.

In the largest internment camp, at Alexandra Palace in London, the well-known anarcho-syndicalist Rudolph Rocker informally led the 3,000 inmates of the camp, delivering no less than 139 lectures to Anglo-German internees in the period 1915–1919 (Butt, 2011). Rocker, after being deported back to Germany, emigrated to America and finally published the influential *Nationalism and Culture* in 1937. The internment was a key part of trauma formation for some families and individuals in both their attempts to avoid it or their experiences of undergoing it. Much more could be said about the experience of internment and its social causes. It was clearly a source of huge resentment and social suffering. There is currently research going on led by the Anglo-German Family History Society to try to establish in more detail what happened and to whom (*Mitteilungsblatt*, 2013, p. 36).

War and famine were significant push factors in migration; an equivalent of the Irish potato famine drove many rural Germans to migrate in the years from 1845 to 1850. Some arrived in London and went no further. The Franco-Prussian War of 1871 produced an unknown number of preemptive migrators and active draft dodgers. Dutch traders made large sums by securing night-time snatches, making clandestine arrangements for young men avoiding the draft, and helping them across the nearest border and exit via Antwerp. Exploitation of vulnerable individuals and families was rife. Just as borders were porous in a Europe struggling to invent and maintain the nation-state, so migration was highly de- and disregulated. Trauma caused by dislocation was made worse by impoverishment caused by the journey and being preyed on by ruthless middlemen offering "safe passage."

The City of Hamburg was one of the first to create a safer regulated environment for migrants, putting ceilings on rents chargeable, and providing regulation of accommodation. Eventually a purpose-built facility, a factory of exit, called the Ballinstadt emigration halls, was built and named after its founder Albert Balin. New York later followed suit. A key function of the incoming centers was to control migrants to test for their "viability" in terms of health and economic prospects. Ellis Island isolated poorer migrants for assessment. The earlier mainland disembarkation point of Castle Garden was retained for middle-class migrants. No such arrangements existed in London. Migrants sank or swam on luck, or on the strength of their preexisting networks. Some who intended to make the journey to America were tricked out of their savings and were left stranded on the East India docks. Some walked to Liverpool for a cheaper passage.

At the outbreak of the First World War, many German families, shaken and displaced by rioting, some responding to a call to arms from Germany, walked from London to Harwich (the main port of exit in the UK for Hamburg). Some of these men, retaining their Territorial Army status, joined the German reserve armies and faced their fellow compatriots across the trenches in 1915. This recently lost familiarity with fellow Londoners may have given rise to a series of events on Christmas Day 1915 which astonished middle-class English officers when men on opposing sides recognized each other, played football, sang familiar songs, and exchanged haircuts. "One Tommy from the 3rd rifle brigade even had his hair cut by his former barber in High Holborn, who was now a Saxon soldier" (Towey, 2004, p. 91). A reluctance to fight, which troubled some British officers, may have been underpinned by familiarity and friendship, a cultural factor in these strange and little understood cease-fires of midwinter, 1915 (Jenny Towey 1914/ personal communication, 8-9-2012).

Another key push factor was anti-Semitic labor laws in Prussia. For migrating Jews there were no embargoes on entry into the professions and trades in Britain. However, middle-class Jews tended to be well naturalized in Germany and there was no significant mass migration of middle-class Jews from Germany until the days of the Third Reich. By contrast, working-class German Jews were subject to all the push/pull factors described above and were also deeply involved in migration to escape the complex embargoes on trades in which Jews were prohibited from engaging in Germany. Searching in the British National Archive in Kew for my own ancestors' nonexistent naturalization papers, I found records of wave after wave of Russian early twentieth-century Jews. They were often poor, and consequently worked in co-ops of joint savings cartels to pay the then very large naturalization fee.

I like to work archives without using an index if I can. This produces contact with the original documents and allows me to search without a purpose (the psychosocial equivalent of free association and being without memory and desire). In these searches I found a German bookseller whose citizenship was cancelled in 1920. It wasn't difficult to imagine what kind of books he had been selling. The records for that year carry many red stamps that indicate deportation. The majority are German, recategorized as "enemy alien."

In short, during the latter quarter of the nineteenth century, and in the early part of the twentieth century, it was so normal and so easy to pass back and forth between Britain and Germany that a new, unofficial international zone had emerged. This was characterized by short-range migration, a proportion of which was also seasonal. This, in effect, gave rise to a sense of cultural and geographical extension for many Anglo-Germans, which may be represented in Georg Kenner's painting composed while interned in Alexandra Palace in 1915 called "My First Christmas" where he depicts himself sitting huddled below a map of Europe "the right way up"; Britain is depicted upside down, where it belongs, as an extension of Europe (Butt, 2011, p. 36). There were, however, many more mundane examples of extended and porous national boundaries where, for example, in my own family, service work was sought and taken for Swiss clients that involved traveling back to Europe while young wives and children remained in London.

The older nonmigrating generation continued to exert a pull on my Anglo-German family both culturally and in terms of business ties. Soaps and lotions vital to the hairdressing trade continued to get imported via small family businesses. Upon the death of her husband, my great-grandmother migrated to London to live with her Anglo-German children and grandchildren, the final seal of approval on a successful three-generational migratory venture started in the 1880s. She died in 1905.

CULTURAL POLITICAL FACTORS: GROWING RIVALRY AND INVASION FANTASIES

As the turn of the century approached, other vital factors started to emerge in Anglo-German relations that had a subtle and sometimes very direct bearing on migrants, particularly those who were becoming better established. The older Victorian sense of two nations joined by family was increasingly disturbed by both economic and military rivalry. The Franco-Prussian War and subsequent German Unification occurred in 1871. As a direct response the first invasion fantasy book, called *The Battle of Dorking* (Chesney, 1871), was published in Britain. In it, the vastly superior German armies land at Worthing, and defeat the British Volunteer Army on Box Hill, in Surrey. England is humiliated and loses its empire. Published as a pamphlet, it rapidly sold eighty thousand copies. While the invasion fantasy is a ready-made English reflex encompassing figures as diverse as Normans, Irish, Spaniards, Barbary pirates, and the French of the Napoleonic era, it is deeply ironic that the story was renamed *Was England Erwartet* or *What England Expects* and issued to German troops in anticipation of their successful invasion of Britain in 1940 (Dorking Museum and Heritage Centre, 2014).

Over sixty different invasion stories were published between *The Battle of Dorking* and the start of WWI. The *Daily Mail* launched its reputation and role as promoter and guardian of British xenophobia with Le Queux's (1906) story *The Invasion of 1910*. It was serialized and accompanied by frequent editorials about the danger of "Germans in our midst" and the growing threat of German naval power. In Germany, the translation of the same *Die Invasion von 1910: Einfallen der Deutschen in England* (Tamm 1906) proved equally popular due in some large measure to the omission of the last chapter where the British push the Germans back across the channel.

Europe was changing. In the last decade of the nineteenth century a strange division of labor started to emerge between Britain and Germany. Britain remained preeminently a nation of extended overseas empire, aloof or buffered at least from continental politics. Germany could be admired, and acknowledged as, the economic leader of all Europe. Between Hamburg and London, the feeling of a single area of trade and migration subtly emerged. It was an illusion but a powerful one for migrants, and London represented a haven for those Germans unable to live with the increasingly centralizing and authoritarian Prussian state. Around 1900, a new dynamic emerged shaking and disturbing this illusion or "imagined community," that of the first proxy war where Germany actively, although mainly in the cultural sphere, supported the Teutonic Boers against the English in South Africa.

Bur und Lord (Boer and English), by Karl Bleibtreu (1900), names and anticipates the struggle between downtrodden Teutonic brethren and the aristocratic and superior imperialist English. "Lords" and "Hun" are part of an emerging language of mutual denigration.

Utopias and Science Fiction in Anglo-German Relations

There is another significant literary genre of the period, broadly known as utopianism or futurism that has a bearing on Anglo-German relations. H. G. Wells is the most well-known proponent of this genre, which also became a part of popular literature that explored Anglo-German conflict via imaginary cultural and technological futures. Ian Boyd Whyte (2006) documents this clash taking place in his essay "Anglo-German Conflict in Popular Fiction, 1870–1914" (Boyd Whyte, 2006). Bridgham's (2006), *The First World War as a Clash of Cultures* edited collection is a good general source on the topic.

Wells's earlier *War of the Worlds* (1898) depicts merciless, androgynous Martians invading the earth and dominating all warring nations. His visionary *War in the Air* (1910) shows the dystopian future as the world is ravaged by technologically driven warfare. Wells's debt to Darwinism is grimly present in the description of the various arms races that express the survival of the fittest. His predictive power of the emergence and then collapse of new world order seems to signal an idea that the First World War was actually the start of another European Thirty Years' War (Neumann, 1946). Wells's predictions cover features of both world wars and the Cold War. This is a broader cultural haunting, an uncanny foreshadowing of events via literature. By the time war was declared in 1914, it had already been fought many times over in popular imagination. Wells even successfully predicted its physical destructiveness, as his character Marcus Karenin says in *The World Set Free* (1913), knowledge and power, not love, are the essential goals of humanity (Wells, 1913).

It was left to the subtle and brilliant imagination of his German contemporary Kurd Lasswitz (1971) to imagine a Martian takeover where both parties are altered forever by the experience and where mankind acquires a new collective identity in its collision with an older but vulnerable civilization. *Zwei Planetum* (1897) was not translated into English until 1971 but was widely read in pre–WWI Germany and was the favorite boyhood read of the famous theorist of culture and the civilizing process, Norbert Elias (1994, p. 17). Lasswitz deals with the Anglo-German conflict as something that expresses an immaturity in man and a misunderstanding of the sources of social conflict. These, for Lasswitz, are about the scientific, economic, and technical failure to tackle scarce resources and at the personal level have to do with the need for renewal in relationships. He wrote *Zwei Planetum* in 1897, in the same Silesian town my family came from, Breslau (now Wroclaw, Poland). In the next section I explore what this emerging sense of danger associated with being Anglo-German meant for ordinary families.

DANGER, NAME-CHANGING, AND SHAPE-SHIFTING

Curiously, my German grandfather's father-in-law, George Capel, was a British Army veteran. He had been in the Indian Army in the mid-1890s: a working-class man who was an expert at handling horses. He lived a few doors down from a Silesian German family called the Sussenbachs. Julius William Sussenbach (my great-grandfather) was a chiropodist and hairdresser, and his two children, Blanche and Percy, were just starting their first jobs; Percy was a chauffeur/mechanic and Blanche was a West End manicurist. Percy probably met George's daughter, Martha, in London's Fulham area while living a few doors down. By the time Percy and Martha got to know each other, the family name of Sussenbach, and also Percy's Christian names, had undergone transformations that would provide a basic puzzle, a century on, in my own ancestry research.

My grandfather, Percy, officially carried a traditional set of three Christian names, the last two being Edwin Adolphus, but was signing himself "Tommy" in his letters. This is a shift not only away from German-ness but also toward a particular brand of British-ness, both inconspicuous and patriotic. Tommy Atkins was the nickname given to the "ordinary soldier" by the Duke of Wellington in the mid-1840s and was the example name used on British army joining papers to show how to fill in the form. One need only read the Kipling poem "Tommy" (1994/1892) to imagine the kind of working-class-hero social currency that my grandfather may have been reaching for. Percy's father, Julius, and his younger brother, Herman, had already adopted the surname Williams by 1901. The middle brother, Carl, kept the German surname, but he was the only one in the migrating generation to marry an English woman, her Englishness offering a palpable prop to his otherwise German-sounding identity when needed.

All my German ancestors had three Christian names, one the same as the grandparents. It was easy to follow through the name of the grandparent of each gender. The three brothers all carried Carl or Karl. The next generation, despite being settled in London, continued to do the same. Here the names Herman, Carolina, and Bertha remained stable and significant for the siblings of the next generation. The parents and the grandparents seem to have been remembered in this way. These naming patterns represent generational signifiers of identity, authority, and origin. Yet origin can become a source of anxiety and shame, and is often overlain with a story about a current and recently acquired or even imaginary identity.

A key signifier of the extinguishing of the familiar aspect of German identity is the stopping of Christian name resemblances. This was achieved in my own family by the reduction of three names down to one. I myself have only one Christian name, even though the English naming tradition is often two. My grandfather took another route: He adopted a nickname. Percy Edwin Adolphus passed as Tommy, and signed his letters the same. His beloved nephew Carel (another Anglo-German) added another disguise in his paintings of Percy; in these he is called "Uncle Joe."

None of my family actually changed their surnames by any legal process, but I can see from various documents that a strain had started to manifest itself in the mid-1890s. Both oldest and youngest brothers had William as their middle Christian name, and they started to use it as an alternative to the deeply southern, middle European sounding Sussenbach. They just added an "s" and the trick was done. This simple reconfiguration signifies the double impulse of the suppressed German identity, which is both subsumed by the new name Williams and yet its haunting trace remains in the transformative "s." "S" marks the cost at which my family remained German sounding and yet appeared British in the written idiom.

WHO MARRIES WHO IN THE SECOND GENERATION

In my family people have maximized or minimized their German-ness as the cultural advantages and disadvantages of being German in London waxed and waned. Marriage and child birth are strong markers of deep level identity and are signs of its shifting and changing. In the migrating generation of my family, from 1880 to 1900, the couples were German. Their children were baptized with the German family name, and all Christian names were of German spelling and origin. The marriage certificates have German sounding friends as witnesses (they were often brothers and sisters in the families). The fathers had clearly stated origins in various parts of Germany.

Another kind of ambivalence made its way in for the next generation. In the decade 1900–1910 something happened that made it desirable to have an Anglo-German marriage. The sons of my great uncles sought English women to marry. The choices of their daughters are not so clear. One remained with a continental choice of partner, one made an English choice. One uncle, a widower, sought and found an English wife for his second marriage in 1910. Now it was desirable, even essential, to have an English wife. The war was on its way. A cultural war had been fought for the previous decade.

Desire, Partner Choice, and Social Mobility

When deaths occur people revert to their old names. When my great-grandmother died in 1905, Rebecca, my middle great-uncle's English partner, signed in her husband-to-be's German name on the death certificate. She was co-habiting but did not marry into the family for another two years! Whose desire was in the signing? Love for the cultural other is always to some extent transgressive and can denote both upward and downward mobility. In the game of cultural snakes and ladders that migrants and their families play, perceptions of downward mobility are equally as powerful as perceptions of upward mobility and they can haunt generations that have no power to alter them. This was true for my father. My English grandmother, speaking of my father about to marry my mother in 1946, is reported to have said: "A nice man Ray, such pity he is descended from those beastly Germans," as she unconsciously echoed both Noel Coward's song of 1943 "Don't let's be beastly to the Germans," and Horatio Bottomly in 1915! (Panayi, 1991, p. 233).

The Role of Romance and Marriage in Changing Identity

In *Howard's End,* E. M. Forster (1910) tells a story of love and betrayal, turned to a story of intergenerational conflict and reconciliation. This is based partly on his experience of tutoring for the family of a contemporary Anglo-German marriage, that between Elizabeth Von Arnim and Henning Von Arnim Schlagenthin. As Forster narrates a series of complex class-based and interethnic relationships with the power to overcome national, ethnic, and class division, he portrays a reconciliation of the idealism and future focus of the Schlegal sisters and the pragmatic self-interested Wilcoxes. It is the women who lead this Anglo-German reconciliation and finally enact it. It is also women who possess a mystical connection to the past and the power to reach out beyond their own social circle, vital for the resolution of complex cultural conflicts.

Elizabeth Von Arnim herself voices a woman's inner experience in a marriage going wrong. She gives ironic and reflective voice to something that is also political and power based. From *Elizabeth and Her German Garden* in 1898 to the more political *Fraulein Schmitt and Mr. Ansthruther* in 1907, she plots a theme of women, first as observers of their "national other" partners, then as free agents in their own right. The personal is being portrayed as political and the theme is voiced by the other major Anglo-German relationship of the period, that of D. H. Lawrence and Frieda Weekly.

D. H. Lawrence is the only Englishman to have been accused and arrested for spying both for the Germans and the British. The first time, it was brought about by his and Frieda's al fresco liaison outside the town of Metz, attracting the attentions of a passing German policeman. The second time, less dramatically, having a German-sounding wife in Zennor, Cornwall, was sufficient (Worthen, 2005). I mention these because Lawrence came to think that the war between nations was like the war between men and women in that it had to be fought out in all its destructiveness before something new could be won. For Lawrence, New Man is born out of the ashes of Mass Man, to restate his refrain of cultural death and rebirth. Lawrence successfully avoided the draft during the war, and felt profoundly rejected by the narrowing horizons of his native England (not least by the banning of his book *The Rainbow* in 1915). For Lawrence, women, by their sensual nature and socially inferior position, can see and bring into being a new world order that goes beyond the miserable confines of industrialism and war. This is summed up in the character of Ursula and her experience of the struggle for personal emancipation in the last lines of *The Rainbow*: "She saw in the rainbow the earth's new architecture, the old, brittle corruption of houses and factories swept away, the world built up in a living fabric of Truth, fitting to the over-arching heaven" (Lawrence, 2012/1915, p. 444).

Lawrence and Frieda escaped to Cornwall. Other Anglo-German families were not so fortunate. Many were separated, the men interned and the women and children left to fend for themselves. In her book *True to Both My Selves*, Katrin Fitzherbert (1997, p. 17) describes the plight of her English grandmother with young children in London after her German hairdresser husband is interned in Alexandra Palace. George Kenner, the German artist, is separated from his German wife. They are repatriated into such poverty in postwar Germany that both their children die. The fate of the Anglo-Germans in Germany postdeportation is another story that has yet to be told fully Katrin Fitzherbert's three-generation story is a lively example that shows, amongst many other rich narrative strands, that the romantic pull and counter-pull of Anglo-German relationships can become a feature of future generation's partner choices.

THE WAR STARTS . . . GERMANS IN THE BRITISH ARMY

The Anglo-German experience of war had a number of variations; established migrants, children of German settlers, were exempt from internment but none were exempt from the need to prove their affiliation to their host nation as a matter of survival. Three of my ancestors entered a London regiment called Middlesex Rifles. In one of their joining papers the name "Sussenbach" is changed to Beck. The regiment was known jokingly as "The Kaiser's Own." While urgently asked questions from liberal pro–Anglo-German Members of Parliament seeking assurances that these soldiers would not have to take up arms against their fellow countrymen, the regiment did go to France. In 1917 my own grandfather Percy/Tommy went on a long convalescence in the countryside, walking perilously close to one of the internment camps in Frimley, Surrey. He successfully avoided the last draft of the war, probably on medical grounds.

Other families caught by direct split loyalties had members fight on different sides of the same conflict. Typically, they were men who had retained their German Territorial Army memberships and left at the outbreak of war to answer the fatherland's call to arms and to avoid internment. This may have given rise to some of the strange and unexpected activities during the Christmas Day armistice of 1915, which I recounted earlier.

Back to the Affective Start of This Research—Another War, a Strange Haunting

My grandfather died in 1940 during the London blitz. He had suffered from bouts of poor health since the years of 1914–1918, and, like many, had a form of incipient lung disease. I heard the story of his death from my father. We were in the garden shed on a rainy day. My father trying, as he often would, to convey something of the existential power of ordinary life, had just said, apropos of nothing, that his father's head had still been warm a while after he died. This somehow got my grudging ten-year-old attention. I listened as he told how his Dad, terrified of the dive-bombers, had discharged himself from the hospital and walked home. There he lay in a daze for several days until one night he woke with a terrible nightmare, "The German aunts have come to get me" he cried out, and proceeded to make a recovery that lasted for a few days. He then died peacefully in his sleep.

I didn't consciously think about this episode, although it remained in my memory until after my father had died. It was only then I asked the question "Who are the German Aunts?" In his memoir, written the year before he died, my father bemoaned the "infuriating incompleteness" of his knowledge of his own family origins. His decision to write was informed by this and, as a result, we have a delightfully full social record of his own life and times as a child, and a young adult in pre–WWII Britain.

The German Aunts

So in 2009, a decade after the death of both my parents, I decided to see if I could "tidy up" some of the missing bits in my father's memoir. This dream-like memory swam up and I could as a researcher, rather than a child, ask who were these women and why should he be so frightened? I had barely started to ask the question when to my surprise, and rather like my grandfather's experience, one of the aunts' descendants came and, figuratively speaking, knocked on my door. Equipped this time with computer, ancestry charts, and narratives, she reproached, "Now, we are not going to lose touch this time, are we?"

I had just tumbled to the fact that there was in my family a sibling system of three brothers, Julius, Adolph, and Herman, starting back in 1880. The moment I had posted the information about the brothers on an ancestry website the aunts, descendants of my great uncle Herman on the maternal side, started to contact me! I think of them now as the first of the German aunts. I surmise now that some of Percy's fear was about hearing the voice of the cultural other, the voice of his mother and her sister and sisters-in-law come to claim him, take him home as it were, after so much of his identity had been built up around denial of "German-ness." As we die, we become what we were. More recently acquired languages are lost, earlier affect-laden memories come to the fore. Percy's story is personal, but it is also a cultural haunting which makes no sense without the actual lost history. This makes a point that intergenerational hauntings are often—perhaps always—about lost information and experience. It isn't that they are failed symbols in the psychoanalytic sense, but they are more like dreams to which the daytime referents have been lost, or which are not directly in view. They make perfect sense, but not to us. To us, in another generation, they simply disturb and trouble.

BACK TO THE FUTURE 1914 AND NOW WITH SOME THEORY

Linking my own family history to broader social history of the period I now think Britain and Germany had a kind of unofficial sibling relationship deeply tied by generations of two-way migration and culture. Perhaps, in some secret familial sense, they had become one nation, too close for comfort—made up of intermarriage, alliance, and counteralliance, as well as the rivalrous projection that arises out of mutual dependency. I think that something like that rivalry may have also occurred in the brother sibling system in my family. I believe this evolved from strong cooperation with elements of conflict in the last decade of the nineteenth century, to increasing rivalry during the first ten years of the twentieth century. The final break between the families occurred in the early 1920s. The conflict of going to war was experienced between both families and nations. I argue that mutual trauma of this kind is a key factor in the erasure of identity in that it necessitates a forgetfulness of who we are.

I propose that the states of mind produced in this kind of trauma are those of silence and then absence, where the names of the brothers and their wives and children must be forgotten, lest their fate and betrayal be revealed. For the survivors on each side the German or the English aspect of their identity must be expunged or radically modified in order to continue. Names must be changed or forgotten forever. Disguises must be donned, then taken for real, and then it must be forgotten that they are disguises. Thus, many Anglo-German descendants no longer know their histories and no longer know that their name and identity was changed or abandoned. At a political cultural level, the British still quickly fall into anti-German stereotypes and seem powerfully attached to prejudices formed during the two world wars. Even today, the German is still firmly seen as the beast. Yet there is a painful echo on the German side, an echo of a long-lost generation when two nations were culturally close, intermarried and intermingled.

Important questions remain for politics and cultural life about whether social representations of traumatic events can allow people and nations to heal. One very clear aspect of this is that the mirroring of what has happened to any group or people has to be accurate. Ancestry research of the kind that informs this study can, if handled in the right way, help this process. This applies as much to the attribution of guilt and the dispensing of justice as it does to the recognition process that allows the working through of a social trauma and identity loss.

The much reviled Prussian state is a good example of the dilemma and deep ambivalence over remembering and forgetting. Seen by the Allies as the cause of all of Germany's, and indeed Europe's, problems, it was abolished in 1947, the only modern nation-state to have suffered this fate

(Clarke, 2006, p. 675). This no doubt has stored up problems, both culturally and in contested geographical/territorial terms, that may yet have bite in the future.

The Personal in the Political and the Ancestral in the Historical

In order to understand the fragmented nature of my family experience it has been necessary to attend to a sense of being haunted by something hidden and incomplete. Nicholas Abraham, and Maria Torok (1994) suggest that trauma leads to psychic cysts; compressed unspoken traumas that are passed down in the psyche. In psychoanalytic terms the problem with such traumas is that they are not amenable to symbolization and hence deplete and haunt the psyche of more contemporary generations. In the classical Freudian sense they also carry an accompanying risk or likelihood of repetition. They haunt, they are ghosts rather than actual ancestors with real experiences and untold stories and unrequited grief of loves and losses. Those who are silenced, the erased and unspeakable, have ways of making themselves known. In the book *History beyond Trauma*, Françoise Davoine and Jean-Max Gaudillière (2004) coin the phrase, "Whereof one cannot speak, thereof one cannot stay silent," and while they tend to concentrate on traumatic loss and dislocation the book ushers in a powerful post-Foucauldian theme of the return of the culturally repressed (Foucault, 2005/1961).

We know that the centrality of procedural memory in the development of identity means that many of the key moments and relationships making up our emotional lives are invisible and only partly remembered. Many bodily memories link to cultural memories—I have always liked pickled herrings and anyone who comes from Hamburg will know why—and by the same token are often only recoverable by reminder, by stimulus, by chance meeting or evocation of a past relationship or experience. This is true even more for group life, which can contain and express profound experiences and then disappear, disperse, and apparently evaporate.

Much complication can also arise through processes of identification where a child identifies with a split off aspect of a parent's personality or experience. This can become an "unthought known" (Bollas, 1987), or an object without a self to realize it. In short this can lead to profound confusion where an experience lives on through a child without them knowing properly what it is. Abraham and Torok (1994) call it "rejected psychic matter," which can take the form of psychosomatic symptoms. I think it is equally the case that unrecognized creative capacities or qualities get locked up by similar processes.

I am proposing something simpler, but also something that promises to extend psychoanalytic thinking. This is that much that haunts us about our past, that which is beyond our immediate living generation, is an absence of information, rather than unsymbolized and therefore primitively disturbing experience. As in puzzling dreams, it's not condensation and displacement that are the missing guests at the party, but the associations about the dream, the thoughts that are part of the person whose dream it is. It is missing associations and missing links that disturb.

This leads to another very useful and sensible concept coined by the American sociologist Charles Wright Mills, that of *The Sociological Imagination* (2000/1959). Mills says we suffer and internalize what we can't imagine socially. We divorce and feel terrible about it, without knowing that socially the odds are stacked heavily against our marriages working. My ancestors experienced shell shock, cowardice, and the disobeying of orders as moral failure. Sociological imagination sees these experiences as ones engendered by powerlessness and mediated by social relations of power. There are many such experiences in need of sociological imagination for healing.

Freud makes the distinction between peacetime and wartime neurosis. The former is more to do with life instincts and their conflict, while the latter is more to do with the death or dissolution of the Self. This theme is evident in and taken up by cultural theorists such as E. Ann Kaplan (2005, p. 35) and Paul Lerner (2003), and clinicians such as Allan Schore (2009). The sociological imagination is very helpful when dealing with radical social discontinuities which may link to the formation of traumatic vertical splits in the psyche where identity is threatened, lost, or utterly misdescribed. All of my latter-day Anglo-German relatives suffer that social fate of identity loss via misdescription, although some have direct and intervening psychological trauma as well. Psychoanalytic thinking is stronger and possibly more helpful where intrapsychic conflict is the focus. Intergenerational healing has to address both aspects and their interrelations. We have to be intergenerational as well as transgenerational in our thinking.

Do I feel different as a result of a decade of research and inquiry? If anyone had told me before any of this broke into my consciousness that I would be working at migrant identities and their implications for relations between nations I would have said no, I am a psychotherapist, I do not do the social, it is too ephemeral. Now I feel enormously increased by it. There seems to be more of me, and I have met many new people. More than anything else I have become more confident that if I look steadily at this new field it will gradually be possible to do what Norbert Elias (1978) in *The Civilizing Process* proposed, which is to establish a practice for and sensibility of the long term, so that the complex histories that make up our conflicted migratory and wartorn planet can be acknowledged as the seed for conflict resolution in neighborhoods, nations, and between nations. Norbert Elias's sociology is an intergenerational project, an evolving commitment to understand

and develop practices both now and in the future that counter splitting and nonconnectivity.

Of course I would be the first in the queue to tell me that this idea is largely illusory and grandiose, but even to have the wish is an achievement and reconnects with my ancestors' conviction that a different and radically better life was possible. I think that tackling intergenerational dynamics in this way has to be in the spirit that the world itself is redeemable, and that the biggest and most profound problems can be solved. The contribution that an understanding of intergenerational dynamics might make is that each person's and each group's past interacts with and in some way articulates contemporary problems. Every attempt at conflict resolution, or, in the therapeutic arena, any attempt to work through a problem, brings pressing opportunities to heal old hurts as well as current ones.

Mourning loss is all well and good, but one person's mourning is another's loss and oppression, when it comes to war, civil conflict, and ethnic cleansing. Care over the details helps a lot; in fact it is the difference between solution and repetition. But first we have to have the courage to look and continue looking; we have to think it is worth it.

REFERENCES

Abraham, N. & Torok, M. (1994). *The shell and the kernel* (N. T. Rand, Trans.). Chicago: University of Chicago Press.

Bollas, C. (1987). *The shadow of the object: Psychoanalysis of the unthought known.* New York, NY: Columbia University Press.

Boyd Whyte, I. (2006). Anglo-German conflict in popular fiction, 1870–1914. In F. Bridgham (Ed.), *The first World War as a clash of cultures* (pp. 43–101). New York, NY: Camden House.

Bleibtreu, K. (1900). *Bur und lord.* Heilbronn: Eugen Salzer.

Bridgham F. (2006). (Ed.), *The First World War as a clash of cultures.* New York, NY: Camden House.

Butt, M. (2011). *Ally Pally prison camp.* Devon: Oversteps Books.

Chesney, G. (1871). *The battle of Dorking.* Edinburgh: Blackwood & Sons.

Clarke, C. (2006). *Iron Kingdom: The rise and downfall of Prussia, 1600–1917.* London: Penguin.

Davoine, F. & Gaudillière, J. M. (2004). *History beyond trauma.* New York, NY: Other Press.

Dorking Museum and Heritage Centre. (2014). The battle of Dorking. Retrieved 1/30/2014 from http://www.dorkingmuseum.org.uk/the-battle-of-dorking/.

Elias, N. (1994). *Reflections on a life.* Oxford: Polity Press.

Elias, N. (1978). *The civilizing process: The history of manners.* New York: Urizen Books.

Fitzherbert, K. (1997). *True to both my selves*. London: Virago.
Forster, E. M. (1954/1910). *Howard's end*. London: Edward Arnold.
Foucault, M. (2005/1961). *Madness and civilization: A history of insanity in the age of reason*. London: Routledge.
Kaplan, E. A. (2005). *Trauma culture—The politics of terror and loss in media and literature*. New Brunswick, NJ: Rutgers University Press.
Kipling, R. (1994). *Collected poems of Rudyard Kipling*. Ware, Hertfordshire: Wordsworth Editions Ltd.
Lasswitz, K. (1971). *Two planets*. New York, NY: Southern Illinois University Press.
Lawrence, D. H. (2012/1915). *The rainbow*. London: Egoist Press.
Le Queux, W. (1906). *The invasion of 1910*. London: Eveleigh.
Lerner, P. (2003). *Hysterical men: War, psychiatry and the politics of trauma in Germany, 1890–1930*. Ithaca and London: Cornell University Press.
Mitteilungsblatt. (2013). Marking the Centenary of World War One—Call for information. *Mitteilungsblatt* 106, p. 36.
Neumann, S. (1946). *The future in perspective*. New York, NY: G.P. Putnam's Sons.
Panayi, P. (1991). *The enemy in our midst*. Oxford: Berg.
Panayi, P. (1995). *German immigrants in Britain during the 19th century, 1815–1914*. Oxford: Berg.
Rocker, R. (1937). *Nationalism and culture*. New York, NY: Covici-Friede.
Schore, A. (2009). Attachment trauma and the developing right brain: Origins of pathological dissociation. In F. D. Dell & J. A. O'Neil (Eds.), *Dissociation and dissociative disorders, DSM-V and beyond*. New York, NY: Routledge.
Tamm, T. (1906). *Die invasion von 1910*. Berlin: Concordia.
Towey, J. (2004). *German hairdressers in the UK: Their effect on the British way of life*. UK: Anglo-German Family History Society Publications.
Wells, H. G. (1898). *War of the worlds*. London: William Heinemann.
Wells, H. G. (1910). *The war in the air*. London: George Bell & Sons.
Wells, H. G. (1913). *The world set free*. London: Collins & Son.
Worthen, J. (2005). *D. H. Lawrence: The life of an outsider*. London: Penguin.
Wright Mills, C. (2000/1959). *The sociological imagination*. Oxford: Oxford University Press.
Wustner, K. H. (2012). German pork butchers. *Mitteilungsblatt* 102, pp. 6–7.
Von Arnim, E. (1900/1898). *Elizabeth and her German garden*. London: Macmillan.
Von Arnim, E. (1983/1907). *Fraulein Schmitt and Mr. Ansthruther*. London: Virago Press.

Chapter 7

Ghosts in the Mirror

A Granddaughter of Holocaust Survivors Reflects the Faces of History[1]

Nirit Gradwohl Pisano

Over the past two decades, researchers and clinicians alike have grown curious about the impact of the Holocaust on the lives of its third-generation descendants. Nevertheless, the literature regarding grandchildren of survivors remains sparse, and repeatedly points to "contradictory" hypotheses and conclusions yielded by pertinent studies in the field. While many inquiries trace the long-sensed and increasingly recognized intergenerational transmission of Holocaust trauma and memory (Felsen, 1998; Rubenstein, Cutter, & Templer, 1989–1990), others underscore survivors' and their offspring's "resilience in the face of adversity" (Sigal, 1998, p. 582). Although "resilience" rightfully honors the struggle and endurance of survivors and their descendants in a post-Holocaust world, it is often interpreted as an absence of Holocaust themes, sensitivities, and reverberations in their day-to-day lives. For example, a number of researchers suggest that the transgenerational transmission of trauma has altogether ceased by the third generation (Bachar, Cale, Eisenberg, & Dasberg, 1994). Such conclusions invite questions about the concept of intergenerational trauma and the apparent efforts to either prove or refute its existence; the hunt for psychopathology versus the pursuit of a broader psychodynamic understanding of the third generation experience; and the implications of tracing "trauma trails" (Atkinson, 2002) two generations following such horrors.

In what way is trauma transmitted intergenerationally across families and entire communities? Can future generations heal the pain of a past they did not personally endure? What are the mechanisms by which a child undertakes her parents' and grandparents' suffering? Fraiberg, Adelson, and Shapiro's (1975) "Ghosts in the nursery" examines these questions within a familial context, where members are "possessed by their ghosts . . . while no one has issued an invitation, the ghosts take up residence and conduct the rehearsal of the family tragedy from a tattered script" (p. 165). The unspeakable past traumas experienced by the parents of Fraiberg et al.'s (1975) case studies were left unnamed and unprocessed, such that their mourning was foreclosed. The unmourned suffering silently escalated in power and magnitude, seizing lead roles in their lives and those of their children. Davoine & Gaudillière (2004) powerfully capture how a child easily and "paradoxically" can become "the subject of the other's suffering, especially when this other is unable to feel anything" (p. 49). Through projective identification, a child unexpectedly and unwillingly reenacts such a "hell" (Davoine & Gaudillière, 2004, p. 50), ensuring that previous unresolved losses are carried into future generations.

Yet, what exactly happens with this powerful unmourned suffering? If the parent cannot recall it and will not speak of it, how does the child *know* its existence? In 1972, Judith Kestenberg initiated use of the term "transposition" to explain the psychological process of intergenerational transmission of massive trauma that occurs unconsciously (Kaplan, 1996). Transposition captures the phenomenon by which a parent's past experiences impinge upon the child's present being. Transposition has two distinct characteristics: first, it speaks to the immense "amount of psychological space" that the parent's history demands, and second, it refers to "reversals of ordinary time" between parent and child that leaves them in opposite chronological positions, with the child exceedingly an element of the parent's past (Kaplan, 1996, p. 224). Thus, the parent's history takes over the child's daily existence, forcing the child to abandon her right to live as an individual. Referencing a poem by Celan (1958), Kaplan writes: "the child suckles 'the black milk' of trauma, relishes and absorbs it, cultivates its bitter taste as if it were vital sustenance—as if it were existence itself" (1996, p. 224). Similarly, as Davoine and Gaudillière explain:

> Many small children have not received the words that would have allowed them to keep at bay the disasters experienced by their parents and ancestors. Rather, like the children of Oedipus or Medea, they were abandoned, sacrificed on the battlefront of hatred, wars, and civil wars; they were armed with rifles, real or psychic, to be sent as human shields to protect the adults who remain in the rear. (2004, p. 75)

That is, the child absorbs her parent's unmourned trauma as her own, devoting a lifetime to working through the internal devastation of their shared past. Because a transposition can arise at any given moment, the survivor parent's Holocaust history looms over the child's daily life:

> Though the mother still cannot remember her starvation, she transmits the emotional experience of starvation through her preoccupation with buying,

> preparing, serving, and eating food. The father transmits the physical degradations he endured by being preoccupied with cleanliness and the elimination of feces. (Kaplan, 1996, p. 226)

At times, specifics such as a child's age may serve to trigger the reenactment of history in the present time; for example, Kaplan (1996) describes a hypothetical scenario of a girl who is "innocently competing with her mother for her father's attention" (p. 226), but happens to do so at the exact age that her mother was when she arrived at the Nazi camps. In Kaplan's example, the mother impulsively reacts by cutting off her daughter's ponytail, as this was done to her by Nazi soldiers. In response to this injury,

> The daughter develops an unconscious fantasy that she has been selected by her mother to perform a special mission. She, and she alone, can repair her mother's trauma by sacrificing her own desires and longings. She becomes obese, thus effectively concealing her beauty under layers of fat. Or she starves herself until her body is transformed into the body of a concentration camp survivor. (Kaplan, 1996, pp. 226–27)

A survivor parent who has lost family members in the Holocaust consciously wishes that her new, post-Holocaust family will replace the family members that were killed; the parent's unconscious wish, however, is that each new child or spouse will serve to reinstate the deceased (Kaplan, 1996, p. 234). For the child of a survivor, "the memorialization of the dead entails his resurrection. . . . The revenant knows she must fall into the interrupted biography of the dead one and complete it before she can carry on with her own life" (Kaplan, 1996, p. 234). In *Maus I and II*, Art Spiegelman (1986, 1992) skillfully captures the memorialization of the dead in telling the personal tale of his upbringing by a Holocaust survivor. Art, the post-Holocaust son, acts as a surrogate for his father's late son, Richieu, to such an extent that Art reports feeling throughout his life that he was in competition with a ghost. Indeed, in the final scene, his father calls Art "Richieu." Similarly, Vladek's new wife, Mala, endlessly falls short of reinstating his late wife, Anja. The enactments are rampant throughout both books: Art mutters that Vladek is a "murderer" for having destroyed his dead first wife's, Anja's, wartime diaries; Vladek yells at Art for making a "mess" with cigarette ash while talking about his experience of being yelled at by SS officers for making a mess in the camps; finally, Art's distance from Vladek sustains in him a sense of guilt for "mistreating" his father (Spiegelman, 1986, 1992).

Beyond all other vehicles, tormented silences serve as the main channel through which parents' unimaginable suffering can be witnessed by their children. Kaplan (1996) captures this immense authority of silence: "At first the child knows only that one or both parents are hiding some terrible secret. And the child wonders, 'What is the meaning of the absence, the silence? What is the truth that must never be spoken?'" (p. 219). Within this context, a survivor's child lives a "double life," in that present experiences bear the undercurrent of past events (p. 231). Everyday situations and mundane occurrences become instantaneously linked to both past and present:

> A loop of cord hanging from a lamp becomes a hangman's noose to the survivor. The child hears the parent gasp and sees the parent frantically rearranging the cord. A policeman approaches on the street; the mother has a panic attack. She clutches the child's hand tightly and stands as still as a statue. Nothing is said, but the child registers the mother's reactions and knows "something" is wrong. The child comes to know that existence is precarious. (Kaplan, 1996, p. 231)

Kaplan (1996) suggests that a child who senses her parent's "terror, shame, and guilt" about something unfathomable is compelled to re-create such scenarios in order to concretize and ultimately cure the parent's trauma (p. 232). In a sense, Kaplan (1996) believes that it is only the survivor's children who can bear witness to their parent's history. Furthermore, a parent's secrecy can, in effect, drive the child's impulse to piece together what happened to the parent. "The parent unwittingly and against her conscious will positions her trauma within the child; the child sets out to cure the parent and undo her trauma by placing himself in the parent's position" (Kaplan, 1996, p. 224). Thus, it is the child's role to cure the parent's suffering through a number of contradictory tasks: "On the one hand, she is fighting to reinstate visions of love and goodness. On the other hand she represents the concretization of hatred" (Kaplan, 1996, pp. 234–35). As a result, "She is expected to carry out and perform for her parent the unfinished work of mourning. Yet she is also expected to avenge the parents for the crimes committed against them by enacting the silenced hatred and rage" (Kaplan, 1996, p. 235).

Clearly, such duties take a toll on the child. At best, the child does not receive the necessary help in integrating her own experiences. At worst, deficits in a parent's empathic attunement to the child result in the child's experiences of overwhelming affect, impaired symbolization of experience, and a complete lack of meaningful integration of her feelings (Charles, 2003). Insufficient emotional development is passed along the generations, as affect remains a foreign and threatening experience. Furthermore, repeated exposure to shameful affects may lead to suppression or denial of those experiences through external tools such as compulsive eating and substance abuse (Charles, 2003). For these reasons, traumatic memories and familial reactions to history may only come to light over the course of several generations

(Auerhahn and Laub, 1998, p. 22). "The barrage of experiences that patently ignore the child's perceived needs or feelings generates a sense of helplessness and meaninglessness before the hands of a cold and unseeing destiny, as the child who is not loved loses himself"—thus, the cycle is repeated (Charles, 2003, p. 72). Finally, because children's self-concepts are shaped by the circumstances of their upbringing, Charles (2003) argues that enactments reveal one's "helplessness in the face of destiny" (p. 73).

In her case presentation of a third-generation survivor named "Ann," Talby-Abarbanel (2011) captures the incessant enactments that occur in the face of unspoken and unspeakable grief and loss. Ann is first described as wrestling with "unintegrated" parts of herself without a framework for the origin of such disintegration (Talby-Abarbanel, 2011, p. 219). While confronting her mother about their tormented relationship, Ann learns of her Holocaust history for the very first time; she is subsequently able to comprehend the root of her past obsession with Holocaust books and films, her lifelong creations of artwork centered on themes of relocation and isolation, and her vivid, complex dreams of "separateness" and "attachment" (Talby-Abarbanel, 2011, p. 233). Talby-Abarbanel writes:

> Ann added that by avoiding the trauma and by refraining from working it through, they [her parents] paradoxically re-created the same atmosphere in their own family, from which she now needed to distance herself. Indigestible non-verbal terror, unbearable pain, and apocalyptic fantasies were always in the air. (2011, p. 230)

Bar-On (2008) relays a personal experience with a student in one of his workshops, who claimed disbelief about the concept of a "second generation" of the Holocaust despite her technically belonging within this group (p. x). Bar-On (2008) recalls the impassioned responses of this woman's peers, who understandably felt their own experiences contested by her bold, dismissive statement. The disagreements within the field of third-generation Holocaust research elicit reactions of parallel intensity, highlighting the personal investment and far-reaching implication of these studies to the individuals conducting them. Bar-On writes: "The ambivalence of researchers in this domain can be understood, as we study a complex phenomenon many years after the original occurrences, effected by several simultaneous processes" (2011, p. xi). Yet, as the grandchildren of survivors are continually motivated to confront their parents' and grandparents' experiences, to articulate multifaceted narratives, and to pursue an intergenerational perspective at once removed from and connected to the Holocaust, it has become increasingly imperative for their traumas to be acknowledged and their voices to be heard.

INTERVIEWS WITH GRANDDAUGHTERS OF HOLOCAUST SURVIVORS

The following is one of ten interviews I conducted with American and Israeli granddaughters of Holocaust survivors. All interviews consisted of one 60- to 120-minute session, depending on the scope of the narrative. The discussions began with my open-ended statement, "Tell me about yourself," as was done by Ewing (2004) in her studies. The conversations then took the form of psychoanalytic interviews, in which I remained as minimalist as possible in my interventions and used my free associations in reaction to the interviewee. Most women spoke fluently and eagerly throughout the interview; however, if a participant remained relatively unresponsive or limited in the depth of her narrative, I posed specific questions in order to stimulate the conversation, keeping the following questions in mind: Who is this person? How does she identify herself? What does she know about her family history? What does she not know and why? Where does she come from? How does that affect her? What is her role within her family? How do the limitations of her knowledge impact her experience? How might she know more? This approach was selected in order to encourage participants to speak openly and freely about their Holocaust history, and to allow me to respond to the content and mood of their stories as well as to my own reactions to the narratives.

Following each interview, I kept a log of my own thoughts, associations, and reactions to the participants' narratives, as well as any feelings or observations that arose during and after the interview. This log served to both keep track of the ideas that were developed throughout the course of the interviews and to engage with my unconscious. The interviews thus became a dynamic event—a process—that explored features of both the transference and countertransference. Furthermore, my exploration was informed by the writings of Packer and Addison (1989), and Josselson, Lieblich, and McAdams (2003), who maintain that underlying narrative research is the belief that human nature cannot be captured by a single theory, much like text analysis cannot be encapsulated by one person's perspective or interpretation. As Packer and Addison explain, "Interpretive research emphasizes that the researcher must *not* act as if he or she is a value-free researcher who can objectively see things as they 'really' are, or that the 'data' collected is, in some way, independent of the person who collects it" (1989, p. 42). Instead, throughout the interview process, the researcher should bear in mind, "I was the one who was taking notes, asking questions in the interview, and selecting what aspects of documents and literature were significant for my purposes" (Packer & Addison, 1989, p. 41). Thus, the interviews represent the spoken and unspoken elements of communication and understanding between two individual people.

In drawing conclusions from the data, I utilized a thematic analysis to examine the emergent themes, both in the actual interviews and in my own reactions to the narratives, which signified responses to Holocaust trauma. I looked for recurring ideas, for metaphors that evoked particular images, and for words that seemed laden with meaning. I also made a point of focusing on both explicit and implicit information—including pauses, repetitions, slips of the tongue, hesitations, laughter, tears, and tone of voice. Hence, the "data" by definition encompassed both verbal and nonverbal features of the narrative. While this method allowed for layers of meaning to emerge, the complexity of analyzing nonverbal aspects of verbal accounts was also the greatest obstacle inherent in this approach. For example, differentiating between what was purposely left unsaid and what was unconsciously avoided was not always possible. Ultimately, however, within an unencumbered space that welcomed words, silences, and everything in between, these women's life stories began to unfold.

LEAH'S STORY

> I'm extremely obsessive compulsive, not the type of person that diagnoses themselves. Like, in high school, I was seeing somebody for it. I schedule everything and plan everything, so whenever something goes off course, big or small, I have real difficulty dealing with it and that tends to make me feel guilty. And I don't know when I developed that OCD or where that came from. Potentially that's related . . .

Leah, a twenty-three-year-old, third-generation Holocaust descendant, tenuously links her personality and lifestyle to her history as the granddaughter of survivors. "Potentially that's related," she half states and half wonders, having just revealed this personal information three-quarters of the way into her hour and a half interview on the topic of intergenerational transmission of trauma. Her insight arrives on the heels of her maternal grandparents' story:

> I know that my grandparents . . . they had a five-year-old son and he was shot on the street by a Nazi soldier in front of my grandmother. My mom wasn't born yet . . . this would've been my mom's brother . . . my mom wasn't born, she never met him . . . so he was killed when he was five and my grandparents were both taken . . . they were already married and had a family . . . they were both taken to Auschwitz, separated, lost each other, and ended up finding each other afterwards.

In the context of her ancestral trauma, Leah's obsessive-compulsive tendencies may serve a number of protective functions: first, she preserves a sense of control in her life by mentally planning every hour of the day, having learned early on that the world is unpredictable and painful. Second, she struggles to master a part of her traumatic history, in order that she might undo her family's tragic loss. Along these lines, she unconsciously imagines that by deliberately inspecting every hour of the day, nothing could feel out of control and no one could catch her off guard; thus, her grandparents' son might be saved. Third, Leah engages in thinking to avoid feeling. Perhaps her mind is absorbed by thoughts and lists such that little time or space remains for the emotional burden of past traumas. Finally, Leah's obsessive-compulsive symptoms provide an observable entity, which she can pinpoint as the cause of her pain. Cyrulnik (2005) describes how a person feels relief when she can finally name the source of her inner suffering: "I can join a group and express what I'm feeling. I can consult a doctor and show him a symptom. I'm no longer alone in the world. I now know what I have to deal with and how to get help from people close to me and from my culture" (p. 101).

Leah herself echoes this sentiment: "I just needed somebody to say, like, 'Oh, you have an actual thing with a name, you can blame that, you don't have to blame yourself.'" However, underneath this assertion, like other third-generation survivors, Leah does to some extent blame herself: "whenever something goes off course, big or small, I have real difficulty dealing with it and that tends to make me feel guilty," she says in the opening quote. Indeed, something "big," or more accurately, of massive proportions, has gone "off course." Until her family's trauma is confronted and, as Leah says, "dealt with," she will continue to exist within the shadows of a ghost.

Secrets

Leah begins her interview by stating, "I actually don't know that much about my father's side of the family. Both of his parents were Holocaust survivors." She explains the absence of knowledge with, "We always just sort of went to my mom's side of the family. We were closer with them anyway and they were more open, and as I'll explain, they have a much more obvious link." She adds, "Even my dad, from what he knows, isn't that good at remembering it or sharing it or as deeply impacted as my mom. She talks about it." The "much more obvious link" Leah is referring to is the ghost of a murdered child who is present every day in the life of this family. In contrast, Leah's father and paternal grandparents were not as "open" and, in Leah's mind, not "as deeply impacted" by their Holocaust experiences. As opposed to her mother, they did not "talk about it." We are left to wonder about Leah's paternal side of the family, who was likely debilitated by internal anguish and unable to give voice to unfathomable experiences. As Judith Herman writes, "The conflict between the will to deny horrible events and the will to proclaim them aloud is the central dialectic of psychological trauma. . . . But far too often secrecy prevails, and the story of the traumatic event surfaces not as a verbal narrative but as a symptom" (1997, p. 1).

Indeed, the denial of suffering and devastating silences mold a family's way of life, implicitly deemed the only tolerable way of life, and pass from generation to generation. When asked about her father's father, Leah recalls:

> He was a very quiet man. He was a very nice man, he absolutely wasn't bitter at all, he was just quiet. He would sit in the chair, we would go to school and come home and he would just be sitting in his chair. He made his own meals. He didn't need anybody to make them for him. He just did his own thing. Even like, he passed away in his sleep, very quietly. You know, he was just this quiet old man.

Leah's assertion that her grandfather "absolutely wasn't bitter at all" and was just "a quiet old man" hints at the possibility of emotional numbing. Perhaps he did not "need" anything or anyone because he found safety in his isolation from the world, going through the motions of life without any real contact or connection. Likewise, Leah has learned to take what she sees at face value, accepting the dynamics at play: "he would just be sitting in his chair." Similarly, in speaking about her relationship with her father, Leah states, "I know much less about him. He's just a more introverted person. But that's the sort of relationship we have; when we're together, we're not speaking about world issues or my life, we're just making fun of people that walk by." Leah's accounts of her father and her father's father are matter-of-fact, encouraging the interviewer not to overstep the surface-level descriptions Leah's family has long upheld. Furthermore, her tone indirectly expresses: this is the way it is; there is no need to question myself or my beliefs. Unfortunately, these boundaries reiterate the family's primary struggle, for denial ultimately fortifies trauma. As the subtitle of Davoine and Gaudillière's (2004) book suggests, *Whereof One Cannot Speak, Thereof One Cannot Stay Silent*.

Alongside silence and secrecy, symptoms persist throughout the generations. Of her father's sister, who lived with her survivor parents until their death, Leah says:

> Oh, I mean like crazy. . . . She hadn't been taking her medications; she had been eating all the wrong things. Like, there was old food thrown around the house. It reeked when my parents first got there. They found something like over $20 in change just in one day strewn about the house. She had bags and bags of, for instance, leather gloves that she had bought, never opened, never worn. She had an entire bag of different pairs of silver earrings. . . . As if you were going out and you wanted a pair of silver hoop earrings so you bought every one you could find and figured you could decide later and return them,

> and she just never returned them. She never cleaned out the house from her parents' stuff, but after my grandfather passed away she moved out of her bedroom into what was their master bedroom, but she so cluttered her own bedroom that they couldn't even open the door. She would go on like business trips and she wouldn't unpack her suitcase when she came home, so she just went and bought another suitcase and packed it with new clothes. She had dozens of packed suitcases with the tags still on them so my parents could tell where she'd been and where she'd gone.

Clearly, this daughter of Holocaust survivors spent a lifetime mired in the internal devastation of her parents' experience. Never having found a place within language, her family's unmourned suffering flooded her post-Holocaust life. One can only fantasize about the significance of silver hoop earrings and leather gloves; do such accessories represent fragments of knowledge, in an existence that unfolds outside of language? What of the numerous packed suitcases, which suggest a preparedness to flee yet an inability to truly escape one's baggage? "She just never returned them," Leah says of the earrings, speaking volumes about her aunt's incapacity to "return" and rework the original trauma. As Cyrulnik writes:

> This is how emotional restriction constitutes a major sensory privation, an insidious trauma that is all the more damaging because it's hard to become aware of it, to make it into an event, a memory that we could confront and rework. When we don't come face-to-face with a recollection, it haunts us, like a shadow in our inner world, and instead of working on it, it works on us. (2005, p. 6)

Consequently, while from Leah's point of view we have not yet broached the noteworthy aspects of her family history, it is impossible to escape the power of a secret, "working on us."

Ghosts

> *N:* I'm really interested in going back to your grandparents' son who was killed. Do you know what his name was?
>
> *L:* Robert.
>
> *N:* Robert. Did his name get reused later?
>
> *L:* My middle name is Rosie; that comes from him. And they had a portrait of him in my grandparent's bedroom. . . . I only saw one apartment, but before I was born they had a few and they always had this picture of him and you can tell—it looks exactly like my brother. My whole family looks alike, like a lot alike. It was my grandfather transferring right into my brother. You can see my mom's face in there; you can see me in there.

> *N:* Wow, what was that like?
>
> *L:* You know, as much as I have heard about it, and I feel like. . . . Not that I understand their experience, but that I'm familiar with their experience. . . . I can't ever imagine it. You know, it's such a horrible loss to not even really get to bury your child because of the circumstances. And I think that their fear of ever losing my mom was so legitimate even though it drove her crazy. You know, he's just this kid that I never met, that I never could have. . . . I definitely can't even imagine as an older child or a man because my mom didn't have any other brothers. There's not like there's somebody that you can see him as. I have no idea what he is to me except that he's just this face in this picture.
>
> *N:* Right, a face with whom you share similarities. I mean, physically, anyway.
>
> *L:* Right, like, you can see my brother in there. I mean, I can't think of it as if it was my brother. I can't even imagine that horrible loss. At this point I've lost all of my grandparents so I've experienced death, but not the way you would losing your baby like that.

Leah and her family exist within the subsistence of a five-year-old ghost. In every picture, every mirror, every conversation with her brother, every interaction with a child, and ultimately every encountered "face," hers and that of an "other," the ghost is present. The concrete, visual similarity makes this ghost entirely unavoidable: "It was my grandfather transferring right into my brother. You can see my mom's face in there; you can see me in there." The "much more obvious link" Leah spoke about previously is better understood with this context—what cannot be spoken in this family is tangible and all-consuming, a truth that resurfaces and repeats itself through time. In his *Specters of Marx* (1994), Derrida maintains that a person's life is shaped by attempts to give voice to inner ghosts. He writes:

> Repetition and first time: this is perhaps the question of the event as question of the ghost. . . . Repetition and first time, but also repetition and last time, since the singularity of any first time makes of it also a last time. Each time it is the event itself, a first time is a last time. Altogether other. Staging for the end of history. Let us call it a hauntology. (Derrida, 1994, p. 10)

"Each time it is the event itself," as the haunted and the haunting become one and the same. Leah states, "He's just this kid that I never met," as though "this kid" is an existing person in present time, waiting to be found. Indeed, he is real; alive within her and directing the course of her life.

The metaphor of the "portrait" of a ghost is a powerful one. Derrida's specter, or revenant, invisibly occupies a space that vaguely exists somewhere between the "occupied" and the "occupier" (1994, p. 172). Leah states,

"Right, like, you can see my brother in there. I mean, I can't think of it as if it was my brother. I can't even imagine that horrible loss. At this point I've lost all of my grandparents so I've experienced death, but not the way you would losing your baby like that." From brother to baby and baby to brother, the past engulfs the present and the present is the past. "A first time is a last time. Altogether other," Derrida writes. Thus, the portrait of a ghost manifests both visible and invisible truths, forever a foreign occupier which Leah cannot grasp. She says, "There's not like there's somebody that you can see him as." In other words, he is me but he is not me, he is everything but he is nothing. "I have no idea what he is to me" she concludes; after all, how well can you really know a ghost?

Within her daily life, and stories about her daily life, the ghost repeatedly shows his face. For example, Leah describes frequent arguments with her mother: "Like, I'll snap at her and she will . . . I don't want to say she goes off because she doesn't yell, but she gives the cold shoulder like a *five-year-old* might. And it's something I've inherited. So then she and I end up in this cold war. . . ." How does a five-year-old give a cold shoulder? Instantaneously, Leah and her mother are transformed, back into the world of a slaughtered five-year-old brother. She turns a "cold shoulder" away from her daughter in the presence of this ghost, and the world turns cold. "So then she and I end up in this cold war," Leah speaks, right back in the original setting, as each time "it is the event itself." Leah continues to show the ways in which the dead remain a part of life:

N: How do you think it impacted your mom that her parents' first child was a boy and their second child was a girl?

L: What do you mean?

N: Any sense of loss of a man?

L: In terms of loss of a man, I don't think so at all. My mom and my grandfather were very close, they used to sit and read the newspaper together and watch TV together, so any of those things were like a father wants his son to do those things. I never got the sense that he felt he missed out on any of that. My grandfather *adored* my brother and he would follow him anywhere and whatever my brother said was wonderful, and my grandmother did with me, which is interesting because in my family it's kind of the opposite. I think we were just the idealized versions of what they didn't think they had. Like, I never thought of my grandmother the way she probably feels my mom did, but at the same time she never understood that me and my mom had a similar relationship to what she had. So I think for them it probably spooked them out that my brother looked so much like this kid and maybe that's what made the connection there really strong. But I don't think it's something they would have ever . . . how can you say someone reminds you of someone that's dead? It's not something like . . . six of us sit down at the table and say, "Hey, everyone realizes they looked alike, right?"

N: They might not have even realized it . . .

L: Yeah, but it's like something where my mom and I commented on it, my brother commented on it. It's that obvious.

N: So the two of you were like the idealized siblings, like the two kids they could've had . . .

L: Yeah, I mean, they, you know, we were their only grandchildren. They fawned over us. We were decent kids—we didn't give our parents any trouble, we get along very well . . . my grandmother always had this real romantic notion that he would end up marrying one of my friends and I would end up marrying one of his friends because we're so close in age. That's something actually I needed to mention: my mom so much hated being an only child that she had my brother and immediately got pregnant with me, obviously, because she just wanted to start trying immediately so that he would have a sibling, and then she wanted to keep going but my dad was like, "We have two babies, chill." Sort of like the only-child syndrome.

What I fail to realize in my questioning of Leah, but what she quickly reminds me, is that sex and gender are insignificant in the memorialization of her dead. Her mother was created to reinstate her lost brother, and do all the things "a father wants his son to do." After all, as Kaplan (1996) explains, survivor parents who have lost family members in the Holocaust consciously wish that their post-Holocaust family will replace the family members that were killed; the parents' unconscious wish, however, is that each new child will serve as the return of a dead one. Leah's mother, therefore, was to complete her brother's prematurely interrupted life prior to carrying out her own. We cannot know to what extent she lived a life in her own right; however, Leah clearly states, "My mom so much hated being an only child that she had my brother and immediately got pregnant with me, obviously, because she just wanted to start trying immediately so that he would have a sibling. . . ." The weight of not having had a sibling was intense, one that her mother was unwilling to repeat for her children. While Leah suggests that her father convinced her mother to "chill" and stop after "two babies," Leah and her brother have in turn been created as the two siblings who might undo the family's past trauma. Leah states, "I think we were just the idealized versions of what they didn't think they had." Indeed, not having two children, a son along with a daughter, was ever-present.

"My mom and my grandfather were very close, they used to sit and read the newspaper together and watch TV together, so any of those things were like a father wants his son to do those things. I never got the sense that he felt he missed out on any of that." Again, a protective screen is in place that limits Leah from fully seeing what she already knows. Because she was not her brother, Leah's mother could never be enough. "My grandfather *adored* my brother" Leah says, though he was "spooked" by the reemergence of his murdered son a generation later. Perhaps, then, my heightened awareness of Leah's mother as a woman, and of Leah as a woman, was related to a sense of gender splitting in this family. ". . . whatever my brother said was wonderful, and my grandmother did with me, which is interesting because in my family it's kind of the opposite." Earlier in the interview, a similar gender divide arose:

> I was in my freshman year of college when my grandmother died and I saw it rip apart my mom and I think a lot of that was that she felt guilty for the way that she had treated her. So what my mom did was . . . she wasn't necessarily protective of me . . . she and I also used to butt heads a bunch . . . there was a stubborn streak. I was always like a daddy's girl and my brother was really close with my mom more so than my father. And she always tried to knock it into me that I had to respect her more.

During the interview, I was left feeling unclear about the details: Who is close with whom? Which child resembles which parent? Why does that matter? What is the significance of this sense of preference for one parent, or one child? Perhaps these gender splits represent the various fragments within each person, or the more general fragmentation of life during and since the Holocaust. Or maybe these questions relate to the shame, pride, and envy associated with Leah's knowledge that she is not a boy, and therefore not like the lost boy so memorialized in her family.

In response to my question about any recent dreams or nightmares, Leah says:

> *L:* Nothing really specific. I mean, I've had nightmares about losing people in our family. But they were never specific, like I don't want to go near water because I had a dream where my mom drowned. Nothing like that.
>
> *N:* But it was usually about one of your parents?
>
> *L:* Usually my brother, actually. You know, we're very close. I think a part of me always felt like that would be the hardest person.

The terror of losing her brother overwhelms her dreams. He is both the special child that the family values and remains worried about, but also unenviable in his constant closeness to death. Having been born a girl, Leah both loses and wins.

And Surrounding Shadows

In explaining how her sense of guilt is related to her obsessive-compulsive tendencies, Leah describes having "dragged out" her brother Friday night, only to result in his losing his coat. "It's not a tragedy," she says, "but I feel horrible about it. . . . I get in my head this is the way things are going to go. I expect everything to be perfect." Similarly, she reveals her need to continuously check certain items and create detailed lists that organize every hour of every day:

> *L:* I'll go back and check things. I have certain routines. Not in like my apartment now, but my bedroom in New Hampshire, the door has to be closed a certain way. I'll schedule—get ready with the same routine every morning.
>
> *N:* Like, shower and then do something?
>
> *L:* Yeah, even like put in the mouthwash, while the mouthwash is in, go back to my room and like take out my hair gel, take off the cap, then go back and spit out the mouthwash, then go put in your hair gel . . . things like that. You know, if my roommate goes in the bathroom when I need to go back, I'll be like . . . ugh.
>
> *N:* You'll walk yourself through like little things . . .
>
> *L:* Yeah, it's always been manageable, it's not like a crazy thing, but it's a little weird . . .

Indeed, losing a coat is not a tragedy. Yet, being out of control has led to tragedy in her family history. While Leah worries that she might be crazy, she also reveals a sense of ownership over her compulsions. After my asking whether her brother shares any of these tendencies, Leah responds, "My parents think he's a little compulsive also, but I just think he's bossy." In a sense, Leah insinuates that this is hers and hers is different. Consciously, however, Leah takes herself out of the competition: "I don't feel upstaged nor do I feel the need to upstage someone else and I don't understand why other people do." She is an actress in an old script, constantly upstaged, but long since taken herself out of the running for a lead role.

Leah goes on to describe how her grandfather similarly "stuck to his routine." She says, "And my mother always attributed that to his experience where they were just so shell-shocked that they just clung to this routine of normalcy that they created for themselves afterwards. Very old-fashioned in that sense." While she does not directly link the "routine of normalcy" to her own life, she indirectly reveals how her daily routine reflects a "shell-shocked" reaction to intergenerationally transmitted experiences. For example, she says, "I fully admit I have no street smarts . . . oh, I get lost everywhere. If I get myself into some situation I'm just not smart enough to get myself out of it. You know, I can ride the train all around the city before I figure out where to get off." Understandably, Leah has "no street smarts," because one cannot have street smarts in a world that allows a five-year-old to be shot on the streets. In these ways, she continues to live within the shadow of the Holocaust in a post-Holocaust world.

Nevertheless, Leah's strength and hope persevere. In thinking about her family's suffering, she also reminds herself:

> It seems to me that the thing that I always found most beautiful is that they found each other again. That they clearly instilled in my mother, their only child, a real sense of Judaism. I think of it as like, I know all I need to know to be really proud of them, and to be happy for them, even though it's been hard for them . . . to think that they succeeded in coming out of it.

While Leah has not come "out of it," she finds herself partaking in an interview, honestly discussing her family history, and entertaining new and conflicting ideas. Exhibiting great courage and resilience, she allows herself to exist fully "inside of it." Similarly, in reflecting on what she might want to do differently as a mother, Leah says:

> My brother and I have always talked about how we want to keep our families close with one another. We didn't have any cousins because my dad had this crazy sister, my mom was an only child, so we're really looking forward to being able to give our kids cousins, which is something that we always talked about. Other than that, I imagine, I'm a lot like my mom who is a lot like her mom, so I imagine I'll be a lot like that.

Like her own mother, Leah wishes to expand the size of her family, thereby welcoming additional players that might bring fresh insight and support. As Leah continues to "butt heads" with history and allows herself to remain fully in it—examining pride but also shame, happiness but also sadness—she evolves from an actress in an old script to a part of something altogether original.

CONCLUDING REMARKS

The above interview provides one example of how trauma trails persist among third-generation survivors and are embodied in their day-to-day lives. The imprints of trauma prevail with or without conscious awareness, with or without our predecessors' attempts at reintegration into the world, with or without our rummaging into history in search of answers. This is not to say that granddaughters of the Holocaust are necessarily debilitated by their links to history. Instead, trauma trails must be welcomed, explored, even fostered, for growth to be achieved. The case of Leah reveals how a strong, open, and hopeful young woman can maintain a protective screen that limits her from fully engaging with and reworking her traumatic history. Consequently, Leah relies upon obsessive-compulsive tendencies to provide her with a sense of order and control. As long as the offspring of survivors attempt to cut off their connection to intergenerationally transmitted trauma, they will undoubtedly be owned by residues of the past. Conversely, the study of meaning, the acknowledgment, exploration, and working through of trauma, allow the granddaughters and future descendants of the Holocaust to own their histories and further integrate their identities.

NOTE

1. This chapter is excerpted from my book *Granddaughters of the Holocaust: Never forgetting what they didn't experience* published by Academic Studies Press in 2012, and reprinted here by kind permission of the publisher.

REFERENCES

Atkinson, J. (2002). *Trauma trails—Re-creating song lines: The transgenerational effects of trauma in indigenous Australia.* North Melbourne: Spinifex Press.

Auerhahn, N., & Laub, D. (1998). Intergenerational memory of the Holocaust. In Y. Danieli (Ed.), *International handbook of multigenerational legacies of trauma*, (pp. 21–41). New York: Platinum Press.

Bachar, E., Cale, M., Eisenberg, J., & Dasberg, H. (1994). Aggression expression in grandchildren of Holocaust survivors: A comparative study. *Israeli Journal of Psychiatry and Related Disciplines, 31*(1), 41–47.

Bar-On, D. (2008). Foreward. In *Echoes of the trauma: Relational themes and emotions in children of Holocaust survivors*. H. Wiseman and J. P. Barber (Eds.), (pp. ix–xiii). New York: Cambridge University Press.

Celan, P. (1958). *Bremen Speech.* Literature Prize of the Free Hanseatic City of Bremen, as quoted in Felstinger translation, translating Celan's last poem. *American Poetry Review* 1982 (July/August), 23.

Charles, M. (2003). The intergenerational transmission of unresolved mourning: Personal, familial, and cultural factors. *Samiksa: Journal of the Indian Psychoanalytic Society, 54*, 65–80.

Cyrulnik, B. (2005). *The whispering of ghosts: Trauma and resilience* (S. Fairfield, Trans.). New York: Other Press (Original work published 2003).

Davoine, F., & Gaudillière, J. (2004). *History beyond trauma: Whereof one cannot speak, thereof one cannot stay silent.* New York: Other Press.

Derrida, J. (1994). *Specters of Marx: The state of the debt, the work of mourning, and the new international.* Great Britain: Routledge.

Ewing, K. P. (2004). Anthony Molino in conversation with Katherine Ewing. In A. Molino (Ed.), *Culture, subject, psyche: Dialogues in psychoanalysis and anthropology* (pp. 80–97). Middletown, CT: Wesleyan University Press.

Felsen, I. (1998). Transgenerational transmission of effects of the Holocaust: The North American research perspective. In Y. Danieli (Ed.), *International handbook of multigenerational legacies of trauma* (pp. 43–68). New York: Plenum Press.

Fraiberg, S., Adelson, E., & Shapiro, V. (1975). Ghosts in the nursery: A psychoanalytic approach to the problems of impaired infant-mother relationships. *Journal of the American Academy of Child Psychiatry, 14*, 387–421.

Herman, J. (1992). *Trauma and recovery: The aftermath of violence—From domestic abuse to political terror.* New York: Basic Books.

Josselson, R., Lieblich, A., & McAdams, D. P. (Eds.). (2003). *Up close and personal: The teaching and learning of narrative research.* Washington, DC: American Psychological Association.

Kaplan, L. (1996). *No voice is ever wholly lost: An exploration of the everlasting attachment between parent and child.* New York: Simon & Schuster.

Kestenberg, J. (1972). Psychoanalytic contributions to the problem of children of survivors from Nazi persecution. *Israel Annals of Psychiatry and Related Disciplines, 10*, 249–65.

Packer, M. J., & Addison, R. B. (1989). *Entering the circle: Hermeneutic investigation in psychology.* New York: State University of New York Press.

Pisano, N. G. (2012). *Granddaughters of the Holocaust: Never forgetting what they didn't experience.* Boston: Academic Studies Press.

Rubenstein, I., Cutter, F., & Templer, D. I. (1989–1990). Multigenerational occurrence of survivor syndrome symptoms in families of Holocaust survivors. *Omega: Journal of Death and Dying, 20*(3), 239–44.

Sigal, J. J. (1998). Long-term effects of the Holocaust: Empirical evidence for resilience in the first, second, and third generation. *Psychoanalytic Review, 85*(4), 579–85.

Spiegelman, A. (1986). *Maus I: A survivor's tale: My father bleeds history.* New York: Pantheon Books.

Spiegelman, A. (1992). *Maus II: A survivor's tale: And here my troubles began.* New York: Pantheon Books.

Talby-Abarbanel, M. (2011). "Secretly attached, secretly separate" Art, dreams, and transference-countertransference in the analysis of a third-generation Holocaust survivor. In A. B. Druck, C. Ellman, N. Freedman, & A. Thaler (Eds.), *A new Freudian synthesis: Clinical process in the next generation* (pp. 219–37). London: Karnac Books Ltd.

Chapter 8

Questions Unasked

The Legacy of Childhood Trauma in the Life Narratives of a Lithuanian Woman Survivor of the 1941 Soviet Deportations

Justina Kaminskaitė Dillon and Michael O'Loughlin[1]

Throughout my (Justina's) childhood, my grandparents, parents, teachers, and textbooks talked about the beauty of my country, Lithuania, my people, and my culture. Past suffering was presented as heroism to be emulated by the younger generation. Curious about this suffering, I began groping around for facts and personal accounts: What did my elders experience and remember? Eventually I stopped asking. Growing up in Lithuania, I learned to live with silence.

Lithuania has been an independent country since 1990, and its prior occupation by the Soviet Union seems distant. It feels strange to tell people that I was born in the Soviet Union, because Lithuania has developed economically, politically, and culturally at a remarkably fast pace in the past couple of decades. Lithuanians are proud of their country's membership in the European Union since 2004. My family never really talks about the terror of the Soviet era, so even details of my parents' and grandparents' lives then are vague. I know next to nothing about what my great-grandparents experienced, felt, and thought when their neighbors were taken away to Siberia in cattle cars, when the land they worked for generations was nationalized, or when their sons became partisans, fighting and dying in the woods in the struggle for Lithuania's freedom. I do know that their lives were hard and that the silence shrouding their experiences is meaningful.

It was only with the perspective of an emigrant, as I pursued college and graduate education in the United States, that I became increasingly aware of how the years of Soviet repression had shaped the mentality of Lithuanians. The remnants of the recent occupation are ever-present in the ways people think, approach the world, make choices, and relate to others—a conviction reinforced by delving into the academic literature on the phenomenon of intergenerationally transmitted trauma (e.g., Abraham & Torok, 1994; Auerhahn & Prelinger, 1983; Davoine & Gaudillière, 2004; Faimberg, 2005; Fraiberg, Adelson, & Shapiro, 1975; Frosh, 2013; O'Loughlin, 2010, 2012, 2013; Schutzenberger, 1998). Rates of suicide and alcoholism in Lithuania remain extraordinarily high, for example, and research makes it difficult not to believe that the killings, persecutions, deportations, incarcerations, and other forms of repression left a mark that can be recognized a generation later (Anušauskas, 1996; Kiaupa, 2004; Vardys & Sedaitis, 1997).

When I think about the roots of my interest in studying the traumatic remnants of the Soviet occupation, I recall my aunt's words: "Your roots, like those of a linden, are deeply seated in the Lithuanian land; you will always be pulled by these roots and come back." Feeling the pull and hoping to better understand the effects of past repression on Lithuanian culture and society, I set out to collect life narratives of a sample of Lithuanian women survivors of the Soviet deportations to Siberian labor camps that occurred in 1941. The purpose of this inquiry, based on their narratives, is to deepen understanding of the psychic trauma experienced by survivors and to preserve memory for future generations.

In 2013, I conducted in-person, semistructured, two- to three-hour interviews with eight women survivors of the Soviet deportations. My research approach is based on an integration of interpretive phenomenology[2] and a clinical dynamic approach[3] to interviewing. The interview scope included childhood memories of family life prior to deportation, memories of the deportation process, life in the far north, return to Lithuania, and reflections on the traumatic aftermath of the deportation experience.

In this chapter, we offer a preliminary report on this work by presenting one woman's story of an innocent childhood, survival in unfathomable circumstances, and her capacity for meaning-making thereafter. Her story is just one of thousands, but it sheds light on the human consequences of the Soviet atrocities and reveals the importance of understanding the legacy of historical trauma. We use this story to illustrate our approach to this specific material, as well as to point out the conceptual/analytic approach that is emerging from this work and that will form the basis of analysis of subsequent narratives.

HISTORICAL CONTEXT

Lithuania was first recognized as a unified nation in the 1200s. By the 1400s its borders extended to the Black Sea in the south. However, as political power shifted over the centuries in Europe, Lithuania shrank in size and was eventually absorbed by Imperial Russia in the late 1700s. Following more than a century of repression, Lithuania was able to achieve independence from Russia in 1918 (Kiaupa, 2004). The subsequent years of independence (1918–1939) were marked by a rise in nationalism and a cultural revival in native language, literature, and education throughout the country. Illiteracy rates dropped from 44 percent in 1924 to 12 percent in 1940. Colleges and academies emerged; social and cultural organizations proliferated (Vardys & Sedaitis, 1997).

The Soviet Union invaded Lithuania in 1939. The occupation was accompanied by a crackdown on dissent and decimation of the Lithuanian elite. People who belonged to banned "anti-Soviet" organizations or had been employed in "undesirable" positions (e.g., leadership roles in the former judicial system, government, etc.) were secretly placed on lists of people seen as objectionable. Soviet law also recognized collective responsibility for illegal activity, which meant that family members of an offender were considered equally guilty (Anušauskas, 1996).

By June 1941, the NKVD (Soviet police) and NKGB (Soviet secret police and intelligence) had registered thousands of "undesirable elements of society" and their families. On June 14, in the middle of the night, NKVD operatives burst into the homes of people to be deported and informed the families that they were being moved to other parts of the Soviet Union. Often the operatives would not allow the families to pack even the most essential items. Anybody who tried to escape was shot (Anušauskas, 1996). Under the two Soviet occupations of Lithuania (1940–1941 and 1944–1990), one in six Lithuanians, a total of 456,000 people, experienced some kind of repression, including imprisonment, deportations, and killings (Anušauskas, 1996; Vardys & Sedaitis, 1997). A total of 132,000 Lithuanians (not including political or criminal prisoners), 70 percent of them women and children, were forcibly deported to Siberia, the Arctic Circle, and Central Asia (Kuodytė & Tracevskis, 2004). During the deportation of 1941, the men were immediately separated from their families and dispatched to the Gulag to replenish the free labor force there. The majority of women, children, and elderly persons were transported to the Altai mountain region, in the west of present-day Mongolia. The trip, in cramped cattle cars, similar to those used for Holocaust transport, took weeks. There was not enough water and food, and the deportees struggled to breathe in the overheated, fully enclosed cars. Upon arrival at labor camps, the deportees had any remaining valuables confiscated, were settled in uninsulated wooden barracks—usually several families per room—and employed in timber harvest, salt mining, brick production, and other labor-intensive industries. For their labor, the deportees were given fourteen ounces of white bread per day, but even that was not guaranteed.

Children, elderly persons, and sick persons were allocated six ounces of bread per day. The living conditions were highly unsanitary and unfit for the cold winters of the Altai mountains, during which the temperatures reached as low as –76°F and featured heavy snowstorms (Anušauskas, 1996; *Encyclopedia Britannica*, 2013). More than half of the deportees died during the trip or shortly after arrival (Kuodytė & Tracevskis, 2004).

In the summer of 1942, almost half of the Lithuanian deportees from the Altai region were uprooted again and transported to the Arctic regions in the general Yakutsk area, about two thousand miles further north (Anušauskas, 1996). According to survivor Dalia Grinkevičiūtė,

> They transported us at a time when we were just getting used to the climate and conditions of the new place, and after we had traded our belongings for potatoes, planted gardens, and the potatoes were just starting to bloom, giving us hope that next winter we would not have to starve. (1990, p. 2)

After a grueling trip of about three months in crammed train cars, trucks, and barges, the deportees were dropped off on uninhabited islands in the Arctic Circle by the Laptev Sea.

Only a handful of the deportees were able to return to Lithuania after Stalin's death, and even then they were not greeted with open arms by the Soviet government that deported them in the first place. In the eyes of the government, they and their families were viewed as "bandits," even though most of the survivors had been children at the time of deportation. They were barred from education, jobs, and housing. Many found their homes destroyed or confiscated. Settling down was a struggle the survivors had not anticipated when contemplating the return to their longed-for homeland. Until Lithuanian Independence in 1990, survivors were forced to hide their traumatic histories, and now many feel that the younger generation no longer cares to listen (J. Puodžius, personal communication, January 2013[4]).

JANINA'S STORY

I was introduced to Janina[5] by the leader of *Lapteviečiai* (trans. "of the Laptev Sea"), a Lithuanian survivor community. Janina was energetic and animated and appeared much younger than her eighty-five years. We met at the outdoor museum of ethnography in Lithuania. We talked on a bench in the area dedicated to commemorating the lives of Lithuanian deportees, right next to an original cattle car that was used in the deportation, and close to a yurt that was an exact replica of the moss houses where the deportees spent their first winters in the Arctic. She pointed to these two items throughout the interview, especially when she felt that I needed help envisioning her past. I listened intently and bore witness to Janina's compelling life story.

Janina had a happy childhood preceding her deportation at age thirteen. She grew up in an upper-middle-class family in Kaunas, the temporary capital of Lithuania, where she lived with both of her parents and a brother, a couple of years her senior. In Janina's home, mealtimes were taken seriously and good manners were important, reflecting the middle-class ambiance of her family. Neither she nor her brother could complain about disliking the food.

> Lunch at our house used to be with rituals according to the understanding of the time—always the dining room, always a starched table cloth . . . rituals for thanking, no chatting at the table. . . . They were bringing us up nicely, although I can never remember that they would tell us to do this, tell us to do that.

Throughout the interview Janina referred to her parents using the familiar forms of "mommy" and "daddy," suggesting the love, affection, and admiration that pervaded her childhood. Janina's parents took her to the opera and ballet, and her childhood recollections are tinged with happy memories of play and camaraderie. Janina also remembers reading all the time, and she was conversant with the works of Dickens, Shakespeare, Goethe, and the fairy tales of Perrault. Janina felt sheltered and protected by her family's love, despite the signs of looming war that she noticed even as a small child.

Janina first became aware of impending war when she was five years old: ". . . everyone was waiting for the war. And my dad was also preparing. In other words, he would be gone for months. He once came back home at night with a company of men. It means they were getting ready."

When World War II began, Janina used to listen to radio transmissions from Poland of the German bomb attacks on Warsaw: "God, how I remember, how that war to me, as a horrible legend, those bombs, those Germans—to me, I don't know, like dragons the most horrid."

Soon after Janina's parents took in a Polish refugee family, the Soviet army invaded Lithuania and initially met with little resistance. Janina was horrified that the tanks had destroyed the road, but even more horrifying, for Janina, at age twelve, was the news that the Soviet soldiers were swimming in the river naked while their female sergeant watched on the shore. Soon after the Soviet army invaded, the arrests started. She recalled her parents getting phone calls from friends about spouses being arrested. Nobody could understand what the basis was for the arrests—there was no pattern, just confusion.

> And you know, when the arrests started, those horrors and those phone calls, and you hear the parents' explanations, consoling words, or plans to go search together in some prison—to help with something as to console because that

> phone is sobbing. You don't know in the end what is happening; it's not your business—they were parents' friends.

Although Janina was only twelve when the Soviet Union invaded, she was not just a passive observer and she tried to rebel in ways, however small, that were still within her control. For instance, when Russian language instruction was introduced at school, Janina refused to learn the new alphabet and the Soviet anthem. When her teacher noticed that she was not singing along with the other students and insisted that Janina join in, she pursed her lips, straightened her shoulders, and remained unmoved, thinking that "my parents will kick out those Russians":

> I was angry and I was not going to. I am a child of a Lithuanian freedom fighter. My father volunteered in 1918 [to fight for Lithuania's independence] and my blood is the same. . . . But then, of course, they deported us. So, yes, we learned to speak [Russian] in the Altai region.

The first memory that Janina recalled from the deportations featured the following image:

> I remember how we walked out the door naked, how my mommy is sitting with a [photo] album in her hand. . . . Father said out loud from the chair, when mommy picked up the album, he says, "Put it down, they'll shoot us soon anyway," then he paused for a bit and says, "maybe our relatives will find it." Mommy put down the album and we walked out in our summer dresses. . . . And so we went that they would shoot, we went that they would shoot.

When the family was taken in the truck, Janina assumed they were being taken to the woods to be shot. She was very surprised when they arrived at a train station instead. There Janina's father and all the other men were suddenly separated from their families. Janina got away from the guards and jumped on her father, clinging to him:

> They only didn't believe that I could do anything, but I did . . . I was a zero. So I caught up with daddy, jumped on his neck, with my legs, with my arms around his waist. I was hit then. They tear one leg off, so I have five more grow out . . . So, they smacked me, tore me off—what of me? There were many of them, gargling in Russian. What do I know?

Until more deportees were brought later that morning, Janina and her family were the only ones locked in the train that night. She was sobbing for her father, listening to the echoes, and not knowing what to expect. She heard that her father was locked into a train car at the front of the train. When the trains were filled with people over the next few days and moved to another train station, Janina managed to escape from her car and run in the direction of the car where she had heard her father was. She was running and shouting his name until she found a car full of men, with him inside. She was able to speak with him through a hole in the wall of the car, and he made this final gesture:

> My dad took off his ring, pushing it through the little hole in the wall: "Maybe mommy will get something to eat." He knows we walked out empty-handed. We didn't need anything to be shot, because dad's words were "put it down, because they will shoot us soon anyway. . . ." So, there is no need for anything. There were socks, a little dress, and sandals by the bed. And then dad's words—I am quoting word for word; he squatted down—they had made room for him by the hole. He pushed through the ring. I took it. Then he is saying "Eat grass. I will eat grass. We must meet again." Then he says, "Tell [your brother] that from now on, in my place, he has to take care of your mommy and you."

Janina never saw her father again.

The Altai Region

When Janina, her brother, and her mother arrived in the Altai region in Siberia after a grueling journey in a cramped train, having eaten practically nothing for a month, their train car was not "bought up"—not selected by a representative of the local industries to be laborers, a process that resembled slave trading. So they spent two weeks in the cold rain before walking for eight more rainy days through the mountains to their labor camp. Janina's brother fell ill and needed to be carried. Her first night at the crowded labor camp was dominated by memories of "trillions of chinch bugs—[nobody] had seen those chinch bugs in Lithuania":

> [They] suck blood and painfully . . . and when they are smashed on the walls, red bloody blotches remain. . . . And here, imagine that my brother has fallen asleep, and he was recovering from an illness. . . . So mommy is kneeling. The lights, of course, were on again. I was screaming until the morning—not with my own voice, standing, kneeling by mommy. And mommy . . . was sweeping [the chinch bugs] off her sleeping son, literally. . . . And I am screaming from that horror . . . a person from a respectable home and here suddenly.

Janina's account of the ensuing winter describes almost unimaginable privation, hard labor, resourcefulness, and luck. Initially, her mother and brother worked felling trees, while she gathered firewood and picked "grass" to boil in water for dinner: "There was no salt, the mush was slimy, but you don't die." Knowing the family could not make it through the Siberian winter laboring in the forest, Janina's mother somehow managed to get an administrative job and then find her son work as a firefighter. As civil servants, they were entitled to buy soup—water with an occasional mushroom or potato—Janina recalls, but "still that is life, because in the winter you have no grass and . . . it would have been a tragedy for us." With the small price they could get for her parents' gold wedding rings, they supplemented the soup with farina and survived the winter.

The Arctic

After a year in the Altai region, half of the deportees—among them Janina, her mother, and brother—were displaced again and transported into the Arctic Circle. People thought that they were going to the United States to be saved. Thus, the half left behind "[w]ere crying . . . maybe their situation will change, they will not be saved, they will be forgotten, they cry, but all of them survived. And all of ours died." The trip to their new deportation destination in the Arctic took over two months of grueling travel by truck, train, and boat, covering thousands of kilometers. The last leg of the trip was by boat down the Lena River. Janina felt it growing colder and colder as they headed north. They were eventually unloaded "a thousand kilometers into the Arctic Circle." She cites the local Yakuts' description of the weather: "Winter is twelve months here and what's left is summer." She said that in the summer ten centimeters of the ground would thaw, but, beneath that, ice would remain.

Fifteen minutes after they were unloaded, Janina's brother was forced to go fishing. In his outgrown coat with sleeves at his elbows, fishing in the stormy waters, he was covered by a growing layer of ice: "He was all ice without ever thawing, but still—not the short sleeves of a high school uniform."

At first, Janina, her family, and a couple of other families lived in a tiny yurt that was made of moss, with ice in place of a window. She described their living conditions:

> Ice yurt with ice walls with one burning thread [candle wick]. . . . I, for example, lie between brother and mommy, let's say, on one side—35 centimeters belong to me. I lie on sticks which are not icy on top, but there is ice at the bottom. My head is by black ice. It's −4°C (24.8°F) inside, without a blanket. But mommy, because she could no longer walk, they let her mend fishermen's nets. So, she stole piece after piece, piece after piece, piece after piece, piece after piece: stole, stole, stole . . . and made this little ball . . . I was the only one who had a pillow under my head under my ear on those sticks that softness. They put their heads directly on those sticks.

Upon arrival on the island, Janina was assigned to the children's work brigade. They had to transport bricks for the guards. Bricks were unloaded from a boat three kilometers from the camp, down a steep riverbank. The work was grueling, and the children took at least ten hours to walk the round-trip distance, slipping, falling, losing the bricks, and gathering them up again and again: "To make stairs in the ice nobody had energy—because they died, they died, they died." Janina's other responsibilities included providing wood for the guards. Since there were no trees in that climate zone, she had to find logs that had washed up onto the shores of the Lena, pull them out, and drag them in pieces long distances into the camp. As Janina spoke about those days, she wondered how she had managed:

> But in the winter, that lumber I would [walk] on my own . . . an axe, a sled, and I into that night I would walk alone, not knowing where and you don't know how you will come back. And until you find it, you may not come back. And you don't know where. And there are neither houses, nor villages, nor those lights, nor electricity. You walk simply into the polar glaciers.

Each person had a quota of bread that they could buy every day. Janina's family, like most others, did not have enough money to buy the full quota, which was a few slices per day. And even when they had saved up and could buy a piece of bread, the process was not simple. They would have to line up by the bakery two hours before work and stand in the wind and the blizzards waiting for the few slices of bread. As a result of starvation, grueling work, and inadequate clothing, people died every day. The deaths of Janina's colleagues and friends were a daily experience:

> [During that] very first, very deathly, first period full of horror, [that] very frost . . . and from my children's work brigade a portion died. One already does not arrive in the morning, so you don't know if he is unable to get up, if he is already pulled out onto the snow lying outside, because there was no funeral. Then everyone floated away with those ice floes in 1943 and it is not clear. And maybe, maybe those feral foxes, maybe, gnawed them up. On one of the islands . . . one Russian used to chop those frozen dead into traps for those white foxes.

Janina emphasized that her mother tried to ensure that she was sheltered from the horrors surrounding them. Thus, Janina felt that she was able to remain a child until her mother died:

> I was no longer shy only when mommy died. . . . Mommy had said . . . either alive here or dead, whoever dies first, but that my brother and I would not be burdened by figuring out how to get that piece of bread, when to eat it. . . . And she said, already in the Arctic, she said "When I die, that will be time enough to grow up." And we struggled, worked [despite] deadly exhaustion, but my

> brother and I—when mommy died, I know, we were watching a pot and asking each other how to know that water is boiling. . . . We used to be protected by that invisible care, that concern.

For Janina and her brother, the death of their mother signified the end of their childhood, and the heartache from this point in her life remains with Janina till this day. In 1989, Janina was able to go back to the Arctic and retrieve her mother's remains. She was quite surprised that eight men, warmly clothed and well-fed, struggled to dig out her mother's grave in the summer. She understood that her brother had carved the grave out of ice in the winter with a "bleeding soul, with bleeding hands, with . . . a bleeding heart . . . in a horrible hopelessness, in the black night." When she returned, she found her mother completely preserved in her icy grave just as she used to be: "That's why I found mommy—my frozen beautiful young mom."

Despite the hardships, however, Janina managed to assert her humanity and agency. For example, during a blizzard, Janina found ways to escape from the daily horrors and to help other children escape. She missed books dearly. So, whenever all of the children squatted and huddled together, "so as not to be the dying children" that they were, she started telling them about the books she had read, shows she had attended, and movies she had seen, in the greatest detail,

> telling so not quickly, not briefly, but simply feeling the pleasure . . . again, running from that blizzard, from that horrific cold, that hunger, or again that to escape somewhere, some internal protection or because you want to relive the emotions of that book, I don't know. I just know that each book used to become a series, each show a series, each movie a series.

Likewise, to preserve themselves from psychic numbness, the children struggled to mark occasions that were reminders of their existence and their humanity:

> We started to want to get together for Easter, little by little for us there was sugar . . . some more money . . . to buy the full quota of bread. Of course, we were still endlessly hungry, but for an entire month we would set aside saving up crumb after crumb, so that when we get together we could bring at least something for the common good, even though you could gobble it up in one lick.

They had to attend an indoctrination group where the guards lectured them about how good they had it there, how they were saved. The children used the group, however, as an opportunity to sing, dance, and tell jokes:

> I was 16 years old; the older ones were teaching me to dance for the first time. . . . We lived really in awful horror around us, but that you would talk

> so much about Lithuania, nobody talks that much [now]. [People] are shy now . . . to say that I love Lithuania. There it wouldn't leave your tongue. Just, of course, right there [we] constantly [talked] about food. And [we would silence] each other so as not to speak. . . . It seems you just finished and someone remembered all over again how to cook this [or that], how each one liked this [or that], what each disliked. "Oh God, shut up." . . . And then again we would [talk] about other Lithuanian matters."

Janina also remarked that no matter how hungry or tired she was, she could always admire the colors, shapes, and the magnificence of the polar lights. It was not uncommon to run inside the yurt and shout out in excitement: "Run, look—beauty!" When Janina struggled to fall asleep at night, she would dream that she had traveled all over the world, that she knew all of the languages of the world, that she had completed all sorts of studies, and that she had accomplished all of this before she turned eighteen.

When Janina was eighteen, she managed to return to Lithuania illegally. She was pursued by the KGB with "nowhere to sleep, nothing to eat, no people that I know, not anything." At night, Janina climbed through balconies to sleep in the dorm rooms of various friends. By day, she spent time on the riverside beach or sneaked into college classes. She described this period of transition as unexplainable: "there are stories after stories, history is silent here . . . I have never explained it." She remained silent about this period in her life during our conversation as well. One can only guess at her feelings and thoughts as she was planning to escape the labor camp in the Arctic, as she was traveling the distance of several thousand miles back to her dreamed-of Lithuania, and as she was first walking down the familiar, yet now Sovietized, streets again. Her silence about this transitional period in her life shrouds her experience of coming back to the occupied Lithuania that was very different from the country of her memories: Stalin was still in power; the secret police was active; the last of the Lithuanian rebels were being captured; deportations continued (Anušauskas, 1996); and Janina was an undocumented young woman who was considered a *bandit* by the institutional establishment. It took twelve years after her return to Lithuania before Janina was able to obtain a passport and start her undergraduate studies.

Janina shared only one episode from her life in Soviet Lithuania. In the 1970s, when Janina's daughter was in high school, a "delegation" came to Janina to inquire why her daughter—"a child of educated parents"—remained the only one in her classroom not to join the Komsomol (a primary communist organization for youths) and why her parents "do not explain the situation" to her. At the time, those youths who did not join the Komsomol experienced difficulties pursuing higher education or finding employment, which meant that membership was voluntary in name only (*Encyclopedia Britannica*, 2014). "Since birth," Janina's daughter grew up "knowing everything" about Janina's deportation and her parents' tragic fates. Thus, she was proud of her daughter for deciding to not become a member of the Komsomol of her own accord as she had not pressured her to not join.

Janina's response to such visits, of which there were several, was illustrative of the passive rebellion that characterized her attempts to preserve a sense of integrity in the Sovietized society. For instance, she pretended that her daughter might not be "good enough" for the Komsomol: "[Her] grades are so so and better [marks] would be appreciated." By that comment, Janina also implied a criticism of her daughter's teachers who were part of the "delegation." However, she did not cross the line enough to warrant heightened surveillance by the government. Aside from such small acts of passive rebellion, Janina also sought the company of other deportees to provide a safe niche in society for herself and her family. Even now, she is actively involved in the activities of various survivor communities.

When Lithuania regained its independence in 1990, Janina was able to break the silence about her family's history of deportations publicly for the first time. She believes that "Mr. God probably wrote down 'may this girl remain'" so that she could inform the world about the horrors and the injustice experienced by her family, friends, and fellow Lithuanians during the Soviet deportations. For the past couple of decades, Janina has worked as a tour guide, sharing her life story almost daily despite the lengthy, grueling commute to work that includes walking five miles, hitchhiking, and taking public transportation at her honorable age. She observed that the other survivors "don't want to remember" because the memories of deportations lead to sleepless nights. "Somebody has to," she remarked, explaining the reason behind her determination and her choice of this second career.

The life she lives today with its preoccupations, surprises, and joys always goes along with another life—that of memories, filled with images of times and people that no longer are. She cannot escape the traumatic past haunting her at the most unexpected moments:

> I, not even one minute, while I am not asleep, I do not live in the present life. Too many of those emotions, too many memories. . . . All of the images are with me. . . . I am telling people here and thinking, "I wonder, how it looks from aside." . . . For me, it's like watching a video, but . . . for them . . . , I don't know. Can a human being imagine? . . . You need to be there to understand.

As she works with tourists of all ages and walks of life, Janina encounters a variety of reactions. It is particularly important for her to educate the younger generations because she worries that the cultural heritage of Lithuanian language, history, and values are in danger of dissipating. For instance, she remarked that her grandson "does much worse with the Lithuanian language than with English, much worse than with English." Janina also observed that her grandchild no longer uses certain letters in the Lithuanian alphabet, like š or ž. She encourages him to read more to improve his Lithuanian language skills, but he is not receptive to her suggestions or gifts of books. Janina similarly lamented that "[People] are shy now . . . to say that I love Lithuania." Thus, while Janina worries that the Lithuania that her parents and her childhood self had known no longer exists, despite Lithuania's newfound Independence, she tries to locate herself in her constantly changing society by bearing witness and hoping that the wealth of her memories will be preserved and understood.

Spectral Memories and Ghostly Signifiers

The narratives of Janina and her peers offer multiple entry points for examining the intersection of trauma, history, and memory, and we offer here some brief markers as to the kinds of analysis that we are exploring. Our goal is to seek to decode the signifiers of such narratives, thereby exhuming and preserving narratives of both individual loss, and of the consequences for collective memory of the tears in the fabric of Lithuanian society caused by the immediate trauma of the Stalinist deportations and the subsequent suppression of memory and prohibition on mourning. This work falls into a tradition of interdisciplinary inquiry in our research group, and a broader understanding of the underpinnings of this kind of work can be found in earlier writings.[6] All of our work is motivated by seeking to understand where unprocessed trauma and unspeakable experience goes. What are the effects on individuals and on whole societies of silence produced by self-censorship? What are the effects on individuals and on whole societies of an externally imposed regime of truth and an iron-fisted prohibition on dissent, or even on remembering? Both of these questions are highly relevant to the Lithuanian situation in view of the Stalinist deportations and the subsequent period of Soviet paranoia and suppression. Most important, perhaps, when those ghosts come back as *revenants*, what form do they take?

In terms of the individual suffering of child survivors such as Janina—and the only living contemporary survivors are people who were deported as children—our work is guided by contemporary psychodynamic theories of trauma and intergenerational trauma,[7] and informed particularly by the contributions of Emery (2002), Green (2001), Kaplan (1996), and Kestenberg (1972). This literature on the mechanisms by which adult psychic trauma leaves a trace on the child is very valuable in decoding historical trauma through the manifestations of that trauma in signifiers that are evident in the preoccupations and eccentricities of children of survivors. Taking a more macro view of the influence of larger sociohistorical circumstances and the sweep of history, Lindy and Lifton's (2001) work addresses the consequences of Sovietization directly, and authors such a Atkinson (2002), Davoine and Gaudillière (2004), and Erikson (1976) offer important guidance on the traumatic consequences of severing social linkages and the insidious role national silence plays in the perpetuation of collective trauma across generations. Fundamentally, following Derrida (1993) and Gordon (1997), we frame this work as an inquiry into hauntology, or the presence of ghosts or spectral presences that, while hidden from view, make their presence felt both in individual lives and in the collective psyche of a group or nation. Stories such as Janina's, therefore, with their narratives of unfathomable suffering and with ruptures and gaps that suggest the presence of *unthought knowns* (Bollas, 1987) lurking in the shadows of the individual and collective unconscious, offer a way to understand the significance of history in the formation of human subjectivity.

NOTES

1. This chapter is a preliminary report on dissertation research being conducted by Justina Kaminskaitė Dillon, under the direction of Michael O'Loughlin at the Derner Institute of Advanced Psychological Studies, Adelphi University.

2. Interpretative phenomenology is a continual process of inquiry and reflection that does not aim at discovering or proving a "truth." Rather, interpretive phenomenological research seeks to explore a broad topic by taking into account the preconceived notions of the interviewer/researcher, the content of the interview, the reflections of the participant and the interviewer throughout the process, and the interpretations—all of which are included in the analysis of emergent themes within and across the interviews (Smith & Osborn, 2003; Kvale, 1996; Misgeld & Jardine, 1989).

3. Clinical dynamic interviewing is detailed by Fowler and Perry (2005) and involves a semistructured approach in the form of a conversation. The interviewer first lays out the frame of the interview and assumes a nondirective stance thereafter, allowing the participant to guide the interviewer through his/her experience. Particular emphasis is also placed on learning about the participant's emotional states as they relate to various life events.

4. Jonas Puodžius is one of the leaders of the Lithuanian survivor community "Laptevіečiai."

5. For confidentiality reasons, a fictional name is used to identify Janina and details of her life have been disguised. All interviews were conducted in Lithuanian and all translation is by Justina Kaminskaitė Dillon.

6. See, for example, the publications by Michael O'Loughlin listed in the reference list of this chapter, as well as the work of Nirit Gradwohl Pisano (2012). Chapters by O'Loughlin and by Pisano in this volume offer further detail also.

7. See, for example, Abraham & Torok, 1994; Atkinson, 2002; Auerhahn & Laub, 1998; Auerhahn & Prelinger, 1983; Charles, 2003, 2012; Cyrulnik, 2005; Faimberg, 2005; Fraiberg, Adelson, & Shairo, 1975; Frosh, 2013; Garon, 2004. For description

of a doctoral level course addressing these issues and offering additional resources, please see O'Loughlin & McLeod, 2014.

REFERENCES

Abraham, N. & Torok, M. (1994). *The shell and the kernel.* (Edited, translated and with an Introduction by N. Rand.) Chicago: University of Chicago Press.

Anušauskas, A. (1996). *Lietuvių tautos sovietinis naikinimas, 1940–1958 metais.* Vilnius: Mintis.

Altai Mountains. (2013). In *Encyclopedia Britannica online.* Retrieved from http://www.britannica.com/EBchecked/topic/17446/Altai-Mountains/47848/Climate.

Atkinson, J. (2002). *Trauma trails—Re-creating song lines: The transgenerational effects of trauma in indigenous Australia.* North Melbourne: Spinifex Press.

Auerhahn, N. & Laub, D. (1998). Intergenerational memory of the Holocaust. In Y. Danieli (Ed.), *International handbook of multigenerational legacies of trauma,* (pp. 21–41). New York: Platinum Press.

Auerhahn, N. C. & Prelinger, E. (1983). Repetition in the concentration camp survivor and her child. *International Review of Psychoanalysis, 10*, 31–46.

Bollas, C. (1987). *The Shadow of the object: Psychoanalysis of the unthought known.* New York: Columbia University Press.

Charles, M. (2012). *Working with trauma: Lessons from Bion and Lacan.* Lanham, MD: Jason Aronson.

Charles, M. (2003). The intergenerational transmission of unresolved mourning: Personal, familial, and cultural factors. *Samiksa: Journal of the Indian Psychoanalytic Society, 54*, 65–80.

Cyrulnik, B. (2005). *The whispering of ghosts: Trauma and resilience* (S. Fairfield, Trans.). New York: Other Press (Original work published 2003).

Davoine, F. & Gaudillière, J. M. (2004). *History beyond trauma* (S. Fairfield, Trans.). New York: Other Press.

Derrida, J. (1993). *Specters of Marx: The state of the debt, the work of mourning and the new international.* New York: Routledge.

Emery, E. (2002). The ghost in the mother: Strange attractors and impossible mourning. *Psychoanalytic Review, 89*, 2, 169–94.

Erikson, K. (1976). Loss of communality at Buffalo Creek. *American Journal of Psychiatry, 133,* 302–5.

Faimberg, H. (2005). *The telescoping of generations: Listening to the narcissistic links between generations.* London: Routledge.

Fowler, J. & Perry, C. (2005). Clinical Tasks of the Dynamic Interview. *Psychiatry, 68*, 316–36.

Fraiberg, S., Adelson, E., & Shapiro, V. (1975). Ghosts in the nursery: A psychoanalytic approach to the problems of impaired infant-mother relationships. *Journal of the American Academy of Child and Adolescent Psychiatry, 14*, 3, 387–421.

Frosh, S. (2013). *Hauntings: Psychoanalysis and ghostly transmissions.* New York: Palgrave Macmillan.

Garon, J. (2004). Skeletons in the closet. *International Forum of Psychoanalysis, 13,* 84–92.

Gordon, A. (1997). *Ghostly matters: Haunting and the sociological imagination.* Minneapolis, MN: University of Minnesota Press.

Green, André. (2001). The dead mother. In *Life narcissism/death narcissism* (Andrew Weller, Trans.). London, New York: Free Associations Books.

Grinkevičiūtė, D. (1990). Lithuanians by the Laptev sea: The Siberian memoirs of Dalia Grinkevičiūtė. *Lituanus: Lithuanian Quarterly Journal of Arts and Science, 36,* 4, Retrieved from http://www.lituanus.org/1990_4/90_4_05.htm.

Kaplan, L. (1996). Images of absence, voices of silence. In *No voice is ever wholly lost: An exploration of the everlasting attachment between parent and child.* New York: Simon & Schuster.

Kestenberg, J. (1972). Psychoanalytic contributions to the problem of children of survivors from Nazi persecution. *Israel Annals of Psychiatry and Related Disciplines, 10,* 249–65.

Kiaupa, Z. (2004). *Lietuvos valstybes istorija.* Vilnius: Baltos Lankos.

Komsomol. (2014). In *Encyclopedia Britannica online.* Retrieved from http://www.britannica.com/EBchecked/topic/321647/Komsomol

Kuodytė, D. & Tracevskis, R. (2004). *Siberia: Mass deportations from Lithuania to the USSR.* Vilnius: Genocide and Resistance Research Center of Lithuania.

Kvale, S. (1996). "Postmodern thought: Hermeneutics, phenomenology, dialectics." In *InterViews: An Introduction to qualitative research interviewing.* London: Sake Publications.

Lindy, J. D. & Lifton, R. J. (2001). *The psychological legacy of Soviet trauma, East European therapists and their patients.* New York: Brunner Routledge.

Misgeld, D. & Jardine, D. (1989). Hermeneutics as the undisciplined child: Hermeneutic and technical images of education. In M. Packer & R. Addison (Eds.), *Entering the circle: Hermeneutic investigation in psychology* (pp. 259–73). New York: State University of New York Press.

O'Loughlin, M. (2013). Reclaiming genealogy, memory and history: The psychodynamic potential for reparative therapy in contemporary South Africa. In C. Smith, G. Lobban, & M. O'Loughlin (Eds.), *Psychodynamic psychotherapy in contemporary South Africa: Contexts, theories, practices.* Johannesburg, SA: Wits University Press.

O'Loughlin, M. (2012). Trauma trails from Ireland's Great Hunger: A psychoanalytic inquiry. In B. Willock, R. Curtis & L. Bohm (Eds.), *Loneliness and longing: Conscious and unconscious aspects.* New York: Routledge

O'Loughlin, M. (2010). Ghostly presences in children's lives: Toward a psychoanalysis of the social. In M. O'Loughlin & R. Johnson (Eds.), *Imagining children otherwise: Theoretical and critical perspectives on childhood subjectivity.* New York: Peter Lang Publishing. [Reprinted in M. O'Loughlin (Ed.), *Psychodynamic perspectives on working with children, families and schools.* (2013), Lanham, MD: Jason Aronson.]

O'Loughlin, M. (2009). An analysis of collective trauma among indigenous Australians and a suggestion for intervention. *Australasian Psychiatry, 17,* 33–36.

O'Loughlin, M. (2008). Radical hope or death by a thousand cuts? The future for indigenous Australians. *Arena Journal, 29/30,* 175–202.

O'Loughlin, M. (2007a). Bearing witness to troubled memory. *Psychoanalytic Review, 94,* 2, 191–212.

O'Loughlin, M. (2007b). On losses that are not easily mourned. In L. Bohm, R. Curtis, & B. Willock (Eds.), *Psychoanalysts' reflections on deaths and endings: Finality, transformations, new beginnings.* New York: Routledge.

O'Loughlin, M. & McLeod, B. (2014). "Thinking beyond our means": Engendering a depth understanding of trauma. In M. O'Loughlin & M. Charles (Eds.), *Fragments of trauma and the social production of suffering: Trauma, History and Memory.* Lanham, MD: Rowman & Littlefield.

Pisano, N. G. (2012). *Granddaughters of the Holocaust: Never forgetting what they didn't experience.* Boston: Academic Studies Press.

Schutzenberger, A. A. (1998). *The ancestor syndrome: Transgenerational psychology and the hidden links in the family tree.* London and New York: Routledge Books.

Smith, J. A. & Osborn, M. (2003). Interpretative phenomenological analysis. In J. A. Smith (Ed.), *Qualitative psychology: A practical guide to research methods, 2nd Edition* (pp. 51–80). London: Sage Publications, Ltd.

Vardys, V. S. & Sedaitis, J. B. (1997). *Lithuania: The rebel nation.* Boulder, CO: Westview Press.

Chapter 9

They Left It All Behind

Psychological Experiences of Jewish Immigration and the Ambiguity of Loss[1]

Hannah Hahn

My grandparents were part of the great wave of Jewish immigration from Eastern Europe which occurred between 1880 and 1924. I knew all four, and three lived well into my adulthood; as an adult, I spent a good deal of time with my mother's parents. Yet I understood little about their subjective experiences as immigrants. As a young child growing up in a gentile, working-class suburb, surrounded by Catholic neighbors, I felt some shame about the visits by the "funny little Jewish people" from my extended family. They talked strangely, and their European table manners seemed uncouth to me. Proper speech was highly valued by my first-generation American parents, and I privately wondered if perhaps there was something wrong with the people unable to speak as I was taught to. I secretly pondered the possibility that they might be retarded. As I became an adult, I began to feel guilty thinking about my grandparents' lack of opportunities and the poverty they had endured compared to all that I had been given. They had sacrificed, I felt, so that I could have the riches of an American life. On some level, I realized that they were "little" because indeed they had been malnourished. Yet none of this was spoken about.

Several years ago, I began a systematic study of how the individuals from my grandparents' generation experienced immigration psychologically. I would also inquire about their childrens' experiences. I realized later that this was an attempt to undo the denial surrounding my grandparents' and parents' histories. Although aspects of my grandparent's stories appear in the lives of the immigrants described here, I did not at first realize how deeply personal this research was to me.

This chapter is part of a larger study concerning psychological aspects of Eastern European Jewish immigration to the United States prior to 1930, as perceived through the eyes of immigrants' adult children.[2] Detailed, semistructured psychohistorical interviews with children of the now-deceased immigrants were conducted in order to explore the immigrants' experiences during the period of transition to life in the United States, as well as aspects of being a child of those immigrants.[3] The first fifteen of the completed interviews, six of men and nine of women, are utilized here.[4]

Interviewees were all college educated. While the majority of the fifteen individuals were in their eighties (but cognitively intact), one was in her fifties, two were in their seventies, one was in his nineties, and one was 104 years old. Two were middle-class, but the remainder were upper-middle class. Most were retired, and their former professions included public school teachers, social workers, attorneys, and scientists; thus, they were educated and articulate. Interviewees were located through synagogues, a Jewish senior service program, and acquaintances. Each had had two immigrant parents.

One-third of the Jewish population of Eastern Europe emigrated between 1880 and 1924, the great majority to the United States (Epstein, 2007). Immigrants came largely from czarist Russia, with a smaller proportion coming from eastern Austria-Hungary, especially Galicia (Schmelz & DellaPergola, 2007).[5] With the industrialization occurring in the latter half of the nineteenth century, traditional peasant economies in which Jews participated were affected, leading to extreme poverty for them (Epstein, 2007, p. 3). Economic strain was further exacerbated by a significant increase in the Jewish population (Schmelz & DellaPergola, 2007).

In this atmosphere of economic uncertainty, the Russian government allowed, or perhaps instigated, attacks on the Jewish community (Epstein, 2007, pp. 3–4). Russian soldiers passing through a town would randomly seize, rape, or kill young Jewish women. Jewish boys were subject to conscription, sometimes as young as age eight. After the assassination of Tsar Alexander II in 1881, discrimination and violence toward Jews worsened, and organized pogroms began. Pogroms were widespread between 1881 and 1906; in 1881 alone twenty thousand Jewish homes were demolished (Epstein, 2007, p. 9; Dawidowicz, 1984, p. 13). Furthermore, in 1881, Alexander III, who hated the Jews, instituted the "May Laws," which attempted to destroy the Jews' shtetl way of life by forbidding Jews to live in towns of populations under ten thousand. Jewish access to higher education was greatly restricted (Epstein, 2007, p. 11), and various edicts were passed restricting the ability of Jews to earn a living.

In Austria-Hungary, Jews suffered anti-Semitic discrimination and political oppression, in addition to poverty, although less organized violence occurred than in Russia (Berman, 1980; Katz & Gelber, 2007). As in Russia, restrictions on means of earning a livelihood and university admissions were instituted.

It is important to note that anti-Semitic violence and discrimination varied from region to region (Epstein, 2007). Therefore, some immigrants came from areas with more stable ways of life than others. Among those who immigrated to America, many were young, but frequently, and much more often than in other ethnic groups, families immigrated together.

Before beginning my psychohistory research, I expected that I would hear about missing the Old Country: that in studying immigrants' feelings about being uprooted I would learn both about a sense of loss and about feelings of longing for old ways of life. I knew that, despite persecution, immigrants felt strong ties to Eastern Europe, which they considered to be home, and that their "sense of uprootedness was keen" (Weinberg, 1988, p. 67; Matt, 2011). Moreover, I had been influenced by immigrants' statements, such as the following, quoted by Elizabeth Ewen: A female immigrant, describing her first year in New York said, "I didn't smile for a long time. Why? Because [here] . . . everybody was for himself, and there was always money, money, money; rush, rush, rush" (Ewen, 1985, p. 62). Furthermore, I had read both scholarly and fictional works depicting the shtetl as a place of community orientation and emotional warmth.[6] My preconceptions about immigrants' sense of loss, derived from sources such as this, have been tempered by listening to my interviewees.

THEY LEFT IT ALL BEHIND

I was curious about immigrants' feelings about being uprooted. More often than not, however, the immigrants' children, denying that their parents missed their former homes, said that their parents wanted to "leave it all behind." A few individuals, in contrast, did speak about their parents' longing for the Old Country or a sense of loss, and some depicted this in heartbreaking ways. In one instance, the same parent experienced both loss and wanting to leave it behind.

Benjamin's parents and Seymour's mother were among those who wanted to "leave it all behind."[7] Benjamin's parents had left a world in which the risk of death was ever-present, and both feared gentiles. Indeed, Benjamin's father always limped because he had been hit by a gentile nobleman. When asked whether she wanted to visit her hometown, Benjamin's mother said: "No, I ran away and I have only bad memories of it."

Seymour's mother never wanted to see Poland again. When she was a young girl living in a small town during World War I (her father was already in the United States), German soldiers confiscated the family's food. Seymour's grandmother attempted to hide food under her house floorboards and was imprisoned because of this. Seymour's mother and her siblings were, consequently, forced to beg or otherwise find food on their own. Seymour spoke of the visual image of his mother holding a baby sibling who had just died of cholera. In the intense anti-Semitic violence of the time, Seymour's mother reported that once, while on a train, she witnessed an old man having his "jaw chopped off."

Thus, when asked about their parents' feelings of uprootedness, many of the interviewees told me about the anti-Semitic violence and poverty which made their parents relieved to escape Eastern Europe.[8] These parents and their children were coping not only with the traumatic losses of migration, but also with memories of the traumas of discrimination, persecution, and poverty. Many of the parents had lived through the upheavals of World War I or the Russian Revolution.

The historical record suggests that, despite discrimination and violence, Eastern European immigrants generally felt the loss of their former homes (Ewen, 1985; Howe, 1976; Matt, 2011; Menes, 1970/1972). What do we make then of many of the immigrants' children insisting that their parents "left it all behind"? There are several possibilities: (1) Some parents indeed might have come from backgrounds so deprived and violent that they felt that there was nothing to miss. (2) Some newly arrived immigrant parents may have used denial as a coping technique. They would not allow themselves to miss their families or familiar surroundings for fear that doing so would hinder them from "making it." (3) In many cases "they left it all behind" may have been the children's own interpretation, helping them to avoid thinking or knowing too much about their parents' traumatic histories or about the losses of migration. In general, for both parents and children, not thinking too much about the past was an important coping strategy in allowing them to move forward in order to build a new life in America (Bar-On & Gilad, 1994).

Had I been able to interview the parents themselves, many of them might have expressed more nuanced points of view about their own pasts than those described by their children. For example, Benjamin's mother, discussed above, carried only "bad memories" of her town, but, at the same time, she "pined" for the siblings she would never see again. Because she and many other immigrants experienced profound loss, along with the relief of having escaped poverty and persecution, we can speak of the ambiguity of their losses.[9]

COMMUNICATING ABOUT THE PAST

Listening to my interviewees speak suggested to me that the denial characterizing my grandparents' stories had to do with the various kinds of trauma in their histories. Because my research is based on what the immigrants told their children and on how the children experienced what they heard, it is essential to know how the parents spoke to their children.

In fact, the quality of how immigrants spoke to their children about their lives in Europe and during the transition to America varied greatly. Jacob, a highly intelligent and curious scientist, said, "They told us kids nothing. They wanted to make a marked transition to the U.S. and dump all that stuff. We're here. Let's forget that." Jacob knew only a few details about his family's life in Europe and was unable to speculate about his parents' psychological transition to the United States He conveyed to me that, for his family, survival was paramount, and, consequently, there was no room for thoughts of happiness. For them, the absence of persecution in the United States was a big improvement over life in Eastern Europe. Jacob's experience was a typical one in that many parents, particularly fathers, said very little about their lives in the Old Country and their subjective experiences upon arrival.[10]

One issue in immigrants' communication to their children about the past is whether and how they transmitted traumatic experiences to their children. This is highlighted in the next two vignettes. For example, Rose, an astute professional woman in her sixties, seemed overwhelmed by her parents' massive sense of loss and trauma, and she felt that her parents communicated in opposite manners about their pasts. Rose's mother, Leah, spoke in detail and repetitively about her own mother's frightening experiences during World War I. When displaced with her young children, including Leah, she courageously chose living with them in an isolated barn rather than living with sick families. In contrast, Rose's father never once spoke of his experiences. As a teenager, Rose begged her father to tell her at least one story; he told her about a recurrent traumatic experience from his childhood. Each day when he and the other Jewish boys from his village walked to school, they formed a circle with one boy walking inside the circle. They were stoned by gentile boys, but the boy in the middle was protected from stoning. Rose sensed that this was probably the least troubling of the experiences her father might have told her.

Rose's father seemed to have sought to protect both her and himself from the experience of trauma by not speaking about it. Moreover, Rose herself let me know that she wanted to separate herself from her parents' terrible communications. Rose's father's silence about his past is reminiscent of the silence of Holocaust survivors. For them, "the impossibility of speaking" was the only way to deal with unspeakable horror (Laub, 1992, p. 65; Kaplan, 1996).

At the opposite end of the continuum from Jacob's father, Elaine's mother spoke a great deal about the family she had left behind in Europe. Like Rose's mother, she spoke in detail about the past. In fact, she flooded Elaine with her story of loneliness and trauma. Another similarity was Elaine's father's silence about much of his past. Elaine herself was an educated, pleasant, soft-spoken, and contained retired professional in her seventies. Elaine spoke slowly, quietly, and in detail, and her account was open, thoughtful, and intelligent. An only child herself, she and her husband had raised three daughters to whom they were close, had done well financially, and currently enjoyed an active and social life.

Elaine began her interview with the words, "My mother had a very, very hard time," thus suggesting the intense impact of her mother's suffering on her. Elaine's mother arrived in the United States at about age twenty without any members of her immediate family. Because she missed her family terribly, after her arrival she cried herself to sleep every night for a couple of years. She had expected to work and save money so that her mother and siblings could follow her to New York. However, because of changed laws, they were able only to immigrate to South America, thousands of miles away from Elaine's mother. To compensate for this, her mother told Elaine so many stories about her sisters and brothers that Elaine felt that she actually knew her mother's family: by doing so, her mother kept them psychologically alive. She so much needed someone to talk to that she flooded her child with her loneliness and sadness.

Elaine's mother also told her about her father's early death from cancer and about the anti-Semitic violence, including a pogrom, which took place in her mother's small city. She made clear to Elaine its traumatic impact on her, emphasizing her hate for everything Polish. Elaine felt this hate deeply. Significantly, the dreadful feelings of loss and emptiness which Elaine's mother experienced during her early years in New York may have been worsened because of the effects of the accumulation of everything that had happened to her before her arrival.

Like Rose's father, Elaine's father spoke little about his private experiences. He was a frustrated man, a musician who worked by day in a belt factory and wished for more education. Although she did not know any details, Elaine believed that there were "difficulties" in his family and that his past was "too painful" for him to talk about. He seemed less resilient than her mother.

The feelings that Elaine experienced with her mother were overwhelming. Elaine said, "I could feel my mother's sadness as a young child," and she believed that her mother never completely escaped from it. Sitting with Elaine, who appeared to be a fulfilled and well-adjusted woman, I had a sense of absence and flatness when she spoke about her mother. Elaine was profoundly affected emotionally and, I thought, traumatized by her mother's feelings of loss.

Elaine's absence and flatness represent the ghost of the immense sadness that she took in from her mother and also suggest her father's silent suffering

(O'Loughlin, 2010). Her mother, having no one else at hand, seemed to unwittingly have chosen Elaine as the child listener who could cure her (Kaplan, 1996; O'Loughlin, 2010). Yet trying to assess the overall effects of her parents' trauma is complicated for Elaine. It appeared possible that, during Elaine's later childhood, her mother might have in part recovered from her loneliness. In fact, at that time contact with her mother's family increased. Furthermore, Elaine reported that her mother was social and had a loving marriage. Elaine appeared to have been securely attached (Main, Kaplan, & Cassidy, 1985) and generally treated sensitively by her parents. This, together with her open attitude during the interview, suggests that she had been able partially to work through her parents' painful communications. Although I believe that her parents' traumas had "reverberations" in her present-day life, Elaine's resilience is attested to by the evidence of her generally fulfilling life (Pisano, 2012, p. 40).

Many immigrant parents spoke very little about their pasts. Often their silence represented an attempt to protect their children from memories that were too raw. Some parents who remained silent, such as Rose's father, communicated their trauma wordlessly (Kaplan, 1996; Laub, 1992). Two of the parents described here utilized a different method of dealing with traumatic memories and losses: they spoke in detail or flooded their children with what had occurred. Overall, many of the immigrants experienced some trauma in Eastern Europe or during the immigration process, which was transmitted intergenerationally. The severity of its impact on the children varied widely, but most of the children proved resilient and successful.

MOTHERS WHO MISSED THE OLD COUNTRY

In migrating to the United States, the newcomers left everything familiar behind. Migration itself is generally inherently destabilizing (Akhtar, 2011; Grinberg & Grinberg, 1989; Lieblich, 1993). For immigrants, emotions arise about the people and places which will never be seen again, and feelings of loss and mourning are expectable (Grinberg & Grinberg, 1989). Indeed, for some, migration is traumatic (Grinberg & Grinberg, p. 15). I was told, however, about only a few immigrants, all mothers, who spoke about missing aspects of their former lives. Interestingly, in this small sample, mothers communicated their sense of loss to their daughters, but not to their sons.[11]

Elaine's mother, discussed in the previous section, missed her family intensely when she emigrated to America. She said that she missed only the people from the Old Country, but not the place, and she adamantly wanted to leave Poland behind. According to Elaine, her mother had left behind a large family and a generally happy home in which she had been her father's favorite. Before her father's death, the family had been middle class. Afterwards, however, the family struggled economically, and, consequently, her mother may have idealized her happy childhood as a sort of golden age. Her mother was not alone in the United States. When she arrived, she lived with extended family who cared about her, and a good friend also emigrated to New York. Yet the inevitable alienation and dislocation of migration must have added to Elaine's mother's inconsolable feelings about the loss of her family.

Helen's mother, like Elaine's, missed her family intensely and arrived in the United States without any members of her immediate family. Helen's mother was lonely for years and homesick after her arrival alone at age sixteen. Helen herself was a gracious, talkative, pleasant woman in her eighties and a people pleaser, though she had a somewhat formal manner. She was a retired professional, an intelligent, active, cultured woman, and she lived in a beautiful house with her second husband.

According to Helen, when her mother traveled to the United States, she had been neither ready nor eager to come, and her intention had been to return to her middle-class family's shtetl. Originally, it had been Helen's aunt, not her mother, who had wanted to travel to America. By the time her aunt's ticket arrived, however, her aunt was away, and their mother then chose Helen's mother to take the trip instead. She chose her precisely because she felt that Helen's mother would later return to the Old Country. Thus, in Helen's account, the trip here was not entirely of her mother's choosing. Furthermore, shortly after her mother arrived, World War I broke out and, consequently, she was unable either to correspond with her family or to return.[12] She felt trapped in the United States and was reportedly "distraught beyond words." Because of the war, Helen's mother's trip turned into a migration.

When she arrived in the United States, not only was Helen's mother lonely and homesick, but she was also afraid; for example, she feared getting lost. Adding to her distress was the fact that the relatives with whom Helen's mother stayed lived a "cheerless" life. In fact, the aunt with whom Helen's mother lived was clinically depressed.

Helen described the family her mother left behind in Europe in an idealized way, as warm and affectionate, full of humor, laughter, and joy. Her mother also idealized her shtetl, seemingly overlooking a pogrom that affected extended family members there. A discrepancy between surface presentation and a negative reality, perhaps representing defensive splitting, characterized not only her mother's way of talking, but also Helen's own presentation. For example, Helen described her mother as having "remarkable assets" and "an incredible facility for language." But later Helen said that she did not get affection from her needy mother, and, moreover, that her mother required her children to listen to *her* when the children arrived home from school, rather than the mother inquiring about her children. She said that her mother never forgot a slight.

Helen's mother's traumatic separation from her family, coupled with the other dislocations of immigration, affected her ability to be responsive as a mother. Perhaps partly because of her own psychological predisposition, Helen's mother seemed unable to fully recover after her arrival in the United States (Grinberg & Grinberg, 1989). Helen herself seemed to have been psychologically affected by her mother's traumatic migration and emotional difficulties. She seemed to have been insecurely attached (Main et al., 1985), and, while in most ways well-meaning, she was somewhat self-serving in her interactions.

Adele was a widow in her eighties, a retired civil servant, who was active and interested in culture. She was deferential and nervous about the interview process. Adele pushed herself to volunteer for the interview because, as the last of her surviving siblings, she saw herself as the "repository" of her family's history. Adele's mother emigrated with other family members, and her family's normal nostalgia contrasts with Elaine's and Helen's mothers' traumatic loneliness.

Adele's mother and aunt expressed a sense of nostalgia and loss both for the countryside they had left and for the closer contact with family they experienced in the Old World. In Eastern Europe, her mother's poor family owned an inn in a farming village in an area replete with anti-Semitism. Local peasants routinely "roughed them up," and, much worse, pogroms occurred. During a pogrom, Adele's aunt was seized and forced to dig trenches. Adele and her now deceased husband suspected that, during this pogrom, her "maiden aunt" might have been raped. A second childhood trauma was that Adele's mother and aunt lived through an epidemic during which several siblings perished.

Despite all this, Adele's mother and aunt spoke about how their apples, bread, and potatoes tasted better in the 'alte heim' (the old home). Adele associated her mother's and aunt's feelings of sadness and nostalgia with their longing for their youth when their parents were alive. Adele pointed out that, although conditions were indeed dire in Europe, there, in contrast to the tenements of New York City, they had space, fresh air,[13] and food that they themselves had grown. In addition to the physical environment, Adele's mother and aunt missed the closeness of family, who were able to spend so much more time together in Europe. There the members of the extended family lived in one small community, while in New York they were scattered, some, for example, in Brooklyn and others in Washington Heights; furthermore, they had to work six-and-one-half days per week. Adele's parents owned a store, and she emphasized the hardship that they endured in the United States.

The mild longing for home that Adele's family felt may be seen as normal. At the same time, this family's nostalgia for an idealized home, such a contrast to its actual drudgery and trauma, can be seen as a response to its loss. Her family preserved the past by making it mythically good (Hoffman, 1999). Interestingly, Adele and her sister reacted to this fantasy version of the past by becoming angry when their mother and aunt spoke nostalgically about it. She commented that indeed her mother remembered nothing joyous from her childhood, so why would she long for it?

According to many historical accounts, Eastern European Jewish immigrants experienced homesickness for their families and towns (Ewen, 1985; Howe, 1976; Matt, 2011; Menes, 1970/1972; Weinberg, 1988). In contrast to the many immigrants' children interviewed, who stated that their parents "left it all behind," a few, discussed above, spoke about their mothers' losses and loneliness. In addition, two daughters whose mothers were middle-class in Europe and poor in America spoke about how much their mothers missed their lives in Europe.[14]

Although in general children reported that fathers tended to speak little about their emotions, some of their children were nevertheless aware of them. A daughter and a son of two separate immigrants, for example, knew that their fathers suffered profoundly after leaving their entire families in Europe.[15] Furthermore, one son realized that his father demonstrated a debilitating sense of loss not in the years after his arrival, but only later on, after his family had died during the Holocaust.

My own family was like many others in that missing the past was spoken about only infrequently; for my grandparents, immigration had been a necessity, and, therefore, talking about it would have been seen as irrelevant. However, for Elaine's and Helen's mothers, immigration was destabilizing, as they left family members forever (Akhtar, 2011). Adele's mother expressed a normal sense of loss for all that she missed about home.

Immigration must by its nature evoke various and ambiguous emotions. For these immigrants, complicating the difficulty of leaving everything familiar was, of course, the reality that the majority had to leave Eastern Europe. Thus one of the problems that the immigrants' children faced in speaking about their parents was the ambiguity of their losses. The children's feelings were complicated because the reality their parents faced in immigrating was a complex balance of gains and losses. For example, Elaine's mother missed her family terribly, but in actuality she needed to leave behind the hated economic struggle and the anti-Semitism of life in Eastern Europe. Adele's mother experienced nostalgia for her previous life, but her daughter reflected that the reality of that life was indeed so difficult. Moreover, the ambiguity of Helen's mother's loss, as Helen told it, was particularly poignant: she missed the family she was cut off from and whom she expected to rejoin. Had she returned, however, she would have died in the Holocaust along with all those members of her family who had not moved to Israel.

TWO INTERVIEWS WITH IMMIGRANTS' CHILDREN

In the two life stories presented in this section, I provide more detailed psychological portraits of two immigrant families and their children, Frances and Ruth. In addition, I try to understand the psychological effects of these parents' lives on their children. Frances' mother was middle-class before she emigrated, and she felt that her life in America could never match her former life. Her unhappiness profoundly influenced Frances. In contrast, Ruth's mother's life in Europe had been full of deprivation and fear. The effects of her trauma appeared to have been passed on to Ruth.

Frances

Frances was an intelligent, modestly dressed, retired professional in her eighties, who was task-focused, detailed, and interesting during the interviews. She was psychologically aware in telling me what was, in many ways, a difficult story. She described her unaffectionate mother sardonically. Frances had raised three children while working.

Frances' parents, Anna and Louis, differed in social status, family backgrounds, and personality, and they were mismatched from the beginning of their relationship. Anna was beautiful, ambitious, and snobbish, while Louis, though intelligent, was an ordinary working man. Anna's family was secular and educated. Her mother was a medical professional and her father was a scholar, while Louis's father was an Orthodox grocer. They were from the same large Eastern European city, although Anna's family lived in a higher-status neighborhood there.[16]

Louis intensely disliked his father's religiosity and rebelled against it. After repeatedly running away from home, he made his way to a large German city, where he made a life as a skilled needle-worker. Anna spent time in Paris in her late teens, and when she returned home she opened a millinery shop. She met Louis later when she traveled to Germany to buy millinery supplies. After they married and had a son, Anna joined Louis in Germany.

According to Frances, in Germany, which she saw as modern and sophisticated, Anna lived a "gay cosmopolitan life," made friends, and had "aspirations to the intelligentsia." She was also a successful businesswoman. In 1921, however, Louis decided to follow his sister to the United States. Anna did not want to emigrate. Not only was she frightened of going to America, but she had a close relationship with her sisters, who had remained in Eastern Europe. Moreover, she would not be joining any close relatives in the United States, as Louis was. Unlike Anna, Louis saw emigration as an adventure. Importantly, at that time leaving Germany was a choice for Louis rather than the necessity that it was for most of the immigrants discussed here.

Once they had immigrated, the easy-going and venturesome Louis did not look back on his past; he had left Europe behind. Anna, however, was miserable and depressed in America, and she reportedly cried for five years after arriving. She missed her sisters and felt alienated and displaced. She experienced her new life in America as a loss, and perhaps she saw leaving Germany as a narcissistic blow. She felt that, in comparison to Germany, New York was dirty and inferior culturally. She did not make friends here, probably because her neighbors in New York were working-class individuals on whom she looked down. Also, according to Frances, Anna had "multiple compaints" about her husband, including that he was "satisfied with so little."

Anna's pronounced difficulty in adjusting to the United States may have been due to several factors (Lieblich, 1993). I hypothesize that she felt so deprived by the loss of the cultural and social sophistication of her adopted German home that she was neither able to give up her attachment to it, nor to find anything similar in the United States (Akhtar, 2011; Hoffman, 1999). Moreover, the fact that Anna's move to the United States was not motivated by persecution gave her less motivation to adjust. In addition, an underlying tendency toward depression left her even more vulnerable than other immigrants.

In the United States, Anna and Louis struggled to make a living, although Anna began working when Frances was three. Louis's needle-working business failed during the Depression, and the family did not recover economically until after the war. Anna and Louis sacrificed economically to help both their children become professionals.

As a child, Frances felt largely ignored; she stated that no one cared whether she was happy or unhappy. In contrast to her blond, blue-eyed, attractive, and considerably older brother, not only was Frances plain looking, but she was also so severely cross-eyed that she appeared to be impaired. Furthermore, she resembled her father, which would have been one more reason for what, according to Frances, was her mother's "great disappointment" in her.

Frances felt that family relationships were painful. As a child, she viewed her beautiful working mother as a "fairy princess" and as inaccessible. Frances felt that her brother was both more important to and worshipped by the family. Frances felt that Anna used her for her own purposes. For example, Frances read precociously at age four, which gratified Anna, but Frances also remembered being "smacked" by her mother for making a reading error. Frances's father was generally fonder and more accepting of her than her mother.

My sense is that Frances had been deeply wounded by her mother's continued disappointment in her and her appearance. She described how, as a young adult in professional training, she first was able to reflect on her mother's treatment of her, and she was extremely troubled by it. The profound effects on Frances's personality are suggested by the fact that, so many years later, Frances continued to harbor very negative feelings toward her mother. Though she was aware of her mother's losses, at many points during the interview she implied that her mother's unhappiness about immigration was an expression of her self-involvement. Frances remained angry at her. Frances's inability to identify with her mother's experiences speaks, in turn, to her mother's marked lack of empathy for her.

Nevertheless, as an adult Frances was able to lead a life with some genuine fulfillment. To some degree she seemed able to recover psychologically. She married a man who was also her friend, had a good career, and three children. Though she stated that she did not make friends readily, she did have friends. She and her husband did well economically.

In reality, Anna suffered a wrenching transition when she arrived in the United States. Athough she probably also had a significant underlying psychological vulnerability, the trauma of immigration and loneliness, of losing her middle-class status, her family, and all that she loved was real. Most likely, Frances was correct in saying that her mother would have been unhappy anywhere she was. Yet Anna would have been more responsive to Frances, and thus Frances would have had a more satisfactory childhood, had Anna not had to leave everything she knew.

Ruth

Ruth's and her parents' story is in many ways the opposite of Frances's. Ruth's mother came from an impoverished and deprived background which was full of fear. Her mother wanted to "leave it all behind." Ruth herself was an intelligent, musically knowledgable, beautifully dressed woman in her eighties who lived in a well-appointed apartment and had three children. Her husband had been very successful financially, and Ruth had held important volunteer positions. Ruth's warm, expansive stance on the telephone contrasted with what seemed to be psychological opacity and stiffness during the interview. It was difficult for her to connect to her own feelings.

Ruth's mother Devorah was the third of four children born in the 1890s in a small Eastern European city. Devorah's own mother died in childbirth when Devorah was two years old. They were very poor, and Devorah began working at age ten, selling sundries at a little street stand. Ruth said that Devorah "raised herself" because she was motherless. Devorah did not talk a great deal about her life in the Old Country. In contrast, however, she "talked enough" about pogroms at the hands of "whimsically ruthless" Russian soldiers. Indeed, Ruth acted out for me Devorah's family's procedure for hiding her younger sister during pogroms. Strikingly, this terrifying piece of her mother's history was alive in Ruth, and Ruth's animation at that moment in the interview contrasted with her flatness and attempts to defend against negative affect.

Devorah and her family had survived not only pogroms, but also war. During World War I, her family was displaced and lived in the forest in a shack in a lumber camp. Devorah's future husband, Harry, did forced labor during the war as a woodsman. He suffered a permanent injury as a result.

In 1921, Devorah and Harry, by then married, immigrated to New York City with Devorah's father and a baby son. There they joined extended family, and Ruth, their third child, was born in 1926. The family's hardship continued during their early years in the United States. They lived a "hand to mouth" existence and were aided economically by extended family members. Harry worked for various store owners, and eventually he and Devorah ran a series of stores together. Ruth stated that her parents "slaved" to make a living.

Ruth emphasized the fear, difficulty, and poverty of her mother's life as a child and young adult in Eastern Europe. As Ruth described her, as an adult Devorah was closed off and very private: she "tended to keep her mouth shut," and, although close to family members, "didn't love a million people." My picture of her was of a woman who had been traumatized by her fear of pogroms and motherless childhood. Ruth described her mother's general strategy for dealing with life this way: "My mother was a coper." "You dealt with what you were dealt and moved on." Ruth related an anecdote about Devorah, then elderly, awakening from anesthesia very agitated and calling for her own dead mother.

Ruth's own distance and remote presentation with me was reminiscent of how I imagined her mother. Her flatness and cut-off quality suggested silence and absence. Moreover, her enactment of her mother's procedure during pogroms represented psychic trauma that had never been absorbed or processed: thus it was an embodied ghost of her mother's past, a transmission of traumatic memory (Coles, 2011; O'Loughlin, 2010).

The hypothesis of Ruth as a recipient of trauma is supported by her use of denial, dissociation, and compartmentalization throughout the interview. For example, in describing her childhood, she said: "It was a difficult life; I didn't give it much thought." She said things like "I can't read [my parents'] minds." Of the difficulty of having parents who were always working, she said, "I tucked it away into whatever little compartment 'til it needed to be looked at." Rather than depending on others emotionally, her style was to keep her own counsel, to make judgments without consulting others.

While Ruth's mother was very private, her father Harry, who was outgoing, loved discussion. When Ruth was growing up, her family spent its entire life in the store, where Harry argued about politics with family and customers alike. A source of pain for Ruth when she was growing up was that all family interactions took place in the store. For example, Harry would sign and publicly comment on Ruth's report card there. Later in life Ruth realized how exposed this had made her feel.

Ruth said that her parents shared the goal of wanting to make a living so that they could send their three children to college. Indeed, they did so, which speaks to their determination and capacity for hard work. Yet for Ruth growing up with parents constantly working in the store had taken its toll. Furthermore, Ruth had absorbed her mother's terror of pogroms, as well as the effects of her mother's deprivation. She may have also been scarred by her knowledge of her father's brutal treatment during World War I. Her mother's shut-off quality and Ruth's cut-off remoteness suggest the silence and absence characteristic of traumatized families. Ruth's enactment of her mother's history with pogroms represents the intergenerational transmission of traumatic memory (O'Loughlin, 2010). This psychic trauma, because of its unresolved nature, might have been passed on to future generations.

Frances's and Ruth's family narratives were quite distinct, and their mothers, in particular, had different trajectories. While Anna missed the Old Country, Devorah, in contrast, was happy to leave her life in Eastern Europe behind and was perhaps typical of those immigrants who felt that there was nothing to miss about their previous lives. Also differentiating the two mothers was that Devorah joined extended family in New York.

The narratives of Frances and Ruth allow us to think about the effects of the parents' hardships on their children. Frances and Ruth seemed to have been very much influenced by their mothers' difficulties, perhaps more so than other immigrants' children. However, the two mothers affected their daughters in different ways. Frances's mother experienced a rupture with her previous life which was traumatic for her, and her losses and unhappiness affected her ability to nurture Frances. Ruth's story provides a more clear-cut example of the intergenerational transmission of trauma. The trauma associated with Ruth's mother's extreme fear and hardship were transmitted to and deeply affected her. Moreover, the unsymbolized, unresolved quality of the psychic trauma she carried suggested the possibility that it might be passed on to future generations.

CONCLUSION: MEMORY, TRAUMA, AND THE AMBIGUITY OF LOSS

Although as a young person I had received a good Hebrew School education, no one had ever taught me about the full extent of the traumatic discrimination, persecution, and poverty which were widespread for the prewar immigrant generation. In conducting this research, I learned about how these had affected my grandparents' generation and, by implication, also my parents' generation. As I began the interview process, I realized my paradoxical relationship to what I was being told: I was at the same time personally connected to it, but also two generations removed from the actual experience of immigration. I hoped that this distance would give me the perspective necessary to explore and understand something about both the immigrants' experiences and those of their children (Pisano, 2012; Bar-On & Gilad, 1994).

In writing this chapter, I have attempted to understand the immigrants' psychological lives through the lens of their children's narratives. Ultimately, however, I only know what the children themselves told me. Had I been able to interview the immigrants themselves, it is likely that most would have expressed more nuanced points of view about the past than did their children. Moreover, I believe that I would have been told more about missing the Old Country. Immigrants' experiences of uprootedness were complex, and homesickness was common (Ewen, 1985; Howe, 1976; Matt, 2011; Menes, 1972/1970; Weinberg, 1988). Although I don't doubt that many immigrants felt that they were glad to be "done with" Eastern Europe, at the same time I believe that much information and much of the complexity of their emotions were lost. This occurred either in the transmission of immigrants' stories to their children or in their children's interpretations of them.

What impeded the transmission of immigrants' memories to their children? As a broad and perhaps imperfect generalization, those who wanted to leave it all behind tended to be those who had suffered more severe anti-Semitic violence or poverty, and these individuals spoke less about the past. Those who intensely missed the Old Country, and thus suffered from migration-related trauma, tended to speak more about their memories. This is true, for example, of individuals who emigrated to America alone, leaving their families in Eastern Europe. Men, in general, were more reluctant to speak about their memories, while women more often talked about them.

Trauma, either because of persecution and deprivation in Eastern Europe or because of migration, led to two different strategies for talking to children. Some parents spoke repetitively and in detail, flooding and overwhelming their children. Others spoke very little about their pasts. In these cases, often parents' silence represented an attempt to protect their children from memories that were too raw. Yet whether this was a conscious strategy or not, silence might have had the opposite effect. A parent's silence might well have communicated his or her trauma wordlessly.

Many parents were reticent about their pasts, impeding the transmission of memories to children, and trauma was only one reason for that reticence. For example, many of the men worked extremely long hours and tended not to speak about feelings. Consequently, they had difficulty communicating with their children about themselves and their experiences.[17] Both men and women may have felt that they had come to America to start anew, so why would they dwell on the past? Overall, the immigrants needed to pick themselves up and move on. They were too busy working to survive to talk about the past.

When immigrants' children said that their parents wanted to leave it all behind, we have lost much of the complexity of their feelings about the past. Parents may have missed early experiences of home and family; they may have missed the countryside around their villages; and a few may have missed aspects of traditional ways of life. Parents' reticence influenced what the children knew about them. In addition, the children's own experiences were important in determining what they said to me about their parents.

Often immigrants' children idealized their parents and their parents' experiences. For example, Benjamin, a rational, even-toned, and outwardly successful man, never said one negative thing about his mother. He felt "devotion, obligation, and thanks" toward both his parents. I suspect that both his gratitude and his inability to be negative were associated with his feeling that his parents had sacrificed so that he could succeed.

The economic, or class, differences between the children—most of whom had become middle- or upper-middle class—and their parents, most of whom had struggled so hard, were significant. These parents had indeed striven and sacrificed so that their children and grandchildren could have better lives. If the children said "my parents left it all behind," perhaps one aspect of doing so was to deny that their parents had missed anything or had left anything valuable in emigrating from the Old Country. Children may not have wanted to think about their parents' sacrifices or their own guilt in having better lives than their parents.

Parents' psychological losses were often massive. One mother's family had struggled economically for many years and she was, as a consequence, sometimes separated from her husband. When, in middle age, her economic difficulties finally eased, and she was looking forward to spending more time with her husband, he died and she had to go out to work for the first time. In her interview her daughter repeatedly denied and minimized the difficulty of her mother's life. Her daughter seemed to want to see it as better than it was. As a member of the middle class, her daughter had come so far, and she may not have wanted to think about her mother's sacrifices.[18]

Therefore, the need to psychologically manage the reality of parents' losses or traumatic histories colored the way their children experienced and described them. Often the children tended to minimize the complexity of their parents' experiences and the ambiguity of their losses. In many cases, "they left it all behind" may have been the children's own interpretation, a defense which helped them to avoid thinking or knowing too much about their parents' traumatic histories or the losses of migration.

What were the intergenerational effects of traumatic persecution and loss among those I interviewed? For both Frances and Ruth, discussed above, during their childhoods their mothers' trauma resulted in damaging difficulties with empathic attunement (Pisano, 2012). Frances's mother had been wrenched from a middle-class life in Europe and, in part due to her psychological predispostion, never recovered. She seemed to feel no compunction about expressing her disappointment in Frances and Frances's appearance. Thus Frances was profoundly affected by a mother who had suffered a traumatic migration experience. On the other hand, Ruth's mother lived through pogroms and deprivation in Eastern Europe. In fact, Ruth enacted during the interview her mother's procedure for saving her younger sister during pogroms. Because the terror of pogroms could not be processed or resolved, it was passed on through the generations undigested (O'Loughlin, 2010). The implications of Ruth's mother's trauma were indeed severe.

The immigrants' experiences varied widely, and, consequently, intergenerational effects took various forms. One mother seemingly suffered a discrete trauma, which she never fully described, in Eastern Europe. In part as a result, her son, a highly successful professional, experienced periodic depressions as an adult. Less severely affected was Elaine, whose mother repetitively spoke about the family she had lost in emigrating. Despite her mother's trauma, and in part because she was securely attached (Main et al., 1985), Elaine was psychologically resilient.

In my own family, privation and war were traumatic for my mother's mother; for my father's parents, close calls with anti-Semitic violence and the effects of having lost many family members in the Holocaust were potent influences. Indeed the trauma experienced by my grandparents deeply influenced my parents. I can sum up the intergenerational effects of trauma on those I interviewed as follows. Among those I interviewed, parents' unspeakable horror affected only a few, but these few seemed scarred by their parents' trauma. Parents' traumatic losses or long-lasting homesickness negatively shaped the lives of several others. The largest category were those who knew something about their parents' traumatic experiences and as a result felt some effects. However, because of their own and their parents' resilience, they went on to have highly successful lives.

Many of the immigrants' children said that their parents lost little in leaving the Old Country. Yet underneath this assertion is the knowledge that immigration of necessity involves a complex web of gains and losses. Consequently, one of the difficult and painful psychological realities that immigrants' children must have experienced was the ambiguity of their parents' losses. Some immigrants felt the pain of leaving their families, but had to do so for survival. Others missed the countryside, where they had light and air, but hated the persecution of life in Eastern Europe. The economic realities of life in Eastern Europe were such that, even in the absence of dangerous anti-Semitism, most of the immigrants felt that they had to leave their homes. For example, one mother mourned her middle-class life in Eastern Europe, but there was little future for her in the Old Country; her losses were essential in order for her to build a new life for herself and her family in America. Although immigrants suffered enormous losses in leaving everything familiar, their children and grandchildren flourished as a result.

This concept of necessary loss reminds me of a memory my grandfather related to my father. As my grandfather was departing from his very poor Galician village, thinking that he would never again see his parents or his remaining siblings, *his* father accompanied him for part of the journey. His father said, "If you remain here, you will not be a human being."[19] My great-grandfather meant that emigration was a necessity because in Galicia there was no way for my grandfather to make a living. Without that, my grandfather would be, in effect, less than human. Thus my grandfather's loss of his family, and his father's loss of a son, was necessary for economic survival. Indeed, though no one knew it at the time, this loss was necessary for my grandfather's physical survival. Those family members who remained were killed in the Holocaust. Thus this loss was profoundly ambiguous for the family.

In many cases, "they left it all behind" is the children's interpretation, a result of their need to manage feelings about their parents' losses in the face of their own successes. Because of their parents' immigration, the children gained prosperity, as well as integration into American society. The immigrant experience is part of the history of many Americans, Jews, and non-Jews alike. I hope that this exploration of the psychology of the immigrant experience can help all of us who are descendants of immigrants to more fully understand something about ourselves.

NOTES

1. I would like to thank William C. Tucker, Eva Fogelman, and Joyce Slochower for their invaluable help, as well as Sydney Stahl Weinberg for the inspiration provided by her book, *The World of Our Mothers* (1988). In addition, I am indebted to the members of my writing group, who provided extremely helpful feedback and suggestions.

2. Although this wave of immigration, which began in 1880, formally ended with the restrictive Immigration Act of 1924, a few immigrants belonging to this group arrived after 1924, particularly if close family members were already in the United States.

3. The five- to six-hour interviews, completed in two sittings, gathered information on the experiential and emotional landscape of the parents' pre- and post-immigration lives, emphasizing the period after immigration. For example, immigrants' feelings about being uprooted, their memories of life in Europe, and the process of becoming American were explored. The interviews also investigated how the immigrants' children believed that their own lives were influenced by their parents' immigration.

4. In the interviews conducted subsequent to these fifteen, the gender imbalance between the subjects discussed in this chapter was rectified.

5. Between 1899 and 1914, 71.7 percent of Jews who came to the United States were from Russia, 16.2 percent were from Austria-Hungary, and 4.2 percent were from Romania (Schmelz & DellaPergola, 2007). Because the Romanian Jews composed a smaller percentage of those who emigrated to the United States, I have not discussed separately their reasons for emigration. However, political oppression of Jews was severe in Romania (Berman, 1980).

6. Examples are the early chapters of *Life Is with People* (Zborowski & Herzog, 1952) and the novel *The River Midnight* (Nattel, 1999).

7. Names of all interviewees have been changed in order to protect their identities.

8. Two fathers did not look back on their pasts in Europe, but they had a milder point of view than the bitterness and hate of the accounts of those who reportedly left it all behind: consequently, they represent a variation on this theme. Interestingly, neither father was fleeing pogroms or the possibility of conscription (the latter was a common reason that men emigrated). Thus these fathers left by choice rather than necessity. Both had very Orthodox fathers and wanted alternatives to the strict, "narrow," traditional Orthodox way of life.

9. The idea of the ambiguity of loss was suggested by Lin Robinson (personal communication, January 19, 2012).

10. My choice of interview subjects was, in fact, skewed against those whose families told their children nothing about the past. Because—in order for me to understand the psychology of the immigrant experience—parents had to have communicated something about it to their children, my choice of interviewees included fewer subjects who stated that their parents had said very little about their pasts (I used some subjects whose parents had said little but had interesting experiences as children of immigrants).

11. The reasons for gender differences—both in that mothers were the ones who conveyed loss and in that daughters were the recipients of their memories—is beyond the scope of this paper. Many fathers spoke little about their own experiences (the old joke is that the Jewish father "didn't have a speaking role"), and some died before their daughters reached maturity. Daughters may have been more receptive to their mothers' emotional experiences than sons, and mothers may have used their daughters, rather than sons, as confidants.

12. Communication and travel between Europe and the United States were cut off by World War I.

13. This was a common complaint for immigrants living on the Lower East Side. Often immigrants came from small towns or villages in Eastern Europe in which, in comparison to the tenements of New York City, they had more space, light, and air.

14. One of these daughters and her mother are discussed in detail below.

15. These two interviews were completed after the fifteen discussed in this chapter. The three children's accounts mentioned in this paragraph will be detailed in future publications.

16. In Eastern European Jewish society, social status, or social class, was an important issue. Religious scholarship was the most important marker of social status.

Money was important, but secondary to religious knowledge in determining social status, or *yikhes*. The classes did not mix, and *yikhes* was traditionally very important in choosing a marriage partner (Weinberg, 1988).

17. A number of the fathers of those I interviewed died when their children were young and thus had little opportunity to talk about memories to their children.

18. One additional reason that Jewish immigrants' children tended to say that their parents left it all behind was the push toward Americanization, which was indeed more pronounced than in other immigrant groups. Jewish immigrants "learned English and became citizens more quickly" than did other immigrant groups (Shapiro, 2008, p. xiii). Because both parents and children tended to want to be Americans—even when parents had complex feelings about having been uprooted—children may have been biased toward saying that they had left it all behind.

19. The actual words his father said were: "Si fun dir nisht machen ah Leute." This appears to be an eastern dialect of German, rather than Yiddish. This comment, to the extent that it foreshadowed the catastrophe to come, was more prophetic than my great-grandfather may have realized.

REFERENCES

Akhtar, S. (2011). *Immigration and acculturation: Mourning, adaptation, and the next generation*. Lanham, MD: Jason Aronson.

Bar-On, D., & Gilad, N. (1994). To rebuild life: A narrative analysis of three generations of an Israeli Holocaust survivor's family. In R. E. Josselson & A. Lieblich (Eds.), *The narrative study of lives: Vol. 2* (pp. 83–112). Newbury Park, CA: Sage.

Berman, M. (1980). *The attitude of American Jewry towards East European Jewish immigration, 1881–1914*. New York: Arno.

Coles, P. (2011). *The uninvited guest from the unremembered past: An exploration of the unconscious transmission of trauma across the generations*. London: Karnac.

Dawidowicz, L. S. (1984). *On equal terms: Jews in America, 1881–1981*. New York: Holt, Rinehart & Winston.

Epstein, L. J. (2007). *At the edge of a dream: The story of Jewish immigrants on New York's Lower East Side, 1880–1920*. New York: Jossey-Bass.

Ewen, E. (1985). *Immigrant women in the land of dollars: Life and culture on the Lower East Side*. New York: Monthly Review Press.

Grinberg, L., & Grinberg, R. (1989). *Psychoanalytic perspectives on migration and exile*. New Haven, CT: Yale University Press.

Hoffman, E. (1999). The new nomads. In A. Aciman (Ed.), *Letters of transit: Reflections on exile, identity, language, and loss* (pp. 35–63). New York: The New Press.

Howe, I. (1976). *World of our fathers: The journey of the East European Jews to America and the life they found and made*. New York: Harcourt Brace Jovanovich.

Kaplan, L. (1996). *No voice is ever wholly lost: An exploration of the everlasting attachment between parent and child*. New York: Simon & Schuster.

Katz, S., & Gelber, N. M. (2007). Galicia. In M. Berenbaum & F. Skolnik (Eds.), *Encyclopedia Judaica: Vol. 7* (pp. 341–45). Detroit, MI: Macmillan Reference USA.

Laub, D. (1992). Bearing witness or the vicissitudes of listening. In S. Felman & D. Laub (Eds.), *Testimony: Crises of witnessing in literature, psychoanalysis, and history* (pp. 57–74). New York: Routledge.

Lieblich, A. (1993). Looking at change: Natasha, 21—New immigrant from Russia to Israel. In R. E. Josselson & A. Lieblich (Eds.), *The narrative study of lives: Vol. 1* (pp. 92–129). Newbury Park, CA: Sage.

Main, M., Kaplan, N., & Cassidy, J. (1985). Security in infancy, childhood, and adulthood: A move to the level of representation. In I. Bretherton & E. Waters (Eds.), *Growing points of attachment theory and research. Monographs of the Society for Research in Child Development 50*(1–2), no. 209.

Matt, S. J. (2011). *Homesickness: An American history*. Oxford: Oxford University Press.

Menes, A. (1972). The East Side and the Jewish labor movement. In I. Howe & E. Greenberg (Eds. and Trans.), *Voices from the Yiddish: Essays, memoirs, diaries* (pp. 202–18). Ann Arbor: University of Michigan Press. (Original work published 1970).

Nattel, L. (1999). *The river midnight*. New York: Scribner.

O'Loughlin, M. (2010). Ghostly presences in children's lives: Toward a psychoanalysis of the social. In M. O'Loughlin & R. Johnson (Eds.), *Imagining children otherwise: Theoretical and critical perspectives on childhood subjectivity* (pp. 49–74). New York: Peter Lang Publishing.

Pisano, N. G. (2012). *Granddaughters of the Holocaust: Never forgetting what they didn't experience*. Boston: Academic Studies Press.

Schmelz, U. E., & DellaPergola, S. (2007). Migrations. In M. Berenbaum & F. Skolnik (Eds.), *Encyclopedia Judaica: Vol. 14* (pp. 207–19). Detroit: Macmillan Reference USA.

Shapiro, E. S. (2008). Introduction. In E. S. Shapiro (Ed.), *Yiddish in America: Essays on Yiddish culture in the golden land* (pp. ix–xix). Scranton, PA: University of Scranton Press.

Weinberg, S. S. (1988). *The world of our mothers: The lives of Jewish immigrant women*. Chapel Hill, NC: University of North Carolina Press.

Zborowski, M., & Herzog, E. (1952). *Life is with people: The culture of the shtetl*. New York: International Universities Press.

Part III

HISTORICAL REMNANTS

Chapter 10

The Silence of the Grandchildren of the Civil War

Transgenerational Trauma in Spain

Clara Valverde and Luis Martín-Cabrera

INTRODUCTION

In the 1960s Manuel Fraga Iribarne, Franco's Minister of Tourism and Information, a position responsible both for the promotion of tourism and for controlling censorship and the media, coined the famous sentence, "Spain is different." The slogan was supposedly a way of attracting more European tourists to Spain. As such, it was both the justification of something unjustifiable—the persistence of a fascist dictatorship at the shores of Europe—and the production of Spain as backward and exotic. Thus, nothing is further from our intention than reproducing Fraga's infamous slogan. But, as Scott Boehm has argued, on human rights issues, Spain is, indeed, different.[1]

Unlike other countries in the world that went through similar social traumas, such as Chile, Argentina, El Salvador, or South Africa to name a few, in Spain there are no truth commissions, no trials for perpetrators of human rights abuses, and very little state-sponsored memorial sites or reparatory justice measures of any kind. As we will explain below in detail, the structure of power established during the forty years of the dictatorship (1939–1975) has remained intact. For instance, in Spain, the state has abdicated its responsibility to exhume the bodies of those who were executed during the war and its aftermath. Rather than assuming its responsibility, the Spanish state and the judicial power have passed this crucial task to the relatives of the victims and the civic associations that support them. This is, as far as we know, a unique situation in the world.

Yet, over the past two decades, a good number of studies dealing with the Spanish Civil War and the dictatorship have been published.[2] Some of these studies focus on the war and the repression as a sociohistorical trauma.

However, none of them deal with the transmission of trauma in the generations who did not live through the experience of the war and the repression. In part, this is the case precisely because we, the grandchildren of the Spanish Civil War, have been busy dignifying the memory of our grandparents, understanding the traumatic legacies of the war and helping with the exhumation of mass graves and other reparatory measures. But this is also clearly a symptom. The obsessive preoccupation or the unconscious identification with a relative who was executed or tortured is grounded in strong ethical principles, but it also points to the transgenerational transmission of trauma. Although the grandchildren have produced an important number of studies and literature about the suffering and the struggles of their grandparents, there is very little self-reflection of this dimension in the multidisciplinary work that has been published in Spain and about Spain so far.

Accordingly, the purpose of this chapter is to investigate the cause without origin, the wound without language: the effects of the transmission of trauma on the generation of the grandchildren of the war. In order to do so, we have divided the chapter in three parts. In the first part, we introduce the problematic of the Spanish Civil War as a sociohistoric trauma and its effects in the different generations. The second part is an in-depth analysis of symptoms and effects of unprocessed trauma in the third generation. This part is based on the interviews collected by Clara Valverde and the *Equipo Aquo.*[3] Finally, the last part is an attempt to see the *indignado movement*[4] and its forms of organization as a first attempt to break with the "acting out" and the unconscious transmission. If war traumas break the social link, as Davoine and Gaudillière argue,[5] the 15M movement or "indignados" may be a first attempt to reestablish the broken dimension of time and space that the coup, the war, the dictatorship, and the transition to democracy have kept broken and kept outside of symbolization.

FROM THE UNSPEAKABLE TO THE UNTHINKABLE: THREE GENERATIONS OF PEOPLE WITHOUT MEMORY

On April 14, 1931, after years of debates and struggles, the Second Spanish Republic, the first fully democratic period in Spanish history, came into being by popular demand. After an astonishing victory of Republican[6] parties in the municipal elections of April, the Spanish masses took to the streets to demand the end of the Bourbon Monarchy and the creation of a federal republic that could at last provide a minimum of justice for the centuries-long excluded masses of the Iberian Peninsula. Faced with the collective desire for a new regime, Afonso XXIII, the great-grandfather of the current King, decided to abandon the country, proclaiming that he was going into exile to prevent a "blood bath." What happened after the departure of the King was by all accounts and regardless of one's political beliefs, both shocking and impressive. From 1932 to 1936, the different Republican governments drafted a constitution; they implemented both agrarian and educational reforms; they built more public schools in those four years than in the previous twenty years of the twentieth century; divorce and civil unions were legalized; labor reform paved the way for the massive unionization of industrial workers and peasants; women obtained, for the first time, the right to vote; Church and State were separated, the military power was severely curtailed, historical regions like Catalonia and the Basque country obtained autonomous independence within a federal construction of the nation-state, etc.[7]

All this is not to suggest that the Second Spanish Republic was an idyllic paradise. The successive republican governments made many mistakes and faced very complicated situations, but the point is that the above-mentioned reforms were violently crushed by the military insurrection launched by Francisco Franco and other generals on July 18, 1936. Unable and unwilling to accept the victory of the Popular Front (a progressive coalition that included socialist, communist, and center left parties) in the elections of February 1936, the landowners, the nobility, the anemic industrial bourgeoisie, and a majority of the Catholic Church, decided to support a Fascist military insurrection in an attempt to restore their long history of class privileges.[8] Unlike what happened in the rest of Europe with Hitler and Mussolini, the majority of the Spanish masses—peasants and workers—and wide sectors of the middle-class loyal to the Second Republic, decided to resist the military aggression. As none of the factions was able to impose itself by force, a long, cruel, and protracted Civil War ensued. By 1939, thanks to the support of Nazi Germany and Fascist Italy, who used Spain as a military training ground to prepare for the war in Europe, Franco defeated the last loyalist troops in Valencia.

This is not the place to analyze in detail the many complicated historical dynamics that involved the unfolding and conclusion of the war. To that end, an oceanic bibliography can be consulted. Our intention here is rather to point out from the outset that the term "Spanish Civil War" is in many ways a misnomer that does not allow us to think through the trauma of the war and the ensuing dictatorship. It goes without saying that there was a war front with two armies fighting each other, but the conflict had nothing to do with a fratricidal confrontation. The family, with its Oedipal conflicts, had little to do with a historical event that was rather a bloody outcome of the "class struggle" and its multiple material manifestations (i.e., landownership, access to education). Furthermore, until very recently, the logical emphasis on the theater of war has obscured the fact that behind the war fronts, in the rearguard, Franco's army and the Falange (the Spanish Fascist Militia) were implementing a carefully crafted plan of extermination. As Francisco

Espinosa eloquently argues: "It is about time to clarify that which we call war in numerous provinces of Spain such as Cádiz, Sevilla, Huelva, parts of Córdoba or Badajoz, consisted in eliminating a certain number of people in order to transfer to different hands the political power lost in 1931" (Espinosa, p. 23, our translation).[9]

Of course, there was violence on the loyalist side too, but the Republican government successfully contained this extralegal violence after the first summer of the war, if only because they wanted to gather the support of the European democratic nations—a support that, unfortunately, never materialized. For many years, it was common sense to deny this "genocide" based on the idea that both sides of the conflict were equally responsible for human rights abuses and that therefore the best thing was to forget and forgive in order to move forward. Fortunately, in the past two decades and even before, the important work of historians such as Francisco Espinosa, Paul Preston, Michael Richards, and many others has completely debunked this myth. Not only did Franco's fascist forces kill more people, but it is also clear now that the repression was carefully planned with the intent of exterminating a part of the Spanish *demos*, the supporters of the Spanish Second Republic.[10]

These extermination and genocidal tactics were directly related to Spain's modern colonial project in North Africa. After the loss of Cuba, Puerto Rico, and the Philippines in 1898, Spain tried to reconstruct its empire in the Rift region, in Northern Morocco. Many officials of the fascist army, including General Francisco Franco, participated in a long protracted war of extermination in these territories. As Sebastián Balfour convincingly argued, this experience had a strong impact on these officers. In his own words:

> The so-called army of Africa crossed the Straits of Gibraltar with a mission to destroy the internal enemy and transform a decadent Spain from outside. The self-appointed agents of Spain's purification were those officers who had fought and won a colonial war, and that war inspired their initial strategy and tactics in the Civil War. The Regime installed by Franco also derived its mythological and ideological underpinning from the colonial experience.[11]

This colonial mentality dangerously coalesced around the emergence of European fascism and its biopolitical notion of sovereignty. In modern European thought, sovereignty is inextricably linked with sovereign decisions over life (biopolitics) and death (necropolitics); the right to kill and the right to live are always intertwined and projected over the horizon of modern political sovereignty. Traditionally—in the works of Michel Foucault or Giorgio Agamben, for instance—the crossing of biopolitical thresholds, where certain lives become irrelevant and can be killed without committing a crime, has been equated with a historical trajectory that culminates in Auschwitz as the supreme incarnation of biopower. Achille Mbembe, however, has argued that European modern sovereignty cannot be thought of without slavery and colonialism as their constitutive framework. In his own words:

> Having become mechanized, serialized execution was transformed into purely technical, impersonal, silent and rapid procedure. This development was aided in part by racist stereotypes and the flourishing of a class-based racism that, in translating the social conflicts of the industrial world in racial terms, ended up comparing the working classes and "stateless people" of the industrial world to the "savages" of the colonial world.[12]

In this respect, linking modern sovereignty and colonial rule is essential to understand the nature of repression in Spain during the war and the dictatorship. The war as a production of death was a combination of colonial violence and fascist terror whose aim was an internal enemy that had to be exterminated in order to purify the "malignant tumors" that threatened Spain as a living organism. To that end, the dictatorship both during the war and its aftermath, in war zones and in the rearward, in times of peace and in times of war, displayed a complex array of repressive tactics in order to consolidate Franco's power over life and death as the new sovereign of the nation-state. The production of death included, but was not limited to, the following repressive and exterminating tactics:

- Arbitrary detentions and executions of political enemies.
- Disappearance of the remains of those executed in unmarked mass graves.
- Forced labor of political prisoners in camps. Among other things, political prisoners built Franco's mausoleum in the "Valley of the Fallen" in Madrid or "El Canal de los Presos" in Andalucia.
- Censorship of any public account that could point out to the perpetration of genocidal violence.
- Abduction of babies and reassignment of these babies to supporters of the regime.
- "Reeducation" camps and orphanages such as the "Hogares de Auxilio Social."
- Torture and denial of basic legal procedures (the practice of torture did not even disappear with the advent of democracy).
- Repression of cultural difference such as national languages and cultures (Catalan, Euskera, Gallego) other than Spanish and Castilian culture.
- The production of "social death" ("muerte civil"). The survivors of these tactics of extermination and their relatives were condemned to social non-existence; they were actively prevented from working in public and private jobs, they could not attend to college nor university, and they did not have access to social welfare programs, among other things.

The bulk of the political executions and political disappearances occurred between 1936, the beginning of the war, and 1945, but terror and repression extended until a couple of years after the end of the dictatorship, in 1975. In this regard, Michael Richards writes:

> While violent deaths in Republican Spain could usually be recorded and collated and the victims commemorated, those killed by the Nationalist forces or by the subsequent Franco regime were often not recorded and could not be publicly remembered during the post-war era. As in other civil war cases, the state granted an exclusive right to patriotic sentiments, public self-justification, a sense of community and of sacrifice, to the victors, not only in the 1940s but throughout its lifetime until the early 1970s. Republican war sacrifices and personal losses in its cause were denied expression, representation and public ritualization: this essentially represented a continuation of the war through symbolic violence.[13]

For our purposes here, this means that neither those Republicans who lived through the war nor their children (the second generation) could elaborate or symbolize the massive trauma of death, torture, incarceration, and disappearance that defined their existence from the beginning of the war onwards. This first generation, according to Abraham and Torok, would be the "unspeakable" generation.[14] What they experienced was so overwhelming that it defies words and the mind's previous ability to elaborate events. Those of the "unspeakable" generation (at that time the population of Spain was twenty-six million) were not able to put words on all the horror that they witnessed. Also they were not able to deal with the extreme feelings that the situation provoked: fear, anger, guilt, sadness, and insecurity. In sum, this "unspeakable first generation" of Republicans could barely survive the lethal violence and repression of the colonial/fascist war machine led by Franco.

The second generation that, following Abraham and Torok's theory, we have termed the "unnamable," continued to live with more or less intensity under the same sovereign power of the dictatorship and, therefore, it could not make sense of the traumatic past either. How can one elaborate a traumatic event if the very same violence, repression, and death that caused the primary trauma continues to repeat itself in the present? This traumatic process added to their inherited inability to construct a verbal representation of what was happening to them and what had happened to their parents. The transgenerational traumas and the repetition of violence and repression kept them from being able to carry out much-needed grieving processes.

The second generation did not dare to ask their own parents what they had lived through during the Civil War. They could see, through their parents' behaviors that their elders had lived through something horrible and were emotionally wounded. Accordingly, these children tried to parent their own parents and tried to cheer them up. They wanted to know what happened to their parents but at the same time they did not want to know because they were afraid of the upsetting information that they might receive.[15] The verbal and nonverbal message in Spanish homes was "don't ask questions," which is so common in families with traumatized parents in other cultures.[16] It also became common sense—that is to say dominant ideology in Gramscian terms—to hear parents of the war generation telling their children "no te signifiques." "Significar" in Spanish means "to produce meaning, language," and hence the categorical imperative to survive was to be "meaningless and insignificant," to lack language, specifically political language.

It goes without saying that not everybody obeyed this categorical imperative. Many of the survivors of the war and their children continued to fight against the dictatorship both inside and outside Spain, but struggling against oppression is not the same as processing or elaborating massive trauma. Precisely because both of these generations of survivors were too afraid or too busy fighting the perpetuation of the same sovereign power incarnated by Franco, they did not have any space, particularly public space, to come to terms with the grief and the pain caused by the excess of death that colonial/fascist sovereignty produced. As a result, both of these generations seemed to be condemned to a subjectless experience of trauma, without words and meanings transmission could only be unconscious and in the form of repetitions, acting out, psychosomatic episodes, and other symptoms of unprocessed trauma.

Unfortunately, with the death of Franco and the advent of democracy this situation did not substantially change. General Francisco Franco passed away peacefully in his own bed November 20, 1975. The fact that he died "undefeated," determined, to a large extend, the outcome of the so-called transition to democracy in Spain. The transition was in fact an elite pact whose main purpose was the perpetuation of the same political and economic model established by the Francoist dictatorship. But politics and economics were not the only things that were perpetuated with this transmission of powers. The impossibility of processing trauma was also perpetuated and established as normal or even desirable.

The amnesty law of 1977 explicitly prohibited the opening of legal prosecution against those responsible for human rights violations and crimes against humanity. As a result of this law and the pacts of the transition period, Spain became a realm of impunity and oblivion. Unlike what happened in many other countries (Argentina, Chile, South Africa, Guatemala, etc.) that went through similar experiences of violence and genocide, the Spanish state did not implement any reparatory policies. Perpetrators of human rights abuses were never tried, no truth commissions were formed, and no public policies of memory were instituted (i.e., museums, memorial parks, educational and other cultural projects). Furthermore this lack of public policies of memory and transitional justice was systematically praised from the state structures as the real reason for Spain's economic success, especially before the most recent economic crisis of 2008. Furthermore, forgetting and forgiving were exported to Latin American countries such as Argentina and Chile that were beginning a transition to democracy as the recipe for economic success within the new neoliberal order.[17]

However, as Davoine and Gaudillère have explained, a historical trauma implies the destruction of social links and markers of time and space which collapse in the face of massive violence. In a social trauma the Real in a Lacanian sense invades reality and renders any notion of normalcy inoperative: here and there, past, present, and future are conflated in the black hole of massive death. As we have explained above, without any public recognition of these gruesome atrocities, trauma cannot find symbolization and therefore the social link remains broken.

This situation was partially reversed around the year 2000 with the creation of a robust social movement that came together around the exhumation of mass graves of those Republicans executed during the Spanish Civil War and the Francoist dictatorship. The Association for the Recuperation of Historical Memory (ARMH) and the *Foro por la Memoria* are the two largest civic associations at the state level working on the exhumation of mass graves and the recuperation of historical memory, but there are many other smaller associations that work on the same issues at the regional and local levels. The main role of these associations has been to create a safe space around the exhumations of mass graves to recuperate the political and affective memory of those who were executed during the war and its aftermath. The heroic work of the associations has forced the state to implement some timid reforms in order to address the return of the specters of the past. The most notable of these initiatives is the so-called Law of Historical Memory, approved in 2007 during the government of José Luis Rodríguez Zapatero. Although the law is the first explicit recognition of this traumatic past on the part of the state, it is also, in many ways, a law that perpetuates impunity and oblivion in Spain. In fact, the law was almost immediately succeeded by the criminalization and expulsion of Judge Garzón from the Audiencia Nacional (the Spanish Superior Tribunal) for opening legal proceedings against those responsible for human rights violations during the war and the dictatorship. This obviously proves that Spain continues to live under the same conception of sovereignty imposed by the colonial/fascist matrix that came out of the war.[18] As long as Franco continues to be buried in his crypt/concentration camp of the Valley of the Fallen, the "law of the father" continues to operate; the right to decide over life and death continues to be the prerogative of this father/sovereign who remains the fundament of the law also in the current democratic order.

In their documents and public addresses, both of the ARMH and the Foro por la Memoria denounce the multiple ways in which the state continues to leave the victims of colonial/fascist violence in a situation of legal abandonment passing the burden of the exhumations and reparations to the families and the civic association. Although both of them agree on that, they tend to disagree in the emphasis they put on the different aspects of the process of reparation and justice. While the ARMH tends to emphasize the recuperation of affect and the possibility of suturing the work of mourning within a global human rights framework, the Foro por la Memoria underscores the political affiliations of the militants that were executed and disappeared during the war and the dictatorship as a necessity to reconstitute radical politics and a better future. The politics and the praxis of both groups are oriented toward the recuperation of the bodies and memories of the generation of the grandfathers (the "unspeakable generation"). Yet, this dialogue between grandparents and grandchildren is one-dimensional. There is no self-reflection in any of these organizations—or in the countless organizations that work toward the recuperation of historical memory. The desire of the grandchildren is invested in repairing what happened to the grandparents, but there is no reflection whatsoever on the effects that unprocessed trauma and structural impunity may have had on them as inheritors of an unspeakable catastrophe.

Following Abraham and Torok's theory, we call this generation of the grandchildren the "unthinkable" generation because they are unable to imagine or put into words what happened to their grandparents and parents. Seventy-five years have passed since the original traumatic process occurred, so there is little connection with the actual facts. But this is not the main impediment for their generation. The main problem is having inherited the unconscious material of two generations. The intense silence and empty words of the grandparents' and parents' generations have resulted in dysfunctional behaviors, symptoms, and manifestations which are seen as "normal" and "cultural."[19] Accordingly, in the following pages we will show examples of ways in which this traumatic past has been transmitted to this "unthinkable generation," the multiple manifestations and the effects that they have in Spanish society and in politics, especially transformational politics.

THE CHILDREN ARE NOT ALL RIGHT: TRANSMISSION AND THE UNKNOWN ELEMENT

More than seventy-five years after the coup d'état which started the Spanish Civil War in 1936, one can walk along the sunny and pleasant streets of any Spanish city or town and be taken by the lively and noisy conversations that fill the outdoor cafes and bars at all hours. But, what are Spaniards talking about? We have observed over the past twenty years that apart from the ever-present topic of soccer, many conversations appear to be about power relations, complaining about power, about abuses of power by politicians, bosses, husbands, etc. "The Monologue," as Doris Lessing would call it, goes along the lines of: "When he told me that, I would have told him. . . ." and "It made me so angry that I would have told him. . . . ," "I would have told him," "I would have."[20] Yet, even in the second decade of the twenty-first century, there is a good chance that the person verbalizing The Monologue will not communicate his or her concerns and complaints to the person being talked about. Instead of "speaking to power," the grandchildren of the Spanish Civil War speak *about* power, which is a form of silence. This noisy silence is one of the many signs of frozen grieving processes.

At a recent mental health congress, Jornadas de Salud Mental del Norte, one of us, Clara Valverde, presented a paper on the Spanish transgenerational transmission of the political violence of the twentieth century to psychoanalysts, psychologists, and psychiatrists.[21] This was one of the first times this topic had been presented in Spain. Some of the comments from the audience after the presentation were: "I have never heard of anything like this," "We do not have this problem here, but they do have it in Kosovo," "Our grandparents were affected by all this but we are not," "You are exaggerating" and "With all the problems we have right now with the austerity measures and you talk about this? You are creating problems where there aren't any." The above comments demonstrated the deeply internalized denial that still exists in Spain about the impact of its recent history.

Far from being banal incidences, all of these comments and daily observations point to an urgent need in Spain. As a society we must investigate the individual and collective impact of the transgenerational transmission of the state-sponsored violence of the twentieth century on the third generation.[22] In the last few years, the Equipo Aquo has been holding workshops on transgenerational transmission arising from the violence in Spain in the twentieth century, in various Spanish cities, for the grandchildren of the Spanish Civil War. Also this team has carried out interviews and distributed questionnaires. The material gathered, including observations and quotes, with the participants' permission, are included in this section.[23]

When these workshops, aimed at the grandchildren of the Spanish Civil War, were announced, the reactions and comments by possible participants tended to be that they do not suffer any negative effects of the Civil War and they emphatically stated that to suggest this was the same as giving another victory to Franco. This is not unique to Spain. Descendents of other political traumas have also feared that to demonstrate the long-term and transgenerational negative impact was tantamount to giving a posthumous victory to the perpetrators.[24] Those few who actually participated in the workshops, although they were not asked to do so, insisted on identifying themselves as grandchildren of Republicans. The facilitators explained that the workshops were on the unconscious impact of the political violence of twentieth-century Spain and so they were open to all participants of the grandchildren's generation, no matter what political affiliation the grandparents had or did not have. Yet the facilitators observed that grandchildren of those who fought on Franco's side (willingly or by force) or from families that, like so many in Spain were divided with members on both sides of the war, with rare exceptions, did not wanted to participate in the workshops but agreed to speak to us in private. CVG, a fifty-seven-year-old woman shared this at a workshop:

> When I was little, I asked my mother why her family home was divided into two with what looked like a brand new brick wall. It was not so much her answer that I did not believe ("the wall has always been there") which altered me. It was her tone of voice full of doubt and anguish and her evasive look, very different from her usual assertive tone. Later on I learned that during the Civil War, one of her uncles was killed by the Republicans and another one by Franco's troops.

In the workshops themselves, of all the feelings, symptoms, and manifestations that were talked about, the one that was totally rejected by participants was guilt. When the topic of guilt—survivor guilt, bystander guilt, or any other type—was brought up by the facilitators, it was rejected and the topic was constantly ignored by the participants. Similar reactions were observed when the words "reconciliation" or "forgiveness" were presented. The highly charged reactions to these concepts included comments about the fact that it would be an act of "treason" toward one's ancestors to in any way consider dialogue with the grandchildren of the grandparents' "enemies," some of whom are in the government right now. Guilt was considered irrelevant by the participants who saw their grandparents only as "victims."

One would think that having unconsciously inherited two generation's frozen grief, sadness would be an important issue to address for the grandchildren of the Civil War. Yet this emotion, as was observed in these workshops, tends to be denied in Spain. There is the cultural belief that sadness is a sign of weakness and that to express it could put one in danger, a nonspecific fear but one that all agree is there.[25] In addition, those who lost the Civil War and those who opposed Franco's regime lived under the constant threat of repression if they expressed their views and feelings. To grieve over a killed, imprisoned, or exiled family member would call the attention of neighbors and authorities and put one at risk of being part of the opposition and therefore open to possible repression. MML, a forty-eight-year-old female nurse who participated in a workshop told us:

> A patient of mine at the health centre, a very old lady, used to come in once a month to get her blood pressure checked. Every time I asked her how she was, she would start crying about her son's death. I thought that he had died a couple of years before, but one day I found out that he had been killed right after the Civil War . . . about 70 years ago!

These difficulties expressing sadness were and are even more complicated in families in which a member was made to disappear during or after the Civil War. The nonplace and nonstatus of the disappeared, being neither dead nor alive, being waited for by the family and not being buried, and the Spanish government's lack of interest in repairing this issue turns a possible healing expression of sadness into chronic melancholy.[26] The lack of research leaves us wondering if the high levels of antidepressant medication use in Spain might be related to this.[27]

Anger

Anger was a feeling recognized and talked about in these workshops. But the conversation was mostly about being afraid of one's anger and other difficulties with this emotion as IRN, a fifty-five-year-old man expressed:

> My father gets really angry and is violent. But he can't help it. He is very angry about what they did to his father during the war (first they imprisoned him, then they sent him by force to the front lines to fight on Franco's side always being watched and then they murdered him). My father gets out of control very easily. Well, I also have quite a temper and I can't control it either.

This next participant's grandfather, a Republican, was sent to fight on Franco's side, and then he was murdered. All this is very powerful material to fuel transgenerational anger. AML, a fifty-three-year-old male commented:

> Yes, what my grandparents lived during the Civil War has affected my family. It has not taught them how to control their emotions. I have seen totally overwhelming anger. Not naming things and keeping quiet has made communication difficult.

Research in other countries has shown that descendents of wars have important challenges managing anger and "not naming things" is another aspect of not managing.[28] RGM, a forty-two-year-old female, for instance, stated:

> Regarding the fact that my grandfather was killed in the trenches, there has always been a lot of silence, a lot of "having to put up with the circumstances," a lot of forbidden issues, a lot of pain that has not been expressed, a lot of

> repressed anger which would come out the few times this was talked about. Especially my father: he is so full of anger that his father was killed and that we have not yet been able to get his remains back, that other family members are not able to talk with him about it.

As other interviewees state, anger gets in the way of talking, and communicating traumatic events from the past. As AZD, a forty-six-year-old woman points out, "anger gets in my way. It does not help me in any way and it makes creativity difficult." Thus, anger becomes for many members of this third generation an impediment to creativity and growth. What does this do to the grandchildren's generation in a whole country? As SLA, a fifty-nine-year-old male, explains, anger makes time freeze and complicates the possibility of moving forward and let the past be past. In his own words:

> It's become more obvious to me with time that I don't forgive those criminals (my uncle was killed in the war and my grandfather was murdered after) . . . it eats me up. I can't stop thinking about all that, with anger, with pain . . . now more than ever.

As theorists like Abraham and Torok have pointed out, time which is not used to elaborate, name, and grieve, does not heal. It tends to deepen complicated feelings. Seventy-five years have passed since the end of the Civil War, yet this grandson's anger and pain is impacting him now more than ever.

Fear

If one adds up the Civil War, the dictatorship, and the violence of the first few years of postdictatorship, life for almost half of the twentieth century, Spain was full of repression, violence, and terror. Because of this, fear and the silence that fear provokes are still present in Spain today. The grandparents' and parents' fear is carried in the unconscious of the third generation so that it seems like a normal part of daily life in which there are manifestations of fear that are out of proportion with reality.[29] MBJ, a thirty-nine-year-old male affirms:

> My grandfather was executed at the end of the Civil War. My father was in prison during the Dictatorship. And my friends criticize me because I won't go to demonstrations with them. They say I am a chicken. . . . If they knew that what I have is not fear . . . it's panic!

In the same vein FPR, a forty-two-year-old male states:

> The result of what my grandparents and parents lived through is silence, the tension for years and years, and those who won the Civil War were left with the fear of the anger and the possible vengeance of those who lost.

Although FPR, a psychologist, did not participate in a workshop, he informed the Equipo Aquo about his family's feelings of fear through a questionnaire. Having had his family on Franco's side of the war still was a source of fear and he added that the fear of the descendants of those who won the war is not talked about in Spain.

> My father survived his prison time during the war and he almost was executed several times. Afterwards, when he got married, I don't think he talked about it, not even with my mother. He was a distant, quiet and serious man. Very cold. . . . I did not find out about what had happened to him during the war until after his death. An uncle told me. My mother knows something but she does not want to talk about it. She is 83 and is well, with no dementia. But if she knew that I was attending this workshop and talking about this, she would kill me! [LJR, male, forty-four years old]

LJR's father never told him about his dangerous experiences during the war. But still, LJR is afraid, at the age of forty-four, of his mother finding out that he is talking about his family history in a safe space, such as a workshop.

Conversations in Spain are full of expressions which seem to be of little importance, but that reflect fear, such as "I can't," "They won't let me," "Be careful of what you say," "Oh little Virgin Mary, may I stay as I am," "What will others say?" and the formerly mentioned "I would have told him." Mobbing, sexual harassment, and other forms of abuse of power are part of the daily reality in Spain which rarely get reported. But there is an intensity and an impunity in these abuses which some say is a cultural part of being Mediterranean. But could it be the product of a society with a repressive history? Further research will be necessary to determine this, but what is clear to us is that fear and abuses of power appeared intertwined in many testimonies like the following one from AA, a thirty-nine-year-old woman:

> In my daily life I am totally overwhelmed by unjust situations and I have not been able to "show my teeth" when faced with unacceptable behaviors. It always catches me off guard when someone treats me badly. It is as though I can't believe it. Then I realize that I have not valued myself enough nor made others respect me.

But how can you value yourself if your parents and grandparents were mistreated, imprisoned, tortured, killed, or disappeared? As CMB, a fifty-six-year-old male states that this creates a paralyzing effect:

> Yes, what gets in my way is fear of power, a feeling of vulnerability vis-à-vis the State and institutional hierarchies, feeling defenseless, a huge anger and hostility towards the Right, towards Capitalism. . . . These feelings are a psychological load that I always carry, it can be paralyzing.

And how do you take your place in the world if, like this participant's mother, you have learned not to "signify" yourself?

> I think that my mother caught on to the need to be silent and to be afraid of verbalizing what one thinks. This can be very dangerous. Better to not be noticed and to be in good terms with everyone. [MIS, female, thirty-eight years old]

These "good terms," when explored in the workshops, did not refer to reconciliation and forgiveness. Not being noticed and keeping silent seemed to be the more common strategy. As MIS noted:

> What really bothers me most of all is when I have to stand up to an authority figure. I feel like I am doing something bad and that I will be punished for it.

Opposing the regime was, for most of the twentieth century, a punishable activity. Is this threat still active in the minds of the grandchildren although it is not a "real" threat? "Fear has kept me from living freely and from being myself" noted MNL, a sixty-year-old female.

Many people in Spain do not realize the role of fear in their everyday life. This lack of conscious knowledge puts them at risk of retraumatization. In a workshop on transgenerational trauma, a participant told an anecdote about a woman in his town. One night she heard people yelling outside her window. She opened up the window and saw hundreds of people shouting while carrying flags. She went into a state of panic that lasted for a few days while she kept repeating, almost in a trance: "Something is going to happen, something is going to happen." In reality those shouting in the streets were celebrating the victory of their soccer team.

Experts in generational transmission of political violence point out that descendants of wars tend to have high levels of phobias and obsessions.[30] The feeling that "something is going to happen" when there is no apparent danger, is actually what happened several generations ago and it is lodged in the grandchildren's unconscious. As RGM, a forty-two-year-old female explains:

> I express happiness in a very contained manner and with fear of what might happen.

With such a presence of unconscious fear, the necessary activism against the present austerity measures and policies in Spain right now is much weaker than in other Southern European countries. Many Spaniards are waiting for these problems to go away by themselves.

> All the feelings that I think of as negative like fear and shame, I have a hard time expressing them, showing them. It really bothers me that I hide my head in the sand and let time pass to see if the problems will go away. But they don't. [AML, male, fifty-three years old]

Confusion

When fear has not been dealt with, when the grieving has not been done, when losses and feelings have not been put into words by each generation, there is the risk of having general confusion and doubt. Confusion about identity and family structure is one manifestation of this symptom.[31]

> My grandmother would get all mixed up and call my father by my great uncle's name, the one who never came back from the war. And my father often calls me by his own brother's name. He does not realize it and he laughs as though it was a joke, but I don't find it funny. [CFG, male, fifty-eight years old]

Who is dead, who is alive, who is buried, and who is still missing? But the doubts go beyond that. Not having grieved leaves the dead relatives in a confusing place in the family tree.

> My grandfather died when I was six years old. Although I was little, I remember that each Christmas he would start crying and he would stay in bed. It did not seem like Christmas. I asked why he was crying and my mother would say that it was because of "those who are not here. No one explained to me who were those who were "not here" and why they were "not here." I don't know why, but I thought that it had something to do with those ghosts I thought were under my bed at night (although I always checked before going to bed." [NMN, male, forty-one years old]

It is like "phantom pain": the family members who are missing and have not properly grieved, hurt, insist, and create confusing feelings.

> About my grandfather's murder my parents know very little about how it really happened. I learned about it much later, in 2005, when I was fifty years old. [SLA, male, fifty-nine years old]

This is a common story heard in the transgenerational trauma workshops: a fifty-year-old participant has just found out what happened to his grandfather. What images did he have of his grandfather all these years? Was he curious about why he did not know about his grandfather? Did he notice that his parents avoided the subject? Confusion and doubt seem to be a "normalized" part of daily life.

Differentiation

Fear and doubt transmitted through generations, result in grandchildren who are not aware of their inherited mistrust.

> My parents learned from their parents the feeling of mistrust of others in general. [APG, male, fifty-four years old]

Among the grandchildren of victims of political traumas the inherited fears also result in the development of symptoms of differentiation that range from mistrust to the pathological need to have enemies.[32] What our grandparents and parents were not able to elaborate manifests itself in an important need to divide, to create barriers, and to separate "them" from "us." Other symptoms include absolutism (to try to be always right, "because I say so"), abuse of authority (creating divisions by putting one's self above others), the destruction of the capacity for empathy,[33] and playing the victim ("I have suffered more than you" to justify divisions and to carry out vengeance). Polarization is part of everyday social relations in Spain, where instead of trying to find a middle ground, there is a tendency to look for enemies not in those who oppress, but in those in one's own social, family, and political milieu.

> I don't know why, but each time we had a team meeting, instead of looking for a consensus, we ended up badly, totally confrontational. And the funny thing is that we got along well and we had similar ideas politically. But instead of looking for a common ground, we looked for disagreements about things that I now realize were small stuff. I don't know why. I am kind of embarrassed to admit it, but as soon as we walked into the meeting room, we got defensive. We even hired a mediator, but he was not able to help us. The team fell apart. It was sad. [RLN, female, forty-three years old]
>
> In the non-government organization where I worked, the coordinator was really awful. None of us could stand him. Finally the board fired him. At first we were all very happy but after a few days a co-worker said: "But now we don't have a common enemy." [JTR, a forty-two-year-old male]

One dangerous outcome of this manifestation is that those in power use this inherited trust to create divisions in the population and manipulate them for their political agendas. This is of special relevance in the politics of national identities.[34]

Repetition

The tendency to create barriers has the danger of repeating itself. Not having elaborated trangenerational traumas of social and political violence can leave a society vulnerable to repeating past mistakes. The sheer force of the unconscious repression returns especially on significant dates: the anniversary of the death or disappearance of a family member, the date of the beginning of a war or coup d'etat, etc.[35]

> Two years ago I went through a rough period. I didn't know why. For about 6 months I had panic attacks and sometimes I couldn't even breathe. I had trouble sleeping. I was very forgetful. The doctor said there was nothing wrong with me and the truth is that there was nothing special going on in my life. My family said that it was probably a "mid-life crisis." One day, while talking to a friend, he asked me how old was my grandfather when they took him away right after the war and they shot him. I told him that he was forty-three years old. I was turning forty-three that year! The weirdest thing is that as soon as my birthday passed, I felt fine again. Weird, eh? [RPR, a forty-five-year-old male]

Unconscious mobilization of significant dates in a state which has been through so much political violence, makes each family a possible time bomb.[36]

> My little sister who was about 4 years old in the mid 1960s, used to have nightmares at night and cry out: "Mom, the enemy is coming! I can hear the enemy!" I don't know why because at home no one used the word "enemy," we did not have a television and the war had been over for almost thirty years. [CVG, a fifty-seven-year-old female]

The unconscious comes up in dreams: In this case, in the dreams of a grandchild of the Spanish Civil War.

When a whole society has a shared past trauma, a particular date can destabilize the whole population. This vulnerability has been used in many countries by leaders to manipulate and impose policies and even to start new wars.[37]

Embodiment

Wars and repression are played out on the bodies of the population. Killing bodies, torturing bodies, capturing bodies, the "body count," is at the center of political violence. Therefore physical symptoms and illness are a logical outcome of such a violent history.

> My Chinese acupuncturist, who had survived the Cultural Revolution in China, the Pol-Pot regime in Cambodia and finally fled to Europe, checked my pulses and asked me with a worried look: "Have you ever been through a war?" I looked at him confused and answered: "Me? No, not me." I did not tell him about my grandparents' and my parents' experience during the Spanish Civil War. At that time in my life I did not imagine that it might be relevant to me. [CVG, female, fifty-seven years old]

If traumas and losses are not put into words, the body often becomes the place where narratives lodge and manifest themselves[38] both through health problems and through self-destructive behaviors.

> My mother (who did not wear glasses), once a year for a few days, she said that her eyes were blurry and she could not read. I checked out the dates and it always coincided with the date that her father was taken away during the war. I told her but she told me that my idea was ridiculous and that I paid too much attention to psychology. [ANT, female, sixty-two years old]

The humiliation that our ancestors lived through during the Civil War and the dictatorship in the form of torture, threats, and general violence, could it be related to the extreme importance that is given to physical appearance in Spain? The high frequency of plastic surgery (Spain is number one in Europe and fourth in the world in plastic surgery)[39] is an interesting fact. Although in Spain this has not been researched, in France it has, amongst the children and grandchildren of the Second World War.[40]

> Most of my women friends have had plastic surgery. Some got a breast enlargement as a high school graduation present from their parents. Others are now in their thirties and are having plastic surgery. Some have had several operations. I say to them, "How many more times are you going to have this done?" I find it really upsetting. [CMT, female, thirty-four years old]

Spain is the European country with the highest levels of eating disorders such as anorexia.[41] Although there are various etiologies for this problem, research with granddaughters of the Nazi Holocaust show that anorexia can be a desperate expression of the suffering inherited unconsciously from grandparents.[42]

> Isn't it something? My parents went hungry after the Civil War, and now that we have no lack of food, my daughter has anorexia. I don't see what one has to do with the other. It's probably just a coincidence. But it does seem ironic, doesn't it? [VMS, female, fifty-eight years old]

In the 1980s, Spain went through a brutal heroin epidemic which ravaged a whole generation with overdoses and created two other epidemics, HIV infection and Hepatitis C, and which, again, put it ahead of other European countries.[43] Much has been published regarding not grieving, transgenerational trauma, and needle-drug use,[44] especially in France with the descendents of the Second World War and the Algerian War. This self-destructive addiction points to a repetition of the harm lived by ancestors and also to a futile way to try to reduce emotional suffering.[45]

> All this (the War, the missing relatives) has affected my brother more than me because he never wants to talk about it. If I bring it up, he feels ashamed and angry. He is addicted to several drugs. [AZD, female, forty-six years old]

Despite these statistics, there is no research in Spain on the relationship between the impact of the political violence of the twentieth century and these somatization disorders.

> Before I got into the methadone program, I shot up heroine every day. Sometimes, twice a day. It really took away all my pain: backaches, headaches and it also took away all the bad feelings, the sadness and the anger about my family. [JJM, male, fifty-seven years old]

The heroin user wants to stop the pain, the transgenerational pain that his grandparents and parents were not able to elaborate nor manage. Overwhelmed by the pain and suffering of three generations, this grandchild of the Spanish Civil War, silently, in his corner, injects himself to get some relief.

But, as has been shown in other countries, there are processes and ways to reduce transgenerational suffering that are life-giving and not self-destructive. They require making the unconscious conscious through the word, through breaking the silence.

FIGHTING NEOLIBERALISM, ALONE, CANNOT HEAL SPAIN'S TRANSGENERATIONAL TRAUMA

How is Spain going to be able to slow down the dismantling of the welfare system and other recently gained rights when its middle-age population is still a wounded generation as a result of the Spanish Civil War?

The current so-called crisis and implementation of brutal neoliberal austerity measures in Spain—measures which go so far as to threaten people's lives[46]—have arrived when the third generation, the grandchildren of the Civil War, are adults who have not yet dealt with the transgenerational trauma of Spain's twentieth century political violence.

The fact that most of the mass graves from that period have not been opened and those responsible for political crimes have been neither named nor tried in court further walls off trauma and makes its impact invisible to most people. The rampant, present-day corruption and impunity of the political class in Spain, while hard evidence of the "sins" of the past, further ensures that trauma stays bottled within the minds and bodies of the third generation.

Against all odds, Spain's fourth generation has sprung into this fraught social/political environment with a new political movement. Single-issue movements (housing rights, The Commons, health care rights) nurtured through the Internet, and with the inspiration of movements in other countries like Egypt's Arab Spring, caused the young indignados (the outraged), on May 15, 2011, to coalesce into a historical sociopolitical movement.

The 15 Movement took over squares in cities all over Spain demanding real democracy and the end of privileges. The 15M, which in turn inspired the Occupy Wall Street movement a few months later,[47] is, according to political theorist Michael Hardt, the most focused on reinventing leadership and demanding real democracy of all the social movements that came to life worldwide in 2011.

> *After the long winter from which we come from, we have left behind old ghosts to start a new process of building the common.*
>
> —Arnau Monterde, #15M activist[48]

Numerous other authors say the 15M is the most important political development in Spain in the last thirty years.[49] The indignado movement is a work in progress. It is reappropriating the political conversation and cracking open issues of inequality and injustice. The 15M is carrying out *heterogenesis*, a concept coined by philosopher Felix Guattari, to define a new composition in a new generation.

How the 15M movement is organized and how it functions is what is most relevant to the issue of transgenerational trauma: horizontally, through stigmergy,[50] with elements of surprise, joy, and decentralization. Their main slogan, "Nobody Represents Us," and the absence of leaders radically challenge the authoritarian and vertical ways of organizing seen since the transition in the Left and union movements.

The antihierarchical and antiauthoritarianism of the 15M are not just slogans. They are ideas that can be seen in the day-to-day functioning of the movement. The 15M thinks that the previous two generations of political activists were inefficient. In their opinion, when their predecessors were faced with injustices, they turned to building structures and nurturing leaders. Committees, parties, commissions were created, large and long meetings were held, long-term plans were elaborated, and leaders were voted in.[51] In contrast, the 15M has created a stigmergic movement.[52] This type of movement focuses on action and on the proven fact that one action modifies the environment which, in turn, attracts further actions and ideas.[53] In other words: energy goes into action and ideas rather than into building structures and nurturing leaders.

The 15M movement seems to break through and clear away some of the symptoms of transgenerational trauma of the third generation. They show evidence of this through their base belief that "difference is not confrontation"[54]—in other words, there is room for a wide range of opinions. Confrontation is viewed as counterproductive. Civil War second and third generations tend to be locked into polarization of issues, the creation of enemies, and division.

So, has the 15M healed Spain's transgenerational trauma? Unfortunately, no. The grandchildren of the Civil War, some of whom have joined the 15M, are still deeply wounded. This can be clearly seen when there are meetings of the Left and unions to which they invite 15M groups. In these events, the indignados are shocked by the authoritarian, polarizing, and inefficient ways of functioning of the third generation. But mostly they are surprised by their elders' fear of new ways of organizing, of improvising, fear of taking a step without having a long-term plan, and fear of the inevitable unknown that is the future. With this fear, the Left ask the 15M in an accusing tone: "But where do you intend to end up with your movement?" To which the 15M answers, quoting Neo, a character in the film, *Matrix*: "I did not come here to tell you how it is going to end. I come here to tell you how it is going to begin."

An important part of this beginning, as research has shown in so many countries, involves a process of carrying out justice, enabling reparation, naming the truth, fostering reconciliation, elaborating mourning, and making the unconscious passed on transgenerationally conscious. The impact of the political violence of the twentieth century is still with us. It is transmitted transgenerationally. There is an urgent need for Spain to unearth, bring to consciousness, and publicly carry out a process that will heal the wounds of the past. Perhaps, in this way, the third generation in particular and the Spanish people in general will walk into a new present and into a new future free from the ghosts and the violence of the past.

NOTES

1. Scott Boehm. "On Human Rights Spain Is Different," *Commondream*, December 10, 2008. Accessed December 8, 2013. http://www.commondreams.org/view/2008/12/10.

2. From the perspective of history see, for instance, Michael Richards, *A Time of Silence: Civil War and the Culture of Repression in Franco's Spain, 1936–1945*. Cambridge: Cambridge University Press, 1998. For a cultural studies perspective see Cristina Moreiras-Menor, *Cultura Herida: Literatura y cine en la españa democrática*. Madrid: Libertarias, 2002, or Luis Martìn-Cabrera, *Radical Justice: Spain and the Southern Cone beyond Market and State*. Lewisburg: Bucknell University Press, 2011. For a psychoanalytical perspective see Ana Miñarro y Teresa Morandi (Eds.), *Trauma y transmisión: Efectos de la guerra del 36, la postguerra, la dictadura y la transición en la subjetividad de los ciudadanos*. Barcelona: Xoroi, 2013.

3. For more information about "Equipo Aquo" see http://www.equipoaquo.com/Information_in_English.html.

4. By "indignado movement" or "15-M movement" we refer to the wave of protests that started in May 15, 2011 in Spain. Following on the doorsteps of the "Arab

Spring," thousands of spaniards took to the streets of Madrid, Barcelona, and other major cities to oppose the austerity measures promoted by the EU and the Spanish government.

5. Francoise Davoine and Jean Max Gaudillère. *History beyond Trauma: Whereof One Cannot Speak, Thereof One Cannot Stay Silent.* Translated by Susan Fairfield. New York: Other Press, 2004.

6. Republican in the Spanish context does not have the same political meaning as in the United States. In Spain, Republican refers to the mostly progressive forces that were in favor of democracy and against the Monarchy.

7. Gabriel Jackson. *The Spanish Republic and the Civil War, 1931–1939.* Princeton: Princeton University Press, 1965.

8. Vincent Navarro. "La herencia nacionalista del fascismo," *Público*, December 3, 2009: http://blogs.publico.es/dominiopublico/1697/la-herencia-nacionalista-del-fascismo/.

9. Francisco Epinosa Maestre, *La justicia de Queipo: Violencia selectiva y terror fascista en la II División en 1936*. Sevilla: Author Edition, 2000, p. 23: "parece ya hora de que quede claro que lo que llamamos guerra, en numerosos lugares de España y en provincias como Cádiz, Sevilla, Huelva o partes de Córdoba o Badajoz, consistió de entrada simplemente en eliminar cierto número de gente y en traspasar a otras manos el poder político perdido en el 31."

10. See, for example, Francisco Espinosa Maestre, *Violencia roja y azul. España 1936–1950*. Barcelona: Crítica, 2010; Santos Juliá, *Víctimas de la Guerra Civil.* Madrid: Temas de hoy, 1999; and Paul Preston, *The Spanish Holocaust: Inquisition and Extermination in Twentieth-Century Spain.* New York: W.W. Norton & Co., 2012.

11. Sebastian Balfour, *Deadly Embrace: Morocco and the Road to the Spanish Civil War.* New York and Oxford: Oxford University Press, 2002, p. ix.

12. Achille Mbembe, "Necropolitics." Translated by Libby Meintjes. *Public Culture*, 15 (1) (2003): 18.

13. Michael Richards, "The Limits of Quantification: Francoist Repression and Historical Methodology," Hispania Nova. Revista de Historia Contemporánea. Número7 (2007), http://hispanianova.rediris.es

14. N. Abraham, and M. Torok, *The Shell and the Kernel: Renewal of Psychoanalysis*, Chicago: University of Chicago Press, 1994.

15. M. Ancharoff, J. F. Munroe, and L. Fisher, "The Legacy of Combat Trauma: Clinical Implications of Intergenerational Transmission." In Y. Danieli, (Ed.), *International Handbook of Multigenerational Legacies of Trauma.* New York: Plenum Press, 2010.

16. G. Fromm, *Lost in Transmission: Studies of Trauma across Generations.* London: Karnac, 2012.

17. For the a comparative analysis of these issues see Luis Martín-Cabrera, *Radical Justice: Spain and the Southern Cone beyond Market and State.* Lewisburg: Bucknell University Press, 2011.

18. Another blatant example of this is the current Spanish justice system which is still based on laws and even managed by judges from the Franco era, see for instance,

C. Jiménez Villarejo and A. Doñate Martín, *Jueces, pero parciales: La pervivencia del franquismo en el poder judicial.* Barcelona: Pasado y Presente, 2012.

19. C. Valverde, Desenterrar las palabras. Transmisión generacional de la violencia del siglo XX en el estado español. *Icaria Editorial.* Forthcoming.

20. D. Lessing, *African Laughter: Four Visits to Zimbabwe*, London: Flamingo, 1993.

21. C. Valverde, *¿De la cuneta a la plaza? Trauma transgeneracional, neoliberalismo y el 15-M.* http://www.aen.es/index.php?option=com_content&view=article&id=569:iii-jornadas-de-salud-mental-del-norte&catid=397:actividades-aen&Itemid=136.

22. The majority of the examples included in this essay come from victims of the fascist repression. We understand reading the bibliography that transmission also occurs between the parents of the perpetrators of violence and their children. Massive violence affects the whole society, but it does not affect everybody in the same manner. The children of the winners of the war are positioned in a different manner vis-à-vis the dark hole of war trauma, but they are nonetheless affected. In this essay we have decided to concentrate on the Republican defeated for two reasons. First, because it is very difficult to get the children of the Francoist families to speak about these matters, and second, because the children and grandchildren of the Republicans are clearly more disempowered due to the perpetuation of state-sponsored impunity.

23. The material used here are direct quotes from participants of transgenerational trauma workshops carried out by the Equipo Aquo in Catalonia, the Basque Country, and Asturias, Spain, between 2010 and 2013. We have also included quotes from some additional individual interviews. There have been over 120 participants in the workshops and 25 individual interviews. The topics were family dynamics and personal emotional coping mechanisms related to being grandchildren of the Civil War.

24. Y. Danieli, "Confronting the Unimaginable: Psychotherapists' Reactions to victims of the Nazi Holocaust. In J. P. Wilson, Z. Harel, and B. Kahan (Eds.), *Human Adaptation to Extreme Stress* (pp. 219–38). New York: Plenum Press, 1988.

25. C. Valverde, *Comunicación terapéutica en enfermería,* Madrid: DAE, 2007.

26. L. Martín-Cabrera, *Radical Justice: Spain and the Southern Cone beyond Market and State,* Lewisburg, PA: Bucknell University Press, 2011.

27. A. Nadler, S. Karvenaki, B. Gleitman, "Transcultural Effects of the Holocaust: Aggression in Second Generation of Holocaust Survivors." *Journal of Consulting and Clinical Psychology*, 53 (1985): 365–69.

28. I. Felsen, "Transgenerational Transmission of Effects of the Holocaust: The North American Perspective." In Y.: Danieli, (Ed.), *International Handbook of Multigenerational Legacies of Trauma.* New York: Plenum Press, 2010.

29. Davoine and Gaudillière, *History beyond Trauma: Whereof one cannot speak, thereof one cannot stay silent.* Translated by Susan Fairchild. New York: Other Press, 2004.

30. V. Volkan, *Enemies on the Couch: A psychological Journey through War and Peace,* Durham, NC: Pitchstone Publishing, 2013.

31. V. Volkan, *Blood Lines: From ethnic price to ethnic terrorism.* Westview Press, 1997.

32. V. Volkan, *Blood Lines.*

33. H. Faimberg, "Le téléscopage des générations à propos de la génealogie des certaines indetifications." In R. Kaës and H. Faimberg, (Eds.), *Transmission de la vie psychique entre générations.* Paris: Dunod, 1993.

34 A. Ancelin-Schützenberger, *The Ancestor Syndrome: Transgenerational Psychotherapy and the Hidden Links in the Family Tree,* New York: Routledge, 1998.

35. Volkan, *Blood Lines.*

36. G. Schwab, *Haunting Legacies: Violent Histories and Transgenerational Trauma*, Columbia University Press, 2010.

37. http://www.elmundo.es/elmundosalud/2006/10/05/mujer/1160033474.html.

38. Davoine and Gaudillière, *History beyond Trauma.*

39. http://www.elmundo.es/salud/Snumeros/97/S262/S262alimentacion.html.

40. J. S. Kestenberg, and M. Kestenberg, *Generations of the Holocaust.* New York: Basic Books (1982).

41. http://energycontrol.org/foro/Foro-sobre-drogas-y-gesti%C3%B3n-de-placeres-y-riesgos/16851-Evoluci%C3%B3n-consumo-de-hero%C3%ADna-en-Espa%C3%B1a-1971–2005.html.

42. J. Braudillard, "L'echange symolique et la mort." Paris: Gallimard, 1976.

43. P. Bruant, "Non-abstinence à personne en danger." *Interventions,* 40, (1993), 41–44. (1993).

44. D. Stuckler, and S. Basu, *The Body Economic: Why Austerity Kills*, New York: Basic Books, 2013.

45. M. Hardt, and A. Negri, *Declaration,* New York: Argo, 2013.

46. A. Monterde, "La potencia de la cooperación en la plaza global" in *Democracia Distribuida: Miradas de la Universidad Nómada al 15M,* http://www.academia.edu/2416872/La_potencia_de_la_cooperacion_en_la_plaza_global (last accessed November 30, 2013).

47. R. Sánchez Cedillo, "El 15M como insurrección del cuerpo-máquina." In *Democracia Distribuida: Miradas de la Universidad Nómada al 15M* (2012), http://www.academia.edu/2416872/La_potencia_de_la_cooperacion_en_la_plaza_global (last accessed November 30, 2013).

48. R. Sánchez Cedillo, "El 15M como insurrección del cuerpo-máquina," 2012.

49. S. Levi, "Notas de trabajo para una R-Evolución." In *Tecnopolítica, Internet y R-evoluciones*, Barcelona: Icaria Editorial, 2012.

50. R. Sánchez Cedillo, "El 15M como insurrección del cuerpo-máquina," 2012.

51. K. Carson, *The Stigmergic Revolution*, Center for a Stateless Society, 2011. http://c4ss.org/content/8914 (last accessed November 30, 2013).

52. R. Sánchez Cedillo, "El 15M como insurrección del cuerpo-máquina," 2012.

53. R. Sánchez Cedillo, "El 15M como insurrección del cuerpo-máquina," 2012.

54. D. Bar-On, *Tell Your Life Story: Creating Dialogue between Jews and Germans, Israelis and Palestinians.* Budapest: Central European University Press, 2006.

Chapter 11

A South African Story of Disavowal

Toward a Genealogy of Post-apartheid Empathy

Ross Truscott[1]

This chapter offers a reading of Pumla Gobodo-Madikizela's (2003) *A Human Being Died That Night: A South African Story of Forgiveness*, her highly acclaimed psychoanalytic account of her interviews with Eugene de Kock. De Kock was commanding officer at Vlakplaas—a farm outside Pretoria where, from the 1970s onward, apartheid's counterinsurgency police unit interrogated, tortured, and murdered anti-apartheid activists, frequently disposing of bodies by burning, burying, or blowing them up—between 1985 and 1993. Gobodo-Madikizela, a clinical and academic psychologist, visited de Kock on behalf of the Truth and Reconciliation Commission of South Africa (TRC) in the Pretoria Central Prison where he is currently serving two life sentences and 212 years.[2] As one would expect, Gobodo-Madikizela expresses dread and anxiety over meeting de Kock, but in contrast to the media-generated image of a cold-hearted psychopath, she finds a vulnerable, remorseful man, a man suffering. "His world," she states, "was a cold world where eyes of death stared accusingly at him, a world littered with corpses and graves—graves of the unknown dead, dismembered or blown up bodies" (p. 47). Indeed, Gobodo-Madikizela finds a man with whom she—much to her horror—comes to identify and empathize.

The identification between Gobodo-Madikizela and de Kock is set in motion and plays itself out over an incident wherein she, moved by his vulnerability, touches his hand during an interview and encounters "a human being capable of feeling, crying and knowing pain" (p. 38). Gobodo-Madikizela recounts how, following his testimony at the TRC regarding the killing of three black policemen in the township of Motherwell, outside Port Elizabeth, de Kock requested a meeting with the widows of the three men. Two of the widows met with de Kock—Pearl Faku and Doreen Mgoduka—and did indeed forgive him. "The image of the widow reaching out to her husband's murderer,"

Gobodo-Madikizela states, "struck me as an extraordinary expression—and *act*—of empathy, to shed tears not only for her loss but also, it seemed, for the loss of de Kock's moral humanity" (p. 15, emphasis in original). It is this empathy on the part of the two widows, we are told, that led her to meet with de Kock in the first place. It is also reciprocal, and Gobodo-Madikizela believes that, by the end of her interviews with de Kock, he has been able to approach something like empathy.

The transformation *A Human Being* bears witness to, participates in, and advocates is—almost to the word—a psychoanalytic "talking cure." At one of the TRC hearings in Cape Town, and following their interview where Gobodo-Madikizela touched de Kock's hand, he tells her that it was his "trigger hand" that she has touched (p. 39). Gobodo-Madikizela suggests that, recoiling from the horror of his own past, he had separated himself from his hand, the guilty party that did the killing, split it off. "Distancing himself and casting away the evil part of his body," Gobodo-Madikizela states, "was an effort at self-preservation. But it was also an illustration of how fragmented he was" (p. 41). It was, as she formulates it, an overdetermined act—"pregnant with so many confusing and contradictory messages" (p. 39)—that recalled the violence of his past, the scenes of violence in which he had been involved intruding into their interaction. First, Gobodo-Madikizela wonders whether de Kock derived pleasure from telling her this, pleasure from being able to imagine her fear. Was this, she asks, an acting out with her of the violence to which he had subjected others, a literalization of the past he was refusing to remember? And second, his violent behavior during apartheid, his very vocation, is read as a repetition of an early childhood trauma at the hands of his drunken father. In which case the question becomes whether telling her this was in fact a confession of his vulnerability. "By touching the troubling murder 'weapon,'" Gobodo-Madikizela states, "I had simply opened the floodgates of unwanted memory" (p. 46), of that which he did, of that which was done to him, as well as the way these had become enfolded within each other. The path to recovery for de Kock—the overcoming of his defensive acting out, of his repetition of a violent past in their relationship—is paved, so this vision of psychic transformation has it, with, if not recovered memories, then at least intersubjective reconstruction of the past, with talk.

A Human Being was largely a response to media representations of perpetrators around the time of the TRC, representations that, as several scholars have argued, enact a disavowal of complicity with apartheid (e.g., Foster, Haupt, & De Beer, 2005). Rather than reading the disavowal of complicity with apartheid as a strictly internal, psychological resistance, it can be seen as an effect of anti-apartheid, post-apartheid nationalism since 1994. The post-apartheid nation has been constituted—quite literally, in the *Constitution of the Republic of South Africa Act 108 of 1996*—as a nation against its own past. The preamble to *The Constitution* begins, "We, the people of South Africa/Recognize the injustices of our past. . . ." These opening lines voice, in an exemplary way, the interpellative address to subjects of the post-apartheid nation, a person becoming one of "the people of South Africa" through the recognition of "the injustices of our past," a past that in the act of recognition *as an injustice* becomes "our past," a common past, but one in which "the people of South Africa" no longer live.

A second level of response to this address, however, upon which admittance to the post-apartheid nation is dependent, entails an insertion of oneself into the statement—"We, the people of South Africa/Recognize the injustices of our past. . . ."—learned by heart, not simply as the recognizing subject, but as the object recognized. That is, one must confess in order to be admitted. To concede too much complicity, then, is to become the other from "our past," dead to the nation yet vital to its constitution; to concede too little is to have not completed the injunction, internalized it. Thus, to be a subject of the post-apartheid nation one must, in the precise psychoanalytic sense, disavow complicity and hold two contrary psychic positions simultaneously.

In such a situation, de Kock has served a crucial function for post-apartheid nation-building, becoming, through his disclosures to the TRC of his acts of interrogation, torture, and murder, the face of the past against which "the people of South Africa" have turned. And it is this projection onto de Kock that has enabled the widespread disavowal of complicity with apartheid. De Kock has become a figure through which subjects of the nation have been able to say—and this is to fill in the blanks in the title of Octave Mannoni's (1969) essay on disavowal, "I know well, but all the same. . . ."—"I know well that apartheid was an injustice, and that I am implicated in that past," but all the same, de Kock is the very "embodiment of hundreds of years of conquest" (Sachs, 2003, p. vii). For "South Africans" who must disavow complicity with apartheid as the condition of admittance, be able to recognize it without it being too recognizable in their thought, conduct, speech, and desire, de Kock is perfectly cast to figure "our" origins inasmuch as his acts of violence were "especially savage" (Parker, 2010, p. 63).[3]

A Human Being countered this as a case study of de Kock's willingness to confront his own past. Through Gobodo-Madikizela's identification with de Kock, she encounters her own capacity to do harm, her own "intimate complicity" (p. 46) with him and with apartheid violence. The disavowal of complicity, Gobodo-Madikizela suggests, is figured in the defense of splitting, which she first reads in de Kock's speech, and then, through her identification with de Kock, she begins to recognize in herself too. But splitting, she argues, is characteristic more generally of what she calls in her sixth chapter "An Apartheid of the Mind" (pp. 104–15); that is, in *A Human Being,* splitting is something close to a national psychic disposition.

There are, then, three itineraries in *A Human Being*. The first, from narcissism to empathy. The second, from the repetition of the past to its remembrance. And then a third, which aims to work through the widespread disavowal of complicity with apartheid violence that took place in the wake of the TRC. The three are, however, intertwined. It is de Kock's defensive splitting that both withholds and, unconsciously, contains the memories he refuses; it is only by remembering that which his splitting conceals that he can begin to empathize, psychically inhabit, to imagine and to feel his way into, the suffering he must have caused others; and it is in splitting that the defense of disavowal is constellated, and, through confession, worked through.

A Human Being has been, at the very least, a timely intervention into a situation of widespread and ongoing racial tension. What Gobodo-Madikizela has done is suggest a way to transform a deeply ingrained pattern of relationship between herself, the woman of her subtitle in the second edition—*A South African Woman Confronts the Legacy of Apartheid*—and one of apartheid's most notorious figures, thus providing a limited case of interpersonal and psychological reconciliation for black and white South Africans, and, if we are to believe her reviewers, for postconflict societies more generally.

The notion of complicity at work in *A Human Being* can, however, be pushed further or at least into an epistemological register. Conceding the important contribution Gobodo-Madikizela makes, as well as the kinds of critical work to which psychoanalysis is frequently set, what I am interested in here, drawing from and contributing to a growing body of literature on the colonial contours of psychoanalytic thought, are the ways in which the use of a psychoanalytic frame can itself be thought of as a form of repetition, an acting out, at an epistemological level, of a relation to the disavowed colonial conditions of possibility for psychoanalysis (Khanna, 2003). If the proposed transformations of *A Human Being* are provided with their armature in psychoanalytic theory, and if colonial thinking is the condition of possibility for psychoanalysis, should we not pause to rethink the stakes of psychoanalysis in South Africa, and in the postcolony? Psychoanalysis has been deployed to formulate and intervene in a disavowal of complicity with apartheid, but how, we might ask, does this formulation itself participate in the very disavowal it names?

We cannot not consider the stakes of psychoanalysis in post-apartheid South Africa; it is already at work, mediating our relation to the past. This is so, particularly, when we consider the TRC's commitment to a "talking cure" (Sitze, 2013; Feldman, 2003; Swartz & Drennan, 2000)—the injunction to remember and, thereby, work through the apartheid past, talk about it so as not to repeat it. That is to say, psychoanalysis, through the TRC, has seeped into the sense making discourses of post-apartheid South Africa, becoming one language, one amongst several, through which South Africans have come to narrate the birth of the post-apartheid nation and its ideal subject. Put differently, the discourse of the TRC, of which *A Human Being* is a part, produces psychoanalytic subjects, with psychoanalytic symptoms. In this sense, Gobodo-Madikizela simply extends a mode of thought already at work, imminent in the TRC and in post-apartheid nationalism.

THE VIOLENCE OF IDENTIFICATION

A Human Being has two related nodes of focus. First, that which enables post-apartheid reconciliation, and although attention is drawn to "an external context" (p. 127), Gobodo-Madikizela is most concerned with "internal psychological dynamics" (p. 127). Second, apartheid violence and its conditions of possibility, and in this regard, too, Gobodo-Madikizela does note structural causes but is more interested in the psychology of apartheid. Despite the risks of psychological reductionism, what makes *A Human Being* remarkable within the copious literature on the TRC is that Gobodo-Madikizela uses the same concept, identification, to formulate both apartheid violence and post-apartheid reconciliation. In positing an isomorphism between apartheid violence and post-apartheid reconciliation, *A Human Being*, I want to suggest, productively complicates its own itineraries, which are also those of post-apartheid nationalism.

In accounting for de Kock's violence, Gobodo-Madikizela pays considerable attention to his early childhood, particularly his relationship to his father. "De Kock's father, a magistrate," Gobodo-Madikizela states, "seems to have had a far greater influence on de Kock than he was willing to acknowledge" (p. 20). In this regard, de Kock's curious but nonetheless absolute refusal to harm children during his counterinsurgency operations is considered alongside his refusal to talk about his own childhood. "Was something more psychologically subtle going on," Gobodo-Madikizela asks, "something to do with his childhood, his helplessness as a child and his own need for protection?" (p. 26).

Drawing on both Sigmund and Anna Freud, Gobodo-Madikizela argues that in situations in which a person is on the receiving end of abuse or subject to the will of an authoritarian figure such as de Kock's father, they will identify with their aggressor. De Kock's violent behavior is then explained as a kind of acting out of the scenes of his own forced submission, a repetition that, as Gobodo-Madikizela argues, entails returning to this scene of subjection but with the roles reversed: de Kock, the son, now in the position of the aggressor, no longer the passive recipient of abuse, now the active abuser. Thus, just as de Kock was subject to the violent rule of paternal law, he subjected apartheid activists to the same law in his repetition of a scene that could never fully satisfy his desire for revenge over his father. De Kock's "life-long pattern of revenge based behaviour" (p. 56) is, thus, framed as a repetition of memories too painful to recall.

The reference in this section of the book is not to Freud's (1914) "Remembering, Repeating and Working-Through," but to his later (1920) *Beyond the Pleasure Principle*. Despite the fact that there is almost no discussion of the text in *A Human Being*, following the drift of Freud's speculative hypothesis, we could say that what Gobodo-Madikizela calls the "temporary relief" (p. 56) de Kock's violence brought him can be refracted through the pleasure principle, inasmuch as "unpleasure corresponds to an *increase* in excitation and pleasure to a *diminution*" (Freud, 1920, p. 2).[4] That is, violence, for de Kock, could be seen as a means of troping pleasure, of providing a repetitive means for reducing unpleasure, excessive stimulation, both from sources external (stimuli that remind him of his vulnerability, threaten him with humiliation) and internal (anxiety). Freud is concerned, though, with the dynamics driving a compulsion to repeat that are, as his title indicates, beyond this economic point of view, a desire not simply to reduce unpleasure, but a conservative drive to return to "an *old* state of things, an initial state from which the living entity has at one time or other departed and to which it is striving to return" (pp. 49–50). That state, from which all living matter forms itself, if one takes the hypothesis to its conclusion, is an inorganic one, leading the subject of the repetition, as Freud famously put it, along a "circuitous path to death" (pp. 50–51).

Indeed, de Kock's compulsion to repeat the scenes of his own humiliation, returning identified with his humiliator in order to master a traumatic experience, to ward off his own death, seems, in a paradoxical way, to hasten the path to his death, at least psychically: he wished for revenge over his father, but *it was himself*, in the substitution of roles, in the displacements of the scene acted out, *that he was killing*, and it is these acts that, retroactively, have become the grounds for the social death he now lives.

There is much to take issue with in this formulation, most notably, as I have already suggested, the risk of psychological reductionism, a risk Gobodo-Madikizela is not unaware of and yet one she takes. We might also say, in Gilles Deleuze's (2009) words on psychoanalysis on fascism, that, in reducing the cause of violence to the father, psychoanalysis has "crushed phenomena of desire on a familial stage, crushed the whole political and economic dimension of the libido" (p. 89). Let us try, then, to locate the violence of identification within a wider frame.

Diana Fuss (1994) suggests that the act of identification might be said to derive its form and force—and its violence—not first and foremost from an originary paternal relation, but from broader formations of colonial domination. Incorporation, frequently associated with Hegelian dialectics but also inseparable from psychoanalytic formulations of "identification as introjection," as Fuss notes, is not only analogous to bodily processes—the alimentary and the excretory—but, as Fuss argues with reference to Robert Young, also "mimics, at a conceptual level, the geographical and economic absorption of the non-European world by the West" (Young cited in Fuss, 1994, p. 23). Identification, Fuss argues, is a kind of psychic geopolitics, "an imperial process, a form of violent appropriation in which the Other is deposed and assimilated into the lordly domain of Self" (p. 23). In this sense, identification should, as Fuss suggests, "be placed squarely within its other historical genealogies, including colonial imperialism" (p. 20). While it is not possible to take on the full implications of Fuss's provocation here, her work is instructive in attempting to lodge the formulation of de Kock's violence as entailing an identification at a more political, economic, and discursive level.

Allen Feldman (2003) notes that during the TRC many testimonies referred to police interrogations wherein a *braai* (barbeque) figured prominently.[5] The *braai* within scenes of apartheid political torture, as Feldman (2003) sees it, was overdetermined, doing many things at once: it was an *instrument of torture*, of cooking, smoking, and burning suspected "terrorists," sometimes entailing the administration of electric shocks as well; it offered a means of normalizing extreme violence, *humanizing* victims within the banal setting of a meal, thereby insulating conscience and, in a paradoxical way, *animalizing* victims, treating them as meat, as prey; and, crucially, it provided a means of *concealment*, of disposing the bodies or rendering them unrecognizable because they were burned. Feldman links "*braai* torture" to the instantiation of white masculine identities during apartheid, arguing that it was but one articulation of the long history of a violent relationship between the South African state and black bodies, an articulation, he suggests, in a moment of crisis, the state's grip on the black body loosening. "*Braai* tortures," Feldman argues, "were a theatre of economic replay and nostalgia for old structural hierarchies that could be replicated in the present state of emergency only through the sensory associations of the masculinist and white barbecue" (p. 253). These scenes are, as Feldman sees them, a kind of acting out of a time when colonial regimes of labor discipline over the black body were tighter, domination more total. Feldman thus examines the irrational motivations driving torture, not first and foremost the extraction of information or the quelling of political revolt, but, rather, the conjuring or acting out of lost forms of colonial, masculinist identity.

Judith Butler's work on identification and genealogy offers one way of extending this formulation of apartheid violence as the repetition of lost modes of masculinity, bringing the question of sexuality more explicitly to the fore. Using Michel Foucault's (1977) formulation of genealogy as, on the one hand, tracing the processes through which an object of knowledge is constituted and, on the other, drawing attention to the processes by which that production is concealed, Butler (1990) suggests that the concept of identification offers a genealogy of the gendered subject's desire, the means by which a gendered identity is formed, with that process of formation effaced.

Butler builds on Freud's concept of melancholia and regressive identification. Freud (1917) argues that in melancholia, to prolong psychically an attachment to a lost or otherwise forbidden object, an object-cathexis is withdrawn into the ego, introjected, establishing "an *identification* of the ego with the abandoned object" (p. 249). Whereas initially Freud (1917) saw this incorporation of a lost love object as pathological, he later (1923) generalized the regressive identification associated with melancholia, positing it as the very condition of giving up lost objects, but also of psychic life in general. Loss, in this later sense, constitutes the ego. Freud (1923) remarks, in this regard, that "the character of the ego is a precipitate of abandoned object-cathexes and that it contains the history of those object choices" (p. 29). As Butler (1997) puts it, commenting on this passage, the ego is no more than "the sedimentation of objects loved and lost, the archaeological remainder, as it were, of unresolved grief" (p. 133), the character of the ego being precisely, and only, the effect of its ungrievable lost objects taken into the ego's economy of drives, an assemblage of fragments and traces of lost objects or parts thereof. We might say that, for Butler reading Freud through Foucault, the ego, no less than any object of knowledge, is "fabricated in a piecemeal fashion from alien forms" (Foucault, 1977, p. 142), that there is no preconstituted ego that is to withstand and mourn its losses.

In reworking Freud's theory of loss and the formation of the ego, Butler argues that, in the case of a young boy, sexual love for the father, forbidden within heteronormative societies and thus "lost," is melancholically transformed into an identification with him, and this identification is what becomes of a lost homosexual bond (Butler, 1990). Thus, in assuming a heterosexual identification with the father, there is, in this melancholic conversion of a homosexual object cathexis into an identification, an always present but never fully experienced loss of homosexual desire. The formation of a heterosexual masculine identity has, then, a genealogy—the conversion of a foreclosed object cathexis into an identification—but that process of formation of a supposedly natural disposition is concealed, the "genealogy of that transmutation fully forgotten and repressed" (Butler, 1990, p. 71).

For Butler (1990), the genealogy of the character of the ego is written on and as the body, the body as a tomb of undeclarable losses:

> Here we see the general strategy of literalization as a form of forgetfulness, which in the case of a literalized sexual anatomy, "forgets" the imaginary and,

with it, imaginable homosexuality. In the case of the melancholic heterosexual male, he never loved another man, he *is* a man, and he can seek recourse to the empirical facts that will prove it. (p. 71)

Apartheid South Africa is perhaps the heteronormative society par excellence, de Kock the heterosexual hard man of apartheid.[6] Gobodo-Madikizela highlights his identification with his father, his aggressor, as a means of mastery, a formulation that can, if we bring it into conversation with Feldman and Butler's work, be posited as an identification that unfolds on the foreclosure of homosexual intimacy. In the face of this foreclosure, we might say, de Kock identified with his father, took the aim and object of his father's desire as his own as a compromise, laying the ground for a later fastening of de Kock to the ideology of apartheid, to its language, its relational patterns of domination.

If torture and murder were, as Gobodo-Madikizela suggests, a displacement of what little intimacy there was between father and son, reenacted as a dissimulated scene in which he, de Kock, plays his father and the tortured victim is thrust into his position, we could argue that the homosexual bond that never was, and was thus never lost, haunts this scene of masculine identity formation, the genealogy of which must be concealed. We could propose, also, that the violent disposal of bodies for which Vlakplaas became so notorious, literalizes the erasure of the never loved and never lost homosexual object in heterosexual masculine identifications. If counterinsurgency operations were performed with the *manifest* objective of protecting a vulnerable feminine subject against the threat of a sexually rapacious, dangerous black male body—dissimulating a scene where the young de Kock protected his mother from his father, or failed to do so (Gobodo-Madikizela, 2003)—treating the black body as an object, a prop in the staging of white masculinist identity—many of these scenes entailing not only violence, but also, crucially, homosociality and, frequently, nudity among men and the application of torture instruments onto the genitals of suspected "terrorists"—then the erasure of the erotics of male bonding is one of the *latent* effects condensed in the act of destroying a body that has become the refuse of the unconscious pursuit of revenge on the father, who never loved that way, and whom one never loved that way. The concealment of the murdered bodies, the burning of the tortured victims, the mutilation of bodies by blowing them up, dismembering bodies, burying them in unmarked graves to be forgotten, had, of course, "practical" reasons; if these scenes of violence can be thought of as reenactments of an intimacy of domination between father and son, though, then the black body here is the displaced site of that intimacy that must be concealed, the burning of the body literalizing the erasure of homosexual desire.

That these were the bodies of black men being interrogated, tortured, and murdered only serves to entrench the identification with an Afrikaner Nationalist, *Broederbond* (Afrikaner Brotherhood) father, such as de Kock's, and the constitution of a white, masculine heterosexual identity. Yet, it is precisely because it was with black men that a homosexual relation was being acted out unconsciously that the need to conceal the genealogy of desire the scene connotes was intensified, leading to a double disavowal of interracial homosexuality the burned, exploded, and dismembered body came to literalize. In Feldman's (2003) terms, "these acts of police cover-up took the form of burning the bodies of victims, in order to conceal both the acts themselves and the identities of the deceased" (p. 243). We could suppose, though, that these acts also conceal and act out a memory of a form of love that never existed, and yet reappears, at least from a psychoanalytic perspective, as an enigmatic kernel from which some of the worst acts of violence in South African history were issued.

THE COMPLICITY OF EMPATHY

Toward the conclusion of *A Human Being*, Gobodo-Madikizela asks:

> What enables some victims to forgive heinous crimes? What distinguishes them from those who feel unable to do so? In addition to an external context that makes reconciliation normative through the language of restoration—a truth commission, for example, or a counseling agency that focuses on victim-offender encounters, or a national dialogue that begins to put in place the symbols and vocabulary of forgiveness and compromise—there are internal psychological dynamics that impel most of us toward forming an empathic connection with another person in pain, that draws us *into* his pain, regardless of who that someone is. The possibility of making an empathic connection with someone who has victimized us, as a response to the pain of his remorse, stems significantly from this underlying dynamic. The power of human connectedness, of identification with the other as "bone of my bone" through the sheer fact of his being human, draws us to "rescue" others in pain, almost as if this were a learned response embedded deep in our genetic evolutionary past. We cannot help it. We are induced to empathy because there is something in the other that is felt to be a part of the self, and something in the self that is felt to belong to the other. (p. 127, emphasis in original)

The key point here is that the condition of possibility for empathy—the "internal psychological," rather than "external," condition—is an "identification with the other." Gobodo-Madikizela states that her identification with de

Kock, "a brief moment of communion" (p. 47) established through a touch, was something akin to a contamination: "I was from now on infected with the memory of having embraced into my heart the hand that had killed, maimed and blown up lives" (p. 40). Gobodo-Madikizela imagines and feels herself into his psychic space, experiencing his fragmentation as her own: "I was aware of a disintegration happening within myself," she states, "I was struggling with that part of myself that made it possible to identify with de Kock—the evil of de Kock" (pp. 41–42). And the process plays out, as Freud (1921) put it, through a "single trait" (p. 49), here the instrument of his violence—his hand, a weapon of apartheid murder—and Gobodo-Madikizela wakes up the morning after she has touched his hand, her arm numb, "as if my body were rejecting a foreign organ illegitimately planted" (p. 41).

Like most psychoanalytic formulations of empathy, *A Human Being* pegs its argument on Freud's (1921) *Group Psychology and the Analysis of the Ego*, specifically on a rather speculative footnote:

> A path leads from identification by way of imitation to empathy, that is, to the comprehension of the mechanism by means of which we are enabled to take up any attitude at all towards another mental life. Moreover, there is still much to be explained in the manifestations of existing identifications. These result among other things in a person limiting his aggressiveness towards those with whom he has identified himself, and in his sparing them and giving them help. The study of such identifications, like those, for instance, that lie at the root of clan feeling, led Robertson Smith . . . to the surprising discovery that they rest upon the acknowledgement of the possession of a common substance, and may even therefore be created by a meal eaten in common. This feature makes it possible to connect this kind of identification with the early history of the human family which I constructed in *Totem and Taboo*. (Freud, 1921, p. 53*n*)

There are multiple resonances between Freud's footnote on empathy in *Group Psychology* and *A Human Being*, though one is worth isolating here.[7] At the end of his footnote, Freud writes, referring back to *Totem and Taboo* (Freud, 1913), of "the early history of the human family," invoked by Gobodo-Madikizela when she posits empathy as "a learned response embedded deep in our genetic evolutionary past." Though "the early history of the human family" appears in the footnotes of *Group Psychology*, it is not a side issue for the formulation of identification Freud offers; indeed, it is quite at the center of Freud's concerns.

Regarding identification between a boy and his father, Freud (1921) states, "A little boy will exhibit a special interest in his father; he would like to grow like him and be like him, and take his place every where" (p. 46). This kind of identification, Freud notes, is "ambivalent from the very first" (p. 47):

> It behaves like a derivative of the first, *oral* phase, of the organization of libido, in which the object we long for and prize is assimilated by eating and is in that way annihilated as such. The cannibal, as we know, has remained at this stand point; he has a devouring affection for his enemies and only devours people of whom he is fond. (p. 47)

The orality of the child's early identifications recalls the cannibalism of an earlier age in the human species, the corollary of which is that cannibals are rendered a peculiar kind of children. To invoke empathy on the grounds of *Group Psychology*, then, one needs to follow the associative thread to *Totem and Taboo*. And as its subtitle—*Some Points of Agreement between the Mental Lives of Savages and Neurotics*—indicates, there is, underpinning *Totem and Taboo*, for those who would want to deploy this particular iteration of psychoanalysis for postcolonial critique, a rather repellent view within which, as Freud (1913) states, "there are people whom we still consider more closely related to primitive man than ourselves, in whom we therefore recognize the direct descendents and representatives of earlier man" (p. 1).

In *A Human Being,* Gobodo-Madikizela suggests that the capacity to imagine the experience of another person is analogous to an infant's growing awareness of the separateness of the figures upon which it is dependent, primarily the mother, a capacity acquired at a certain point in life, which, once lost in a regression to narcissism—in the case of de Kock, participation in the violence of apartheid was narcissistic inasmuch as he saw himself in the children he refused to kill and himself, the helpless little boy subject to the whims of his father, in his victims—can be restored. It is not simply a developmental passage, though; it is also an evolutionary one: this capacity recalls the distant unremembered prehistory of the human species in which an evolutionary threshold was crossed. Thus, the formulation of identification, and the empathy it enables, folds the phases of man's evolution into the stages of individual psychic development, a schema within which the child relives in its maturation the evolution of the species, the thesis, in other words, that ontogeny recapitulates phylogeny.

De Kock, on these grounds, comes to occupy the position of the "primitive," not simply inasmuch as his defenses—most notably splitting—are psychically primitive, but also in how he figures the "primitivity"—indeed, the cannibalism—from which "the people of South Africa" have ascended and to which we could once more regress.[8] De Kock becomes, that is, the "savage" with an infantile capacity for imagination, who in "the calm violence" of the transference relationship (Foucault, 1970, p. 376) is civilized, admitted into the community, incorporated, on the grounds that he has developed a more subtle and refined capacity for empathy. Along the lines of this reading, Gobodo-Madikizela, with the psychoanalytic frame she deploys, leads her readers to discover a prototypical post-apartheid subject in the rebirth of de Kock: his violence, which exemplifies the violence of apartheid, now renounced, now remembered, worked through and forgiven rather than acted out, is the form of "our" birth as national subjects. Thus, de Kock marks the constitutive limits of post-apartheid South Africa, which must be excluded, but is also its exemplary subject.

As we have seen in the previous section, identification is central to Gobodo-Madikizela's thinking on the violence of apartheid. As I suggested in the introduction, it is this that sets *A Human Being* apart in the TRC literature. The corollary, understated in the text, is that post-apartheid reconciliation bears the trace of precisely the violence it seeks to transcend:

> For at the moment when the perpetrator begins to show remorse, to seek some way to ask forgiveness, the victim becomes the gatekeeper to what the outcast desires—readmission to the human community. And the victim retains that privileged status as long as he or she stays the moral course, refusing to sink to the level of evil that was done to her or him. In this sense, then, *forgiveness is a kind of revenge, but revenge enacted at a rarefied level.* (p. 117, emphasis added)

If empathy is conceptually grounded upon identification, the transformed relationship itself becomes a displaced site of colonial violence, a quarantining of the violence of the past within a transferential circuit, a sublimation, as it were, bearing a trace of the aggression the act forgoes. Even the forgiver, the argument seems to suggest, is complicit through the act of forgiveness. This is the psychoanalytic interpretation par excellence, in which empathy might be said to be animated by colonial violence, even as it marks a break with it.

DISAVOWING THE COLONIALITY OF PSYCHOANALYSIS

Gobodo-Madikizela's identification with de Kock, which allows her to empathize with him, is said to have led back to memories of her participation in anti-apartheid violence. However, if we take colonialism not as an event but as an episteme, perhaps it is the history of the system of thought *A Human Being* uses to make sense of the persistence of the past, the unconscious of psychoanalytic discourse, that ought to be recollected and worked through. Complicity, in this sense, becomes not only participation in the violence of colonial rule and anticolonial struggle, but also a resonance between the ideas deployed to transcend the violence of the past and those ideas that are the conditions of possibility for that violence.

To the question of how, precisely, the subject interpellated by the TRC came to be figured as what Jacques Derrida (1998) calls, in a different context, "Homo psychoanalyticus" (p. 77), Feldman (2004) argues that the "talking cure" dimensions of the TRC were driven largely by "the white-dominated media" (p. 174) and by "key actors in the TRC, as they negotiated their post-commission careers" (p. 184)—*A Human Being* would be a perfect case in point. By contrast, however, Adam Sitze (2013) argues that this psychotherapeutic aim of the TRC has a quite different genealogy, an argument warranting consideration, particularly in the context of a volume dedicated to the stakes of remembering and forgetting.

Sitze notes that transitional justice scholarship usually differentiates the TRC from Nuremburg-style trials on the one hand and from the blanket amnesty offered in Latin America on the other. The claim in transitional justice scholarship is that the TRC was unprecedented on two levels: the individualized conditional amnesty offered to perpetrators, and the centrality in the proceedings of the testimonies of victims. What Sitze establishes, however, is precisely the *colonial precedents* of the TRC. Regarding conditional individual amnesty, Sitze draws attention to colonial jurisprudence of indemnity, later repeated in apartheid jurisprudence to authorize the very state violence that the TRC took as its object of knowledge, as that which it sought to work through. Regarding victim testimony, Sitze focuses on colonial commissions of inquiry, which were quite explicitly meant to attend to the voices of victims of state violence following the suppression of riots and rebellions.

"What then does it mean," Sitze asks, "that we can find so many of the defining attributes of the TRC operating under conditions defined not by democratic transition but by colonial and even apartheid domination? Did the TRC simply repeat this colonial legacy?" (p. 16) "The hypothesis we shall entertain in this book," Sitze states:

> is that this forgetting is neither accidental nor politically neutral. It is what Sigmund Freud, writing in 1901, called "motivated forgetting." It is the inability to remember something unpleasant, threatening, or even painful. In particular, it is the forgetting of a jurisprudence that transitional scholars cannot possibly want to remember, much less inherit or assume, and the truth of which they indeed cannot possibly acknowledge being a constitutive part of their analyses of so humanitarian an institution as the TRC. (pp. 44–45)

Reports on commissions of inquiry, written in the wake of the excesses of the state's violence in its suppression of revolts "were texts," Sitze states, "which were almost therapeutic in their intense interest in the gradations and thresholds internal to hatred" (p. 166). The logic of the commission of inquiry was that if the anger that drove revolts could be better understood, they could be prevented.[9] It is here that Sitze inserts psychoanalysis into the picture:

> Prior to any integration of psychoanalysis within the administrative apparatus of the TRC, after all, the Tumult Commission already itself interpreted the etiology of political conflict within a manifestly therapeutic horizon, searching for the psychological antidotes that colonial administrators could apply to dissipate the "fevers" of hatred that always were at risk of swelling into open rebellion. But this turn to the therapeutic is anything but novel; to the contrary, it reactualizes the therapeutic discourse already at work in the apparatus of the Tumult Commission, only now in a different idiom, by inviting individuals and collectives alike to self-identify as trauma victims. (p. 206)

A similar point can be made regarding *A Human Being*: while it troubles the widespread disavowal of complicity with apartheid, there is, perhaps, too little recollection of the resonance between the psychoanalytic frame and that which it has been deployed to move beyond for it not to reinscribe colonial violence back into post-apartheid reconciliation, intentionally or inadvertently, and into the birth of the post-apartheid subject over which it presides. *A Human Being*, then, while setting itself against post-apartheid disavowal, also tightens the knot of disavowal in which post-apartheid subjectivity is configured.

Sitze's reading, while critical of the "watered-down psychoanalysis" (p. 99) of transitional justice scholarship, and of the dangerous psychotherapeutics of commissions of inquiry, is at least in part dependent on psychoanalysis, abiding by what could be taken as a more rigorous form of psychoanalysis hinged to a project of genealogy. Following Sitze, we needn't suggest that psychoanalysis has no place in working out the transformations of post-apartheid South Africa. If, as Sitze argues, the audacity of the theoreticians of the TRC was to inhabit the very discursive terrain of colonial jurisprudence, setting it against itself, then this move, discernable in *A Human Being*—the invocation of a concept that bears the formal features of precisely the object of its critique—might be Gobodo-Madikizela's audacity, too, as well as where we might locate her text's postcolonial gesture of reiteration, of repetition with a difference.[10] While *A Human Being* can certainly be read critically as a text symptomatic of the concessions of psychoanalytic theory under the influence of humanistic ego psychology, one has to concede the nerve of using, in Audre Lorde's (1984) famous phrase, the master's tools to dismantle the master's house.

Indeed, the deliberate choice here, in reading *A Human Being*, has been to remain within a psychoanalytic frame, to subject psychoanalysis to its own thought, implicating my reading of *A Human Being*, inasmuch as I am thinking psychoanalytically, to a similar critique I make of the book. By repeating psychoanalysis against itself—by asking what it as a discourse forgets and repeats, by turning it on itself in order to recollect its own violence, to work through its own disavowals, its own dependence on the very colonial thinking against which it so frequently rails—psychoanalysis in post-apartheid South Africa may have a role to play in the academic project of postcolonialism. Reiterating the commandment that those deploying psychoanalysis undergo a personal analysis, twisting it, the condition of post-apartheid psychoanalysis, from a postcolonial perspective, might be that it undergoes an impersonal, genealogical analysis that throws into relief the historicity and the epistemological freighting of its concepts. In this particular instance, this would not preclude the continued use of the concept of empathy, but only mark the stakes of its usage and draw attention to the colonial histories out of which it was forged, overdetermining its deployment.[11]

This is, admittedly, a highly selective reading of *A Human Being*. I hope it is clear, though, that I see this text as worth reading, worth taking seriously, and I hope also that this paper might join a conversation on the post-apartheid moment in which we find ourselves, one in which many have been declaring—in violent protest and melancholy resignation—that the "new South Africa" was delivered stillborn, a failed promise of new life, that apartheid has only ended officially, that it still lives. My aim has been to address the stakes of the psychoanalytic thought through which we speak of this birth that was not a birth, this rupture that is being called, in different quarters, a repetition.

NOTES

1. This chapter was greatly assisted by readings from friends and colleagues. Many thanks to Michael O'Loughlin, Tammy Shefer, Derek Hook, Qadri Ismail, Maurits Van Bever Donker, Paulo Israel, and John Mowitt for generous feedback, criticisms, and comments. The NRF SARChI Chair for Social Change at the University of Fort Hare is duly acknowledged for financial support during the writing of this chapter.

2. De Kock testified before the TRC and was granted amnesty—the TRC granted amnesty for full disclosures of gross human rights violations in the period between 1960 and the first democratic election, later extended to May 10, 1994, the date Nelson Mandela was inaugurated as president of South Africa—for all but two of his operations. Gobodo-Madikizela also wrote her doctoral study (Gobodo-Madikizela, 1999), at least in part, on her interviews with de Kock.

3. The language here is crucial to the diagnosis of disavowal. On the one hand, apartheid violence is repudiated, complicity with it refused; on the other, the language of the repudiation dwells within the logic and grammar of colonial discourse, which is what, at an epistemic level, enabled the violence being denounced to occur in the first place. The more one insists, in the language of colonialism, that de Kock was "especially savage"—that he was, thus, primitive relative to one's own civilized position—the more the repudiation works against itself, the more complicit one becomes, at least at an unconscious, symptomatic level (see also Foster, Haupt, & De Beer, 2005).

4. It is important to note that Gobodo-Madikizela does not accept the death drive, a stance she takes more strongly in her (1999) dissertation. Much of the tension and contradiction in the book is issued from this refusal.

5. On Feldman's (2003) account, anti-apartheid activists would be driven to a remote spot—including Vlakplaas—and would frequently be made to collect wood for the fire that would later become a prop in the theater of their own interrogation and torture. Apartheid police officers frequently drank heavily during these *braais*.

6. An important backdrop to this is the coconstitution of race and sexuality in colonial and apartheid South Africa—and, if we follow Gunkel Henriette (2010), post-apartheid South Africa too. Significant here is Tammy Shefer's and Kopano Ratele's (2010) argument on "the exceptionality of South Africa as one of a few places where sexuality was flagrantly entwined with legislated race ideology and policy" (p. 28). Indeed, the numerous acts of apartheid formed a dense network of legislation that was underpinned as much by heteronormativity as by the ideology of racial superiority. Although desire for gender *difference* was normalized during apartheid—indeed, lawfully enforced—it was a desire for sexual difference designed to reproduce racial *sameness*. Thus, not only was racial mixing prohibited, as this risked the contamination of the purity of the *volk*, but so too was homosexuality, as this stood as an obstacle in the path of the reproduction of whiteness, biologically but also socially.

7. Many of the resonances are self-evident so I won't list them, but there are also some pronounced differences despite appearances. Consider how Freud writes of "the acknowledgement of the possession of a common substance," while Gobodo-Madikizela writes of an "identification with the other as 'bone of my bone.'" It is worthwhile marking the difference between the ego in the Freudian—and Lacanian—sense, an ego that is at its core alien, other, to itself, its desire issued from elsewhere, and the humanistic iteration of psychoanalysis in *A Human Being*. That is to say, the "sheer fact of his being human," which we are called to recognize, posits a kind of raw humanity, in the terms of structural anthropology. Yet, as Butler (1990) pithily notes, that which is "supposed to be most in the raw, proves always already 'cooked'" (pp. 37–38). Cooked here seems appropriate given that Freud speaks of a meal as the means by which a "common substance" is produced, lasting perhaps only as long as the meal is within the bodies of both parties. It is appropriate also given Gobodo-Madikizela's term, "bone of my bone."

8. "The *braai* torture," Feldman (2003) states, "was a pleasure inducing experience in which the subordination of racial Others was explicitly linked to heightened moments of commensality, object-choice, and virtual or symbolic cannibalism" (p. 253).

9. Citing a parliamentary address by South African statesman, Jan Smuts, Sitze is attentive to the way commissions of inquiry produced sympathy for the subject in rebellion. As Smuts stated regarding the Bondelzwarts Commission, "I have a certain amount of sympathy with them. I can understand that with their psychology, their past and their character, how they came to view things in the light they did, but even so they were not justified, and that, I take it, is the result that the majority of the Commission has arrived at, and that Commission was influenced by very real sympathy with them" (cited in Sitze, 2013, p. 166). It seems notable that Smut's (1925) *Holism and*

Evolution is the first South African text, to my knowledge, to invoke psychoanalytic theory, however wildly.

10. Sitze (2013) in fact pays close attention to *A Human Being*, and I must acknowledge a debt to his reading. He is, however, less concerned with her deployment of psychoanalysis than her elaboration of a concept of *Ubuntu*.

11. This chapter offers a few steps in the direction of such an analysis, but must leave several threads hanging, and I note just two here. First, the longer genealogy of empathy—or, rather, *Einfühlung*, from which empathy is a recent translation—in German Romanticism. Such a genealogy would allow the fetishism that resides within the conception of empathy to be underscored, particularly in Herder's anticolonial relativism. Given that apartheid ideologues such as Geoffrey Cronjé would elaborate in the 1940s the imperative for racial separatism upon the grounds of Herder's philosophy, at least in part, this seems crucial to a more sustained post-apartheid genealogy of empathy. Second, if the enactment of the violence of identification entails, as argued above, a foreclosure on, and an unconscious acting out of, homosexual desire, then the itineraries of subjectivity written into psychoanalytic conceptions of fellow feeling as the sublimation of narcissism, specifically the sublimation of homosexual desire as a form of narcissism (Freud, 1911), suggests a further isomorphism between conceptions of apartheid violence and conceptions of post-apartheid reconciliation implicit in the psychoanalytic logic to which post-apartheid South Africa has unwittingly committed itself. The work of Eve Kosofsky Sedgwick (1990) and Eric Santner (1996) on Freud's (1911) Schreber case would no doubt aid this line of analysis and complicate it too.

REFERENCES

Butler, J. (1997). *The psychic life of power: Theories in subjection.* Stanford, CA: Stanford University Press.

Butler, J. (1990). *Gender trouble: Feminism and the subversion of identity*. London & New York: Routledge.

Constitution of the Republic of South Africa Act 108 of 1996. Downloaded June 16, 2011 from http://www.info.gov.za/documents/constitution/1996/a108–96.pdf

Deleuze, G. (2007). In flux (Interview by Maurice Nadeau with Felix Guattari and Gilles Deleuze). In S. Lotringer (Ed.), & D. L. Sweet, J. Becker, & T. Adkins (Trans.) *Chaosophy: Texts and interviews, 1972–1977, Felix Guattari*. Los Angeles, CA: Semiotext(e).

Derrida, J. (1998). Geopsychoanalysis: ". . . and the rest of the world." In C. Lane (Ed.), *The psychoanalysis of race* (pp. 65–90). New York, NY: Columbia University Press.

Feldman, A. (2004). Memory theaters, virtual witnessing, and the trauma-aesthetic. *Biography, 27*(1), 163–202.

Feldman, A. (2003). Strange fruit: The South African truth commission and the demonic economies of violence. In B. Kapferer (Ed.), *Beyond rationalism: Rethinking magic, witchcraft and sorcery* (pp. 234–65). New York & Oxford: Berghahn Books.

Foster, D., Haupt, P. & de Beer, M. (2005). *The theatre of violence: Narratives of protagonists in the South African conflict*. South Africa: HSRC Press.

Foucault, M. (1977). Nietzsche, genealogy, history. In D. F. Bouchard (Ed.), *Language, counter-memory, practice: Selected essays and interviews by Michel Foucault* (pp. 139–64). Ithaca, NY: Cornell University Press.

Foucault, M. (1970). *The order of things: An archaeology of the human sciences*. London: Vintage Random House.

Freud, S. (1911). Psycho-analytic notes on an autobiographical account of a case of paranoia (dementia paranoides). In J. Strachey (Ed. & Trans.), *Standard edition of the complete psychological works of Sigmund Freud*, 12 (pp. 3–82). London: Hogarth Press.

Freud, S. (1913). Totem and taboo: Resemblances between the psychic lives of savages and neurotics. In J. Strachey (Ed. & Trans.), *Standard edition of the complete psychological works of Sigmund Freud*, 13 (pp. 1–161). London: Hogarth Press.

Freud, S. (1914). Remembering, repeating and working-through. In J. Strachey (Ed. & Trans.), *Standard edition of the complete psychological works of Sigmund Freud*, 12 (pp. 147–56). London: Hogarth Press.

Freud, S. (1917). Mourning and melancholia. In J. Strachey (Ed. & Trans.), *Standard edition of the complete psychological works of Sigmund Freud*, 14 (pp. 243–58). London: Hogarth Press.

Freud, S. (1920). Beyond the pleasure principle. In J. Strachey (Ed. & Trans.), *Standard edition of the complete psychological works of Sigmund Freud*, 29 (pp. 7–64). London: Hogarth Press.

Freud, S. (1921). Group psychology and the analysis of the ego. In J. Strachey (Ed. & Trans.), *Standard edition of the complete psychological works of Sigmund Freud*, 28 (pp. 69–143). London: Hogarth Press.

Freud, S. (1923). The Ego and the Id. In J. Strachey (Ed. & Trans.), *Standard edition of the complete psychological works of Sigmund Freud*, 19 (pp. 12–66). London: Hogarth Press.

Fuss, D. (1994). Interior colonies: Frantz Fanon and the politics of identification. *Diacritics*, *24*(2–3), 20–42.

Fuss, D. (1995). *Identification papers*. London and New York: Routledge.

Gobodo-Madikizela, P. (1999). *Legacies of violence: An in-depth analysis of two case studies based on interviews with perpetrators of a "Necklace Murder and with Eugene de Kock."* Unpublished doctoral dissertation, University of Cape Town-South Africa.

Gobodo-Madikizela, P. (2003). *A human being died that night: A South African woman confronts the legacy of apartheid*. New York, NY: First Mariner Books.

Gunkel, H. (2010). *The cultural politics of female sexuality in South Africa*. London and New York: Routledge.

Khanna, R. (2003). *Dark continents: Psychoanalysis and colonialism*. Durham, NC: Duke University Press.

Lorde, A. (1984 [2007]). The master's tools will never dismantle the master's house. *Sister Outsider: Essays and Speeches* (pp. 110–14). Berkeley, CA: Crossing Press.

Mannoni, O. (1969). "Je sais bien, mais quand même . . ." In *Clefs pour l'imaginaire; ou L'autre scène* (pp. 9–33). Paris: Seuil.
Parker, A. (2010). *Fifty people who stuffed up South Africa.* South Africa: Two Dogs.
Sachs, A. (2003). Preface. In P. Gobodo-Madikizela, *A human being died that night: A South African story of forgiveness* (2nd ed.) (pp. vii–xi). South Africa: David Phillip.
Santner, E. (1996). *My own private Germany: Daniel Paul Schreber's secret history of modernity.* Princeton, NJ: Princeton University Press.
Sedgwick, E. K. (1990). *Epistemology of the closet.* Berkeley, CA: University of California Press.
Shefer, T. & Ratele, K. (2011). Racist sexualisation and sexualised racism in narratives on apartheid. *Psychoanalysis, Culture and Society, 16*(1), 27–48.
Sitze, A. (2013). *The impossible machine: A genealogy of South Africa's truth and reconciliation commission.* Ann Arbor, MI: University of Michigan Press.
Smuts, J. (1925). *Holism and evolution.* London: Macmillan and Co.
Swartz, L. & Drennan, G. (2000). The cultural construction of healing in the truth and reconciliation commission: Implications for mental health practice. *Ethnicity and Health, 5*(3–4), 205–13.

Chapter 12

Specters of Genocide

Mass Graves, Horror Film, and Impunity in Post-Dictatorship Spain

Scott Boehm

In this chapter, I will discuss three elements of Spanish culture—mass graves, horror film, and impunity—in order to paint a picture of postdictatorship Spain that challenges common ways of depicting and perceiving a country that has successfully marketed itself as a fun tourist destination full of beautiful sunny beaches, cultural idiosyncrasies, and *mucha alegría*, that unique Spanish brand of happiness and contagious zest for living. Indeed, despite suffering several brutal years of economic crisis, staggering unemployment rates, and massive political corruption, in 2013 Spain regained its position, briefly usurped by China, as the world's third most popular tourist destination, welcoming a record 60.6 million international tourists. It would appear that the opportunity to run with bulls, catch a late night flamenco show, or marvel at the architectural wonders of Antoni Gaudí have not lost their global appeal in spite of the hard times that have fallen on Spain. Nor has the government's harsh austerity policy, which has cut health care services, education budgets, and social programs, translated into a shortage of funds to finance Madrid's quixotic quest to win the Summer Olympics, even though Barcelona hosted them as recently as 1992.

Not incidentally, during Spain's official presentation to the International Olympic Committee (IOC) in Buenos Aires in September 2013, Ana Botella, Madrid's conservative mayor and wife of former Spanish president José María Aznar, one of George W. Bush's key allies during the highly unpopular war in Iraq, repeatedly stressed the fact that life in Spain is "fun." Indeed, her appeal largely hinged on this seemingly immutable quality of Spanish culture, in sharp contrast to the country's staggering unemployment rate, which reached a record high of 27.2 percent during the first quarter of 2013, with youth unemployment peaking at 56.1 percent in August of that year (Burgen, 2013). It was the third consecutive bid for the summer games that Madrid lost, and the second during the final round of IOC voting, this time to Tokyo, a city that boasts, rather ironically, more flamenco bars than all of Spain. While Botella's performance was highly criticized within Spain for her poor English pronunciation and affected speech—and ridiculed to no end for her use of the instantly iconic "Spanglish" phrase "a relaxing cup of *café con leche*"—I would suggest there are much deeper issues at stake in her "typical Spanish" representation of Spain on the global stage at this crucial point in the nation's history; issues that relate specifically to the ethics of remembering and the consequences of forgetting the horrific genocide that took place during the 1936 fascist military coup that led to the Spanish Civil War and that continued under the repressive rule of General Francisco Franco from 1939 to 1975, making his dictatorship one of the longest—and bloodiest—in modern history.

Botella's speech is an object lesson in how Spain continues to sell itself to the world while completely effacing the country's recent genocidal past, which includes 114,266 certified cases of enforced disappearance. However, it is anything but new; Manuel Fraga Iribarne, the powerful Minister of Information and Tourism under Franco, popularized the slogan "Spain is different!" in the 1960s, a statement that simultaneously exoticized Spanish culture while legitimizing the dictatorship (Crumbaugh, 2010). Yet Botella's speech occurred precisely at a moment when the historical trauma of genocide in Spain has come under increased international scrutiny on two different fronts: the United Nations and an Argentine judge. Shortly after Botella left Buenos Aires empty-handed, departing the continent flanked by Spanish president Mariano Rajoy and Spain's crown prince, the United Nations Working Group on Enforced or Involuntary Disappearances visited Spain and concluded that "the State must assume a leadership role and engage more actively to respond to the demands of thousands of families searching for the fate or whereabouts of their loved ones who disappeared during the civil war and the dictatorship" (UN Human Rights Office of the High Commissioner, para. 2). This followed Argentine judge María Romilda Servini de Cubría's decision to issue international arrest warrants for four former officials of the Francoist dictatorship for their involvement in crimes against humanity, a legal act that cut straight through the official discourse of "Spanish fun" reproduced by the twenty-first-century Spanish flotilla to Latin America.

Judge Servini de Cubría's investigation of torture and other human rights violations during the Francoist dictatorship is the latest example of how specters of genocide haunt post-dictatorship Spain. Initiated in response to a criminal lawsuit filed in Buenos Aires in April 2010 by Darío Rivas and Inés García Holgado, both of whom have family members who forcibly disappeared in Spain, the case is the first time the international law principle of universal jurisdiction is being employed by a foreign judge to investigate crimes in Spain. Importantly, it was none other than former Spanish judge Baltasar Garzón who first tested the principle when he issued an arrest warrant for Chilean dictator Augusto Pinochet in 1998. Pinochet was subsequently placed under house arrest while traveling in England but was allowed to return to Chile by British Home Secretary Jack Straw who rejected Garzón's request for his extradition to Spain, citing Pinochet's poor health. In 2005, Garzón invoked universal jurisdiction again in order to prosecute former Argentine naval officer Adolfo Scilingo for genocide and other crimes against humanity. Found guilty of numerous charges, Scilingo was sentenced to 640 years in prison, which he is currently serving in Spain.

Following that success, Garzón opened a historic investigation of the Francoist dictatorship in 2008, citing universal jurisdiction in order to circumvent Spain's 1977 amnesty law, which prohibits the prosecution of crimes committed during the dictatorship. However, in this case, Garzón was quickly forced to close the investigation and suspended from the Spanish Criminal Court by a vote of his peers, and later made to stand trial in the Spanish Supreme Court for charges of "*prevaricación*," or knowingly abusing one's legal jurisdiction. Ironically, when dealing with crimes against humanity, the Spanish judiciary extended Garzón's jurisdiction to Latin America, but swiftly curtailed it when he set his sights on Spain itself. Such a glaring inconsistency raised red flags among the international law community and human rights groups, but particularly affected the family members of the disappeared in Spain who, at the time, saw the case as their first, and only, possibility for justice. Servini de Cubría's investigation revived those hopes; four years after Rivas and Holgado filed the original suit, it now has 120 plaintiffs.

The double standard applied by the Spanish judiciary to Garzón's investigation of crimes against humanity in Spain signals the country's institutionalized refusal to deal with the specters of genocide created by the Francoist state. That genocide was forcibly forgotten during the country's "transition to democracy" after Franco's death in 1975. Known simply as *la Transición* in Spain, that sociopolitical process orchestrated by cultural elites with strong ties to the dictatorship had been considered sacrosanct within Spain and hailed almost univocally by historians and political scientists as an exemplary model for how to peacefully establish democracy in the wake of dictatorship. The 1977 Amnesty Law was a key piece of legislation of the Transition that officially mandated the enforced forgetting of genocide under Franco and impeded any possibility for achieving substantive justice in post-dictatorship Spain. However, in December 2000, the first public, mass grave exhumation that brought the specter of genocide back into the national spotlight took place on the outskirts of Priaranza del Bierzo, a small village in northern Spain. As Emilio Silva (2003), the journalist responsible for that exhumation and the founder of the Association for the Recovery of Historical Memory notes in his account of that ground-breaking moment in post-dictatorship Spain, the exhumation disrupted celebratory narratives of the Transition: "Without being completely aware of it, the work we were doing contained an implicit critique of the Transition" (p. 135, translation mine). In fact, the Transition was never as peaceful as its proponents had suggested, nor did it provide a means to reckon with the exterminatory violence of the recent past, which produced wounds that continue to fester nearly forty years after Franco's death (Sánchez Soler, 2010; Moreiras-Menor, 2002; Vilarós, 1998).

On the contrary, the "success" of the Transition was rooted precisely in the twin cultural pacts of silence and forgetting that made it impossible for such a reckoning to occur since politicians and the mass media agreed not to speak about the traumatic past (Navarro, 2009; Cardús i Ros, 2000). In lieu of a truth and reconciliation commission or a national dialogue on the crimes against humanity that occurred during the dictatorship, the Transition "was possible to a large extent because it guaranteed the continuity of the fundamental institutions and apparatuses of the state, particularly the Civil Service, and especially those that had played a central role in the previous regime, as was the case with the state police force, the *Guardia Civil*," as Salvador Cardús i Ros has noted (Cardús i Ros, 2000, p. 21). Instead of human rights, the Transition granted Spaniards the "right" to look toward the future, which superseded desires for transitional justice in Spain. As President Mariano Rajoy stated in a 2008 interview while campaigning for the office he now holds, "I believe that all Spaniards have the right to look towards the future and not generate tension or division, as we decided in 1978 [the year the Spanish Constitution was approved]" ("Rajoy," translation mine). As an answer to a question about whether the family members of the disappeared have the right to recover their remains, Rajoy's statement succinctly summarizes what I will refer to throughout this chapter as "Transition ideology," the culturally ingrained injunction to forget the crimes of the past and to focus on a united Spanish future.

Transition ideology implicitly carries the command to ignore the personal pain and social tensions related to the on-going injustice produced by genocide with effects that are perpetuated by the culture of impunity that characterizes post-dictatorship Spain. Unfortunately for the surviving family members of the victims of genocide—and put in the terms of Raymond Williams (1977)—while an ethics of remembering has emerged from the Priaranza exhumation, Transition ideology remains dominant in Spain. Transition ideology has been passed on from one generation of Spaniards to the next, while the specters of genocide continue their ghostly struggle for recognition in the national imaginary. In recent years, they have done this most forcibly by haunting the present through mass grave exhumations that disrupt the smooth functioning of ideology, and more subtly, their apparition in a Spanish horror film. But before touching on both of those topics, it is necessary to provide an overview of the genocide I have been referring to, since unlike the Holocaust or the thirty thousand *desaparecidos* produced by Argentina's "Dirty War," the genocide that took place in Spain remains relatively unknown, or at least underappreciated in terms of its scope, despite its similarities, and convergences with both of those historical traumas.

THE GENOCIDE OF *"LOS ROJOS"*

We must extend terror, it's necessary to leave the sensation of domination, eliminating—without hesitation—all those who don't think like us.

—General Emilio Mola (July 19, 1936, *Bando Adicional*, Seville; Qtd. in Armengou & Belis, 2006, p. 28, translation mine)

General Emilio Mola, also known as "The Director," was the key organizer of the 1936 fascist military coup against the Second Spanish Republic, which led to the Spanish Civil War (1936–1939). In the quote above, he minces no words in the orders given two days after the coup broke out in Spanish Morocco on July 17, a day before its scheduled launch across Spain. As Mola makes clear, from the beginning, the coup was intended to be much more than just a power grab or another *pronunciamiento* of the kind that was common in Spain during the nineteenth century; rather, it was a violent exercise in the total elimination of dissent from the retrograde ideas about what characteristics constituted "Spanishness" and who belonged to the Spanish "race" held by Mola, Franco, and the handful of generals who led the coup. As Michael Ugarte (2007) has pointed out, "racial and ethnic conflicts and tensions have received little attention in the otherwise multilayered social and literary historiography of the Spanish Civil War" but that "race in all its complexity, both as a real marker of human existence and as a construction, played an immensely important role in the war" (p. 109). The racial ideas held by the rebels during the coup were rooted in nostalgia for the national spirit that animated Spain's "glorious" colonial past, the last remnants of which—Cuba, Puerto Rico, and the Philippines—had been lost to the United States during the Spanish-American War in 1898. Based on cultural, rather than biological, conceptions of race, "they refer to a cultural race from which the national community creates racial myths founded in the idea of a 'racism without a race,'" as noted by Cristina Moreiras-Menor (2007, p. 124). However, it is important to point out that the racial ideas behind the genocide that took place in Spain were developed in the blatantly—and biologically—racist colonial context of North Africa between 1898 and 1936 and then violently mapped onto social, economic, and political tensions on the Spanish Peninsula.

The majority of the military officers involved in the 1936 coup had spent significant time during the 1920s engaged in ruthless military campaigns in Morocco in an attempt to reclaim national honor lost during what was popularly known in Spain as "the disaster of '98." Led by the Spanish Foreign Legion, which Franco helped found in 1920, the colonial occupation of North Africa served as a crucible for the development of a racialized national identity forged through the massacre—and frequent beheading—of Moroccans who were considered subhuman barbarians by Spanish troops (Balfour, 2002). The sense of racial distinctiveness and superiority that this violent colonial experience engendered in the leaders of the military campaigns was, in turn, mapped onto the Spanish domestic context of the 1930s, during which the Spanish working class began to enjoy a share of political and economic power. This shift threatened the hierarchical social order that had been dominated for centuries by the Catholic Church, the monarchy and large landowners supported by the military and caciques, local political bosses who wielded significant power over election results. As Helen Graham (2005) has observed, "what was deadly about this new interpretation of imperial defense was that it came to be directed against other groups of Spaniards who symbolized the social and economic changes occurring in the towns and cities [of Spain]" (p. 3). One of the coup's principal aims was to resubjugate the Spanish working class and to restore the old order by employing colonial military tactics developed in Morocco. This was easy to do, since, as Paul Preston (2012) notes:

> The leaders of the rebellion, Generals Mola, Franco and Queipo de Llano, regarded the Spanish proletariat in the same way they did the Moroccan, as an inferior race that had to be subjugated by sudden, uncompromising violence. Thus they applied in Spain the exemplary terror they had learned in North Africa by deploying the Spanish Foreign Legion and Moroccan mercenaries, the Regulares, of the colonial army. (p. xii)

In order to understand the genocidal dimension of the violence unleashed by the 1936 coup, it is necessary to keep this colonial context in mind. The coup was, in large part, the deadly inward turn of racialized violence to eradicate the threat of a perceived internal Other in order to save the nation and restore the traditional social, economic, and religious order. According to such logic, it makes sense that Franco referred to the Spanish Civil War as "a crusade."

That crusade was waged specifically against those who, in the minds of the rebel conspirators, had stealthily taken the country captive through the "foreign" apparatus of the Second Spanish Republic, the first truly democratic period in Spanish history, which lasted from April 14, 1931, until the end of the Spanish Civil War on April 1, 1939. Among other things, the first

Republican government carried out projects that included the redistribution of political and economic power, the revoking of privileges traditionally enjoyed by the Catholic Church, liberal educational reforms, and the construction of new, secular schools, as well as attempts at agrarian reform. Because these sweeping social changes came so rapidly and because they occurred in Spain, a country with a long history of militant Catholicism, the Republic was viewed by its enemies as a frontal assault on traditional Spanish society. Not surprisingly then, the desire to save Spain from what was perceived as a foreign political invasion with roots in French revolutionary thought, European liberalism and Russian bolshevism drew further inspiration from the *Reconquista* that ended centuries of Islamic rule in Spain with the expulsion of the Moors in 1492, a date that concurrently marks Spain's inauguration as an imperial power.

Thus, religiously tinged and racially charged nostalgic desires for domination and the recuperation of imperial greatness, linked historically to both 1492 and 1898 converged with modern fascism to destroy the Republic and eliminate its supporters through genocidal violence. These forces would ultimately converge into a dictatorship composed of heterogeneous, and sometimes volatile, elements bound together by a shared sense of who belonged to the Spanish "race" and who had become traitors to it. Such "race traitors" were referred to as *los rojos* ("the reds"), who constituted *la anti-España* ("the anti-Spain"). The consequences of such classification had far-reaching effects that included the mass expropriation of property, imprisonment, torture, slave labor, summary execution, and involuntary disappearance. In 1938, Antonio Vallejo Nájera, a Nazi-trained psychiatrist and one of the founders of the Spanish Psychological Society, even began experiments with concentration camp prisoners in order to search for "the red gene" (González Duro, 2009). His eugenic policies led to the theft of at least thirty thousand "red" babies, oftentimes after the mothers had nursed them for several months while in prison. The mothers were frequently executed afterwards, and the babies were given to Francoist parents to be raised with what were considered to be proper Spanish values. This strategy was intended to improve the Spanish stock and regenerate the Spanish "race" (Armengou & Belis, 2006).

The division of Spaniards along such constructed racial lines was not fleeting, and there is evidence that suggests they have not entirely vanished from the psyche of the victors and their offspring in post-dictatorship Spain. As dictator, Franco sought to preserve these constructed racial divisions not only through fierce repression, but also through ideological cultural production. By far the most conspicuous example of this is the story he personally wrote for the screen under the pseudonym Jaime de Andrade. The film *Raza/Race* (Sáenz de Heredia, 1942) was Spain's first superproduction. The story follows the decisions and subsequent fates of four siblings during the Second Spanish

Republic and the Spanish Civil War. Significantly, it begins with the death of their father, a navy captain, during the Spanish-American War in 1898 and concludes with a happy fascist ending that includes real footage of Franco's victory parade through Madrid in 1939. In effect, *Raza* narrates the triumph of the "Spanish" will from devastating colonial loss to their modern *Reconquista* of Spain. To underscore the reconquest narrative, Franco draws selectively on Iberian history and elevates *Los Almogavares*—Christian foot soldiers from the thirteenth and fourteenth centuries who fought during the *Reconquista*—to mythical status. Before his death off the coast of Cuba, Captain Pedro Churruca tells his four young children a heroic version of the *Almogavares* legend and claims that they were "elected warriors, the best representatives of the Spanish race: firm fighters, agile, and determined in maneuvers." Pedro's son José, a cinematic surrogate for Franco played by Alfredo Mayo—the Antonio Banderas of his day—demonstrates the *Almogavare* spirit throughout the film, making his character the intended ideological point of identification for mass audiences. At the same time, it glorified the 1936 coup and depicted the Spanish Civil War as a heroic struggle of epic proportions that confirmed Spanish racial superiority over the anti-Spanish *rojos*.

As *Raza* demonstrates, for those who posited themselves as the chosen defenders of the true Spanish race, and who imagined themselves engaged in a modern crusade against foreign ideas that had invaded Spain during the first third of the twentieth century, *los rojos* embodied a racialized political identity that consisted of various traits and affiliations deemed antithetical to the spirit of the Spanish race. Specifically, *los rojos* included people associated with the "Bolshevik," "Jewish," and "African" ideas of democracy, liberalism, socialism, communism, anarchism, trade unionism, and freemasonry. They also included the landless rural poor, day laborers, urban workers, liberal teachers, gays and lesbians, feminists, atheists, gypsies, even nudists, and vegetarians (Preston, 2012). Seen as threats to the nation and denounced—without irony—for their *ideas avanzadas* (advanced ideas), *los rojos* were targeted for elimination in the plans laid out for the 1936 coup. Two weeks before the coup unleashed widespread exterminatory violence across Spain—much of which was carried out by members of *La Falange*, the Spanish fascist party—General Mola issued the following order: "Eliminate the leftist elements: communists, anarchists, sindicalists, masons, etc." (Espinoza Maestre, 2007, p. 59, translation mine). The content and syntax of this statement echoes that most haunting line of Western literature found in Joseph Conrad's *Heart of Darkness*, Kurtz' order to "Exterminate all the brutes!"

Spanish historian Francisco Espinoza takes such instructions as evidence of the "genocidal spirit" of the 1936 coup. He claims that "for the rebels, [the reds] were infrahumans who were not to be considered prisoners, nor even Spaniards" (p. 59, translation mine). Espinoza, who is from Badajoz, the site of one of the most brutal episodes of repression during the Spanish Civil War, was one of the first historians to argue that the exterminatory violence generated by the coup merits the classification of genocide. Referring to the 2,500 *desaparecidos* in the province of Huelva alone, Espinoza states:

> The word to define the action that ended their lives should be crime against humanity or genocide in the sense originally given to it by its creator, the Polish lawyer Rafael Lemkin, of systematic criminality against a group, or in the dictionary definitions: the systematic extermination of a social group for racial, religious or political motive. (p. 59, translation mine)

Like Espinoza, I maintain that genocide is the most appropriate term to describe the type of mass extermination that took place not only during the coup and the Spanish Civil War, but also during the particularly repressive early years of the Francoist dictatorship, a period that British historian Michael Richards has dubbed "a time of silence" due to the traumatic nature of the "purification" that took place during those years (Richards, 1998), which persisted throughout the duration of the dictatorship. For although it is true that the level of state repression decreased as time went on, we should remember that Franco notoriously ordered the execution of five members of Euskadi Ta Askatasuna (ETA), the armed Basque separatist organization, and El Frente Revolucionario Antifascista y Patriótico (FRAP), the Revolutionary Antifascist Patriotic Front, while on the verge of death himself on September 27, 1975, thirty-nine years after the coup. It's also true that it was not necessary to keep up the level of repression maintained from 1936 to 1945 since the genocide carried out during those years was so thorough. Furthermore, at the end of the Spanish Civil War, thousands of *los rojos* fled Spain and lived in exile never to return to the country until Franco's death if ever. This is to neither forget nor minimize the constant acts of daily resistance to the dictatorship—armed and otherwise—but to highlight the fact that the genocide of *los rojos* was as devastating as it was extensive.

By the numbers, conservative estimates of that genocide include the extra or quasi-judicial deaths of over 150,000 people (Preston, 2012). These deaths occurred not on battlefields, but on the outskirts of small villages or in Franocist prisons. Richards cites official state reports from 1939–1944 that list 192,684 cases of persons who were "executed or died in prison" (Richards, 1998, p. 179). At least another 100,000 died at the front lines defending the Republic against the Spanish rebels who were supported and supplied generously by Hitler, Mussolini, and the Texaco Oil Company from 1936–1939 (Preston, 2012). Hundreds of thousands more died during the mass aerial bombing of "red" cities, such as Gernika, Barcelona, and Madrid, as well as from disease, hunger, suicide, torture, and forced labor in prisons and concentration camps in Spain, France, and Germany (Lafuente, 2002; Rodrigo, 2003). As noted earlier, thirty thousand babies were stolen from their "red" parents in order to improve the nation's "racial hygiene," a crime included in the definition of genocide found in the Convention on the Prevention and Punishment of the Crime of Genocide adopted by the United Nations and the International Criminal Court. Judge Baltasar Garzón's 2008 investigation of the dictatorship certified 114,266 cases of enforced disappearance, though the actual number of *desaparecidos* is certainly much higher. Through the mass grave exhumations that have become ubiquitous throughout Spain since the exhumation at Priaranza del Bierzo in 2000, the ghosts of those that Franco, Mola and the other coup organizers sought to eradicate completely from national memory have returned to haunt post-dictatorship Spain much in the same way Joan Ramon Resina claims, "a memory that will not let up, that insists on being there in its paradoxical nonpresence, is the territory of the ghost" (Resina, 2000, p. 102).

MASS GRAVES AND THE RETURN OF THE DISAPPEARED

There are few things as horrifying as peering into the depths of a mass grave. Bones piled randomly on top of each other elicit primal fears of arbitrary death, abandonment, and postmortem anonymity. Skulls gaze back at you, eerily interrogating your stare with their unspeakable knowledge. Bullet holes in the back of craniums bear witness to human brutality, scenes of which are involuntarily imagined through the instant recall of black and white images of summary executions and concentration camps, collective memories fixed by film footage of atrocities committed during the long twentieth century. Femurs, tibias, and vertebra strewn haphazardly in the dirt testify to the violence and disdain with which those deemed undesirable were made to disappear. Fragments of ribs and tiny finger bones reveal the fragility of the human skeletal structure hidden beneath the surface of our seemingly impenetrable skin. Teeth still sparkling among the dirt, become uncanny reminders that such prostrate remains were once full of life—life abruptly denied the right to exist by a firing squad.

Standing at the edge of a mass grave is to find oneself on the precipice of the real lurking in everyday experience, where a picturesque field of wheat is suddenly transformed into a crime scene. A frightening abyss is exposed beneath the apparently peaceful pastures where sheep roam oblivious; picturesque rural landscapes take on a sinister, haunted appearance. Such proximity to the remains of violent death incites feelings of dread because it explodes notions of personal security and cultural stability. Looking closely at a mass grave is to risk putting comforting notions about historical progress in jeopardy. It is a precarious act, in which traumatic memories of the past flash up, revealing the present as a moment pregnant with the seeds of danger, sown with hate.

Like Walter Benjamin's angel of history, who sees a catastrophe buried under triumphal narratives of historical progress, submitting oneself to the gaze of the undead is to become burdened by the human wreckage covered up by official history and national myths (Benjamin, 1955). It is to become a witness to genocidal violence that challenges dominant cultural fantasies that predetermine ways of perceiving and interpreting "reality." It exposes unsolved crimes and demands retributive justice. Such an encounter is akin to finding oneself in the middle of a horror film in broad daylight, far from the enveloping darkness of a movie theater or the comfort of one's home.

Also, like a well-made horror film, mass grave exhumations provoke a multitude of effects that endure long after the initial shock fades away. The labor of forensic archeologists, cultural anthropologists, and dedicated volunteers not only cuts through land and soil, transforming the physical landscape; it also breaks cultural taboos. This results in the suspension of the laws and social practices that have constituted the symbolic order up until the steady work of picks and shovels disrupts the doxa of involuntary disappearance as a naturalized, unspoken phenomenon, underpinning the social relations of the rural village or the small town where the exhumation takes place.

Until—and unless—their remains are located, exhumed, identified, and reburied, the disappeared are nothing less than the living dead, trapped between life and death. They are condemned to haunt the present with their demands for justice, while waiting for the dignified burial they were denied by their executioners. Significantly, commemorations of the disappeared whose remains have been recovered take various forms, but almost always contain a public dimension however small. This makes them an ethical act of remembering the victims of genocide—and whatever political beliefs, class associations or racialized traits had made them a target for elimination—while reclaiming their human dignity and inserting them back into the symbolic order from which they were banished for decades.

Such acts are crucial for reinscribing the disappeared into the fabric of the local community's memory, as well as the memory of the nation. As Slavoj Žižek has observed:

> The funeral rite exemplifies symbolization at its purest: through it, the dead are inscribed in the text of symbolic tradition, they are assured that, in spite of their death, they will "continue to live" in the memory of the community. The "return of the living dead" is, on the other hand, the reverse of the proper funeral rite. While the latter implies a certain reconciliation, an acceptance of loss, the

> return of the dead signifies that they cannot find their proper place in the text of tradition. The two great traumatic events of the Holocaust and the Gulag are, of course, exemplary cases of the return of the dead in the twentieth century. The shadows of their victims will continue to chase us as "living dead" until we give them a decent burial, until we integrate the trauma of their death into our historical memory. (Žižek, 1991, p. 23)

What is true of the Holocaust and the Gulag also holds true for the genocide of *los rojos*, which should be understood within the same framework of twentieth-century European, and even world, history. The fact that it is overshadowed by those two monumental events does not diminish its status as a deeply traumatic event that continues to have repercussions well into the twenty-first century.

Furthermore, due to significant international involvement in the Spanish Civil War and the mass exile of *los rojos* from Spain after the fascist victory, what is often considered an isolated national trauma is not contained within the borders of Spain. It is transnational in the sense that its legacy can be traced from Spanish communities in southern France and Latin America to the few remaining volunteers who traveled to Spain to fight against Franco from countries as varied as England, Germany, Japan, Brazil, Mexico, and the United States in the International Brigades. The lack of recognition for the genocide of *los rojos* in post-dictatorship Spain is a testament to the "success" of the Transition, which, as I have discussed, sought to actively forget how genocide brought Franco to power and the state repression that kept him there for five decades through pacts of silence and forgetting imposed on society by cultural elites with ties to the dictatorship. But this does not account for why this particular historical trauma—and the Spanish Civil War in general—has been largely forgotten, or at least overlooked, by the rest of the world. In the case of the Western democracies that constituted the Allied forces, this can be explained by the fact that the Spanish Civil War disrupts celebratory narratives of the democratic victory over European fascism since the Allies not only failed to invade fascist Spain and remove Franco from power as they did in Italy and Germany, but also failed to support the democratic Spanish Republic during the 1936 coup and throughout the Spanish Civil War. The U.S. case is particularly egregious, since it lobbied for Francoist Spain's inclusion in the United Nations during the 1950s and legitimized the dictatorship during the Cold War since the genocide of *los rojos*—although never referred to as such—served as irrefutable proof that Franco was one of the world's most proven anticommunists.

In contrast with these different forms of cultural forgetting and historical negligence, the living dead who have returned to haunt post-dictatorship

Spain through the specter of mass grave exhumations, are being greeted with a desire to recover their memory not only by a significant sector of Spanish society, but also by a set of global volunteers whose diversity reflect a new iteration of the original International Brigades. This ethics of remembering is nothing less than the praxis of hospitality that Jacques Derrida prescribes in *Specters of Marx*, the inspiration for the title of this chapter (Derrida, 2006). In that book, Derrida theorizes the particular "ontology" of the living dead, which he names "hauntology" since the disappeared have been reduced to the status of ghosts. According to Derrida, the living have a debt to such specters, and as such, the ethical response to the ghosts of the disappeared is to provide them with the hospitality they were denied in both life and death, to grant them respite by recognizing and publicly mourning their loss, effectively inscribing them into Spanish—and global—cultural memory. In an important essay that reflects upon hauntology within the Spanish context, Spanish cultural critic Jo Labanyi cites Derrida when she claims "ghosts must be exorcised not in order to chase them away but in order 'this time to grant them the right [. . .] to [. . .] a hospitable memory [. . .] out of a concern for justice'" (Labanyi, 2000, p. 66).

However, since it is at odds with the cultural common sense manufactured by the Transition, the recovery of historical memory in Spain has been met with significant resistance not only from admirers of the dictatorship and the extreme right, but also from political moderates who have internalized Transition ideology. Perhaps the most pernicious example of this is PSOE, Spain's socialist party, which, while in power from 2004 to 2011, consistently retracted its support when the demands of the historical memory movement went beyond passing pieces of hollow legislation and paying lip service to the cause, despite protests from the right to the contrary. Yet at the same time the recovery of historical memory has been met with resistance, it has also heightened cultural anxieties, particularly through mass grave exhumations, since by their very nature exhumations stage confrontations with the traumatic real that dramatically return the living dead to cultural consciousness. Haunting photographs of mass graves capture the horror of genocide, and such glimpses of the real are regularly printed alongside portraits and accounts of the disappeared in Spanish newspapers and magazines. Accompanied by a steady stream of books, documentaries, and public acts dedicated to historical memory, they have made post-dictatorship Spain an uncanny place where cultural common sense is being contested. What had been regarded as familiar for decades is slowly coming undone (Ferrándiz & Baer, 2008; Ferrándiz, 2006). This may explain, in part, why Spain has experienced a renaissance of horror film production over the past fifteen years since the uncanny, ghosts, and cultural anxieties have always been the raw materials of the genre.

SCREENING TRAUMATIC MEMORIES: SPANISH HORROR FILM RENAISSANCE

In *The Horror Genre: From Beelzebub to Blair Witch,* film scholar Paul Wells claims "the history of the horror film is essentially a history of anxiety in the twentieth century" (Wells, 2000, p. 3). I would suggest that such a history shows no sign of changing course during the twenty-first century, and I would go so far as to claim that whoever writes the history of Spanish cinema a hundred years from now will undoubtedly see how the Spanish horror films of this century's first decade are unconsciously tied up with cultural anxieties elicited by the recovery of historical memory. In this section, after providing a brief overview of the Spanish horror film renaissance, I will discuss two horror films made by Spanish directors as examples of how such anxieties are projected on the big screen, with very different results.

If we are currently seeing a renaissance in Spanish horror, then it is a revival of a genre that saw its first boom in the late 1960s, which lasted until the mid-1970s. Aside from a few exceptions, particularly Narciso Ibáñez Serrador's *La residencia/The House That Screamed* (Ibáñez Serrador, 1969) and *¿Quién puede matar a un niño?/Island of the Damned* (Ibáñez Serrador, 1976), as well as Jorge Grau's *No profanar el sueño de los muertos/Let Sleeping Corpses Lie* (Grau, 1974), the first boom of Spanish horror was dominated by Jess Franco's countless B movies that often verged on soft pornography, as well as a slew of werewolf and vampire films, many of which starred Jacinto Molina Álvarez—better known as Paul Naschy—that also included a reliable, if fleeting, dose of female nudity. It is easy to understand how such films were popular at the time since they provided an escape from the harsh realities of life under the dictatorship while allowing viewers—particularly working-class male viewers—the possibility of fantasizing alternatives to their social castration and thwarted desire for control. These were fantasies often—though not always—played out at the expense of women, who were frequently treated as celluloid sex objects ready made for projecting male heterosexual aggression through gendered violence and recurrent sadomasochism.

By the end of the 1970s, however, Spanish horror film production had slowed significantly. It is impossible not to note that the drop in production follows Franco's death in 1975 and coincides with the period of the countercultural movement called *la movida madrileña* ("the Madrid scene"). That artistic, music, and social scene identified most closely with Madrid, but that included several other Spanish cities, launched the career of Pedro Almodóvar, Spain's most well-known film director. While Almodóvar's *oeuvre* is complex in the ways it handles the Francoist past—and it could be argued that his 2011 film *La piel que habito/The Skin I Live In* (Almodóvar, 2011) constitutes part of the Spanish horror film renaissance—his early films reflect the free spirit of the times after Franco's death, when Spaniards celebrated the freedoms denied during the dictatorship, in many cases to dangerous excess. The sudden lifting of state repression resulted in channeling decades of repression—and the cultural anxieties that repression produced—into an explosion of sex, drugs, and rock and roll rather than a desire for horror. Horror film production reached its lowest point in the 1980s when the socialist government introduced policies that allocated state funding for establishing what cultural elites considered a serious national cinema of "quality." Since horror did not meet such criteria, production ground to a near halt. It wasn't until the mid-1990s when a new generation of young Spanish filmmakers began experimenting with horror, most notably Alex de la Iglesia and Alejandro Amenábar, whose films *El día de la bestia/Day of the Beast* (de la Iglesia, 1995) and *Tésis/Thesis* (Amenábar, 1996), announced bold new possibilities for innovative work in the genre, laying the groundwork for the current renaissance. While directors such as Juame Balagueró, Nacho Cerdá, Agustí Villaronga, and Santiago Seguro all made horror films of note during the 1990s, Amenábar's English language horror film, *The Others* (Amenábar, 2001), is often seen as marking the arrival of a Spanish horror film renaissance due to its massive international box office success.

The only other horror Spanish language film made by a Spanish director that was an international hit is Juan Antonio Bayona's *El orfanato/The Orphanage* (Bayona, 2007), the first film I will analyze in some detail. However, at this point it may seem strange to readers who are familiar with Spanish horror that I have not mentioned either *El espinazo del diablo/The Devil's Backbone* (del Toro, 2001) or *El laberinto del fauno/Pan's Labyrinth* (del Toro 2006). While those films certainly form part of the renaissance in Spanish horror and deal explicitly with the trauma of the Spanish Civil War and the Francoist dictatorship, as a Mexican director, Guillermo del Toro approaches these subjects from the perspective of an artist who was not raised under Franco or inculcated with Transition ideology. This liberates him from the cultural anxieties that Spanish directors face; the result is the direct ways in which del Toro treats these subjects, in marked contrast with his Spanish counterparts who tend to make horror films in which the traumatic material remains latent rather than manifest, and in many cases apparently the result of unconscious artistic choices. However, it should be added that in addition to the very conscious films he has directed, del Toro has also played a major role in the Spanish renaissance in his capacity as producer, serving as executive producer for *El orfanato* and as a producer for *Los ojos de Julia/Julia's Eyes* (Morales, 2010), the second film I will examine briefly.

El orfanato, Juan Antonio Bayona's first feature film, charts the tragic fate of a married couple, Laura and Carlos, and their adopted child, Simón, who is HIV positive. The family moves to a large, abandoned house that previously housed the orphanage where Laura (played by Belén Rueda) grew up. Laura and Carlos, who is a doctor, plan on turning it into a residence for children with special needs. During the launch party for that project, Simón, who claims to have made contact with ghosts in the house, disappears. The rest of the film follows Laura's increasingly desperate search to find him, which leads her to the brink of madness. In order to highlight how *El orfanato* is tied up with the historical trauma of genocide, as well as how horror film can stage virtual encounters with the real in which viewers are forced to confront the unconscious remains of such traumas, I will focus on a crucial sequence that sets up the last act of the film.

The sequence begins with a shot that recalls Hitchcock's *Psycho*, as we observe Laura, who is perhaps already going crazy, descend the staircase of the orphanage and exit the house, heading toward an abandoned storage shed below. She enters the shed, an abject memory space full of antique remains where times has been suspended, in search of the next clue in a game she believes the ghosts have organized in order to lead her to Simón. The game involves linking a chain of apparently unrelated signifiers, unwittingly involving her in a spectral game of cognitively mapping her surroundings, which has the effect of transforming the familiar into the uncanny. While searching the shed, something out of place on the floor catches her eye. She recognizes it as a pendant worn by Bengina, a suspicious old social worker who was killed in a violent traffic accident, and she remembers that she had a bizarre encounter with Bengina in the shed after the woman came to visit her, uninvited. Laura makes an association between the pendant and what looks like an oven in a crematorium of a Nazi concentration camp, and here, we should note that tens of thousands of *los rojos* were deported to Nazi camps; more than seven thousand of them were sent to Mauthausen in Austria, where a large percentage of them died (Wingate Pike, 2000). Laura struggles to break through the locked door of the oven, an ideological barrier standing between her and the traumatic real, preventing her from seeing the whole of reality. When she finally breaks through, she finds herself peering into a black hole. She illuminates the darkness, sees a few sacks behind a row of bricks. Laura bravely enters the hole, physically placing her entire body within the dangerous zone of the real and starts removing the sacks one at a time. Just like breaking through the ideological door, it's not easy work, but she continues, propelled by the urgency of finding her disappeared son.

In a series of shots filmed with the camera mounted from within the depths of the oven, we see Laura as if viewing her from deep inside the Lacanian gaze, observing her actions from the position of the real. The door is transformed into an eye that remains hidden, which subsequently reveals the horror that ideology concealed: Laura is shocked by the discovery of human bones that have fallen out of a ripped sack and she becomes frightened that her dead son's remains might be among them. She proceeds to empty all the sacks. In the process, she converts the space into a virtual mass grave exhumation site. Foreshadowing the end of the film, Laura herself is transformed into a ghost when she unknowingly smears white ash across her face with the back of her hand.

In addition to simulating a mass grave exhumation, this sequence demonstrates the power of horror film to transmit emotions related to traumatic material, which is accomplished by our identification with Laura's loss and desire to recover her disappeared son. It is also an example of what film scholar Adam Lowenstein calls an "allegorical moment," which he defines as "a shocking collision of film, spectator, and history where registers of bodily space and historical time are disrupted, confronted, and intertwined" (Lowenstein, 2005, p. 2). Following Lowenstein's appropriation of Walter Benjamin, I see remnants of *Trauerspiel*, the Baroque German mourning plays that Benjamin used to formulate his thoughts of allegory, in this sequence of *El orfanato* and in much of recent Spanish horror (Benjamin, 1998). Benjamin claimed that in those German tragic mourning plays, allegory represented history as a "petrified, primordial landscape" of "decay," best encapsulated by the recurring symbol of the "death's head" (Benjamin, 1998, p. 166). I would argue that within the Spanish horror renaissance, a subgenre of "Spanish tragic mourning films" reflect a similar view of haunted history that employ many of the tropes and the specific melancholic mood of allegory that Benjamin describes. Additionally, for Benjamin, an allegorical moment is also "a moment of danger" in which an image—a memory—of the past flashes up suddenly, momentarily making evident the ways in which the past and the present are linked (Benjamin, 1955, p. 255). Like Laura's act of breaking through the oven door, an allegorical moment cuts through the blinders of ideology that prevent us from recognizing how the present is structured by past historical tragedies and traumas.

Thus, for Laura, the shock of her experience in the shed represents a point of no return. From this point on, her character behaves like a historical materialist lifted straight from Benjamin's "Theses on the Philosophy of History" (1955) as she seizes hold of the memory of the disappeared children whose remains she exhumed from the sinister oven. She realizes they were the remains of her childhood friends from the orphanage, and in a nod to *The Innocents* (Clayton, 1961), which Bayona cites as a key influence on *El orfanato*, Laura sends her doubting husband away and re-creates the conditions of the past, hoping that will allow her to see the ghosts with her own eyes. When the past is fully brought into the present—after Laura cleans the orphanage, decorates it just as it was thirty years earlier, puts on an orphanage uniform and prepares food for the ghosts, in effect, providing them with Derridean hospitality—the ghosts, do indeed, appear to her while playing the childhood game that opens the film in a brief flashback to Laura's youth at the orphanage.

The ghosts lead Laura to Simón's corpse lying in a hidden basement. She realizes she was responsible for her son's death by unknowingly blocking the door with a heavy object, converting Laura into the archetype of the monstrous mother. She responds by committing suicide by taking an overdose of Simón's HIV medication, and in a final twist, lives on in the spectral world, seemingly content surrounded by Simón and her childhood friends, although in her transformation, Laura has become a desexualized ideal mother figure trapped in a melancholic Neverland, much like Wendy in Peter Pan.

This, of course, is not the ending Benjamin would have liked to see; viewed from this perspective, it is a tragedy for historical materialists and a happy ending for conservative ideologues. However, the film's ending illustrates a vital point for understanding the disciplinary dimension of Transition ideology in post-dictatorship Spain, a concise summation of which is found in the frequently repeated maxim: "no remover el pasado para no re-abrir las heridas," which can be translated as "don't dig up the past to avoid reopening wounds." Throughout *El orfanato*, the two characters whose principal function is to support Laura—her husband and a female police psychologist—repeatedly instruct her to abide by this cultural common sense, to forget about finding Simón and to move on with her life after a relatively short period of time. Laura disobeys these patriarchal symbolic authorities, refusing to give way on her desire, but ends up paying the ultimate price. One way of interpreting the film then, is as a postmodern morality play inspired by Transition ideology that cautions viewers against digging up the past. In such a reading, Laura's suicide dramatizes the consequences of not adhering to Transition ideology and serves as a warning to those who would dare to follow her example.

In sharp contrast, Belén Rueda demonstrates a clear alternative to such an ending in her subsequent performance in *Los ojos de Julia*, another horror film released three years after *El orfanato*. In this film, directed by Guillem Morales, Rueda plays Julia, a woman with a degenerative eye disease that will eventually leave her blind, like her twin sister Sara, who is murdered in the first scene of the film. Just as in *El orfanato*, Rueda's character disobeys patriarchal symbolic authorities and investigates the murder, which the police quickly rule a suicide. Following the well-worn path of what feminist film scholar Carol Clover has termed "the Final Girl," doing so leads her into danger, but it also saves Julia from the hands of a psychopath who she discovers has murdered a large number of women in her sister's small community (Clover, 1993). Julia's digging in the past leads the psychopath to commit suicide in order to avoid arrest. Here, we have a message and an ending that are diametrically opposed to *El orfanato*: If you investigate crimes thoroughly, the truth will be uncovered and the agents of violence will self-destruct. Furthermore, the film demonstrates how Transition ideology prevents people from seeing the violence surrounding them, which will continue to constitute part of Spanish daily life unless viewers follow Julia's example and ignore symbolic authorities that—often through ignorance, negligence, and inertia, but sometimes quite consciously—are complicit with the maintenance of an unacknowledged culture of impunity.

While *Los ojos de Julia* can be analyzed from several perspectives—i.e., feminist critique, gender, and disability studies—what is most pertinent for my purposes is how the film exposes the dangers of widespread impunity. The failure of symbolic authorities to investigate a series of apparent suicides that turn out to be a string of homicides is precisely what allows the film's monster to terrorize his victims and their families without raising the eyebrows of the community. Until the film's climax, the police simply do not seem to notice that there is a murderer on the loose. In this way, *Los ojos de Julia* holds a mirror up to the culture of impunity that characterizes post-dictatorship Spain in which those responsible for genocide have enjoyed the protection afforded by relative anonymity due to the Transition's injunction to forget the crimes of the past, as well as by interventions by state authorities that have prevented those crimes from being investigated. Along these lines, I will end this chapter with a discussion of a few of the ways impunity is palpable in post-dictatorship Spain.

THE CULTURE OF IMPUNITY IN POST-DICTATORSHIP SPAIN

Judge Baltasar Garzón's historic criminal investigation of the Francoist dictatorship took place two years before *Los ojos de Julia* was released. That case marked the first attempt by a Spanish judge to investigate the crimes against humanity that formed the basis of the genocide of *los rojos*. As I noted earlier, Garzón was forced to close his investigation just a few weeks after he opened it. He was subsequently suspended from the Spanish judiciary, and later tried by the Supreme Court for *prevaricación*, or knowingly abusing his legal authority to investigate the dictatorship. Incredibly, the Supreme Court brought Garzón to trial, in part, based on a lawsuit prepared by *La Falange*, Spain's Fascist Party and one of the key agents of the genocide during the 1936 coup. The presiding judge, Luciano Varela, even personally helped members of *La Falange* modify the lawsuit when it was submitted to Spain's highest court with errors. While that suit was later dropped, two others put forth by Far Right organizations were accepted. Not surprisingly, they argued that "without doubt Judge Garzón has reopened wounds which we Spaniards—whatever our political beliefs—had totally recovered from," citing that sacred piece of Transition ideology nearly word for word (Spain's Franco-era probe, 2012, para. 15). Garzón was acquitted in this case, but only after he was convicted of the same charge in another case involving a massive corruption scandal involving Spain's Popular Party, the conservative party currently in power, led by Spanish president Mariano Rajoy. Garzón's conviction resulted in an eleven-year suspension from the bench.

Here it should be pointed out that Manuel Fraga, the Francoist official who popularized the "Spain is Different!" slogan while serving as the dictatorship's Minister of Information and Tourism, founded the Popular Party shortly after Franco's death. Until his own death in 2012, Fraga, who, like Franco, was from the northwestern autonomous community of Galicia, enjoyed a political career in the post-dictatorship that included long tenures as president of Galicia and as a senator in the Spanish Parliament. The fact that this former member of *La Falange* remained a fervent Franco admirer until the end, while holding such high political offices as late as 2011—at the age of eighty-nine—is, in fact, perhaps the most egregious example of the culture of impunity in post-dictatorship Spain. That Fraga was also a coauthor of Spain's 1978 constitution is further evidence of how the grounds for such impunity were laid by political agreements forged during the Transition. While it is hardly surprising that a leading Francoist official would not wish to investigate crimes committed by the dictatorship, it is telling that such a figure could flourish to such an extent in the democracy he helped shape.

Not long after Fraga's Popular Party won the presidential elections held conspicuously on November 20, 2011—the shared anniversary of the deaths of Franco and José Antonio Primo de Rivera, the founder of *La Falange*—President Mariano Rajoy cut the already meager state funding that had been allocated for mass grave exhumations by the Socialist government that had been in power since 2004. This dual blow to the historical memory movement—Garzón's suspension, which signified the end to hopes for a Spanish-led investigation of genocide in Spain, and the elimination of the mass grave exhumation budget—has not stopped it from continuing to make demands for justice and to find alternative sources of funding for exhumations. However, they illustrate how the culture of impunity that exists in post-dictatorship Spain is a consequence of decisions made at the highest levels of the state.

By now, it should be clear that such decisions are mediated by Transition ideology and have their roots in decisions made during the Transition itself. For in addition to preserving the fundamental bodies of the state, such as the Civil Service and the *Guardia Civil*, Cardús i Ros highlights the fact that the Transition also ensured the continuity of "other areas of administration and service, from state teachers or university professors to the administration of the judicial system" that "had, at different times and to different degrees, been accomplices to Franco's regime, which explains their enthusiastic collaboration in the task of hiding the footprints of compromising facts" (Cardús i Ros, 2000, p. 21). I would add that the injunction to forget the traumatic past has ensured not only that the perpetrators of crimes against humanity are free to walk the streets—and hold political office—in Spain, but that their victims and the family members of the disappeared are unable to enjoy such peace of mind or wield such political power. One result of this is that nearly forty years after Franco's death, asymmetries of power and social belonging that existed during the dictatorship, and that have their origins in the racial ideas of the 1936 coup organizers, remain. Those constructed racial divisions, which were brought to life on the Francoist big screen in order to retroactively justify the genocide of *los rojos* are still perceptible on the Spanish landscape.

A symbolic example of how these divisions have not been erased during the post-dictatorship period is that Antonio Vallejo Nájera, the Nazi-trained psychiatrist who led the search for the "red" gene and was responsible for initiating the theft of at least thirty thousand red babies as part of a state-sponsored eugenics policy, still has a street named after him in the center of Madrid. Like other key figures of the dictatorship—including Franco himself—the memory of Vallejo Nájera lives on in Spain's capital while street names that mark the memory of those who resisted fascism and the dictatorship are noticeably absent. Furthermore, two of the few existing examples of fascist architecture in Europe, Franco's Victory Arch, situated in the center of Madrid, and the Valley of the Fallen, Franco's monumental resting place located in a mountain range outside the city, have neither been destroyed, nor converted into museum spaces that offer critical pedagogical interpretations to the millions of tourists who visit or walk past these sites every year. They remain just as they did during the dictatorship, still maintained by the Spanish state. To put this in the plainest of American political terms: Spanish tax euros support the maintenance of fascist monuments constructed with slave labor instead of financing the exhumations of mass graves containing the remains of the victims of a genocide organized by fascists.

To conclude, the state-supported culture of impunity that exists in Spain means that Fraga's popular marketing slogan, "Spain is Different!" rings as "true" today as it did in the 1960s. While it was first employed as a means to justify—and efface—the Francoist dictatorship to foreign tourists as just another aspect of an exotic country full of entertaining traditions not to be found elsewhere, now it encapsulates Spain's paradoxical application of the legal principle of universal jurisdiction. Likewise, as Ana Botella's speech to the International Olympic Committee made clear on the world stage, Spain continues to sell itself unabashedly as a destination of exceptional fun while disavowing the blatant injustices that exist in post-dictatorship Spain. This lamentable state of affairs can be directly attributed to the calculated failure of the architects of the Transition to take an ethical position on addressing the genocide of *los rojos*. This was considered a success for Spanish democracy and is celebrated as such to this day by a majority of Spaniards due to the widespread internalization of Transition ideology that continues to dominate post-dictatorship Spain. Yet despite continued efforts to forget, ignore, and dismiss the historical trauma lying at the heart of Spanish society, the specters of genocide will continue to haunt Spain and its institutions until the state decides—or is forced—to recognize the criminal foundations upon which it is constructed.

If horror film has anything to teach us in such a context, it is that ghosts are hungry for recognition and that their appetites for hospitality do not disappear quite as easily as their bodies were once disposed of.

REFERENCES

Almodóvar, P. (Director). (2011). *La piel que habito*. [Motion Picture]. Spain: El Deseo.

Amenábar, A. (Director). (1996). *Tesis*. [Motion Picture]. Spain: Las Producciones del Escorpión.

Amenábar, A. (Director). (2001). *The Others*. [Motion Picture]. Spain: Las Producciones del Escorpión.

Armengou, M. & Belis, R. (2006). *Los fosas del silencio: Hay un holocausto español?*. Barcelona: Debolsillo.

Balfour, S. (2002). *Deadly Embrace: Morocco and the Road to the Spanish Civil War*. Oxford: Oxford University Press.

Bayona, J. (Director). (2007). *El orfanato*. [Motion Picture]. Spain: Rodar y Rodar Cine y Televisión.

Benjamin, W. (1955). Theses on the Philosophy of History. In H. Arendt (Ed.), *Illuminations: Essays and Reflections*. New York: Schocken Books.

Benjamin, W. (1998). *The Origin of German Tragic Drama*. London: Verso.

Burgen, S. (2013, August 30). Spain youth unemployment reaches record 56.1%. *The Guardian*. Retrieved from http://www.theguardian.com.

Cardús i Ros, S. (2000). Politics and the Invention of Memory: For a Sociology of the Transition to Democracy in Spain. In J. Resina (Ed.), *Disremembering the Dictatorship: The Politics of Memory in the Spanish Transition to Democracy*. Amsterdam: Editions Rodopi.

Clayton, J. (Director). (1961). *The Innocents*. [Motion Picture]. USA: Twentieth Century Fox Corporation.

Clover, C. (1993). *Men, Women and Chain Saws: Gender in the Modern Horror Film*. Princeton, NJ: Princeton University Press.

Crumbaugh, J. (2010). *Destination Dictatorship: The Spectacle of Spain's Tourist Boom and the Reinvention of Difference*. Albany, NY: State University of New York.

de la Iglesia, A. (Director). (1995). *El día de la bestia*. [Motion Picture]. Spain: Canal+ España.
del Toro, G. (Director). (2001). *El espinazo del diablo*. [Motion Picture]. Mexico: Tequila Gang.
del Toro, G. (Director). (2006). *El laberinto del fauno*. [Motion Picture]. Mexico: Tequila Gang.
Derrida, J. (2006). *Specters of Marx: The State of the Debt, the Work of Mourning and the New International*. New York: Routledge.
Espinoza Maestre, F. (2007). *La columna de la muerte: El avance del ejército franquista de Sevilla a Badajoz*. Barcelona: Crítica.
Ferrándiz, F. (2006). The Return of Civil War Ghosts. *Anthropology Today*, 22(3), 7–12.
Ferrándiz, F. & Baer, A. (2008). Digital Memory: The Visual Recording of Mass Grave Exhumations in Contemporary Spain. *Forum: Qualitative Social Research* 9(3), Art. 35.
González Duro, E. (2009). *Los Psiquiatras De Franco: Los rojos no estaban locos*. Barcelona: Ediciones Península.
Graham, H. (2005). *The Spanish Civil War: A Very Short Introduction*. Oxford: Oxford University Press.
Grau, J. (Director). (1974). *No profanar el sueño de los muertos*. [Motion Picture]. Spain: Star Films.
Ibáñez Serrador, N. (Director). (1969). *La residencia*. [Motion Picture]. Spain: Anabel Films.
Ibáñez Serrador, N. (Director). (1976). *¿Quién puede matar a un niño?* [Motion Picture]. Spain: Penta Films.
Labanyi, J. (2000). History and Hauntology; or, What Does One Do with the Ghosts of the Past? Reflections on Spanish Film and Fiction of the Post-Franco Period. In J. Resina (Ed.), *Disremembering the Dictatorship: The Politics of Memory in the Spanish Transition to Democracy*. Amsterdam: Editions Rodopi.
Lafuente, I. (2002). *Esclavos por la patria: La explotación de los presos bajo el franquismo*. Madrid: Temas de Hoy.
Lowenstein, A. (2005). *Shocking Representation: Historical Trauma, National Cinema, and the Modern Horror Film*. New York: Columbia University Press.
Morales, G. (Director). (2010). *Los ojos de Julia*. [Motion Picture]. Spain: Antena 3 Films.
Moreiras-Menor, C. (2002). *Cultura herida: Literatura y cine en la España democrática*. Madrid: Ediciones Libertarias.
Moreiras-Menor, C. (2007). War, Postwar, and the Fascist Fabrication of Identity. In N. Valis (Ed.), *Teaching Representations of the Spanish Civil War*. New York: Modern Language Association of America.
Navarro, V. (2009). *Bienestar insuficiente, democracia incompleta: Sobre lo que no se habla en nuestro país*. Barcelona: Anagrama.
Preston, P. (2012). *The Spanish Holocaust: Inquisition and Extermination in Twentieth-Century Spain*. London: Harper Press.
Rajoy cierra la Oficina de Víctimas como prometió en el 2008 (2012, March 2). *El Plural.com*. Retrieved from http://www.elplural.com/.

Resina, J. (Ed.) (2000). *Disremembering the Dictatorship: The Politics of Memory in the Spanish Transition to Democracy*. Amsterdam: Editions Rodopi.

Richards, Michael. (1998). *A Time of Silence: Civil War and the Culture of Repression in Franco's Spain, 1936–1945*. Cambridge: Cambridge University Press.

Rodrigo, J. (2003). *Los campos de concentración franquistas: Entre la historia y la memoria*. Madrid: Siete Mares.

Sáenz de Heredia, J. (Director). (1942). *Raza*. [Motion Picture]. Spain: Cancilleria del Consejo de la Hispanidad.

Sanchez Soler, M. (2010). *La transición sangrienta: Una historia violenta del proceso democrático en España (1975–1983)*. Barcelona: Edicciones Península.

Silva, E. (2003). *Las fosas de Franco: Crónica de un desagravio*. Madrid: Temas de Hoy.

Spain's Franco-era probe judge Baltasar Garzón on trial. (2012, January 24). BBC News Europe. Retrieved from http://www.bbc.co.uk/news.

Ugarte, Michael. (2007). The Question of Race in the Spanish Civil War. In N. Valis (Ed.), *Teaching Representations of the Spanish Civil War*. New York: Modern Language Association of America.

United Nations Human Rights Office of the High Commissioner. (2013). "U.N. experts urge Spain to do more to ensure justice for relatives of disappeared persons." Retrieved from http://www.un.org/.

Vilarós, T. (1998). *El mono del desencanto: Una crítica cultural de la transición española (1973–1993)*. Madrid: Siglo Veintiuno de España Editores.

Wells, P. (2000). *The Horror Genre: From Beelzebub to Blair Witch*. London: Wallflower Publishing Limited.

Williams, R. (1977). *Marxism and Literature*. Oxford: Oxford University Press.

Wingate Pike, D. (2000). *Spaniards in the Holocaust: Mauthasen, Horror on the Danube*. New York: Routledge.

Žižek, S. (1991). *Looking Awry: An Introduction to Jacques Lacan through Popular Culture*. Cambridge, MA: MIT Press.

Chapter 13

"Each of Us Bears His Own Hell"

A Window into Venues of Trauma in Central Eastern Europe

Reinhold Stipsits

Quisque suos patimur Manes—each of us suffers his own spirit

—Virgil, Aeneid, Book VI, line 743

In this essay, I base my exploration on the ideas of Egon Friedell (1878–1938) on cultural historiography. Friedell describes a threefold approach—aesthetic, ethical, and logical—to writing history. The first one aims at vivid description, the second at a pragmatic intentional description with a "moral" of application, while the third is genetic or developmental and is dominated by a logical moment.

I offer three experiences demonstrating aesthetic, ethical, and logical ways of dealing with trauma and history. The first one is linked to the Sathmar Swabians, a German-speaking minority in Romania; the second is linked to an almost forgotten war of resistance in Lithuania; and the third refers to the current situation in Moldova, where traumatized children are gathered in a city of orphans.

Based upon personal experiences, and encounters at sites where traumas have occurred, the memorials speak, lest we forget. This essay depicts meanings that are retained within the aura of buildings of historic importance, and their relevance to previous traumas.

IN THE LION'S DEN

From time to time, lecturers come from Babes-Bolyai University at Cluj-Napoca, the major city in Transylvania, to Satu Mare (as it is called in Romanian; Sathmar in German and Yiddish, Szatmárnémeti in Hungarian), to present a paper and stay overnight. Several students from tiny villages in the countryside take advantage of distance learning and so are grateful to be able to hear lecturers in town. Usually, professors from Cluj-Napoca rotate their turns at Satu Mare. It is quite a strain to travel to the province by train or by car to meet with just a handful of students. Still, it is a privilege to be invited to lecture to a small group of Sathmar Swabian students, and I was given this privilege. Indeed, it is a very rare opportunity for someone from the West who knows little about the history of the Romanian-Hungarian border area. Students wait impatiently to hear a lecture in German or, better, to have an opportunity to speak German. They are capable of speaking German, learned from their forefathers, but due to the current political situation, they speak German mainly at home and less in public. My lecture led to an intense group discussion. It was held just in time, before all the students of German had left, since many were moving abroad. After lectures in a jerry-built house, we bade each other farewell and I had to find my way to the university guesthouse.

The guesthouse is located on a side street of a suburb of Satu Mare, if a provincial town could ever claim to have a suburb. It is a villa that used to serve as lodgings for Ceausescu, the much-feared former Romanian dictator, whenever he visited the area. Designed in a charming provincial *nouveau-riche* style, the somewhat run-down building now serves as a guesthouse for the University of Cluj-Napoca.

Ceausescu's villa attracts little attention among the neighbors, but one should look at it carefully. The house is fenced in by neatly clipped hedgerows; a paved track leads to an unspectacular wooden door. Beyond the entry hall there is a fully equipped spic-and-span kitchen. Next to the kitchen, which seems not to have been used for a long time, there are guest rooms along a corridor. Stark walls with no pictures give the corridor an eerie atmosphere, reminiscent of Roman Polanski's (1965) film *Repulsion.* Shadows in the dim light reach out from the walls like hands trying to grasp at any newcomer. The odor of cheap cleaning supplies hovers over the floor. Farther down the corridor, a door opens into a very large living room furnished with heavy dark brown leather armchairs. This leads on to a gloomy reading room, which appears to once have housed a library though not a single book or journal remains on the shelves.

Next door there is a bathroom: strange dark brown tiles from top to bottom, a sink and an oversized tub with gold-plated mountings, and mirrors with gold-plated frames—pure *Kitsch.* The mirrors are mounted at the eye-level of a short person; any look in the mirror reflects a blurry image.

Next, in the bedroom there is a king-size bed, centrally positioned. The windows are locked tight and darkened with shutters. The air is musty and moldy. Next to the bedroom, there is a kind of a dressing room with walk-in cupboards. I open the door of one of the walk-in cupboards only to see a square hole on the floor. From there, a steep and narrow metal staircase leads into the dark of the basement, obviously an emergency exit. An underground walkway leads directly from the bedroom, its entrance well hidden in that walk-in-cupboard, through to the basement and out of the house into the garden or elsewhere. There is a haunting feeling of paranoia. If someone wanted to escape from the bedroom and out of the house, then it was also possible for someone to intrude from outside and enter the house and the bedroom. For example, any possible assassin of a tyrant could do so. Any way of escape could also become an access. Whoever protected a despot could also become the biggest threat to his life. Despotism is built upon a regime of terror and a network of agents. As long as distrust and weak egos reign, brutal force is needed to remain in power. And there has been much distrust and many stool pigeons. Informers were abundant in Ceausescu's Romania. The *Securitate* was at the top of the system. Ever-present in the villa in Sathmar is the *Ungeist*, the demon, the evil spirit of Nicolae Ceausescu, the "Conducător," the Genius of the Carpathians, the Titan of the Titans, the Son of the Sun, the Lion—all titles he bestowed on himself—a short person with a fifteen-year-long career as a despot.

As a guest professor, I was given the privilege of sleeping for two nights in the bed of the dictator! The advantage of this compared to ordinary citizens was disputable; I hardly found rest or sleep at all. Hallucinations and visions haunted me. Anxiety has never been a good counselor or instructor. Eerie daydreams, horrible nightmares were, to put it mildly, sensations I experienced. Did I step into the lion's den? Certainly the paranoia of the "Conducător," the "Great Leader," had an immense impact on the aura of this villa. And, I cannot deny the lingering impact on my awareness. In the lion's den, I took notes on the recollection of the stories the Sathmar Swabian students had shared with me.

Unresolved trauma tends to repeatedly occur like a haunting nightmare. It must have been so for all the Sathmar Swabian people, a minority within even a linguistic minority who spoke German more colored by the influence of the Swabian dialect rather than German itself, already a language not spoken in the region. Additionally, Swabians were seen as a minority with different customs and a peculiar ethos of being hard working. Driven by the pursuit of happiness and out of poverty they set off from their homes on barges, floated down the river Danube in the year 1712. They live somewhat constrained between and among Hungarian and Romanian people. They seem to have had a great talent for wrong choices, at least as proven by the course of history. Alas, they were punished or had to pay a high price for the wrong choices they made. Sathmar Swabians often opted for the "losers" in history by taking sides and thus made themselves losers.

I shall try to examine the trauma, the thoughts that still haunt people's minds. At some point, every choice made seems to have been a mistake. The official history, if ever told, consists of personal stories, those that are handed over to the next generation. All history is, first of all, a personal tradition. Personal stories are embedded in tales. Let me briefly summarize the history.

Transmigration seems to be the ongoing destiny of Sathmar Swabians. About three hundred years ago there was the Swabian Trek, which brought the people from what was known as Upper Swabia, Vorderösterreich, from cities such as Biberach in today's Germany, into the region between the rivers Thisza and Szamos (using Hungarian spelling) in the old area called Pannonia, north of the Danube (Hauler, 1997). Most of them were farmers and they prospered. The abolition of serfdom in the year 1848 strengthened the position of the Swabian people. In 1867, the Austro-Hungarian Compromise led to the dual Austro-Hungarian Monarchy and changed the situation. Ethnic minorities faced severe pressure of "Magyarization." Non-Hungarian people were forced to adopt a Magyarized (Hungarian) personal name and surname; Stefan became István, for instance. Places were renamed in Hungarian. Geographical terms had to change (e.g., Sathmar turned into Szathmárnemeti). Schools were closed down by law (*Lex Apponyi*) when they offered classes in any language of the minorities. Only teaching in Hungarian was accepted. World War I can be seen as a tragic result of the fight for national ideas, national rights, and a battle for national languages. In the year 1919, the Swabian population sympathized with the idea of Great Romania and with no longer being connected with Hungary. The Treaty of Trianon (1920) joined the area of Northern Transylvania to Great Romania. In the year 1920, the label Satu Mare came up, just a phonetic translation of Sathmar into the Romanian language. Unfortunately, this part of Romania developed very slowly.

Within less than a lifespan, the people were faced with the *Wiener Schiedsspruch* (Second Vienna Award, due to the Vienna Arbitration in 1940), with the result of "reforming" the Treaty of Trianon on behalf of Hitler in favor of Hungary, to change the borders again. Sathmar Swabians had taken a stand for Great Romania in the hope of regaining the freedom of speaking German (Schmied, 1976). It seemed to work well, even when the Vienna Award was declared null and void during World War II. Due to ethnic disturbances, however, the region of Northern Transylvania faced ongoing harassment, ethnic massacres, mass exodus, and the population suffered terribly. Most of the Jewish people were sent to concentration camps; Romanians were expelled, including Hungarian Romanians. Ethnic Germans formed a bond within the Romanian army and joined voluntarily the German army *Wehrmacht*. Nevertheless, the dreams of a Great Germany of ethnic Germans evaporated when Romania changed sides on August 23, 1944. Overnight, the state of Romania allied itself with the Red Army and the Allied Forces against Nazi Germany. The Swabian people would be blamed for having acted as military partners of Nazi Germany.

Soon after 1945 at the end of World War II, Northern Transylvania again became part of Romania. For the new rulers, a time of Romanianization gradually become a reality. In other words, the new majority could take revenge through language to force people to change their names into Romanian, to punish those who had believed in the new Romanian state under the Second Vienna Award by which Northern Transylvania had been reassigend by Nazi Germany and Fascist Italy from Romania to Hungary. István now became Ştefan (pronounced as ʃtefan). Swabians in Northern Transylvania, the Satu Mare area, as well as in the Banat, the southern part of Transylvania, due to their language, were seen as former collaborators of Hitler Germany and sent off to labor camps east of Bucharest. Again, a new totalitarian regime, this time under the banner of communism, traumatized people and forced them to transmigrate. At the end of the line, there was Ceausescu, infamous, hated, and feared. And the guesthouse in Satu Mare exuded his vapor.

Sathmar Swabians were faced with developments that pulled them back and forth, asked to trust new promises never kept by people in charge. I pondered all this throughout my fretful time on the premises in Satu Mare. Students from the group I worked with had shared their personal stories in truly amazing ways. They did not deny the facts from the past. On the contrary, they acknowledged the problematic decisions some of their forefathers had made. What really struck me were their personal memories. I asked the students if some would be willing to share their memories from around Christmas time of 1989, when Ceausescu was assassinated.

In 2006, here in the premises of Dictator Ceausescu, a place full of haunting visions, I remembered a student sharing his experience of fleeing with his mother when he was nine years old. Sandor was raised in a trilingual environment. He learned Romanian from his mother, Hungarian from his friends at elementary school, and a childlike German from his father's side. Ceausescu had planned to steamroll the farmhouses of all non-Romanian minorities in the villages to build huge agricultural production cooperatives. Local farmers were forced to leave their homes and were promised work places in factories. The megalomaniac dream of a despot instilled trembling fear. Sandor's family was forced to leave home. So, they tried to escape. Sandor's mother carried him piggyback when they waded through a river to the western border, to freedom in Hungary. But Sandor fell off and as he fell, he yelled for help, in Romanian! The getaway ended in an asylum camp in Austria. That was where his Christmas memory was anchored. Being traumatized, he refused to talk, as he spoke no language of any use. But he had to start to learn German. As his parents did not find a permanent job in the area, they moved to the south of Germany where Swabian was spoken. At school, he mastered German quickly. Then his father lost his job and again, the family moved back to Romania. There he had to start afresh, with the old languages, Romanian, and for the first time, he had to learn to write in Hungarian. He intended to study journalism, in Cluj-Napoca, at the Department of German Language. And—traumatized by his childhood years—he still fervently expressed one wish: "Please do not talk about this background story in a negative way that might make somebody think badly of Romania. I forgive them, since the State of Romania provides me an opportunity, gives me an education!" What a noble mind, shaped by traumatic events.

Anxiety, power, and occupational career are closely intertwined. From Smelser (2004, p. 53), we take hints from Freud (1933), Krystal (1988), and Caruth (1995): There is a strong dual tendency to avoid and to relive. There are different forms of amnesia: forgetting, denial, difficulty in recalling, or unwillingness to contemplate or dwell on the traumatic event, and the compulsive tendency to avoid situations that resemble the traumatic scene or remind the victim of it; but, at the same time, there is an equally strong compulsion to repeat the trauma or to relive some aspect of it. We recall the powerful lines from Bob Dylan (1968) reminding us that we ought to take care of our memories, for we cannot relive them. The work of a journalist is mainly concerned with language. To switch between languages is an established ambivalence between attraction and repulsion. Somehow, Sandor could not avoid his fate of becoming a man of letters. And he never wanted to take sides. Nobel Prize winner Joseph Brodsky (1972) states: "I do not believe in political movements. I believe in personal movement, that movement of the soul when a man who looks at himself is so ashamed that he tries to make some sort of change—within himself, not on the outside" (p. 11).

The vivid description of every personal history reveals the aesthetic moment (in Greek: *aisthesis*) of a given situation. The perception of a situation stems from an aesthetic intention of awareness. A sense of belonging is developed under the most twisted circumstances. Shelter and protection are never guaranteed, and therefore one may doubt that they ever exist in a lion's den.

A review of historical facts is not merely a sentimental reminiscence. In the microtale, there is the nucleus of the tall tale. As we learn from psychoanalysis, to interpret carefully is most relevant for traumatized people, to listen to the individual story so as to gain and to provide understanding. Anxiety, fear, power, and individual history are firmly linked. Locations as places of traumas have an almost magical power, as if there were an inherited curse reactivated where the traumas occurred. It does seem to be rather consistent that traumatized people are silenced when they reenter sites of previous trauma experiences. Names and language can be such a locus of traumatic experience that people need to rediscover. Sathmar Swabians certainly can bear witness.

At the cultural level, there are instances alternating between compulsive avoidance and compulsive attraction, concerns kept alive by some individuals and groups through songs and myths. Even those repressed by a totalitarian regime remember positive aspects of their lives, and as we know from effects like the "Stockholm syndrome," may even experience a traumatic bonding. Political polarization results when opposing modes of scission confront one another, where one is favored over the other, or when there is a struggle over the meaning and assessment of the trauma. The Conducător Ceausescu, in his weird megalomania, surely did not see Sathmar Swabians as his brothers, but neither did he count on the Hungarian or Romanian population in the area. It would be a virtue to accept the ambivalence of an ambiguous situation, even as a lion in its own den.

REAR WINDOW TO HORROR

Vilnius, capital of Lithuania, is a city with a rich cultural heritage. The University of Vilnius hosts an excellent library dating back to 1579, and is in walking distance from the former ghetto. In the city center, there are still remarkable buildings from the time when Vilna (Vilnius) was called the Jerusalem of the North. Churches of many denominations are abundant. The Jewish community was almost entirely annihilated and a significant change in population has happened since World War II. In 1991, the state of Lithuania declared its independence and boasts that it has been a member state of the European Union since 2004. With a history of atrocities, a good balance between national pride and economic difficulties has always been a delicate political issue. The emigration rate is significantly high.

For a visitor, it is bewildering to see that one of the former synagogues—officially deconsecrated—now serves as the embassy of Austria. However, the building that caught my interest most is a former state prison. Today it is the Museum of Genocide Victims.

The architect of the prestigious building, designed in 1888 and completed in 1890, was Mikhail Prozorov. He must have had good standing with the hierarchy since, in 1895, he also designed and built the Orthodox Church of St. Michael the Archangel in Vilnius in the Russian Revival style.

Construction started in the spring of 1897 and was completed two years later. The new building, however, did not become a symbol for justice. Up to the reestablishment of independence on March 11, 1990 (and even until the demise of the Soviet Union after the August 1991 putsch), it continued to house one or another state institution of the occupying regime.[1]

It is startling that the various despotic regimes have always had similar requirements for the building. The main message of the building and its purpose was "justice." Today it serves as a "memory in stone." But who decides what justice is, which aims are to be fulfilled, which hopes destroyed? No one really can count the victims of so-called liberation movements.

Let us enter the Museum of Genocide Victims with an eye to its didactic purpose (of historiography), as Friedell suggests (Friedell, 1997 [1927], p. 5). The ethical way or ethical intention exposes a collection of traumatic events that bring tears to one's eyes.

The first impression of the building is that it is a majestic gesture. Here is where the goddess of law poses on her throne. In old Roman law, the goddess of law, Justitia, stands for justice. Her symbols may have varied over the course of time, but, usually, she is sculpted with scales, a sword, and sometimes a blindfold. Justitia stands for impartiality, weighing carefully competing claims. The sword represents her power.

In contrast with other statues of Justitia, here in Vilnius, the capital of Lithuania, there is no sign of justice. Justitia must have been blind. She had no difficulty with the crimes and massacres before her eyes. In fact, totalitarian headquarters used the very same location not just to exhibit power, but to execute it in extremis.

Lithuania seems to be like a pendulum gaining momentum from huge forces outside the country. Under the Russian occupation, when Lithuania was part of the Russian Empire, the building was intended to impress as a courthouse of the Russian province of Vilnius. It quickly changed and served the occupying German institutions from 1915–1918. Then, under the occupying Polish regime, it changed from a conscription center to a remand prison. Then, under the Soviet Government until the Nazis took over, it went from a remand prison to a prison for mass reprisals. Under Hitler, Germany's Special Unit for the City of Vilnius, mass executions of Jews were ordered on those premises. From that building, which then housed Gestapo headquarters, Nazi henchmen pursued local Jews as well as thousands of people from other nations. In that same building, bloodhounds killed patriots from Lithuania whenever regimes changed. In 1944, the Soviets took over and the instruments and chambers of torture remained in operation until 1991. The building served as the Lithuanian branch of KGB headquarters. From 1959, when it was renamed as a prison, the facilities were used as interrogation cells. Today, the death chamber is still there in the basement. Where victims stood on sand before being shot, there is now a glass bottom. Visitors walk in and see traces of shoes in the sand. The torture rack in the basement can almost be touched, as if a museum is likely to be more convincing if there is a realistic experience.

A pragmatic intention of such museums is clearly indicated: To remember, never to forget. The moral is an appellative cry for an ethos of humanity. A museum like the Museum of Genocide Victims in Vilnius is a site of enlightenment in its best sense. The site bespeaks experiences of trauma. We face the horror and we cannot abdicate from our responsibility to remember—we must walk the line.

Pragmatic enlightenment is the core idea of education in general. Sigmund Freud's psychoanalysis intends nothing other than *Nacherziehung* (after-education, reeducation). In the *New Introductory Lectures on Psycho-Analysis*, he alludes to and suggests multiple applications of psychoanalysis in the mental sciences at large, and points out some of his concerns. To discuss one particular application in greater detail, he defines the goal and claims that: "education" is "the upbringing of the next generation" (Freud, 1933). Good education can only be achieved if the balance is maintained "between Scylla of noninterference and Charybdis of frustration" (p. 149). It takes courage to explore the Museum of Genocide Victims. Many visitors are not prepared to confront the dark past. Yet, visitors lurk in the basement of the museum as if they were on a film set.

A moral commitment, however, justifies the exhibition of a chamber of torture. Zygmunt Bauman (1992) alerts: "The Holocaust was not a picture on the wall, but a window which made things visible, which usually remain undetected" (p. 1).

The main question in the Museum of Genocide Victims, as it is called today, is whether we can bear witness to what must have been traumatizing episodes that defy a simple narrative. We can see representations of things, some of them, for example, closely linked with torture and murder. In a way, we have to trust our eyes to see what they can no longer see (because the events chronicled were not possible to bear witness to at the time), and most likely never would want to see at all. In another time, there were shattering experiences by victims of the Holocaust or the repressive system of the KGB. Although we may know these events to be true, nevertheless, we only really believe what we see.

In the Museum of Genocide Victims, we approach "collective memory." And we approach the past in a way that reveals much about society and how it desires the past to be understood and remembered. As Christopher Browning put it: "A museum tells us more about the present than the past" (2013, p. 153). The most we can learn from an "authentic museum" is that we become able to judge through our own senses. In that respect, we get close, but we can never be close enough. It would seem that we approach the evidence of torture merely as a representation of torture.

When we are confronted by the collective memory of a country, it may reveal what we did not face before. We might have read about the Holocaust and might be convinced about its unique and incomparable status (see Bubnys, 2008; and Margolis, 2008). People from a so-called civilized nation killed according to an industrial plan of extinction called the Final Solution.

We are also aware that the Nazis managed to involve a relatively large number of Lithuanian institutions and local people into carrying out the killings. This is explained by the fact that, unlike Western and Central European countries, Lithuania had experienced the Soviet occupation before the Nazi occupation. The pain inflicted during the Soviet occupation made a large part of the Lithuanian population, nurtured by false hopes, enemies of Bolshevism and supporters of Germany (see Bubnys, 2008, p. 50). One cannot ignore these multifaceted discussions without being blamed for ignorance. Humanity was at stake and historiography changed from the history of the vanquished into the history of victims. We become aware how ordinary men can turn into killers (cf. Browning, 2010).

Furthermore, we might learn that, from 1944 onward, a new occupation took place that caused new traumas in the Lithuanian population. The relatively unknown war of resistance against the occupying communist regime is well documented in that building initially intended for the courts of the Vilnius province, but which instead, since its creation in 1899 housed successive state institutions of occupying regimes and never became more a site of imprisonment and reprisal than one of justice. The resistance hoped for liberation by the West, trusting that the Atlantic Charta would be implemented and would demand freedom for the occupied nations. The disappointment of the partisans became acute. From 1944 to 1953, Lithuania fought its war entirely alone. The West did not dare raise a voice in protest against the destruction of the Lithuanian nation. Partisans came to be known as forest brothers and about twenty thousand people died as local heroes in the guerrilla war within one year (Kuodytė & Tracevskis, 2006). A nation cried for help but, alas, that cry went unheard. Another trauma occurred. But the question remains the same as in the case of the Holocaust: How is the collective memory of a population to be managed if we are to be able to understand the situation of the partisans, those volunteers who fought for freedom? Like Christopher Browning, I support the idea of the representation of microhistory. Microhistory covers everything. In a way, one may claim that general history is embedded in the history of a single person.

Collected memories, as Christopher Browning intends to gather in documents, reduce the gap between the past and the present. From the outside, we look through a window into places of trauma, but we always will remain at a distance. We never can get close to either the perpetrators or to their prey. Even tears, of which nobody would have to be ashamed, cannot bridge the gap. Therefore, we need the items of such a collection to build up our memory. A kettle, a tin bowl, an army knife, a tattered tent, a rosary, some underground papers, create a vision for ourselves to be able to form a vague insight into what it must have meant to live in the woods under an occupation that went on for months and years.

What is real and what is virtual? These questions stimulate discussions by historians and other scientists. We also invent our narratives with and through the items of a museum. There is a message that must go out to the world, one inherent in the artefacts. Yet, who decides about an item, an artefact, and what can the message become that we might learn when we stroll in such a place of collected memory? Visitors could get lost between the changing despots of the country. A guideline is formed by the tools and instruments every defender in the occupied country needed that contextualizes what otherwise might be viewed as tools for camping holidays.

A pragmatic idea includes a moral of application. In this respect, we see Freud's idea of an educational aim when dealing with trauma. To work through it is only possible if one can get close to the real objects. The tools a partisan had to survive in the woods of Lithuania reveal what it meant to be a partisan. Instruments, such as paper and ink, have the same moral weight of resistance, as do weapons molded for combat and self-defense. And a footprint in the sand of the death cell recalls both prey and perpetrator. What for? To remember, to repeat and to work through the classical steps of psychoanalytical work (Freud, 1933 [1914]). Trauma work becomes quite evident and is an irrefutable task in the Museum of Genocide Victims.

PIRITA: THE CITY OF CHILDREN

The trip from Chisinau Airport in Moldova to Pirita takes a bit more than half an hour by car. Passing the "Gates of Chisinau," an impressive, huge achievement of real socialism built from extraordinarily ugly concrete, the paved road with unexpected holes turns into the hilly countryside. A few miles later, one approaches the River Nistru. All drivers are forced to slow down there to pass the bridge guarded by mighty Russian tanks, one on each side of the bridge. Martially dressed and grim looking officials check our papers. Then we continue to a remote area, into a fertile bucolic landscape. Pirita, a type of exclave, is situated across the banks of the Nistru, in Transnistria. Yet, there is poverty all around. A wooden horse carriage run by a boy of about ten years old carries some hay bales and is the only vehicle on the road. A brick wall appears, flags on poles in the wind, one of Moldova, the European flag, the village flag, and a flag of a private patron, all decorate the entrance where a fenced gate opens into a square resembling a parade ground. About two hundred children wave paper pennants in their hands. They perform as a choir the welcome shout of Pirita, the city of children. *Miki spune*. A big blackboard on the side shows, in white chalk, what has been said: "Miki spune," the little ones say; "Welcome Mr. Such and Such." As a visitor, I cannot deny that seeing my name written in chalk on the blackboard made me shudder at the rhythmic singsong. The children greet the visitor. They themselves are never likely to have the opportunity of being welcomed in a similar way. Pirita provides shelter, an oasis of cleanliness, and safety. What about the trauma? Where is it. What caused a trauma?

Evidence from developmental psychology takes for granted, affirmed by insights from psychoanalysis, that a spoiled childhood causes trauma and pain. A disregard for children, a lack of a minimal stable relationship, leads inevitably to insecurity. In Moldova we find children left completely to their own devices, living in private houses, their parents having left the country by the thousands to join cheap labor forces abroad. These are hard facts in Moldova, but they represent a nightmarish report which could be one from another planet.

Notwithstanding, Moldova is considered an independent nation. The truth is that the country is largely unknown to the East and to the West. Its 3.5 million inhabitants are cut off between Ukraine and Romania. There is only limited traffic between Moldova and its Western neighbor, Romania, and yet, there remains some close relationship. The Moldovan language is related to Old Romanian, but just a little darker in pronunciation. Many people in Europe are confused by the name. There is a region in Romania that is also called Moldova; both areas just have a common border.

The political connection to the neighbor states is almost nonexistent. The European Union does not permit people from Moldova to work within the Union, and only a few exceptions are made. The influence of Russia is enormous. In particular, there are grudges held against developments in a country that recently switched from the Cyrillic alphabet to the Latin one and claimed independence.

Russia, as the successor state of the former Soviet Union, "penalized" the young independent Moldova as if it were a naughty child rebelling against the former brother state. Russia's main interest is to take advantage of the fertile agricultural land. Moldova itself boasts of producing not only millions of hectoliters of wine a year, but also says that it is excellent. In 2006, Russia blocked all wine imports from Moldova and completely ruined the country's poorly developed economy. Under the former Soviet regime, the Moldovan nation was the pride of the USSR and had the largest gross income of all the satellite states. Their relative wealth had been destroyed under repression. Almost from one day to the other, the Moldovan people saw that the nation had became dirt poor. The experiment of "real socialism" with large cooperatives in the agricultural sector had gone astray. An "agricultural paradise" fell apart. The trauma of literally losing the basis of existence was superseded by another trauma that went from a collective trauma to a trauma on the individual level, severe poverty.

The result is work emigrants. In general, illegal employment abroad over the last decade has led to a lack of workforce at home. Furthermore, parents in prison, abroad, or due to the insufficient health care situations died at a young age. Children were left behind and became leftovers. In no other country in Europe are there as many real orphans or so-called social orphans as in Moldova. Street kids are a by-product of state monopoly capitalism in less-developed countries. In an independent state, as Moldova declared itself to be, resistance against Western or foreign help is prevalent. Both major players in the European scene, Germany and the long arm of Russia, are met with distrust among the population. Too deep are the wounds from when the German *Wehrmacht* occupied the banks of the River Dnjestr (today Nistru). The Russian Front was right there in the nowhere lands of Moldova, along the River Nistru with its Moldovan name.

The Red Army, too, has left, but memories remain. A camp for young pioneers was established in Pirita, with a fortified wall to avoid direct contact with the local village people. In the hot Moldovan summer days, young pioneers were proud to have an outdoor swimming pool for relaxation. A red brick wall at the pioneer camp bears the inscription in Russian and in Cyrillic letters: *Nation's pride*. Involuntarily or forced, the heyday is now gone, leaving today the remnants of an outdated ruin.

Nearly everyone is aware of the immense poverty, but the state seems helpless to do anything about it. However, a private initiative—an association called Concordia—gathers orphans into the city of the children, in the village of Pirita. The trauma of these children is separation. The trauma of separation for children is that they have to bear the brunt even when they are gathered together in a child-friendly ambience, such as in Pirita. It seems to be a logical way of dealing with trauma. Children are left on their own or have to stay with sick grandparents, so someone has to look after their survival. Grants from abroad permit the survival of these children. In 2004, the city of children was founded on that former campground by an Austrian pioneer, Father Sporschill, a Jesuit, who worked with street kids in Central Eastern Europe. (He has since moved to Bulgaria for other projects.) Private and public funding from Austria allows maintaining the city of children. There are now about thirteen houses and an outpatient department, which provide homes and shelter for up to two hundred and fifty homeless youngsters in Pirita.

The children in Pirita have to start from scratch after their bad experiences. And they have to learn to overcome their unwanted experiences. Organized in the style of family houses, responsibilities are shared. Duties are divided by age group. A housemother takes care of the daily needs, such as cooking and providing meals. Up to twenty children of all ages between four and seventeen years live in a single house together. A voluntary helper provides temporary support for their activities. Sometimes these helpers come from abroad, acquiring practical experience over a minimum of three months. Language is an issue: Moldovan (Romanian), Russian, Ukrainian, or some German is welcomed and heard in the village. However, the children have to attend the local school. This is difficult for quite a number of them. Some never had the chance to learn an alphabet, others had no home where they learned a daily hygiene routine. When they became separated from parents, some fell into shock, became wayward, and survived through juvenile delinquency. Some were picked up randomly by social workers from the state and through negotiation were given medical checkups and given access to stay in the city of children. We cannot deny, however, that trauma remains. Where former pioneers enjoyed happy weeks of summer camps, today there is the herculean task of helping poor children regain trust in relationships.

Trauma in Moldova is linked to separation. As a state, Moldova itself suffers from the separation and division represented by Transnistria. It would be arrogant to argue from outside in favor of a unification either with Russia, Ukraine, or with the European Union. Nevertheless, the move to independence from the Soviet Union has had a high price.

Separation can be seen as the ultimate goal of becoming mature and independent. It is also a painful experience, which begins with the very first separation, the trauma of birth. We need to recall Otto Rank and his brilliant study on separation (see Rank, 1996, 1998 [1924]). In fact, that study was written much to the dismay of Sigmund Freud. The trauma of separation became a pivotal issue among the inner circle of the Wednesday Psychological Society in the days of Freud's Vienna (see also Lieberman & Kramer, 2012). Rank saw the trauma of birth as a general biological factor ". . . to prove to be the deepest foundation for an essential part of our whole cultural development" (Rank cit. Kramer, 1996, p. 81).

How to start afresh is the ultimate aim of every great artist. Orphans have a history, but as if they are reborn every day, there can be new chances. Every child born is a blank slate, a new start, and a start from scratch. Orphans begin with separation from a traumatized past and seek a future union. One motto in Pirita is: "Pentru parintii nostri—For our parents."[2]

Empathy is needed to understand the trauma of separation. However, adults cannot understand children fully (see the radical position of Rousseau's [1979/1762] novel *Emile, or On Education*). Thus, we remain strangers to the psyche of a traumatized child.

In general, there is an optimistic spirit in Pirita. The children teach us a lesson. "Miki spune," the little ones say. "We ask for respect! Yet, each of us bears his own hell." They speak of the hell afforded by our apparent incapacity to improve their lot. We cannot relieve them of their trauma, one they share with us. And it is this point of impossibility we need to respect.

The student in the lion's den does not want people to speak badly about Romania. The architecture of terror becomes a curated site for the visitor to engage with past traumas. And, in their own hell, the children cry out, albeit silently, for empathy and respect. Overall, the psychoanalytical intention to work with trauma by shared memories seems to be rewarding. One can state that with reference to venues of former tyranny, horror, or a regained man-made environmental paradise of childhood—each of us suffers his own spirit.

NOTES

1. http://www.genocid.lt/muziejus/en/273/c/.
2. http://www.socialintegration.org/network/social-projects/.

REFERENCES

Bauman, Z. (1992). *Dialektik der Ordnung. Die Moderne und der Holocaust*. Hamburg: EVA Europäische Verlagsanstalt.

Brodsky, J. (1972). There is a murderer in every one of us. *New York Times*. Retrieved August 16, 2013, from http://bookhaven.stanford.edu/2013/06/joseph-brodsky-and-the-point-of-vertical-takeoff-there-is-a-murderer-in-every-one-of-us/

Browning, C. R. (2013). Reply to Daniel Fulda. In N. Frei, & W. Kansteiner (Eds.), *Den Holocaust erzählen* (pp. 151–64). Weimar: Wallstein Verlag.

Browning, C. R. (2010). *Remembering survival: Inside a Nazi slave-labor camp*. New York: W.W. Norton & Company.

Bubnys, A. (2008). *The Holocaust in Lithuania between 1941 and 1944*. Vilnius: Genocide and Research Centre of Lithuania.

Caruth, C. (1995). *Trauma: Exploration in memory*. Baltimore, MD: Johns Hopkins University Press.

Dylan, B. (1968). Open the door, Homer. From http://www.bobdylan.com/us/songs/open-door-homer.

Freud, S. (1933a). New introductory lecture on psycho-analysis, in vol. 22 of *Standard edition of the complete psychological works of Sigmund Freud* (Ed.) and trans. James Strachey et al. (London 1953–1974), Lecture XXXIV, "*Explanations, Applications, and Orientations.*" (Originally published, 1933, Aufklärungen, Anwendungen, Orientierungen. Vorlesungen zur Einführung in die Psychoanalyse und Neue Folge.)

Freud, S. (1933b). Remembering, repeating and working through, in vol. 12 of *Standard edition of the complete psychological works of Sigmund Freud* (Ed.) and trans. James Strachey et al. (London 1953–1974), 209–41 (Originally published, 1914, Erinnern, Wiederholen Durcharbeiten.)

Friedell, E. (1997, 12.Aufl.). (Originally published, 1927.) *Kulturgeschichte der Neuzeit. Band 1. Die Krisis der europäischen Seele von der schwarzen Pest bis zum Ersten Weltkrieg*. München: Deutscher Taschenbuch Verlag.

Hauler, E. (1997). *Tausend Jahre deutsche Siedlungen in der Region Sathmar.* München: Verlag der Donauschwäbischen Kulturstiftung.
Krystal, H. (1988). *Integration and self healing: Affect, trauma, alexithymia.* Hillsdale, NJ: Analytic Press.
Kuodytė, D. & Tracevskis, R. (2006). *The unknown war. Armed anti-Soviet resistance in Lithuania in 1944–1953.* Vilnius: Genocide and Resistance Centre of Lithuania.
Lieberman, J. E. & Kramer, R. (Eds.). (2012). *The letters of Sigmund Freud and Otto Rank inside psychoanalysis.* Baltimore, MD: Johns Hopkins University Press.
Margolis, R. (2008). *Als Partisanin in Wilna. Erinnerungen an den jüdischen Widerstand in Litauen.* Frankfurt/Main: Fischer Taschenbuch Verlag.
Polanski, R. [Director]. (1965). *Repulsion.* [Motion Picure]. United States: Columbia Pictures.
Rank, O. (1998). (Originally published, 1924.) *Das Trauma der Geburt und seine Bedeutung für die Psychoanalyse.* Leipzig, Wien, Zürich: Psychosozial Verlag.
Rank, O. (1996). *A psychology of difference: The American lectures.* (Selected, edited, and introduced by Robert Kramer.) Princeton: University Press.
Rousseau, J. J. (1979). (Originally published, 1762.) *Emile, or on education.* (Trans. Allan Bloom). New York, NY: Basic Books.
Schmied, S. (1976). *Die deutsch-schwäbische Volksgemeinschaft Sathmar. Ein Beitrag zur Geschichte der Sathmarer Schwaben von 1918–1940.* Im Selbstverlag: Kempten.
Smelser, N. (2004). Psychological and cultural trauma. In J. Alexander, R. Eyerman, B. Giesen, N. Smelser & P. Sztompka, (Eds.), *Cultural trauma and collective identity* (pp. 31–59). Los Angeles, CA: University of California Press.
Virgil, (19 B.C.E). *Aeneid, Book VI.* http://classics.mit.edu/Virgil/aeneid.html.

Chapter 14

Battling with History

Collective Memory in the War Narratives of Israeli Soldiers

Naama de la Fontaine and Kate Szymanski

The study of transgenerational trauma is particularly relevant to the Jewish nation. Due to Jewish history of persecution and displacement, and repeated prohibitions limiting Jewish religious practice, storytelling, and oral teachings have always been a necessary and central method of communication (Schram, 1984). While in diaspora, Jews utilized stories of persecution and resurrection to warn their children of the dangers lurking outside the Jewish quarters and instill in them a recognizable need for hope, as well as a connection to the Jewish people, as persecutions were likely to recur. Stories were traditionally embedded in religious practices and also functioned to strengthen Jews' shared narrative and collective identity in the context of spiritual beliefs. In this manner, direct telling of Jewish suffering and miraculous salvation became integral to the survival of the Jewish nation, both physically and psychologically. At the same time, implicit messages conveyed through unspoken communication have also been powerful in shaping common aspects of Jewish identity for generations (Keller, 1988; Rowland-Klein & Dunlop, 1998; Sorscher & Cohen, 1997).

The establishment of the state of Israel in 1948 encouraged increasing emigration of Jews from around the world searching for a safe haven in the land of Palestine. Whereas powerlessness, in all its forms, has been a repeated theme in Jewish history, many Jews perceived the establishment of the state of Israel in the immediate aftermath of the Holocaust as an almost messianic end to the suffering and displacement of the Jewish nation (Cohn-Sherbok, 2002, p. 8). However, even as Jews escaping persecution from around the world sought refuge in the young state, fatal threat from surrounding Arab countries simultaneously called for immediate unification and formation of a military organization. Hence, as Jews focused on Zionism and protecting their young state, emphasis on traditional religious practices became less salient, and communication of Jewish history through religion became secondary for many (Liebman & Don-Yehiya, 1983). As a result, military service, mandated of all capable eighteen-year-old civilians,[1] became a central and unifying experience in contemporary Israeli society.

Since its inception, shortly after the establishment of the Israeli state and in the midst of the War of Independence, the Israeli Defense Force (IDF) has symbolized an unprecedented Jewish movement toward active self-defense. Historically a relatively passive and studious people, Jews became daring fighters, capable of using force to defend their people and property (Gal, 1986). Given the dominance of trauma in the collective Jewish narrative, the IDF has held, and continues to hold, a highly venerated role among Jews and Israelis as necessary defenders of the Jewish people and state (Ben-Eliezer, 1995). Direct teachings of soldiers by the Instruction and Education branches of the IDF complement this common social attitude by ensuring that every soldier is taught Jewish and IDF history, thereby increasing soldiers' identification, sense of belonging, and personal responsibility (Kalil Hahoresh & Nizri, 2013). Consequently, the IDF has become an important vessel for the transmission of Jewish narrative (Grossman & Kaplan, 2006). Therefore, examination of soldiers' experiences, attitudes, and beliefs can shed light on spoken and unspoken messages, transmitted across generations. These messages now impact and motivate young Israeli men and women to put their lives on the line in the name of their identity and state.

In this chapter, we discuss the presence and impact of these messages as evident in the war narratives of Israeli soldiers who participated in the 2006 Second Lebanon War. The Second Lebanon War erupted in the context of the ongoing Israeli-Palestinian political conflict. The war followed Hezbollah's[2] ongoing rocket firing into Israel's territory, along with the kidnapping and killing of Israeli soldiers (Inbar, 2007; Kreps, 2007). In turn, the IDF army invaded Lebanon by foot while the air force dropped numerous bombs, causing significant destruction to Lebanese territory, and leading to the dislocation of many Lebanese civilians (Gross, 2008). As Hezbollah attacks intensified in 2006, there was increased civilian pressure for political and military response. Once a decision to send troops into Lebanon was made, IDF soldiers faced a complex situation in which they were called to engage in battle with a paramilitary resistance movement rather than with a formal army, exemplifying modern-day warfare and redefining the meaning of "defense forces" (Schmitt, 2007). Compared to previous wars fought by the IDF, the Second Lebanon War is distinguishable both by Israel's position of relative power in the face of the Hezbollah attacks, and by the less pervasively existential nature of the war. Additionally, given the Israeli advantage in military resources, this war was planned to be a swift and contained military operation. Instead, there were many unexpected military casualties that left Israeli soldiers and civilians, on both the Israeli and Lebanese sides, in a state of apprehension. Thus, the Second Lebanon War was met with extreme criticism given the military casualties and the failure to achieve any long-lasting objectives regarding national security (Kober, 2008). Both Israeli and international media harshly criticized wartime decisions made by the IDF and the Israeli government, while soldiers returning from battle reported operational failures in the field. Following the war, reserve soldiers took action in establishing the 2006 Israeli Reserve Soldiers' Protest, a movement that called for the resignation of the government and the formation of a state commission of inquiry into what, they argued, were crucial failures experienced during and after the war. The war, along with its surrounding controversies, exemplifies the evolution of the Jewish narrative. Jews, who have experienced themselves as the subject of persecution for generations, were expressing the struggles that accompany a newly acquired sense of agency along with its associated conflict and responsibility.

In this chapter we examine the transmission and impact of transgenerational trauma as reflected in the war narratives of Israeli soldiers who fought in the Second Lebanon War. As part of a qualitative research study assessing the impact of war exposure on soldiers' ideological beliefs and mental health functioning, I (Naama de la Fontaine) interviewed twenty-four male,[3] Jewish, Israeli soldiers (ages twenty-two to twenty-nine). All study participants had served as active mandatory or reserve soldiers in the IDF during the Second Lebanon War. Participants had experienced missile attacks or live-fire at the Israeli-Lebanese border, and/or had crossed the border into Lebanon for the purpose of completing missions or engaging in combat. I conducted semistructured interviews in August 2009, and utilized Hill's (1997) Consensual Qualitative Research (CQR) method of analysis to identify common themes. For the purpose of this chapter, a fellow clinical psychologist and I reviewed quotes from pertinent domains identified through the CQR analysis (e.g., Ideology, Motivation, Hopes for Future). In particular, we sought to identify quotes that illuminated the ways in which the Jewish narrative has been transmitted and continues to impact the perceptions, self-concept, and coping of Israeli soldiers. In order to ensure consensual agreement between the raters, we first individually reviewed all participant quotes and then discussed each quote to achieve agreement regarding dominant themes and interpretation. The findings that I report in this chapter demonstrate emergent themes common amongst the combat IDF soldiers I interviewed. They are, by no means, meant to represent all IDF soldiers or citizens; rather, they offer an illustrative sample of the ways in which transmission of Jewish transgenerational trauma can impact IDF soldiers.

Sasson-Levy (2008) suggests that, within democratic societies whose liberal values seem to contradict coercive militaristic values, men are motivated to participate in war by careful creation of shared motive on the part of national government and leadership. To do this, states create nationalist feelings by constructing collective identities based on (real or invented) traditions, a common origin, and a shared sense of threat (Furman, 1999). In the case of Israel, a collective identity has been cultivated for generations. This identity has emerged from religious traditions, and has been further reinforced by a shared history of persecution. Memories of persecution are now combined with the possibility of an actual external threat, emanating from current political conflict in the Middle East. As a result, many Israelis experience threat as ongoing, relentless, and beyond nonviolent resolution. One study participant, Daniel,[4] related the following:

> I'll tell you what that drive is . . . after the war we were told not to return our equipment, that we were going for a second tour. And I asked my commander,
>
> "What will happen? Again, the same story?" . . . So he said, I'll summarize it for you: "They want to kill you because you are a Jew on the land of Israel." Suddenly, he spoke to me in terms of the land of Israel, of Jews. . . . I recalled that on the yellow flag of the Hezbollah it says that they're also releasing Jerusalem, so, it's like something I can fight for . . . it gave me perspective. I recall suddenly feeling confidence . . . gaining perspective: You are now fighting for your land, for your identity. They're not just fighting over territory somewhere, they are fighting for Jerusalem.

Linn (1999) refers to this outlook as the Israeli soldier's "siege mentality," a mentality currently linked to Arabic protest against the fundamental right of Israel's existence. And yet, this mentality can be traced as far back as biblical stories of Jewish defeat. The Holocaust and Spanish Inquisition serve as powerful, more recent examples reinforcing the notion that perceived threat of persecution is indeed a realistic worry. Linn (1988) concludes that this sense of threat has generated an army based upon ". . . personal, internal discipline traditionally ascribed to the strong norm of self-sacrifice for the sake of national security out of the realization of a 'no choice situation'" (p. 144). Gideon, a study participant, described this link between perception of threat and devotion of soldiers in the following way: "It's people who are totally willing to give . . . they're here because . . . there is an existential feeling that this war holds something existential, just like every Israeli war. . . ." Ofer, another participant, also highlighted this notion when he described how the call for duty forced him to contemplate the depth of his personal commitment to the national cause:

> [It was] the first reserve experience after my discharge from the military . . . it was accompanied with a difficult deliberation, since my wife was 9 months pregnant and, where I serve, we had the privilege of deciding whether to join (the war) or not. . . . And I chose to join the war. Out of an assumption that everyone has their personal situation in life. And this is a particular point in time in which it is necessary for each to put in their vision, each one needs to place things aside, and join together for a particular cause which, let's say, belongs to us all and is for the good of all of us.

As part of their interviews, I asked soldiers to reflect upon whether they identified a motivation to participate in the war, aside from their legal requirement to do so. In their responses, the majority discussed a sense of a shared cause, repeatedly referencing the popular Israeli slogan, "Righteousness of the Way" (in Hebrew, *Emuna Btzidkat Haderech*). This slogan, often cited in the context of IDF missions, was referenced by Chief of General Staff Gabi Ashkenazi, who identified it as the Jewish right to live as a free nation, safe in its country. Ashkenazi commented that the message conveyed in this slogan has been transmitted throughout generations of IDF fighters, and serves as the basis for their strength (Channel 7, 2007). Indeed, the mere existence of such a slogan gives voice to a shared cause, to the need for its collective justification, and to the oral transmission of shared ideals.

When asked to elaborate on the *personal* meaning ascribed to this slogan, most soldiers alluded to a shared cause originating in a collective national narrative infused by trauma and threat. Thus, the majority of soldiers I interviewed revealed that they were mainly motivated by the sense of *existential threat* posed by the enemy and by their *need* to protect the safety of the Israeli people, including their own families. Many perceived this need and eternal threat as unique to the Jewish/Israeli people, as Nadav expressed:

> [After the war] the IDF realized that it's not enough to be a professional military now . . . with the most innovative missiles, it's not what works. An internal drive is needed. That would provide values, that would provide some type of reason to fight, Righteousness of Way, whatever you want . . . this subject is so important to me because I think it's the secret of our existence here. If it will end . . . we will not remain here. . . . [we've become a] hedonistic society and are supposed to be an idealistic society. Under these conditions, there's no chance that we'll succeed. It'll take a year, two years, 10 years, but they have patience and belief in whatever they believe.

Many participants identified a second interpretation for the Righteousness of Way. These participants discussed a need to protect the Israeli *identity,* which they believe relies upon the independence of the state of Israel. Barrak, another participant, elaborated on this notion:

> Look, it's a type of belief in the "Righteousness of the Way," more than faith . . . it's certainly not a religious faith . . . it had several meanings, it happened on Tisha B'av [a fast day] . . . but, I felt that I was doing it more because . . . I believe in where I am, I believe in the military, I believe in . . . that the IDF needs to protect the state of Israel.

Barrak's mention of Tisha B'av, the day that commemorates the destruction of both Temples and that has been recognized in Judaism as a day destined for tragedy, is of note. His ambivalence regarding the role of religion in his motivation to fight serves as a testimony of the inevitable presence of religion, along with past trauma narratives, in the ethos of many Israeli soldiers.

Gideon, another participant, exemplified the continued commitment to this shared cause and the relics of religion in the collective memory among current generation IDF soldiers in his words:

> It's part of a larger life ideology that I have. That I'm not just some lonely person wandering here in Israel . . . the history and past of this nation is important to me, and what's next is also important to me. As an Israeli, and as a religious person. We can talk about definitions, I don't define myself as a banal religious person, but . . . I was educated that there is some awareness of the collective . . . it begins with lending help to others . . . it's something I grew up with, that's developed in me . . . the awareness of the environment, of the People, and that everyone must join, that also helped me and guided me to join the war, and not to place . . . my personal life before that.

Thus, the ongoing, relentless perception of existential threat has been transmitted to modern-day soldiers. This narrative has nurtured the emergence of idealized soldiers, who continue to exemplify the uncompromising devotion that has characterized IDF soldiers since the State's inception.

Throughout societies, once a threat and common purpose has been established, the need for an idealized savior, or an identified "hero," deepens. Not only does the socially constructed hero image serve as a focal point for national identification, the hero also embodies the finest qualities that a society wishes to impart to subsequent generations (Baumel-Schwartz, 2010). Hence, an analysis of a society's idealized figure can yield an increased appreciation of the collective memory, the perceived threat for which the hero ideal was constructed, and the pressures experienced by those who have inherited the role of hero. Throughout years of diaspora, the Jewish hero was captured in the image of a studious religious leader who preserved the spirit of Judaism in the face of growing Jewish assimilation (Bokser, 2001; Magid, 2012). Though stories of Jewish bravery and active resistance are certainly interwoven within the nation's narrative, evident in biblical times as well as in testimonies of more recent atrocities, Jewish heroism was not historically equated with acts of courage at war. Baumel-Schwartz (2010) discusses the various archetypes of Jewish heroism, and points out that, for centuries religious martyrdom was the most prevalent form of heroism. In fact, Edrei (2006) argues that, historically, the lack of power experienced by the Jewish nation ". . . created an ethos of opposition to the use of force, an idealization of the reality of powerlessness and a world of values in which the use of force was not an option in both a normative and an ethical sense" (p. 193). This adaptation to diaspora and repeated persecutions led both Jews and non-Jews to perceive the nation as incapable of engaging in its own active defense (Almog, 2000).

A shift toward more active resistance has occurred in recent generations, epitomized in the partisans and ghetto fighters[5] who fought bravely to the death. As Baumel-Schwartz (2010) highlights, however, these heroes sacrificed themselves in honor of their identity but with no chance of actually overcoming their enemies and protecting the nation. Following the atrocities of the Holocaust, and with the establishment of the Israeli state, society reconstructed its narrative, shifting its focus to that of a heroic figure in the form of the pioneer-soldier, a figure more fit to meet the perceived needs of the new country and the Israeli people. Gal (1986) describes this as an almost diametrical shift:

> Only with the establishment of the state of Israel as a homeland for the Jewish people has there come the sense of something tangible and worth dying for. A new kind of heroism has emerged with the birth of Israel—the heroism of those who defend their homes and "wouldn't let it happen again." Indeed for many of the young Israeli natives (Sabras) who very distinctly perceived themselves as so different from their ancestors in diaspora, accepting the type of passive martyrdom as heroism was incomprehensible. . . . For them the new Israeli image, of the tough, non-capitulating Israeli hero is actually an antithesis of, and even perhaps a reaction against, the old stereotype of the weak Jew who responded with helplessness and passivity to adversities. (p. 191)

This new Israeli hero, characterized by strength, assertiveness, and protective power, is exemplified in the image of the IDF soldier. Harrell, another study participant, provided a description of his entry into Lebanon, which captures the identification of soldiers with this idealized image of an active, fearless Jewish fighter:

> The massive entrance [to Lebanon] was on foot and is hard to try and explain because . . . like the entire brigade entering at once, like by foot in a line, there were the Armored Corps, there were the planes, there were the Artillery Corps and there were also the helicopters. And you don't witness things like that often and like . . . there was a kind of feeling, like it's an amazing feeling, partially

> positive, and I was surprised by how much . . . it's like, it's power . . . not alone at all . . . people I know, on most of them I relied . . . like after this I understood those generals who start conquering all kinds of places.

While it is common for soldiers in most militaries to report similar feelings of exhilaration and power, as Gal clearly describes, this active stance is novel for the Jewish people. It has become synonymous with the "new" Israeli Jew, who charges his enemies, rather than awaiting his destruction. The Jewish admiration for the revised "Jewish Hero" is also expressed by Sasson-Levy who states:

> Israel's Jewish community perceived the military as the emblem of pure patriotism and as one of the major symbols of the collective. In this militaristic culture, the (Jewish) combat soldier has achieved the status of hegemonic masculinity and is identified with good citizenship. (2008, p. 298)

The idealization of IDF soldiers plays a significant role in soldiers' motivation to put their lives on the line. Across many cultures, fallen and injured soldiers and others willing to jeopardize their lives for their country or cause have repeatedly been cast in the treacherous role of hero (Bilu & Witztum, 2000)—often at the cost of gravely limiting their actual recovery (Herman, 1997; O'Brien & Hughes, 1991). In the case of Israel, society's admiration of fallen IDF soldiers is clearly enhanced by the transmission of a traumatized collective narrative that is particular to the Jewish people. With a long history of Jews killed for no reason other than their religion and ethnicity, dying for a cause has become strongly linked to salvation and victory (Weiss, 1997). Barrak conveyed this sentiment in his interview: "There were those people who were killed at war . . . those are model people . . . and you always want to be, want to be at war let's call it. Want to be that hero. Want it."

Given these pressures, it is understandable that the thought of losing this responsibility—and with it, guaranteed honor—is almost unbearable. As Daniel reflected:

> The worst that could have happened to me, now and in my mandated service would have been to say to me, "Man, you're not a fighter." What does that mean? Like . . . the best thing that happened to me, the most joyous thing that happened to me supposedly, in terms of ideology as well, is being a fighter, being a soldier, being a hero . . . it's a type of fulfillment of your ideologies.

The shift from the idealization of Jewish scholars to focusing on IDF soldiers was cemented in the motivational speeches of Ben-Gurion, Israel's first prime minister and one of the main figures responsible for the establishment of the state and the IDF (Azaryahu, 1992). And yet, even with the shift toward a more active, militaristic hero, religion continued to factor into the Jewish narrative. For example, Ben-Gurion expressed his belief that biblical heroes serve as ideal role models for soldiers, and often drew comparisons between biblical heroes and Israeli soldiers (Liebman & Don-Yehiya, 1983). In so doing, Ben Gurion invoked not only a profound sense of belonging and personal responsibility, but also a renewed sense of agency and power. Rather than the oppressed survivor, Ben Gurion retrieved the image of the fearless Jewish fighter from the collective memory of a nation caught in a cycle of victimization and passivity. Ben Gurion's speech also demonstrates the continuous dialogue between the modern-day Jewish narrative and its religious origins.

Themes that emerged from postwar narratives of study participants revealed that soldiers turned to religious notions, such as collective responsibility, attachment to the land of Israel, and God's constant presence, as motivators that enabled coping and perseverance throughout the war. Dor, another participant, provided an example of the constant presence of religious faith and its function in facilitating interpersonal connection and processing:

> I remember lots and lots of conversation . . . about meaning, about religion. . . . I was originally raised religious at home. . . . I stopped observing at age 17. And I have another very good friend from my unit who is the opposite; he became religious at age 19. I remember that somehow this entire topic surfaced. . . . I would also prepare kosher dishes for him at every house we arrived at, he didn't know how it's done. . . . I remember one situation, we were standing by a window . . . during the first three days . . . and like (there were) lots of explosions, and like you know, sort of like . . . some kind of Hollywood movie, like we would sit by the window and see all the explosions and shots. . . . And then, my friend said to me: how could you see all this and think that there is no God? I responded: how could you see all this now and think that there is a God? And I remember like, it was very . . . suddenly it evolved into discussions that were . . . very thought provoking.

Dor's narrative demonstrates the dual role of the Israeli soldier, and mirrors a conflict felt among many nations in which religion is part of the cultural and historical narrative. While performing his duty at battle, the Israeli soldier continues to grapple with religious notions. Moreover, religion provides a meaningful and uniting context for his experiences at war. This anecdote also depicts the implicit presence of the once idealized pious Jew, who continues to live on within the shared unconscious of the modern-day Israeli soldier-hero.

Daniel shared the following anecdote, which speaks to the merging of the Jewish spirit, and which has been preserved and transmitted throughout history, with that of the modern-day IDF fighter:

> I remember receiving the Sabbath while in Lebanon, the sun is setting, the room is completely dark, because you're not allowed to turn on a light, there is some stick light covered in luggage so that no one can see us, and I remember that I'm praying and weeping, telling myself that this might be my last reception of the Sabbath.

Daniel also reflected on how, as for many Jews throughout history, war has put his faith to the test:

> It made me question a great deal of my faith . . . it caught me by surprise. . . . I suddenly had to stand behind my words . . . I mean, you believe in one thing and then reality shows you another . . . reality is terrifying.

Israeli soldiers are particularly susceptible to carrying the trauma of their families and the larger society because they are not experienced as distant or inaccessible heroes. Rather, they are enmeshed in the social fabric, while also carrying the duty of preserving the very body to which they belong. The fact that all men and women are mandated to serve in the IDF when they reach the age of eighteen (with exceptions as previously described), and that reserve soldiers continue to serve several weeks per year and in cases of emergency, creates an army comprised of almost all adult Israeli citizens. In almost every family, there is a son, daughter, father, or husband who has served in the IDF, or is currently on active duty. As a result, the historical national narrative becomes a contemporary one that is infused in the familial, personal narrative as well. Naturally, then, IDF soldiers are typically fully supported, and virtually sheltered, even when there is strong citizen and/or veteran opposition to military actions.

Tensions between the various economic, religious, and ethnic groups within Israeli society have continuously impacted the country's social climate. However, mandated service and with it, the shared support of soldiers, transcends these differences, creating a strong sense of identification and unity. On the other hand, those who do not share in the collective narrative tend to be categorized as Others. As in societies worldwide, this dichotomy serves to further enhance cohesiveness among members by providing a contrast against which the group identity can be sculpted and juxtaposed (Silberstein & Cohn, 1994). One participant, Myron, demonstrated the dichotomy between self and Other, differentiating between the idealized Israeli soldier and his stereotype of the American soldier. Myron also explained how this very differentiation further enhanced his motivation to participate in the Second Lebanon War:

> I watch military shows . . . of the American air force, or the American military and it disgusts me, it repels me damn . . . Rambo, that's not at all the thing. That there is a soldier, and an Israeli soldier, who defends the land of Israel, . . . his

> nation, after the awful Holocaust . . . the memory of the Holocaust is very powerful for me, not because I have family from there, I'm Sephardic[6] [it] doesn't relate to me. And suddenly you're a soldier, after 60 years that . . . that we were under the incinerators, suddenly you wear the IDF uniform and defend your nation. Wow. That's like a thing that you have to be part of.

Myron's words depict a complex picture, which may represent some soldiers' internal conflict with regards to their militaristic role. Myron rejects and externalizes the sense of excitement and exhilaration, despite it being clearly evident within this sample of IDF soldiers, as in military populations worldwide. It can be argued that soldiers who carry this need to distinguish themselves from their perceived Other jeopardize their ability to engage in objective self-reflection. Though such tendencies are present in many cultures and militaries, Jewish culture has long struggled to observe itself from the outside and recognize the commonalties between Jews and other nations (Diesendruck, 1939). This struggle can be traced back to biblical writings, distinguishing the Jewish people as "a light to all nations." With regard to its transmission through generations, this message might be understood as a highly effective defense mechanism that has served the Jews for centuries. Namely, it has provided a religious rationale for the long history of trauma. At the same time, this message has contributed to a culture in which suffering is often idealized, as it has been associated with promised distinction, holiness, and national resurrection (Bowker, 1975).

Social rejection, both explicit and implicit, is often the fate of those (particularly men) who, in refusing to join the IDF, also refuse to take on the idealized role of soldier-hero. In Israeli society, the ultraorthodox have regularly been exempt from mandated military service for "conscientious reasons." This faction claims a unique role in ensuring national safety through strict religious adherence, including daily study and prayers (Heilman, 1992). In this manner, they perceive themselves as responsible for keeping alive the studious Jewish hero who safeguarded spiritual existence throughout generations of diaspora. However, their exemption has led to ongoing conflict and protest within Israeli society. Intolerance toward military refusal for *nonreligious* reasons originates in the historical Jewish existential threat and the consequential shared responsibility in national defense (Linn & Gilligan, 1990). Thus, voluntary refusal to participate in the IDF is often perceived as betrayal, not only of present-day soldiers and society, but also of Jewish victims throughout history. In this way, military refusal represents opposition toward the very right of Jews to defend their physical and psychological existence and, thus, a colluding with the Other in all its viciousness. This collective perception often leads to an immense sense of guilt among individuals refusing duty, and even in soldiers who enlist in positions in which they are spared the experience of risking their lives in the line of duty. In reflecting on whether he would wish for his son to become an IDF fighter like him, Dor highlighted the pressures associated with possible refusal:

> Such a hard question, like I am unable to answer it for myself. Like, it's clear to me that if I live here and that if he will grow up here then yes, then he needs to go to be a fighter and to be there with everyone else. And like now my thought is to leave the country and spare him of it. So that he won't fulfill this duty. This social duty. So that the guilt will be on me and not on him . . . and perhaps the stares will be on me as one who left the country, but at least he won't . . . he won't be there. Won't feel this obligation.

Despite the tendency of Israeli Jews and their soldiers to sharply dichotomize self and Other, there are times when a critical voice emerges, and forces the nation to engage in a difficult, yet familiar process of self-reflection. The Second Lebanon War was one of these times. In Judaism, personal and communal confession are perceived to be challenging and sacred practices. Though they exact a significant emotional toll, they also carry poignant cathartic potential for both the individual and the Jewish collective seeking redemption (Frankel, 1998). Originating in religious tradition and passed on through shared narrative, self-reflection remains a defining feature in the modern ethos of the Jewish people. This tradition of self-reflection, along with heightened sensitivity toward external criticism, has at times led the Jewish people to question the boundaries between their identification with the role of hero-soldier versus that of potential aggressor. This distinction is of utmost importance, since, in the narrative of Jewish history, the word aggressor has been synonymous with "Other."

As society's couriers of both power and protection, IDF soldiers are frequently forced to grapple with profound moral dilemmas regarding issues of power, privilege, protection, duty, and loyalty. On one hand, they carry the relentless fear of threat emanating from a history of persecution and the desire to take on an active fighting role to ensure the nation's endurance as an independent state. At the same time, however, IDF soldiers have also inherited nonviolent principles originating in Judaism and central to the ideals of the organizations from which the IDF was founded. For instance, the Haganah[7] called soldiers to "Keep their weapon pure," conveying a historical urge to avoid violence when at all possible (Gal, 1986). And yet, for years, Israel has been criticized, both internally and internationally, for various military actions, including its ongoing occupation of Palestinian territories and activities in Gaza, as well as its use of military force on the Israel-Lebanese border. Thus, the task of reconciling inherited messages with present-day actions is difficult. This conflict epitomizes the struggle accompanying an increased awareness of the transgenerational transmission of trauma and its impact.

Self-questioning was particularly salient during the Second Lebanon War. Throughout the war, the Israeli media repeatedly articulated this self-reflective, critical stance. The media questioned the rather impulsive, disorganized, and reportedly targeted use of Israeli military force in an attempt to defeat Hezbollah targets. Given the strong identification of Israeli soldiers with the IDF and its mission, soldiers' reactions to media criticism were dominated by themes of loyalty and betrayal. Study participants stated that the media's critical position had a direct and detrimental impact on soldier morale, as well as on citizens' support of war efforts. Nathan's narrative depicts the intersection of historical discourse and current-day conflict:

> I was very angry at the media. It's people who are totally willing to give . . . they're here because . . . yes, there is an existential feeling that this war holds something existential, just like every Israeli war . . . and the morale is important, and . . . the moments in which that was injured, was when . . . we watched the news . . . people . . . sitting and analyzing for you what is occurring in the field . . . you feel like, how immense the gap is between the motivation of those in the field, versus what the media supposedly attempts to reflect. . . .

Reaction to the seemingly immense gap between those in the field and those spared the experiences of war is not particular to Israeli soldiers. Yet, for Israeli soldiers carrying the legacy of intergenerational trauma and, with it, the ever-present sense of existential threat, the task of incorporating criticism and self-reflecting is particularly challenging.

Whereas it is often easier to express rage at such a distant voice, soldiers expressed greater personal pain when faced with the criticism of close family members or friends. The impact of such incongruency of views is conveyed in the words of Barrak, who was temporarily dismissed from the field in order to attend his brother's wedding:

> I sat with my cousin, and he began talking about all the things that were talked about later, that were very true, about this war lacking, and nothing is being done, and there is no organized operation . . . and I recall that I was so angry, I already really felt like . . . punching him in his face . . . I felt that . . . I'm not being supported . . . because as a soldier, you feel, "I am doing everything I can" . . . and you see yourself immediately, when the military is discussed, that's you. *You, you are the military at that moment.*

Unwavering identification of combat soldiers with their unit members and with their military body is certainly not uncommon across societies. Nevertheless, it can be argued that the extent to which criticism is intolerable, and the need to justify IDF actions—at times, blindly—reflects the unity emergent from a shared trauma-induced narrative (Aronoff, 1999).

Within a tightly joined collective, individuals are constantly faced with the need to balance their loyalty to the nation with their shifting individual needs, aspirations, and beliefs. As is a hallmark of intergenerational trauma, this conflict often causes deep realizations to be suppressed or silenced, as individuals feel unable to act upon them due to a profound, historically based need to maintain alliances and preserve unity at all costs (Wiseman, Metzl, & Barber, 2006). However, despite the difficulties of separating themselves from the nation under the circumstances of perceived ongoing threat, many of the soldiers I interviewed reported that their experiences changed them in some manner. The majority disclosed experiencing personal change in the form of decreased irritability, and about half perceived this to be both a positive and negative personal change. Those who perceived postwar change to be negative reported experiencing increased sensitivity toward others, fear of loss, avoidance of painful affect, and a constant need to maintain control in social interactions. In terms of positive personal change, participants also reported that war evoked new realizations and meaning, as well as improvement in their personal relationships and their ability to prioritize life goals, as Benny articulated:

> War causes you . . . to ask questions, existential questions . . . that begin with, what am I doing here, what is my role here, what is this life, what . . . is the meaning of life, war? . . . Perhaps on a lower level, what do I want to accomplish in my life . . . how do I want to see myself, with whom do I want to live my life

Several soldiers stated that war reminded them that they are not immune to danger, a realization that caused them to become more grateful for what they had in life thus far. From their stories, it is clear that internal changes prompted soldiers to reevaluate their life choices and to act on their goals without delay postwar. This gained insight is reflected in the following quote provided by Oren:

> When I take myself back to that place . . . before the war . . . to the moments of terror and fear . . . your entire life in fact loses its importance. Remaining are only the truly important things. When you tell a human being that he has five minutes to live, an hour, two more days to live, suddenly all priorities change, suddenly all the things he cares about, that are important to him change completely . . . so I didn't care about anything but the things that appear in front of a man before his death.

Despite these profound realizations, participants' responses also captured the complexity of translating change from internal to external. This struggle mirrors a broader challenge in Israeli society as a whole and the resistance to internal change that occurs in individuals affected by intergenerational trauma. For example, one participant, Re'uven, stated that his desire for peace increased due to his war experience, yet that it had limited impact on his political stance in actuality:

> After you see that war is something so, let's call it, even disgusting, and so terrible, that there is nothing more terrible than war in the world, then . . . on the contrary, my belief in . . . my desire for peace, is much greater, not that I think it needs to be done . . . in short, my political views haven't changed.

Thus, although individuals are often affected by present-day trauma and capable of shifting their perspectives to an extent, their loyalty and attachment to the collective shapes their ability to respond authentically and fully to their experiences.

In conclusion, Jewish history is characterized by repeated external persecution along with internal perseverance and resurrection. The Jewish narrative involves the transmission of this history, along with its associated affect and reactions, within each generation. The collective narrative is passed down in the form of explicit storytelling, as well as through silenced truths and religious traditions that carry with them implicit messages. This narrative influences both self-perception and the perception of others, yielding a unique national identity that is contrasted with the perceived identities of other nations. For the Jewish people, past traumas, and the Holocaust in particular, have solidified the nation's view of itself as a victim in need of heroic, internal defense against an ever-threatening aggressor. In the midst of attack and in the immediate aftermath of Nazi horrors, the first Jewish Israeli military was formed, and the IDF soldier emerged as a much-needed symbol of strength, protection, and perseverance.

At present, the IDF serves as a melting pot for the Israeli people, where young men and women negotiate their diverse backgrounds with the modern-day narrative of Jewish heritage and unite to fulfill their part in Jewish history. As we have shown through the personal narratives of Second Lebanon War soldiers, for many young Israeli males, the need and desire to fulfill this role is immense, as they too carry with them the national narrative inherited from their ancestors, along with the guilt of surviving generations, and the fear of repeated persecution. Sent to battle, Israeli soldiers are thus armed, not only with the weapons on their bodies and the trainings they have mastered, but also with the spoken and unspoken narrative that, through their duty, has become their own. While this collective transgenerational narrative provides the indispensable uniting element needed for their functioning and survival, it also confines their ability to view themselves and their actions within a more objective reality, and to grapple with the reactions and conflicts that often accompany trauma-related military experiences. In this way, the Israeli soldier represents a strong example of the struggles and pressures faced by most Israeli Jews, influenced by the collective memory and intergenerational trauma of their families and the Jewish people as a whole.

The root of enactment, on both individual and societal levels, is grounded in blindness. The inability to observe oneself is particularly salient where trauma dictates affect and actions, and where denial and repression dominate. In this manner, repetition is likely to ensue. Self-reflection has been an important component of traditional Jewish culture, originating in religious principles and practices. Yet individual and group self-reflection in the time of perceived threat, especially when coupled with traumatic memories, is particularly challenging, as issues of loyalty and identification are prominent. In this manner, repetition of past cycles are likely to recur, further cementing a culture of silencing, avoidance, and retraumatization. In this chapter, we set out to identify the impact of transgenerational trauma on the perceptions and behaviors of Israeli soldiers. In a culture dictated by trauma, we believe that there is a paramount need to give explicit voice to the transmission of trauma and by so doing, raise an awareness of recurrent cycles. Ultimately, such awareness will increase individuals' and society's capacity to move forward and react to present-day conflict with greater perspective and freedom.

NOTES

1. According to the Defense Service Law, all eighteen-year-olds living in the territory of the state of Israel are obligated to serve in the IDF. However, the following populations are legally exempt from IDF service: mothers and pregnant women or women who find military service contradictory to "reasons of conscience"; individuals suffering from physical or mental disabilities; ultraorthodox men through Tal Law. (Røislien, 2013).

2. The Hezbollah, or "Party of God," is the Shiite fundamentalist organization, identified by the U.S. State Department as a terrorist group since the 1980s. According to Harik (2005), the organization has since evolved from a radical, primarily militant group, to a moderate mainstream political party, which also includes a resistance wing that has been fighting Israel for the past seventeen years.

3. The number of female IDF fighters is considerably smaller compared to males. As a result, I was unable to recruit a representative sample of female participants. Therefore, I excluded females from the study altogether.

4. Names of all study participants presented in this chapter have been changed in order to ensure their confidentiality.

5. Jews who fought in active resistance units operating against Nazi Germany and their allies in France, Belgium, the Ukraine, Belorussia, Lithuania, and Poland.

For more information on Jewish resistance during WWII see Berkowitz (2006) and Kopel (2007).

6. Sephardic refers to Jews who trace their origin to North Africa and the Middle East.

7. The Haganah (the Hebrew Defense Organisation in Palestine) is one of several organizations from which the IDF emerged. Formed on June 12, 1920, the Haganah was a direct response to increasing Arab attacks on Jewish cities throughout Palestine. Adhering to humanistic-social principle, the Haganah was primarly dedicated to the ongoing protection of the lives and property of Jews in Palestine (Bauer, 1966).

REFERENCES

Almog, O. (2000). *The sabra: The creation of the new Jew*. Berkeley, CA: University of California Press.

Aronoff, M. J. (1999). Wars as catalysts of political and cultural change. *The military and militarism in Israeli society*. New York: SUNY Press, 37–57.

Azaryahu, M. (1992). War memorials and the commemoration of the Israeli war of independence, 1948–1956. *Journal of Israeli History, 13*(1), 57–77.

Bauer, Y. (1966). From cooperation to resistance: The Haganah, 1938–1946. *Middle Eastern Studies, 2*(3), 182–210.

Baumel-Schwartz, J. T. (2010). *Perfect heroes: The World War II parachutists and the making of Israeli collective memory*. Madison, WI: University of Wisconsin Press.

Ben-Eliezer, U. (1995). A nation-in-arms: State, nation, and militarism in Israel's first years. *Comparative Studies in Society and History, 37*(2), 264–85.

Berkowitz, M. (2006). The Nazi equation of Jewish partisans with "bandits" and its consequences 1. *European Review of History—Revue européenne d'Histoire, 13*(2), 311–33.

Bilu, Y., & Witztum, E. (2000). War-related loss and suffering in Israeli society: A historical perspective. *Israel Studies, 5*(2), 1–31.

Bokser, B. Z. (2001). *The wisdom of the Talmud: A thousand years of Jewish thought*. New York, NY: Citadel Press.

Bowker, J. (1975). *Problems of suffering in religions of the world*. Cambridge, UK: Cambridge University Press.

Channel 7 (2007). The righteousness of the way—The basis of our power. Channel 7. Retrieved from http://www.inn.co.il/News/Flash.aspx/177571.

Cohn-Sherbok, D. (Ed.). (2002). *Holocaust theology: A reader*. Exeter, UK: University of Exeter Press.

Diesendruck, Z. (1939). Anti-Semitism and ourselves. *Jewish Social Studies, 1*(4), 399–408.

Edrei, A. (2006). Law, interpretation, and ideology: The renewal of the Jewish laws of war in the state of Israel. *Cardozo L. Rev., 28*, 187.

Frankel, E. (1998). Repentance, psychotherapy, and healing through a Jewish lens. *American Behavioral Scientist, 41*(6), 814–33.

Furman, M. (1999). Army and war: Collective narratives of early childhood in contemporary Israel. In E. Lomsky-Feder and E. Ben-Ari (Eds.), *The military and militarism in Israeli society* (141–68). Albany: State University of New York Press.
Gal, R. (1986). *A portrait of the Israeli soldier (No. 52)*. New York: Greenwood Press.
Gross, M. L. (2008). The second Lebanon war: The question of proportionality and the prospect of non-lethal warfare. *Journal of Military Ethics*, *7*(1), 1–22.
Grossman, G., & Kaplan, R. (2006). Courage to refuse. *Peace Review*, *18*(2), 189–97.
Harik, J. P. (2005). *Hezbollah: The changing face of terrorism*. London: I.B. Tauris.
Heilman, S. C. (1992). *Defenders of the faith: Inside ultra-orthodox Jewry*. New York: Shocken Books.
Herman, J. L. (1997). *Trauma and recovery: The aftermath of violence from domestic abuse to political terror*. New York, NY: Basic books.
Hill, C. E., Thompson, B. J., & Williams, E. N. (1997). A guide to conducting consensual qualitative research. *The Counseling Psychologist, 25*(4), 517–72.
Inbar, E. (2007). How Israel bungled the second Lebanon war. *Middle East Quarterly*, *14*(3), 57–65.
Kalil Hahoresh, H., & Nizri, I. (2013). Following fighters: For the people, the land and the state. In D. Avidan (Ed.), *Workshop for Battle Heritage* (pp. 2–4).
Keller, R. S. (1988). Children of Jewish Holocaust survivors: Relationship of family communication to family cohesion, adaptability and satisfaction. *Family Therapy: Journal of the California Graduate School of Family Psychology*, *15*(3).
Kober, A. (2008). The Israel defense forces in the Second Lebanon War: Why the poor performance? *Journal of Strategic Studies*, *31*(1), 3–40.
Kopel, D. B. (2007). Armed resistance to the Holocaust. *Journal of Firearms and Public Policy*, *19*, 144.
Kreps, S. E. (2007). The 2006 Lebanon War: Lessons learned. *Parameters*, *37*(1), 72.
Liebman, C. S., & Don-Yeḥiya, E. (1983). *Civil religion in Israel: Traditional Judaism and political culture in the Jewish state*. Berkeley, CA: University of California Press.
Linn, R. (1999). In the name of the Holocaust: Fears and hopes among Israeli soldiers and Palestinians. *Journal of Genocide Research, 1*(3), 439–53.
Linn, R. (1988). Terrorism, morality and soldiers' motivation to fight—An example from the Israeli experience in Lebanon. *Studies in Conflict and Terrorism*, *11*(2), 139–49.
Linn, R., & Gilligan, C. (1990). One action, two moral orientations—The tension between justice and care voices in Israeli selective conscientious objectors. *New Ideas in Psychology*, *8*(2), 189–203.
Magid, S. (2012). From sainthood to selfhood in American Judaism: Artscroll's new Jewish hero and Jewish renewal's functional rebbe. *Modern Judaism*, *32*(3), 270–92.
O'Brien, L. S., & Hughes, S. J. (1991). Symptoms of post-traumatic stress disorder in Falklands veterans five years after the conflict. *British Journal of Psychiatry*, *159*(1), 135–41.

Røislien, H. E. (2013). Religion and military conscription: The case of the Israel Defense Forces. *Armed Forces and Society*, *39*(2), 213–32.

Rowland-Klein, D., & Dunlop, R. (1998). The transmission of trauma across generations: Identification with parental trauma in children of Holocaust survivors. *Australian and New Zealand Journal of Psychiatry*, *32*(3), 358–69.

Sasson-Levy, O. (2008). Individual bodies, collective state interests: The case of Israeli combat soldiers. *Men and Masculinities*, *10*(3), 296–321.

Schmitt, M. N. (2007). Change direction 2006: Israeli operations in Lebanon and the international law of self-defense. *Michigan Journal of International Law*, *29*, 127–64.

Schram, P. (1984). One generation tells another: The transmission of Jewish values through storytelling. *Text and Performance Quarterly*, *4*(2), 33–45.

Silberstein, L. J., & Cohn, R. L. (Eds.). (1994). *The other in Jewish thought and history: Constructions of Jewish culture and identity*. New York: New York University Press.

Sorscher, N., & Cohen, L. J. (1997). Trauma in children of Holocaust survivors: Transgenerational effects. *American Journal of Orthopsychiatry*, *67*(3), 493–500.

Weiss, M. (1997). Bereavement, commemoration, and collective identity in contemporary Israeli society. *Anthropological Quarterly*, *70*(2).

Wiseman, H., Metzl, E., & Barber, J. P. (2006). Anger, guilt, and intergenerational communication of trauma in the interpersonal narratives of second generation Holocaust survivors. *American Journal of Orthopsychiatry*, *76*(2), 176–84.

Chapter 15

Trauma, Community, and Contemporary Racial Violence

Reflections on the Architecture of Memory

Ricardo C. Ainslie

Whether we acknowledge the past or deny it, it is with us daily in our lives as a silent, spectral presence.

—Michael O'Loughlin (2013, p. 249)

Over the past twenty years, I have spent significant time in several Texas communities (Anson, Hempstead, and Jasper) where the "spectral presence" of which O'Loughlin speaks, in this case a conflictual and traumatic racial history, has been palpable even as the direct referents to that past have at times been obscured under a variety of motives. There is no question that significant social progress has been made in these communities since the end of Jim Crow and the passage of the 1964 Civil Rights Act. While racial segregation and racism itself continue to haunt these communities (and, indeed, the United States more generally), the more blatant and blunt manifestations of racism, such as legally required segregation of schools and other public facilities or the prohibition of interracial marriage, have been removed. All three of these communities, for example, had witnessed the rise of African American or Latino political leadership, among other signs of social progress. However, the residues of a brutal racism that had ground entire communities down and made them the object of individual and collective violence was still in evidence, reflected in severe economic and power disparities, for example, and yielding to underlying racial tension and mistrust which remains present. For this reason, and notwithstanding indications of social progress, repairing the sociohistorical fabric in these communities remains an ongoing challenge for contemporary society. In this chapter I examine a racially based hate crime and its embeddedness within a broader history of racial violence. The hate crime served as a contemporary reference point to a collective experience of trauma that was supposed to be "past." This present-day enactment illustrated the extent to which a spectral horror continued to cast a shadow upon the community. I will also use this incident as a point of departure for a reflection on our assumptions about the relationship between memory and trauma and differences between individual and collective trauma when it comes to memory and memorialization.

THE MURDER OF JAMES BYRD, JR.

In June 1998, in Jasper, Texas, three white men participated in the murder of James Byrd, Jr., a middle-aged African American man. The victim had been walking home from a party around midnight when he accepted a ride from the men in a pickup truck. Unbeknownst to Byrd, two of them had only been out of prison six months, where they had been leaders of a white supremacist gang called the Confederate Knights of America. The prison, where they'd served time, the George Beto Unit in Palestine, Texas, was known as a "gladiator unit"—virtually all of the inmates were violent offenders between eighteen and twenty-five years of age, and racial violence was endemic within the prison.

It appears that Byrd was hoodwinked into believing that the three men were simply taking him along for a night of fun as he rode along in the bed of the pickup truck (he knew one of the men, and his DNA was later found on cigarette butts and on a beer bottle). The friendliness was clearly a ruse to lull the unsuspecting victim: Byrd was taken to a remote, secluded area, where he was brutally assaulted before having his ankles chained to the back of the truck and being dragged for over three miles, much of it over an asphalt-covered lane called Huff Creek Road.

Huff Creek Road is home to a small, rural community, the majority African American, and many of whom had lived in the area for several generations. The area is pastoral in its beauty and lush with wildflowers and dense woods. An African American cemetery and church anchor the end of the narrow country road. The brutally disfigured and, by then, decapitated remains of James Byrd were left early on a Sunday morning in front of that African American church, presumably to be discovered as families arrived for services later that morning.[1] A distinct trail of blood covered some two miles of Huff Creek Road, beginning at the point where the men had dragged Mr. Byrd from a clearing in the woods onto the paved road.

The sheer brutality of the manner in which James Byrd, Jr. was murdered suggested that it was an act of racial hatred. That thesis found further support when Jasper law enforcement officers entered the apartment shared by two of the perpetrators following their arrest some fourteen hours after the discovery of James Byrd's remains[2]: the officers found white supremacist literature and membership forms for the Confederate Knights of America. The evidence of a hate crime was so irrefutable that the Jasper County sheriff immediately sought the involvement of the Federal Bureau of Investigation.

Jasper lies in deep East Texas, near the Louisiana border, and its population is nearly evenly divided between white and African American residents. In interviews conducted in the aftermath of the Byrd murder (Ainslie and Brabeck, 2003; Ainslie, 2004), it was evident that the incident was profoundly traumatizing to the entire community of eight thousand. Geographically and culturally, East Texas is more akin to the American South when compared to the rest of Texas. It is here that slavery flourished and cotton plantations were a driving force of the economy. Because the Mexican constitution outlawed slavery, it was prohibited in Texas until the state's independence from Mexico in 1836. Between 1840 and 1860, however, the slave population in Texas grew from 11,000 to 182,000 (Ross, 2010). Texas was annexed as a slave state into the United States in 1845. As I have noted elsewhere (Ainslie, 1995), in west and south Texas, race relations bear the imprint of the psychodynamics of victor-vanquished relations, given that Mexicans lost lands (not infrequently via violent means) as well as social and political power after the Texas War of Independence. In many of these communities, Jim Crow laws were later imposed upon people of Mexican ancestry. In east Texas, race relations are predominantly shaped by the legacy of slavery, the Civil War, Reconstruction, and Jim Crow and thus governed by the psychodynamics attendant to slavery and white oppression, including violence directed toward African Americans. In other words, the reigning paradigms for race relations in different parts of Texas have been shaped by distinct historical and cultural contexts.

HATE CRIME AND COMMUNITY TRAUMA

The murder of James Byrd, Jr. contained all of the essential elements that some theorists argue are the undergirding for experiences of extreme trauma: It was an intended act of violence that had an impact beyond the specific victim, instilling terror and helplessness upon an entire community. This is evidenced, for example, by the fact that Mr. Byrd's horribly disfigured remains were left in front of an African American church on a Sunday morning as well as by the white supremacist literature, including membership forms for their racist organization. Varvin and Rosenbaum (2003) cogently sum up the relationship between significant trauma and intentional acts of brutality that create profound individual and collective anxiety:

> Extreme traumatization is a special and complicated sequence of events; it is the result of an intentional, malignant act or acts committed or designed by persons, organizations or states in order to cause damage to the individual and to social organizations, in order to produce a state of fear and helplessness and to produce prolonged and long-standing destabilization . . . aimed at specific groups such as ethnic communities, political movements or social groups. The aim is to produce fear on a mass basis and destroy or destabilize social links. (Varvin and Rosenbaum, 2003, p. 5)

Thus, the hate crime committed in Jasper, Texas, in the summer of 1998 contains all of the elements identified by Varvin and Rosenbaum as essential to the formation of extreme trauma. Indeed, in subsequent interviews with members of Jasper's African American community, there was ample evidence of such collective traumatization (Ainslie and Brabeck, 2003).

THEORIES OF TRAUMA AND MEMORY

The concepts of trauma and memory are deeply entwined in psychoanalytic theory. Freud's classic formulation linking symptoms to overwhelming experiences that have been subjected to a variety of dislocations in relation to memory is obviously seminal to this thesis in which trauma produces severe narrative discontinuity (Freud, 1954). Whether by repression or some other defensive mechanism, memory is no longer a reliable reference point because the integrity of the self requires that the traumatic experiences remain fully or partially disconnected from awareness.

The classic Freudian prescription for ameliorating symptoms focuses on the reintegration of the exiled, traumatizing experiences into the "ego" or the self. As noted, it is this state of dislocation that is understood to be responsible for symptoms and the thrust of psychoanalytic interventions often center on the removal of the obstructing defensive operations so that memory might be restored. Central to these foundational formulations is the idea that unconscious processes govern the tensions between trauma and memory. In other words, a motivational process is at work in the failure to remember.

These formulations have been rich and fertile ground for theorizing about trauma, its relation to representation, and strategies for helping resolve the profound psychic consequences of trauma. Numerous influential theorists have articulated variations on this idea, including Judith Herman (1997), Cathy Caruth (1995, 1996), Felman and Laub (1992), Michael O'Loughlin (2008, 2010), and Volkan (1997). One illustration of this line of theorizing is O'Loughlin's (2010) discussion of the presence of trauma in children's lives, where he states the following: "Since we are often rendered mute by our own traumatic experiences—or those ghosts of ancestral trauma we unconsciously embody—there is consolation in the fact that healing may be possible through the unconscious transmission of our unspeakable experiences to a receptive Other who can then give them back to us in speakable form" (p. 3). Similarly, in their chapter titled, "Amnesia, Dissociation, and the Return of the Repressed" Van der Kolk and Kadish (1987) remark that the "walling off the memories of the trauma" occupies a central place in the symptomatic consequences of that trauma (p. 181). They go on to note that: "Memories and feelings connected with the trauma are forgotten and return as intrusive recollections, feeling states (such as overwhelming anxiety and panic unwarranted by current experience), fugues, delusions, states of depersonalization, and finally in behavioral reenactments" (p. 185). These ideas are a common point of reference for psychoanalytic theorizing about trauma. It is almost axiomatic in psychoanalytic thinking that trauma leads to repression of memories which, in turn, result in problematic and hobbling symptomatic outcomes which cannot be resolved as long as the victim of trauma remains so deeply disconnected from those overwhelming experiences.

INDIVIDUAL TRAUMA, COLLECTIVE TRAUMA, AND MEMORY

Notwithstanding the power and utility of traditional psychoanalytic formulations regarding the psychodynamics of trauma, there is reason to believe that collective trauma operates somewhat differently from individual trauma, especially as it relates to the role of memory and repression in the formation of the emotional nucleus of trauma. In his seminal article, "Loss of communality at Buffalo Creek," Kai Erikson (1976) cogently argues that individual and collective trauma each are organized along a separate axis. Individual trauma occurs when there is a blow to the psyche "that breaks through one's defenses so suddenly and with such force that one cannot respond effectively" (p. 302). The consequence of such trauma is withdrawal, numbing, fear, vulnerability, and isolation and it includes the range of defensive operations that psychoanalytic theorists have long recognized.

Collective trauma, on the other hand, "is a blow to the tissues of social life that damages the bonds linking people together and impairs the prevailing sense of communality" (p. 302). Erikson argues that the two kinds of trauma are distinct and autonomous—either can take place without the other, even though the two often occur hand in hand (a large scale trauma may simultaneously be an individual trauma, for example). My argument in this chapter is that because collective trauma is organized along different lines, it plays a different role in psychic life. In particular, rather than psychodynamics that revolve around the repression and dislocation in memory of traumatic experience that we see in relation to individual trauma, I hope to illustrate that in collective trauma we often witness the opposite: a compelling need to remember and a demand for acknowledgement and memorialization of those traumatic experiences. In other words, not all trauma is unsayable or unknowable (except in the sense that all representations of experience are incomplete and elusive), much less unconscious.

Because psychoanalytic theorizing about trauma has centered on individual psychodynamics, it has been difficult to see how collective trauma might operate along different lines. However, we have a great deal of evidence to suggest that that is the case as I will illustrate below. Vamik Volkan's (1997) theorizing bridges the conceptualizations of individual and collective trauma by helping us understand how individual and collective identities intersect. Even as individuals and family groups are always operating, psychologically speaking, within the framework of broader sociocultural forces that shape and "hold" them, it is easy to overlook the place of these broader forces in our intrapsychic lives until events activate the "large tent" conflicts within which individuals and families exist (Volkan, 1997). I suggest that once they are activated (via acts of collective terrorism, for example), they play a different role in our psychic organization, a role that has to do with the relationship between individual and group identity that not only allows but in fact requires memory and memorialization of those experiences of collective trauma. Thus, groups often weave those very experiences into ritualized forms of remembrance and insist on their not being forgotten. Indeed, as Bohleber (2007) argues, in the aftermath of some forms of collective trauma, remembrance becomes "a special moral requirement" (p. 331).

Thus, we might argue that within psychoanalytic theorizing about trauma we must leave room for two major variants. In one, formulations regarding individual trauma are ultimately derived from classical psychoanalytic theorizing and emphasize the ways in which memory is repressed or otherwise abridged in the service of psychic survival. Here, psychological processes problematize aspects of memory and representation. In the second, trauma is actually thoroughly inscribed in memory, and groups who have been the victims of such collective trauma mobilize to insure that the memory of those events does not get erased or they otherwise work to actively maintain the presence of those representations in collective awareness. I believe that this is the case for African American communities in the United States with respect to the legacy of slavery, Jim Crow, and the brutality to which that community was subjected. The murder of James Byrd, Jr., and its reading as a "modern-day lynching" serves as an illustration of this thesis as I hope to illustrate in what follows.

LYNCHING AND THE GEOGRAPHY OF FEAR

The murder of James Byrd, Jr. took place within a clear, distinct historical context that helped frame its meaning and the way in which the community understood it. In late nineteenth-century and early twentieth-century Texas, collective violence was one of a variety of means that were used for exerting control over African Americans. The history of lynching in Texas provides a window into this reign of terror, as racial violence played out following the Civil War and into modern times. This history also forms the experiential reference point for what took place in Jasper in 1998.

Texas ranks third in terms of the number of lynching victims in America, second only to Mississippi and Georgia. In Texas, there were 468 officially recorded lynching incidents (defined as an extra official mob action that resulted in the murder of the victim) between 1885 and 1942 (Ross, 2010). Of these, 339 (72 percent) of the victims were black, 77 (16 percent) were white, 53 (11 percent) were individuals of Mexican-origin, and 1 is listed as "Indian," which more than likely means Native American (Ross, 2010). The great majority of these lynchings took place in the forty-year interval between 1885 and 1925, that is, between the time that Reconstruction was dismantled and Union troops left the state, and the height of Jim Crow. This tally is most certainly an underestimate, given that it only includes lynching incidents that were officially documented (as I note below, in Jasper, for example, on several occasions white and black residents described two lynching incidents involving African American men that took place in the area, neither of which appears in the state's official tally). In addition, it should be emphasized that lynching is only one facet of the many ways in which violence, including murder, assault, and rape, was used against non-whites. In many Texas communities, such violence often went unreported to local law enforcement officials for fear of reprisals.

The link between the pattern of lynching and specific historical contexts is clear in Texas. For example, half of the white lynching victims were killed in the immediate aftermath of the Civil War (within ten years) and presumably related to score settling of one sort or another. Similarly, half of the Mexican-origin lynching incidents took place around 1915, when Jim Crow laws were being implemented in communities that had once been Spanish or Mexican territory (perhaps targeting Mexican-ancestry individuals who resisted the imposition of Jim Crow laws). However, it is telling that lynching activities directed toward African Americans were not only much more prevalent, they also spanned a much longer period of time, from Reconstruction to the early 1930s (other brutal acts against African American communities have obviously continued beyond that time). The communities in Texas where lynching of black victims were most likely to take place were also those where slavery had been at the heart of the social and economic system. For example, all but fifteen of the officially documented lynching incidents involving black victims took place in East Texas (Ross, 2010). The farther east one goes in Texas, the more lynching-prone was the geography. Virtually every East Texas county witnessed lynching activity between Reconstruction and the 1930s. In other words, lynching was a pervasive mechanism of social control and Jasper was in the heart of the most violent part of the state with respect to lynching activity.

Following the murder of James Byrd, Jr. between the fall of 1999 and the end of 2002, I conducted an ethnography in Jasper that included many interviews in the community. A primary focus of these interviews was to map the impact of the hate crime on the broader population. On three occasions, I took a team of doctoral students into the community to conduct semi-structured interviews with white and African American residents. Many of these interviews were done in Jasper's white and black churches. In addition, I conducted extensive, in-depth interviews with a variety of residents, including friends and family members of two of the three perpetrators. As I have noted elsewhere (Ainslie & Brabeck, 2003), my team and I found substantial narratives of traumatization in these interviews.

In the course of my work in Jasper, I was struck by the fact that numerous people (both white and black) spontaneously mentioned that in the 1920s African American men had been lynched in two neighboring counties (St. Augustine County and Newton County). Altogether, six men had been lynched in these two incidents. In the Sabine County lynching, similar and converging accounts indicated that five African American men had been hanged by a mob. In the St. Augustine lynching, there had been one victim. A white man whom I interviewed told me that his father had witnessed the St. Augustine lynching and that some of the perpetrators had been named in his father's account, individuals whose descendants still lived in the area. A further detail of the St. Augustine lynching appeared to suggest its possible relationship to the murder of James Byrd, Jr.: a black man had been dragged around the county courthouse behind a pickup truck (his alleged transgression was that he'd had a relationship with a white woman). In Jasper, where these lynching incidents were part of the collective, if unofficial, memory of the community, one could not help but wonder if, in fact, the St. Augustine lynching might have served as a template for the murder of James Byrd, Jr., whose murder was uncannily similar.

The many accounts from the Jasper interviews in which the region's history of racial violence and, in particular, lynching activity, were present help us understand the emotional context within which the murder of James Byrd, Jr., widely described as a "modern-day lynching," took place (Ainslie, 2006). This act of violence was immediately understood as a recognizable and familiar form. Labeling the brutal murder a "lynching" obviously placed it firmly within a known and existing construct for racialized violence, while the concept of a modern-day lynching evoked the notion of something from the past transposed into the present.

This brutal act of racial violence was situated in the collective perception of the community as a contemporary version of the reign of terror under which African Americans had lived for generations. As I have noted elsewhere in relation to the lynchings that had taken place in the two neighboring counties:

> The perpetrators of those lynchings had never even been accused, much less tried in a court of law, but the incidents had not been forgotten. On the contrary, accounts of the lynchings had been handed down from generation to generation within Jasper County's white and black families, woven into the lore about the region's dark history of racial animus . . . they formed part of an uneasily shared past, living on as part of a collective, if unofficial legacy. (Ainslie, 2004, p. 118)

It was this contextualization of what had taken place on Huff Creek Road that also drove some of the community responses to the murder. For example, the Jasper District Attorney who handled the prosecution of the three men arrested for the murder of James Byrd, Jr. told me in an interview that, in the immediate aftermath of the murder, when tensions were extremely high and the town's atmosphere volatile, he had taken the unusual step of presenting the Probable Cause document to the members of Jasper's Ministerial Alliance. This organization was comprised of the ministers from the area's white and black churches and the district attorney had gone to them because, as he put it, "We had to satisfy them that this was not 1920." (Ainslie, 2004, p. 118).

Within the community of Jasper (and presumably elsewhere), the murder of James Byrd, Jr. was not the object of individual or collective repression or amnesia. Beyond the sheer brutality of the murder, what rendered it traumatic was precisely that its architecture drew from terrain that was all too familiar, reflecting and, in fact, amplifying, something ever so recognizable and known. That the hate crime reimposed upon individual and collective awareness something horrific and familiar is what helped make it so powerfully traumatic. In other words, the murder reactivated a broader experience of collective trauma, giving it an exponential power to undermine stability and instill anxiety, fear, and rage. That broader experience was not an unremembered past. Rather, it was an all too familiar past, albeit a past whose sense of immediacy had, arguably, become attenuated.

In this respect, the murder of James Byrd, Jr., as a collective experience, represents a variation on Freud's notion of the uncanny (1919). The hate crime was simultaneously profoundly shocking and, in this sense, foreign, while also psychologically deeply familiar as an action that perfectly fit the mold of historical acts of terror against the black community. A collective history of brutal violence was forced into awareness by the act of three white men who murdered a black man on a whim fueled by deep racial hatred. Byrd's murder made present something that was supposed to be past. It was impossible to separate the understanding of the brutal murder from the broader context in which this incident of racial violence had taken place. Both African Americans and whites spontaneously and instinctively drew the parallel. Thus, the hate crime was immediately recognizable as something familiar and known, yet foreign, as something that was supposed to be past. That past was brutally enacted in the present, tearing off the protective layers of distance and time. The protective illusion of lynching as something of the past was shattered by the Sunday morning horror of a black man chained and dragged to his death behind a pickup truck.

COLLECTIVE TRAUMA, TRANSGENERATIONAL TRANSMISSION, AND IDENTITY

This history of racial violence against African Americans is clear and until recent times the threats were ever-present. All around, a pattern of massive social violence was being played out against this community. The scale of the violence was enormous, and lynching was only its most raw manifestation. White on black violence in the form of murder (as opposed to the mass attacks that defined lynching), assault, and rape, in addition to a complete absence of recourse for any other grievance (e.g., exploitation or not being paid for services, etc.), all formed part of a culture of victimization in relation to which the black community was essentially powerless. In Texas, the Texas Slave Code of 1858, a statute that provided, for example, that "the insolence of a slave will justify a white man in inflicting moderate chastisement, with an ordinary instrument of correction, if done at the time when the insolent language is used" (Glasrud, 1974, p. 49) continued in force as a social practice if no longer inscribed in law. Similarly, the post-Reconstruction Texas Constitution stipulated that "persons of color shall not testify, except where the prosecution is against a person of color; or where the offense is charged to have been committed against the person or property of a person of color" (Glasrud, 1974, p. 51). In other words, in Texas, as in the rest of the American South, blacks were utterly defenseless, disenfranchised, and had virtually no legal recourse in relation to whites.

Judith Kestenberg, uses the term "transposition" to describe the psychological process of unconscious, cross-generational transmission of massive trauma:

> Transposition describes the uncanny experience where the past reality of the parent intrudes into the present psychological reality of the child. Transposition is an anomalous version of the ordinary psychological process whereby the wishes, desires, fantasies, ideals, and experiences of a parent are unconsciously transmitted to a child. (1998, pp. 223–24)

Along similar lines, O'Loughlin describes the ways in which parental trauma may be handed down, making its presence known, as a kind of socio-historically constituted and ancestrally located experience (O'Loughlin, 2012). Volkan (1997), too, has described processes of transgenerational transmission of trauma in groups. However, I would argue that in the context of collective trauma, the transgenerational transmission is often more direct and less driven by unconscious processes (which is not to say that there are no unconscious processes at work within it) because of the ways in which individual and collective identity processes interact. Psychoanalysis theorizes about the relationship between history and identity and about the costs of dislocated, repressed, or otherwise sealed off experience. However, the lynchings in East Texas were not repressed; rather, they existed within the fabric of collective memory, handed down and, within the black community, embodying aspects of what Volkan (1997) might describe as "Chosen traumas" around which group identity constellates. They had a different status within the white community, where the uncanny nature of the Byrd lynching, thrusting the past into the present, was perhaps disquieting for different reasons. Here, at least for some, the constellations of shame and guilt participated in a different way in the psychodynamics of memory and dislocation.

COLLECTIVE TRAUMA AND CONTESTED MEMORY

The ways in which trauma is remembered and represented becomes a site of contestation. In an individual context, there are conflicts and defenses operating out of the realm of awareness that shape and propel how trauma becomes positioned, psychologically. In a collective context, the conflicts around how such experiences are represented and remembered also become sites of contestation. The fact that different motives lurk within the processes attendant to memory and in relation to the impulse to erase or affirm these experiences, makes the memory of collective trauma contested territory and renders contestations themselves dense with implication, for they point to varying positionalities in relation to power and with respect to the problem of guilt, responsibility, shame, and rage.

One illustration can be found in the use of historical markers. In communities and locations that have been sites of trauma, such markers serve to sustain memory; they insist on an acknowledgement and they invite awareness of traumatizing experience. However, as noted, often these acts of memory are themselves contested. For example, in January 2014, the *New York Times* published an article about a controversy in Montgomery, Alabama, over the placement of historical markers indicating the sites where the slave trade had been conducted within the city. Members of the African American community and Civil Rights groups sought to have those sites memorialized with historical markers, while some segments of the city's white community were anxious that such markers might prove to be "divisive." Montgomery became a site for contested memory. Or, better said, the move to publicly register that history brought into the open processes of political (rather than psychological) repression that had been silent undercurrents in the community's treatment of the legacy of slavery. Here, the victims of the collective trauma of slavery, African American descendants of the slave trade, were the voices insisting on remembrance, while some in the white community explicitly or implicitly resisted in favor of what was in effect an attempt to suppress that history. The efforts to repress ("we do not want to acknowledge the violence that took place here in our city") was in the service of assuaging the guilt and sense of responsibility on the part of those who felt an identification with the historic perpetrators of the atrocity of slavery. However, this repression and the attempted erasure of memory were not in the service of protecting the victims of that injustice from the anxiety of memory. On the contrary, the descendants of those victims and others in the community were insisting on the preservation of that memory.

Similarly, in Jasper, following the murder of James Byrd, Jr., there were community disagreements over how to memorialize him. For example, a proposal to name a school after him drew heated debate. One camp argued that Byrd's life was anything but exemplary, given that he'd been arrested on several occasions and had served prison time, while others argued that the act of racial brutalization required some form of substantive acknowledgement, irrespective of the victim's personal traits. Eventually, a small, vacant patch of land in a part of Jasper known as "The Quarters" was designated the James Byrd, Jr. Memorial Park. Though the park had a basketball court, a playground, and picnic tables, it was set in a part of town where few whites were likely to encounter it: The Quarters was the area in Jasper where slaves had lived prior to the Civil War (hence its name) and it continued to be predominantly African American. It was also the part of town where James Byrd, Jr. had been picked up by the three perpetrators. Thus, the park's geographic marginalization reflected the African American community's marginalization. This latter observation would seem to echo de Kok's reflection that the custody of memory is highly contested (de Kok, 1998). It illustrates the fluid, "mobile current" within which individuals and communities make and remake their meanings (de Kok, 1998).

CONCLUSION

Notwithstanding the psychoanalytic privileging of a narrative of trauma as linked to the repression of experience or experience being otherwise exiled from memory, we have, in fact, a bifurcated body of theory of trauma. Groups that have experienced collective trauma have a powerful need to keep the memory of the traumatizing experiences that have befallen them alive and in awareness. Indeed, as noted earlier, some forms of collective trauma turn "remembrance into a special moral requirement" (Bohleber, 2007, p. 331). This is why traumatized groups frequently insist on remembrance. It is for this reason that we have the September 11 Memorial in New York City, why the Cherokee nation conducts annual Trail of Tears memorial walks, why African Americans demand historical signs that mark the sites of the slave trade in Montgomery, Alabama, why Armenians observe Genocide Remembrance Day all over the world, and why we find Holocaust museums in the United States, Europe, and elsewhere. The examples, in fact, are countless. Unlike individual trauma, which often seeks to elude and distance trauma, collective trauma insists on memory and memorialization.

Individuals whose traumatization has taken place in the context of collective trauma, may well resort to a variety of defensive processes that are well known to psychoanalytic theorists in an effort to help manage the overwhelming nature of those experiences. Holocaust survivors, survivors of genocidal wars, and even veterans returning from wars, where they have experienced profoundly overwhelming events, often resort to strategies of isolation, compartmentalization, numbing, and silence, as part of their efforts to shut down their emotional connection to traumatic experiences in order to psychically survive them. This is different from forgetting. While individual responses to trauma may often include repression as salient aspects of their strategies for psychic survival, collective responses to trauma appear to often require the opposite: they are metabolized via processes of memory and memorialization. It is within such ritualized remembering that collective identities are affirmed for members of the group. Those groups thus repudiate the efforts to erase their experienced trauma from public and collective memory; on the contrary, they insist on honoring that memory through ritualized forms of recollection, including the placement of historical markers and memorials, the creation of museums, the creation of holidays marking important dates, and other forms of remembrance.

NOTES

1. Two of the three perpetrators were Jasper residents and both knew the Huff Creek area well.

2. The third man had only been in Jasper for two weeks. He was in town visiting the man who would subsequently be identified as the ringleader in the murder.

REFERENCES

Ainslie, R. (1995). *No dancin' in Anson: An American story of race and social change*. Northvale, NJ: Jason Aronson.

Ainslie, R. (2004). *Long dark road: The story of Bill King and Jasper's murder.* Austin, TX: University of Texas Press.

Ainslie, R. (2006). Psychoanalytic ethnography, racist violence, and Jasper, Texas: An introduction. *Psychoanalysis, Culture and Society, 11*(1), 97–98.

Ainslie, R. C., & Brabeck, K. (2003). Race murder and community trauma: Psychoanalysis and ethnography in exploring the impact of the killing of James Byrd in Jasper, Texas. *Journal of Psychoanalysis, Culture and Society*, *8*(1), 42–51.

Bohleber, W. (2007). Remembrance, trauma and collective memory: The battle for memory in psychoanalysis. *International Journal of Psychoanalysis*, *88*, 329–52.

Caruth, C. (Ed.). (1995). *Trauma: Explorations in memory.* Baltimore, MD: Johns Hopkins University Press.

Caruth, C. (1996). *Unclaimed experience: Trauma, narrative, and history.* Baltimore, MD: Johns Hopkins University Press.

De Kok, I. (1998). Cracked heirlooms: Memory on exhibition. In S. Nuttal & C. Coetzee (Eds.). *Negotiating the past: Making memory in South Africa.* Cape Town: Oxford University Press.

Erikson, K. T. (1976). Everything in its path: Destruction of community in the Buffalo Creek Flood. *American Journal of Psychiatry*, *133*, 3.

Felman, S., & Laub, D. (Eds). (1992). *Testimony: Crises of witness in literature, psychoanalysis, and history.* New York and London: Routlege.

Freud, S. (1954). Studies on hysteria. *Standard edition of the complete psychological works of Sigmund Freud.* Vol. II (1893–1895).

Freud, S. (1919). The "Uncanny." *Standard edition of the complete psychological works of Sigmund Freud.* Vol. VII (1917–1919).

Glasrud, B. (1974). Jim Crow's emergence in Texas. *American Studies*, *15*(1), 47–60.

Herman, J. L. (1997). *Trauma and recovery: The aftermath of violence from domestic abuse to political terror.* New York, NY: Basic Books.

Kestenberg, J. (1998). The echo of trauma and the trauma of echo. *American Imago, 55*(3), 319–47.

O'Loughlin, M. (2008). Radical hope or death by a thousand cuts: The future for indigenous Australians. *Arena Journal, 29/30*, 175–201.

O'Loughlin, M. (2010). Ghostly presences in children's lives: Toward a psychoanalysis of the social. In M. O'Loughlin & R. Johnson (Eds.), *Imagining children otherwise: Theoretical and critical perspectives on childhood subjectivity*. New York: Peter Lang Publishing.

O'Loughlin, M. (2013). Reclaiming geneology, memory and history: The psychodynamic potential for reparative therapy in contemporary South Africa. In G. Lobban, M. O'Loughlin, & C. Smith (Eds.), *Psychodynamic psychotherapy in Contemporary South Africa: Theory, practice and policy perspectives*. Johannesburg, South Africa: University of Witwatersrand Press.

Robertson, C. (2013, December 9). Before the battles and the protests: The chains. *New York Times*. Retrieved from http://www.nytimes.com/2013/12/10/us/before-the-battles-and-the-protests-the-chains.html?_r=0

Ross, J. R. (2010). Lynching. *Handbook of Texas online*. Austin: Texas State Historical Commission. Retrieved from http://www.tshaonline.org/handbook/online/articles/jgl01

van der Kolk, B., & Kadish, W. (1987). Amnesia, dissociation, and the return of the repressed. In B. van der Kolk (Ed.), *Psychological trauma*. Arlington, VA: American Psychiatric Publishing.

Varvin, S., & Rosenbaum, B. (2003). Extreme traumatization: Strategies for mental survival. *International Forum of Psychoanalysis, 12*, 5–16.

Volkan, V. D. (1997). *Bloodlines: From ethnic pride to ethnic terrorism*. New York: Farrar, Straus, and Giroux.

Chapter 16

Managing Collapse

Commemorating September 11 through the Relational Design of a Memorial Museum

Billie Pivnick and Tom Hennes[1]

COLLAPSE

What was it that was so shocking about the attacks of 9/11? The event began in strangeness[2]: rumors of an airplane flying into the World Trade Center. As television cameras were trained on the burning North Tower, the world rapidly began to take notice. When the second hijacked airliner careened into the South Tower, all doubt about what was going on—whether it was an accident or an act of terrorism—vanished. A group of military and civilian personnel in the Pentagon was watching the event on television when a third airliner crashed into the office where they sat, instantly killing many of them as well as others nearby. Meanwhile, a drama the world wouldn't know about until later unfolded on a fourth airliner above the skies of Pennsylvania, ending in a column of black smoke rising above rolling farmland.

We remember the images of people jumping from the towers. We remember the horrific flames and the gaping holes venting roiling black smoke. Those of us who were watching the unfolding event live remember the questions that most certainly were on all of our minds: How would people escape from so high a building? How could anyone put out these fires? The answer came when the first tower—the South Tower—vanished in a cloud of dust. We remember the feeling of foreboding watching the fires burn in the North Tower that was still standing, now impossibly alone. And then it was over: where only 102 minutes before, two shining towers had stood in the brilliant morning sunlight, there was only a cloud of dust and smoke drifting high above lower Manhattan and Brooklyn, casting a bustling city into a pall of grey dust as an impossible quantity of paper fluttered slowly downward.

Over mass media, we watched in rapt horror the endless replay of the second impact, captured from every imaginable angle, and then the video of the first impact that emerged later in the day, serendipitously captured by a film crew traveling with a fire company not far from the World Trade Center. And we watched the collapse, over and over again, of the two towers. It was surely the collapse itself, with its unfathomable force, the uncountable number of souls within it, and the utter destruction of these icons of American bravado, that most shocked us, making us numb and yet compelling us to rush in, each of us in our way, to do something, anything, to help. We waited for the wounded to be pulled out and brought to St. Vincent's Hospital, where hundreds of medical personnel were awaiting the ambulances that never came. Instead, missing posters, by the thousands, appeared on walls and fences and lampposts across New York. Vigils assembled spontaneously. But with the exception of 23 survivors pulled from the vast pile of wreckage, almost nothing of the 2,763 missing victims of the New York attack ever emerged from the wreckage of the Towers.

What visibly collapsed on 9/11 were buildings, symbols, defensive systems, and response systems—those of a nation plunged into uncertainty and those of so many around the world attempting to comprehend what had happened. But what also collapsed was society's capacity for reasoned dialogue and tolerance of views that dissented from a rapidly crystallizing narrative of outrage and inchoate revenge. And for many, what further collapsed was the ability to symbolize what had happened, buried like so many bodies in the hot, smoky, heavy rubble at Ground Zero. As the emotions evoked by the events were transmuted into retaliation, reinvigorated defenses, and sometimes paralytic fear of repetition, time also collapsed the distinction between present, past, and future—in debilitating ways for some of those most affected, more subtly for a vast number of others whose sense of the world was set akimbo by the collapse they sensed or feared all around them. These kinds of responses to the events, in turn, collapsed for some the ability to engage an alive interplay with others' ideas, sensations, and emotions.[3]

REANIMATION

In the hours, days, and months after 9/11, not all was collapse. Running counter to it was the mobilization of defenses, the rush to rescue victims and then, in New York, to recover the dead, to dig through the pile, to clear the site, and eventually, to rebuild and return life to a place of destruction. In the fractious process of the ensuing years, while the "war on terror" raged within the United States and around the world, the design for a memorial was chosen from among 5,201 entries and the space beneath it was designated as an archaeological site and museum. In 2006, what was then called the World Trade Center Memorial Foundation issued a request for proposals for the museum's exhibition design.

I (Tom) am the principal of Thinc Design, a firm that specializes in the creation of museum exhibitions. Though I was deeply skeptical that the 9/11 museum project could easily become a jingoistic remaking of the events and their aftermath into a two-dimensional caricature, similar to the rhetoric around the wars in Afghanistan and Iraq, I was nonetheless drawn to it upon reading the museum's multifaceted prospective narrative in its Request for Qualifications, the first stage of competition for the design. Having worked at the time for four years already on a complex memorial and museum in a project of national reconciliation in South Africa, the Freedom Park, it occurred to me that this could be a platform for reinstituting thoughtful dialogue in the aftermath of 9/11—an opportunity to carry some humanizing aspects of the work in South Africa into my own country. I invited Billie to be a part of the team, primarily in anticipation of the potentially traumatizing impact of the museum on its users.

Not only was I (Billie) a psychoanalytic psychologist who had worked extensively with firefighters and other traumatized people after 9/11, I also had a varied background in dance therapy and art therapy that gave me added capability to work as a creative partner on what would undoubtedly be a complex design process. Moreover, we had worked together before in a fruitful collaboration on another museum project, and Tom sensed that I would be able to assist the museum and his team of designers to formulate a museum with a greater chance for revivified dialogue around multiple perspectives on the events.

The two of us joined forces, together with Thinc's media partner, Local Projects, in what became a successful bid for the exhibition design of the museum. As we began to traverse the social, political, historical, and psychological landscape of 9/11 and its many constituencies, we were to develop a sense of what such a museum might accomplish within its walls and for the larger society of which it would be a part. We also came to develop a perspective on the museum that located its ethical center in the intersubjective negotiation of meaning through the representation of multiple experiences and perspectives of the events (Lichtenstein, 2014). Its theoretical basis was a relational field[4] created jointly by those who had experienced the events, represented on video and through audio recordings and text, those who created the museum through the design of space, the curation of artifacts, and the selection of narrative material, and those who would attend the museum, each with an "entrance narrative,"[5] sense impressions, and, for most, numerous gaps in awareness, knowledge, or experience. We believed that by building what amounted to a holding environment[6]—unlike but not unrelated to a consulting room—in which each user could safely negotiate a field of varied experience and narrative of 9/11, we could to some degree facilitate the uncollapsing of time, of play, and of symbolization so that people in the museum could gain a more fully conscious sense of their own experience of

9/11, and thereby greater flexibility and tolerance for the complex world that has emerged from it (Bernstein, 2000).

AN EMERGENT UNDERSTANDING

Although history is typically thought of as a systematically gathered, continuous narrative of the past of a particular group of people or a place or time, the defining linearity of history has been reconsidered by cultural scholars (Blanchot, 1980/1995). Given the traumatic context of so much of what's memorable enough to be written and transmitted to future generations, such a chronicle has typically been so distorted by the dissociation of semantic and sensate memory and disorientation in time that some scholars have concluded that history can no longer be considered a linear story (Caruth, 1996). If history is instead seen as nonlinear, it must be understood as emerging in the present moment from multiple partial views, which can eventually be brought together into a collective awareness before and even as it is being inscribed. So even if a coherent understanding of the scope and significance of that history is not yet possible, the story can be told by attending with others to its emerging story fragments, strands, and images.

Memorial museum storytelling can be considered a first draft of history. Records of traumatic testimony often emerge as fragmentary representations. They bear witness to the pain of victims, but require being listened to, observed, or reexperienced by others to serve a socially or psychologically reparative function (Boulanger, 2007; Davoine & Gaudillière, 2004; Felman & Laub, 1991; Gerson, 2009). Yet they serve even more than this crucial psychological function. As collective repositories of narrated experience, together they also form an important record from which present and future members of society can derive and negotiate the evolving meaning of historical events (Beebe, McCrorie, & Pivnick, 2013; Halbwachs, 1941/1992).

If a memorial museum's task is to represent and help repair what happened during a catastrophic communal loss, then a contemporary museum that attempts to represent history has to include multiple narratives, multiple subjectivities, and the interpenetration of curatorial and user participation. Fundamentally, such a memorial museum must be about the cocreation of narrative meaning through intersubjective experience. At the same time, representing all the facets of the collapse from multiple points of view requires enormously complex thinking. By applying relational theory to the development of the exhibitions in what we came to call "relational design," we believed we could create an environment in which the multiple subjectivities of all those who contribute to it—whether as represented subjects, exhibition creators, or museum users—asynchronously interpenetrate each other through the experience in the museum. Unlike a more conventionally organized exhibition, in which the frequently stated goal is for the user to understand and "correctly" interpret the curatorial messages embodied by it, this exhibition, as the product of relational design, would be subject to many possible interpretations emerging as the product of the things users encounter and their own prior experiences. Its most fundamental purpose is to assist users in locating themselves within a field of potential meaning. The museum should thus be able to construct a scaffold that stretches users' capacities to engage complexity as they journey through it. As a museum user becomes more able to empathically experience others' perspectives, while also continuing to witness and give meaning to her own unique and potentially conflicting experience, she may develop an enhanced ability to think paradoxically about these contested events.

What we discovered in the years of working toward the finished museum was a sometimes overpowering tension between our urge to uncollapse the events and their narratives—shared by many in the museum development team as well—and other constituents' or team members' urge to recollapse them. We encountered the effects of trauma at nearly every turn, in places both expected and surprising—even within our own experience. The museum that opened in May 2014 is an embodiment of that tension, with elements that breathe life back into a place of death and others that bear down with a chaotic intensity that can become overwhelming. Far from perfect, it is the product of more hands than can be counted, often motivated by unseen psychological currents that sometimes erupted into the turbulence of internal discord and sometimes very public conflict.

BEGINNINGS

In the first days of the design process in 2007, both the design team and the curatorial staff of the museum listened to various experts and toured important sites related to the work we were about to undertake. The first of these was an enormous hanger at Kennedy Airport in New York, simply denoted "Hanger 17," where the Port Authority, which owned the World Trade Center site and the buildings on it, had stored thousands of pieces of wreckage noted for significance and held for a possible museum. The second was a room in the downtown building that housed the Memorial Foundation offices, which contained memorial objects and tributes placed there by families of the victims. Called the "Family Room," it was closed to the public and provided a place for families to visit and overlook the site during and after the recovery. The third site was Ground Zero itself, which was at the time an enormous, open hole, sixteen acres in area, and seventy feet deep. These encounters were meant to orient us to the project and to locate a discussion of important design principles within the physical spaces of the events.

While visiting these sites, and in what became hundreds of meetings with the museum development team, advisors, board members, public officials, and a town hall-style discussion series with stakeholders, we gradually became deeply immersed in the world of 9/11, in the ways in which its effects permeated the world around our work, and in the ways that it shaped both the understandings and emotional dynamics of the people inside and near the project. Our continual attunement to both the verbal and nonverbal context of these myriad working sessions and discussions became critical tools to shape an exhibition with a heightened potential for factual and emotional accessibility, authenticity, and utility for a wide range of future users.[7] We were alerted at several key moments to the importance of what we came to call "managing collapse." In this section, we will provide four significant vignettes, each of them illustrative of a different sort of collapse, and each followed by a theoretical discussion.

NOT THE FIRST TIME

We were alerted to the importance of collapsed time to the design process during our first visit to Hangar 17, the repository of the artifacts that included, among many other things, eighty thousand square feet of steel, sorted by type and stacked neatly on wooden blocks. The effect of all these rusty, often twisted beams standing guard over objects like a torqued bicycle rack minus its bike riders left viewers nearly speechless. The maimed remnants of the giant antenna that stood atop the North Tower looked like the Skylab space station from the same era as the Towers. Fire trucks, some crushed and twisted, one of them shiny and nearly intact at one end, burned and rusted at the other, sat among flattened cars and an ambulance whose roofless interior was burned away and filled with ash. Remnants of a huge Calder sculpture were laid out along with fragments of Rodin figures that seemed like actual blackened, torn bodies. The conservator of these objects greeted us by saying, "This will not be your first visit. . . ." We assumed he meant, "This will not be your last visit" since most of us were there for the first time. We mused that the narrative pancaking pointed to by his confusion of temporal terms could, if opened, become a space where we would see history emerging—and where the nascent story of 9/11 would begin, scaffolded in now-wounded steel that told a story devoid of verbs.

Stories help us to anticipate and organize the passage of time (Heidegger, 1927/2008; Ochs & Capps, 2001; Ricoeur, 1984). The narrative structure in the museum would begin with the way the attacks disrupted the expected

Figure 16.1 Hanger 17 at Kennedy Airport, Where Wreckage from the World Trade Center Was Stored. *Credit*: Tom Hennes.

state of things and show how people coped with their new reality. The stories told in the museum would necessarily be in dialectical tension between what might otherwise have been and what actually happened. The outcome of the story—the process of recovery—would, we hoped, help us to anticipate further trouble and imagine future probabilities. We hoped, too, that if users told and listened to stories, they would come to better understand others' ways of making sense out of such a seemingly senseless event. Furthermore, their sharing of stories might create a sense of community essential to reciprocal social interactions. Over time, sharing stories might even help the museum's users create and maintain both their individual and group identities, while seeing how interconnected they are (Al Ramiah & Hewstone, 2013).

THE GROTTO IN THE TIMELINE

We were alerted to the disruption of narrative structures nearly immediately. In an orientation meeting, the creative director, when describing a dark narrow corridor that had been nicknamed "the grotto" that was thought to be a good place for a "timeline" of the events of the day of 9/11, stated "the grotto in the timeline" instead of "the timeline in the grotto." This *parapraxis* reaffirmed that we needed to anticipate the visitors' needs to pause for reflection at different points in their museum journey. There was again the gap in time that we had glimpsed in the conservator's speech at Hangar 17.

These communicative gaffes reflected what Freud (1920) called "a break in the mind's experience of time." He saw this temporal discontinuity as more disruptive to a person's defenses than the actual escape from extreme danger in traumatic situations. Usually the action of *nachträglichkeit,* or retranscription, would attempt to restore continuity through compulsive repetition (Freud & Breuer, 1895). Because the effects of trauma are, in this way, deferred to a later time,[8] enacted repetitions, however painful and unanticipated, bridge those gaps through action. Given that actions can reveal which emotions need translation into linguistic links, telling stories that depict those actions to others can therefore reintegrate procedural and semantic memory and prevent repeated disruptions. Freud (1914) called this process "repeating, remembering, and working through." Attending to their effects on communication can also help reestablish "social links" among people and institutions (Davoine & Gaudillière, 2004; Pivnick, 2013a).

But traumatized survivors often fail to envision a connection to an interested other, so both intrapsychic and interpersonal dialogue could be precluded in the museum, making intersubjective space uninhabitable.[9] Being a victim of the malignant trauma created by destruction at other humans' hands could make it difficult to restore trust, faith, and fidelity in human relationships and social institutions (LaMothe, 1999; Lear, 2007). These sorts of ruptures in our interpersonal connections often reflect denial of permanent loss, which, when coupled with a wish for reunion with things and people we lost, produce a state in which "there is no death, only a change in communication" (Krupp, 1965, p. 311). Therefore, telling stories to remember, commemorate, honor, educate, and mourn, could prove to be problematic.

The Presence of Absence

Even in 2007, six years after the attacks, our visit to the Family Room was painfully moving and dislocating. We could see families' ongoing anguish at the loss of loved ones and, for so many, the utter absence of any physical remains. The messages in the visitor book were still addressed by family members to their deceased relatives as if they were alive. To paraphrase: "The children miss you. I tell them what a great father and hero you are." The walls and windows were decorated with a collage of missing posters, floral wreaths, and pictures, both emphasizing the importance of the spatial enclosure and blotting out any view of the outdoors, which consisted of the construction site at Ground Zero. In the core of the room were brightly colored plastic toys, a table and chairs, balls, and blocks; but they were so new, unused, and lifeless, it was as if they embodied the death at the core of the

9/11 experience. I (Billie) came away with the realization that the museum journey had to shift Museum visitors "from shock to think." As we continued to discuss our work, the hole in the spatial organization came to stand not merely for the gap in the narrative but also for the importance of representing the paradoxical journey from "the absence of presence"—a dissociated state of shock—to accepting "the presence of absence" through memorial activities.

We also understood this as an ethical obligation. Keeping absent others in mind shows ongoing concern for them, but memory, if not scaffolded in ritual or story, lasts only a short time, perhaps a generation or two, before forgetting sets in. Bringing explicit memories of those lost into the museum space, would not only help people to *know* those lost but also aid them in forming the *beliefs* that would emerge from that knowledge (Margalit, 2002). Reasserting these beliefs through both story (explicit memory, often written) and ritual (implicit memory, usually noninscribed) is one form of recovery following cultural trauma (Connerton, 1989).

Injunctions to remember a dead person's name have been passed down from Biblical times. Remembering someone's name is a way of evoking that person metonymically and, from a religious perspective, confers a kind of immortality. But the secular importance of memory is a matter of demonstrating caring, a basic attribute of being human. Looking after someone, in commemorating, we have to plan, as well. This reminder that we live in time can help us remain oriented in the face of sometimes disorienting emotions. In addition, caring is an intersubjective act.

The chain of repeated genocides of the twentieth century teaches the importance of remembering the emotions members of society once experienced together as they faced a common threat. These reactions are typically expressed in story form. Because there is no single perspective on these complex occurrences, but rather many views of the same events, multiple stories must be told. The involvement created in this shared experience facilitates mutual caring and concern for each other as well as for victims—the principal features of an ethical community. By bearing witness publicly to acts of mass murder and catastrophe, as well as to the suffering they induced, a memorial visit can help us to reorganize as an ethical community of memory. Being witnessed in this way enables hope and meaning to be possible again (Margalit, 2002). Observing the suffering of others with an awareness of "the one in the many and the many in the one" has indeed been considered by psychoanalysts (cf., Ulanov, 2010) to be the prime ethical charge to people in this age of overstimulation (Huyssens, 2003).

Stories that remind us of how to avoid or cope with a catastrophic event, and that can help bridge the gap between what was and what could have been are of two sorts. One kind emphasizes memories of individuals and the power of their lives as lived. A second type tells the facts of what happened, often alerting us to vulnerabilities that need repair and highlighting not only suffering, but also acts of heroism that helped us triumph over radical evil; this is destined to become historical narrative. Both types of story would have to be a part of the museum.

A SANCTUM WITHIN A SANCTUM WITHIN A SANCTUM

In attendance at one of the Conversation Series meetings organized by the museum for the purposes of obtaining feedback on the developing exhibitions from important stakeholders that included people from the local community and family members, we were struck by the comments of two participants. One was the request from a community member that our design reflect the enormity of the buildings and the vast space they contained. Another was the desire of a young adult who had lost his brother in the attack on the towers and who, like many family members, had no remains to bury, that the museum provide a sense of containment for his grief. He requested that the museum contain a space that would be like "a sanctum within a sanctum within a sanctum." Struck by the degree to which these spatial desires contradicted each other, we became aware of the need to accommodate in the design the likelihood of binary thinking so common after traumatic loss. Realizing that feelings of unsafety could complicate the path of mourning and recovery from bereavement, we kept both these suggestions in mind as we worked on the memorial exhibit design, but aspired to contain them in more paradoxical form. We also realized more generally that we would need to pay careful attention to implicit (unconscious, procedural) phenomena as well as explicit (declarative) ones.

Memorial practices aim to enfold the remembered into the community of living or the community of living into the remembered (Olin, 2003). A multifaceted encounter with the authentic narrative and artifactual remains of the event in the memorial museum can help museum users remember the fallen and pay tribute to rescuers and rebuilders. But it may also help with inner repair by stimulating emotions like grief and sorrow. Because artifacts evoke particularly powerful feelings, they signify stories, as well. An intersubjective "aesthetic moment" occurs when we are in such deep rapport with an object (whether person, text, painting, or composition) that time seems to disappear and space crystallizes, creating the illusion of fit with the object. This can trigger an existential memory of being with someone in a deep affective dialogue (Bollas, 1989). Similarly, a work of art can be viewed as incomplete without the participation of the viewer/reader/listener's perceptual and emotional state, called "the beholder's share."[10]

If, as Langan posits, "where you choose to place your mind determines what place is" (2000, p. 77), then each individual's unique intentions, beliefs, and lived experiences would shape the encounter with objects in the museum (cf. Hennes, 2010) and with the museum staff's itinerary for their visit in idiosyncratic ways.

Becoming and being a biographical and cultural self by incorporating aspects of other peoples' activities and beliefs is the same neurobiological process as responding to and incorporating other aspects of the world (Damasio, 2012). Nevertheless, the self emerges not just in a physical presence, but also in narrative form. Thus, if we are engaged with hearing others' narratives, their ideas become part of our extended selves. The melding of the first- and third-person perspectives of the same phenomenon leads to "shared representations" and a "shared self" that finds itself in the eyes of another.[11] Neuroscientists and moral philosophers now posit this process to be the basis of ethics (Ravven, 2013).

However, differing perspectives mean divergent narratives. And many of these storylines about 9/11 are contested by others with differing points of view (Greenwald, 2010). By offering users the opportunity to see multiple points of view while also cocreating with the storytellers an overarching position, memorializing becomes not just a chance to notice our tendency to forget (Spitz, 2005) but also an intersubjective ethical act (Kafka, 2008).

Visiting a memorial, listening to the stories, and viewing the scope of the destruction provides a means to recognize the shifting sands on which we still stand, to "stand in the spaces" among dialectically organized perspectives (Bromberg, 1998; Pivnick, 2011). Intersubjective witnessing can reduce the defensive projection and concretization that enables groups to reduce other people to caricatures who fit just one social category, rather than seeing them in all their multiple roles and life narratives (Pivnick, 2011). Such variegated understanding can help diminish the demagogic claims and the wish to find a scapegoat that can lead to violence and victimization in trauma's aftermath (Sen, 2006). Memorials, in this way of thinking, can help nations in the wake of acts of mass murder and catastrophe to reorganize as caring communities of memory rather than to resort to grandiose and ultimately destructive identifications with the aggressor (Ferrell, 1995). Since, as Freud (1914) instructed, we are doomed to repeat what we do not remember, memorial visitors are essential to the intersubjective process of healing mass trauma.

STORYTELLING, PROCESS, AND DESIGN

In this section, we begin with a brief description of the physical context of the memorial and the museum that is situated beneath it. Then we will highlight four examples of the ways storytelling and our working process resulted in design solutions for the memorial museum.

Michael Arad and Peter Walker's design for the two memorial pools and the plaza surrounding them at ground level is by now well known. These squares-within-squares are sited directly above the original "footprints" of the Twin Towers, which are seventy feet below them in the Memorial Museum. Named "Reflecting Absence," these voids, with their immense waterfalls cascading into pools that themselves cascade into square "voids" at their centers, inversely represent what were once immensely tall structures. The design of the architectural space of the museum utilizes the twin volumetric structures of the pools to create a simulacrum of the towers, reproduced metaphorically as hovering solids that descend toward the footprints, enabling people in the museum to circumnavigate the archaeological remains beneath the volumes. Conceived by Davis Brody Bond, the architects of the underground portion of the museum, and designed prior to our engagement as exhibition designers these "present absences" became defining features of the museum spaces and shaped differentiated exhibition design approaches throughout.

People enter the museum through a pavilion designed by Snøhetta that is located on the Memorial Plaza between the two pools. The path of descent into the museum begins with a stair and escalator that leads past two ninety-foot high "tridents"—the tall, remnant steel arches that defined the Towers' ground floor lobbies and became so iconic in the wreckage of Ground Zero. This is where Thinc's exhibition design work really begins. The descent continues along a more than four-hundred foot ramp that conveys people from a subterranean concourse level, past overlooks into the surrounding museum spaces, to a stair and escalator that lead to the main exhibit space at the "Bedrock" level where most exhibition spaces are.

The entry sequence is a procession that begins with reminiscences by hundreds of people about where they were when they first heard about the attacks—an audiovisual presentation of voices and words projected onto a map of the world. The pathway leads through a series of physical artifacts and digital images that bring people from those distant points of witness ever closer to the center of the site itself, a vast chamber at the Bedrock level called Memorial Hall. From there, they can explore the two Tower Footprints beneath the overhanging volumes formed by the structure of the Memorial voids, enter into the more contained exhibition spaces within the North and South Footprints, or pass westward through the Grotto (now called the Center Passage), which is populated by some of the largest artifacts of the wreckage. Moving on, they enter Foundation Hall, which is dominated by a remnant of the huge slurry wall—the original, containing foundation wall of the World Trade Center that still surrounds the entire site and became a symbol in the aftermath of 9/11 of standing fast in the midst of collapse. There they can see

Figure 16.2 Two Ninety-Foot High "Tridents," Once Part of the Lobby Structure of One of the Towers, Mark the Entrance to the Museum. *Credit*: Tom Hennes.

Figure 16.3 The Introductory Exhibition Is a Soundscape of Remembrances of People First Hearing about the Attacks, with Their Words Projected as a World Map. *Credit*: Tom Hennes.

the Last Column, which became a locus of memory for the recovery workers on the site, and the Signing Steel, which provides people in the museum with a chance to write their thoughts and reflections on a digital screen at the site.

MOURNING AND MEMORIALIZING

During the Conversational Series meetings, we noticed that several of the family members repeatedly professed that they would never stop feeling angry or move on past their grief. After some time, others professed acceptance of their losses and even proudly introduced their new spouses to the group. We were struck by the polarity of some family members' expressed wish to hold on emotionally to the memory of particular lives and the reflective telling of stories that helped other family members let go. Held in relation, we thought, the two contradictory impulses could help mourners establish meaning for lives that ended in deaths both senseless and nearly intolerable (Freud, 1917; Shabad, 2000).

We worked within this paradoxical field of absence and presence in the design of both the vast Memorial Hall and the comparatively intimate memorial exhibition that came to be called *In Memoriam*. Memorial Hall is dominated by an enormous concrete wall that literally divides the living from the dead; it conceals a permanent repository of more than fourteen-thousand unidentified human remains recovered from the site, too burnt to provide the DNA evidence needed to return them to their respective families. This almost unbearable presence of absence—the missing people whose very remains could not be claimed—is counterpoised by a promise, drawn from Virgil's Aeneid: "No day shall erase you from the memory of time." We struggled, along with the museum, for nearly two years to shape this space and create something meaningful within it. As the design team arranged and rearranged artifacts, developed treatments for the wall, and composed the quote, it became apparent to us that the very emptiness of the space and the strength of the promise were in fact the essence of what we had to make. On Thinc's recommendation, the museum commissioned the sculptor Tom Joyce to forge the letters for the quote out of recovered World Trade Center steel that he folded over itself, burnished, and transformed into an enduring commitment to memory. Placed against the emptiness of the concrete wall, we, as designers, felt the strength and beauty of the transformed letters carried sufficient power to contrast with the emptiness of the space that embodied the absence of presence. Yet this was not ultimately to be. Nearly two years after the design had been accepted, some of the family members objected to the use of the quote.[12] Others objected to the rawness of the concrete we felt was so deeply expressive of loss. Still others objected to the very presence of remains in the museum; even though the public would not be able to view the remains, they felt their loved ones were being put on display.

The museum leadership ultimately invited several artists to propose works that would occupy the blank space of the wall. The artist who was chosen, Spencer Finch, developed a work with 2,983 blue-painted squares of paper attached to a metal grid—a variegated expression of attempts to remember the color of the blue sky on the morning of 9/11 that reiterates the number of people who died in the 9/11 attacks and in the Trade Center bombing of 1993. Developed largely in secret, this was ultimately presented to Thinc's design team and to Tom Joyce as a fait accompli, a filling-in of what we interpreted as an absence they felt was too unbearable to allow. Billed as temporary, it crowds the once-prominent Virgil quote, papering over the blankness and filling in the void. The unoccupied, three-dimensional space in this vast hall, between the people there and the promise of Virgil's poetry, is thus collapsed into the two dimensional space of the wall itself, flattened into a predetermined affective mode (remembering the blue sky) rather than expanded into a manifest void in which absence could be actively contemplated and, perhaps, reckoned with.

Figure 16.4 The Quote from Virgil, Created by Sculptor Tom Joyce out of WTC Steel, Surrounded by Spencer Finch's Installation. The Entrance to the Memorial Exhibition, Beneath the Silvery Exterior of the South Memorial Pool, Is at Upper Right. *Credit*: Tom Hennes.

We envisioned the design of *In Memoriam*, the memorial exhibition, on the other hand, as expressing the absence of presence. Responding to families' desire to share a sense of who their loved ones were and how they had lived, it would be populated with recorded personal recollections and photographs—taking on a profoundly human quality. Locating it at the corner of the South Tower volume, we designed it to repeat the square-within-square form of the pool above it in a way that divides it into two zones: the zone of The Many, and the zone of The One. Entered from either of two sides, the periphery of the space, between the outer and inner squares of the exhibition, is lined with portraits of all of the victims (including the three sites of 9/11 and the 1993 World Trade Center bombing), embodying the space of The Many. The display of photographs is an example of a noninscribed or incorporative practice (Connerton, 1989). The serial nature of the formal structure conveys order. Its recapitulation of the many photos of the missing seen in the aftermath of the disaster also transmits a message in the here and now of continuity in time and tradition. This area outside the inner chamber also includes digital tables where selected images may be called up and explored in detail. Conversations among museum users can become part of the rerepresenting and retranscribing process.

Figure 16.5 The Innermost Chamber of the Memorial Exhibition, the "Zone of the One." The Outer Chamber, the "Zone of the Many," Is Visible in the Background.
Credit: Tom Hennes.

The innermost square is a chamber lined with benches surrounding a glass floor through which a jagged remnant of the original "bedrock" concrete slab can be seen. In this literal "Ground Zero," individuals lives are displayed through projected photographs donated by family members and recorded recollections of family and friends. These offer brief impressions of not only individual people—The One—but also the web of relations that constituted their lives. It is a place to bear witness to their intimate lives, as well as their deaths, where the meanings of their lives to those who loved them can echo (Rynearson, 2005). Within this contemplative, quiet sanctuary, the inward-facing seating supports communal witnessing; the softly upholstered and sound-absorbing physical enclosure provides a literal and intersubjectively present containing function intended to provide a safe environment for emotional openness and a lowering of defenses. Tissue boxes, built into the wooden seating, offer implicit permission and support for the feelings of grief that will inevitably arise. In contrast to Memorial Hall, this design was fully accepted by the museum and the families, and has opened exactly as designed. The perhaps yearned-for uncollapse of time, and of the terrible compression of the pile in which so many perished, has in some measure been realized through the creative reanimation of memory (Ornstein, 2010).

THE COMPOSITE

On our first visit to Hanger 17 in 2007, we were taken into an air-conditioned tent to see what was perhaps the most enigmatic of the remains of the towers, several meteor-like boulders of fused concrete, steel, and fragments of furniture, wire, and the mundane materials of office desks. The largest of these was about the size of a Volkswagen, mounted to a concrete base that stabilized it, with tags hung from points along its surface to monitor whether it was truly consolidated and stable or gradually splitting apart. The Composite, as this object came to be known, yielded its nature only on close examination. It was a broken chunk of five floors of one of the towers—it was impossible to say which—that had fused together under the compression of collapse in what was estimated by the forensic analysts to be the more than two-thousand degree heat of the subterranean fires that burned for weeks within the pile, before they had finally consumed everything that could burn. Sitting impossibly atop the Composite were carbonized fragments of paper, one with the word "expenses" clearly legible on it.

From the time the Composite was recovered, it was a subject of contestation. Some relatives felt the museum had an obligation to display what they considered to be an essential embodiment of what happened to their loved ones in the collapse. Others, convinced that the Composite contained human

Figure 16.6 Closeup of the Surface of the Composite. Printed Words, on Scattered Fragments of Carbonized Paper, Are Still Clearly Visible. *Credit*: Tom Hennes.

remains, protested that the museum should in all cases refrain from exhibiting the remains of their sons, daughters, husbands, and wives. Forensic analysis of the object revealed no remains or DNA, and the Office of the Chief Medical Examiner, responsible for all human remains on the site, asserted that the heat that had fused the Composite together, close to a thousand degrees hotter than a crematorium, would have obliterated any remains that might have been there. Disputes erupted, families challenged the report and suspected a cover-up, and the decision about whether or how to include the composite was repeatedly put off.

The museum had originally intended this most collapsed of objects—a literal embodiment of collapse—to be located in Memorial Hall, set in relation to the Virgil quote. This was swiftly abandoned as the design work began and numerous other locations were explored. The Composite was the subject of an entire, raucous session of the Conversation Series that included the results of a second, independent forensic analysis (it also revealed no remains or DNA) and fervent pleas on both sides of the issue. Ultimately, the museum decided to display the object, in a protected and semisecluded space, within the context of the exhibition about the recovery period in which it was discovered. There was no ultimate consensus, but within the space of contestation there was a process by which all views were expressed, heard, and deeply considered. What became a genuinely intersubjective context, in this case, provided sufficient room for negotiation to enable the work to continue without further obstruction.

ENCODING OVERWHELMING AFFECT

In contrast to psychotherapy, which moves patients' attention from the physical realm to a symbolic one, we instead used symbolization theory[13] to craft the kind of physical space a complex museum journey requires. Well-conceived encounters with artifacts and processional movement through represented aspects of the events might help transform people's impressions of 9/11 that were too present into something more distant, like keepsakes or photos. The design itself became progressively more symbolized to scaffold that process, though not in an entirely conscious way. From time to time, members of the design team reacted emotionally to the photos and audio testimony we reviewed for months and sometimes years on end, as part of the development work. Over time, we came to see this as a parallel process to what museum users would encounter on their physical journey. When we found ourselves confronting in the design a disjunction between the story of the actual event and how it was represented—or within the narrative itself, the larger teams' dynamics, or our own internal dynamics—we realized that this gap might signify the presence of absent emotions, perhaps due to dissociation. If, after consideration, that proved to be true, we tried to translate these now conscious emotions back into a more formulated (Stern, D. B., 2013) story in either exhibition structures or in words, with the intent of helping users to "mentalize" (that is, verbally reflect on the states of mind expressed in) frightening images and emotions (Fonagy & Target, 1996).[14] This helped us create coherent stories—within an implicit, overarching narrative that integrated design and storytelling—that visitors could internalize as thinkable thought.

A spectacular example of this occurred one day when we were reviewing designs with Thinc's internal team. I (Tom) found myself uncharacteristically flying into a rage at what I perceived to be the emptiness of the design, telling my team they had simply arranged, not designed the exhibition. I then stormed across the office with a board in my hand and forcibly drove it through a large panel in our model shop to demonstrate what had occurred to me. "That," I said, "is what's missing." In the discussion that followed, aided by Billie's observing and participatory presence, we came to realize that in our efforts to spare museum users any danger of retraumatization—we had literally omitted from the design anything that would signify the violation—and violence—we ourselves felt in that moment. In other words, we found that the exact thing that was absent—a vocabulary for imaginatively encoding the most difficult aspects of the attacks into the design—found expression in my enactment within the team. Within a very short time, we had developed a new design language, based on new forms that conveyed vitality and enlivened what had felt flattened.[15] Elements jutted intrusively into the space. Artifacts were arranged radially—explosively—from the center. Photos of witnesses rose attentively from the floor, signifying heightened arousal. As Billie noted, wherever there is an integrative failure—a gap in the narrative—there is something lurking in that collapsed space, something missing that has to emerge in a more creative and useful form. It was only by standing back from the moment and observing carefully what was and was not happening that we were able to discover the element missing from our work. We encountered this again and again in the course of time.

This reexpansion of the collapsed space of imagination and affect was initially received with enthusiasm by the museum as we brought the design to a nearly complete stage. Our intention was to return to this first section of the exhibition, which focused on 9/11 itself, after other sections about precursor events, the plot, and the recovery, were completed. We planned to further incorporate whatever insights would inevitably occur over the coming months of design. Nine months later, however, the director of the museum stunned us by announcing that she was bringing in another designer to complete a layer of interpretive design on top of the conceptual base we had completed. Her feeling, she explained, was that the design did not adequately express the story she was currently telling about the exhibition in her presentations to constituents.

This startling rupture had repeated aftershocks. I (Tom) withdrew Thinc from the project. After an extended appeal to return, I agreed on the condition that I be able to review the design work that was to come. Soon thereafter, I walked out again, this time on the basis of what I perceived to be broken agreements. After securing an agreement to enter into a process of mediation, I agreed to bring Thinc back to complete the 80 percent of the project that remained within our scope. When I reviewed the first iteration of the new design for the Historical Exhibition, I was again surprised. It had become congested, both through a denser arrangement of artifacts and through the introduction of many new exhibit walls intended to prevent "giving away the story." In contrast to the plan we had developed, which maintained sightlines throughout the experience specifically to enable people to orient themselves and to anticipate[16] what was around the next corner, this design, as it was ultimately built, crowds the space and in many ways recapitulates the confusion and claustrophobia of the pile on Ground Zero itself. Rather than encode emotional affect in a structured design language, it re-creates it through theatricality and immersive sound and light. Only time, experience, and careful research will reveal whether it is as effective as the museum believes it will be, or as overstimulating and potentially retraumatizing as we believe it is likely to be. By recollapsing the event in this literal way, and by collapsing a diverse narrative into a more structured, definitive history, this more immersive version of the exhibition—still bearing numerous aspects and the primary organization of the original—seems a manifestation of a repetition compulsion to re-create and master the original collapse. We believe it is likely to have the contrary effect of reiterating the traumatic impact and compelling a significant number of users to retreat into a more collapsed emotional space due to a feeling of overwhelming affect.

A NARRATIVE ARC

By the time we neared the end of the design phase, we had become more aware of how to utilize "vitality forms" as design elements.[17] This caused us to revisit an earlier formulation of the narrative arc of the user's journey through the museum. The introductory exhibition at the entry ramp utilizes spoken testimonies recorded by hundreds of individuals to create a narrative environment with which people in the museum can intersubjectively engage. It visualizes these narratives by projecting the spoken words as text onto a series of panels that form them into a map of the world that people literally traverse as they enter into the exhibition. This acknowledges that a large portion of those coming to the museum in its early years will have experienced 9/11 in this way. For those who know of it only through their parents' or other adults' descriptions, it links the museum to what they have likely heard. Seeing and hearing these stories that are simultaneously diverse in their origin yet recognizably stereotypic in their patterns of disbelief and dawning awareness could validate an individual's entrance narrative by proclaiming, in essence, that we are all, in some way, witnesses to 9/11, wherever we were then. For the ending, working with the museum team, we had developed a commemorative activity focused on a huge, folded-over piece of bent World Trade Center steel, around which individuals could write their thoughts onto touchscreens in view of the Last Column, the structural column from the South Tower, marked with insignia and messages from recovery workers, that had become a locus of commemoration among those who were clearing Ground Zero.

While this activity was still in development, it gained added resonance for both of us during sessions in which we were first writing about the museum in the summer of 2011. We realized that our feelings of having been either too present or not-present-enough in the events of that day had a tremendous bearing on our own sense of self thereafter and on the work we had been doing together. In New York, I (Billie) had been separated from my young children in Brooklyn and had to cross over the Manhattan Bridge on foot with thousands of others on the afternoon of 9/11 in order to reunite with them. I (Tom) was stranded in San Francisco, working on a museum project. Because of our different experiences, we ourselves were embodying this emotional polarity in opposition—one having felt a need to come close to Ground Zero, the other needing distance. Through our growing understanding of the paradoxical needs each of us felt to maintain a safe distance while simultaneously approaching the heart of the event, we came to a different formulation of what that final act might mean to the Museum's narrative arc, and a reshaping of this final gesture. We recommended a change in the activity from a communal gathering to a leaving behind of a mark on the site itself. By reorienting the activity on one side of the beam, facing the Slurry Wall rather than each other, we were able to incorporate a visible display of what had been written. This projected display reiterates the map of the world in text from the Introductory Exhibition, now incorporating messages written at the end of many

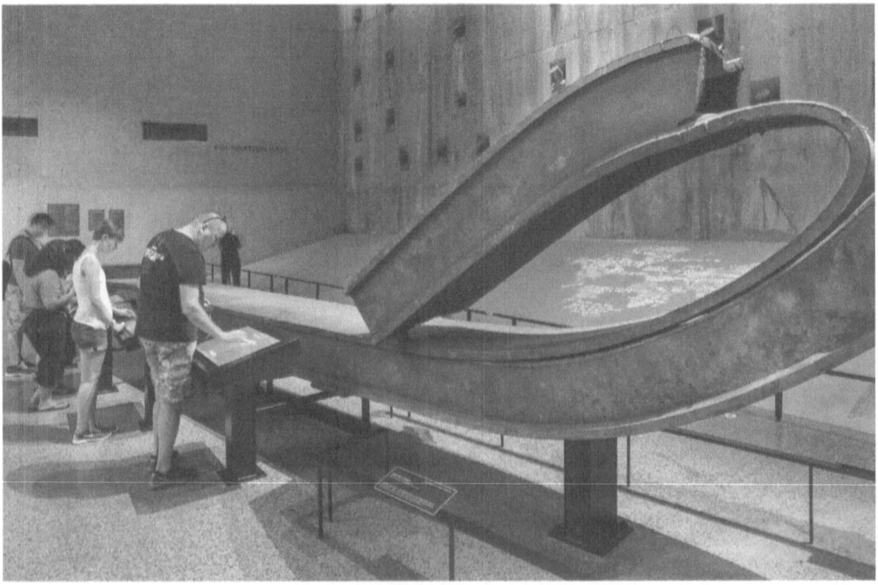

Figure 16.7 As People Write on Touchscreens at the "Signing Steel" in Foundation Hall, Their Words Are Projected onto a World Map Directly onto the Base of the Slurry Wall, at the Location They Give as Their Home. This Mirrors the Projected Words of the Introductory Exhibition. *Credit*: Tom Hennes.

users' visits. It also created an opportunity to "turn passive into active," a mechanism for reversing the helplessness inherent in overwhelming experience. To summarize the new narrative arc: Each person then would have had the experience of entering the museum with the narrative of where we were when it happened—"I was there then." Having carried feelings of having been too absent or too present onto the site, this final gesture could become an important opportunity to assert "I am here now"—in a witnessed, leaving-behind of something of herself and her experience of 9/11 and the museum. By giving time a spatial representation through a physical narrative sequence, with beginning, middle, and end, this arc aims to assist users in maintaining a sense of time undistorted by post-traumatic collapse.

THE ENVISIONED AND THE REAL

Just as there are many and varied 9/11 narratives, so, too, there are many and varied museums within this single museum. They represent many different aspects simultaneously and paradoxically, in essentially the same space. These include idealized aspirations of healing and knowing one's experience more fully, split-off aspects of trauma, anger, revenge, and identification with the aggressor, and the result of pragmatic negotiations among multiple groups with a common interest in its success but often with competing needs and visions for what that means. The museum also contains the expressions of competing visions for what such a museum should be: either a means to set the record in place for this and the next generation or a relatively safe and common ground for the negotiation of meaning as society emerges from the most immediate phase of the event. Finally, it is a multifaceted aesthetic expression, by many artists in a few styles, of what a public exhibition and gathering place should look and feel like.

When we began our work, we believed it possible to bring all these competing needs into a single vision and aesthetic, but, in retrospect, it is hard to assert that this aspiration could have been possible given the raw contestation that still, at the time of the museum's opening, swirls around 9/11 and often erupts into one or another enactment. The truly intersubjective museum we had envisioned became a source of contestation—which itself can be seen in retrospect as the active ground of negotiation which recapitulated the collapse and uncollapse of 9/11 in repeating, discontinuous, and nonlinear ways. In the making of the museum, decisions often reflected unstable binary thinking that quickly oscillated. This repetitive destabilization of seemingly decided points of view played out within the team, within the community, and in public arenas and the press. As we noted above, these switches sometimes occurred without warning and sometimes as much as several years after issues had seemingly been settled. Painful as it often was, we have come to understand this contestation as an essential part of the making of this museum, standing in no real way apart from the larger contestation of meaning of the event evidenced in our global society.

We were, in fact, able to realize a museum that admits mixed feelings while incorporating many of the features of 9/11 that emerged in the process of making it. These include presence and absence; physical and symbolic loss; the collapse of time; the multiplicity of perspectives on the events; the potential of overwhelming affect and narrative incoherence arising from split off aspects of experience; and a history that is indeterminate, evolving, and contested. We arrived at many design solutions through intuitions that had grown out of our respective experiences, application of clinical praxis, and seemingly spontaneous inspiration but came to gauge their appropriateness and usefulness through an increasingly formulated theoretical framework. Our guiding principles have the primary objective of supporting a wide-ranging relational field in which all of the participants—those who contribute objects and narrative, those who organize the experience, and those who participate in the course of a visit—attain the means to come to know their own experience more fully and to more confidently locate themselves within the larger field of collective experience.

This complex and contested memorial museum is specific to a particular event and a particular time. Yet its implications reach well beyond 9/11 and the way it has shaped our world. Traumatic disorientation means that history is relocated through trauma from a linear concept to one consistent with a nonlinear accumulation of the multiple perspectives contained in collective memory that can be held by a museum and witnessed there. Leveraging as it does a psychoanalytic perspective that is freed from the consulting room, this conception of a museum seeks to assist society in reconstituting the dialogue that is at the heart of a functioning democracy. It uses design to bring polarizing narratives and emotions into paradoxical juxtaposition, so they can be creatively explored within the relative safety of a containing, relational frame. This model of design builds equally upon a body of progressive museum theory (cf. Hein, 1998, 2012; Falk & Dierking, 2000; Hennes, 2010; Rounds, 2012) and intersubjective psychoanalysis.

As a prototype for a more genuinely intersubjective museum, it is a step toward an emergent form. Conceived through the principles of democracy and psychology outlined in this chapter, and developed through relational design, such a form has the potential to transcend the classical and constructivist ideals that dominate the museum field and redefine museums of history as ethically informed places in which society may safely work through areas of contestation, reanimate discourse, and operate more fully within a field of knowing.

NOTES

1. The authors wish to thank Dr. Zahava Doering, who read early drafts of this chapter and provided invaluable feedback. It should also be noted that no museum—especially this one—is created by a design team in isolation. The National September 11 Memorial Museum has a dedicated curatorial, exhibition development, and education staff that were deeply involved and inspirational throughout the building of the museum, along with the creative director, Michael Shulan, the museum director, Alice Greenwald, a very active board of trustees and advisory council, as well as leadership from the City of New York. Creating this project was thus the work of many, with whom we are grateful to have been able to participate in this project.

2. Strangeness as a state has a long history in psychoanalysis, beginning with Freud's writing on "the uncanny" in a (1919) paper of that name. Translated from the German, *unheimlich,* with linguistic roots in both "home" and "secret," it literally conveys a secret *wish to find the familiar in the unknown*, and so is used here in a nonironic way. Freedman (1985) asserts that the creation of a symbol, or a name, resolves the spookiness and contextualizes antagonistic perceptions and attitudes, thus permitting a new shared reality to take shape. In relational psychoanalysis, when the polarities can't be contained as mixed feeling states within an individual, they instead are experienced as being enacted by therapist and patient in a power struggle. In a psychoanalytic treatment, these repeated dialectic conflicts in a patient's thinking continually evolve through a process of thesis, antithesis, synthesis, much as Ricoeur (1970) described, but crucially involving the therapist in an intersubjective interaction. In Freedman's view, transformation is achieved through many such transitions that lead to reorganization of the structure of thought at a more symbolized level, thus building psychic structure. Sigmund Freud's grandson, described in his paper, "Beyond the Pleasure Principle," helped us see the manifestations of increasingly symbolized meanings less abstractly. His charming "fort-da" play in his mother's brief absence illustrates a number of levels of symbolization simultaneously. Like smoke coming out of a chimney, his play alerts us to the presence of absence. It is thus indexical, signaling his distress through its repetitiveness and the emotion evoked in a viewer. At the same time, it bears an iconic relation to the event in its resemblance to the mother's to and fro movement. It is symbolic in that it joins opposites, there and here. It is intersubjective in that his playing was in the presence of Freud himself, who mentalized the sounds "oo" and "ah" as "fort and da," making it memorable even a century later. Attachment researchers used "strangeness" as an experimental condition in which a mother's and infant's attachment systems can be most activated for study. So strangeness can also be thought to challenge people to *find the familial in the unknown,* too, in a rather literal way.

3. We identified five forms of collapse that had to be managed: physical, symbolic/cultural, narrative, temporal, and intersubjective.

4. In psychoanalysis, the term "relational field" is a metaphor for a system of relationships that are jointly constructed through the interpenetration of the patient's and the analyst's individual subjectivities at an unconscious level. A coconstructed field is seen

as a container that also interacts dialectically with other containers; it has a dynamic quality in that each person is affected by their changing context and the context in turn shapes each person. Its function is to transform sensory and emotional experiences into thought and meanings. It is a means of communication that aims to find a balance between immersion and interactivity. Therapeutic progress is the outgrowth of both the analyst and the patient utilizing this joint unconscious to learn with each other about their intersubjective reality in ways that repair gaps in the patient's self. The analyst's attunement to subtle shifts in the field—often experienced as feelings that arise in her own emotional state—enables her and eventually the patient as well to gain awareness of the patient's dissociated emotions and sensations (Civitarese & Ferro, 2013).

5. Entrance narrative is a term used within the museum community. It denotes the individual experience that each museum user brings to the present experience of the museum, shaping as powerfully as any other single factor how that person will use and understand the material of the exhibition.

6. Psychoanalyst D. W. Winnicott (1953, 1971) described the safe containment provided by the analyst as a holding environment. In that safety, the analyst and patient create a "transitional space," full of the potential for sharing meanings. We similarly aimed to create a space in which diverse users could feel safe to explore unexpected and potentially threatening new realizations (Bromberg, 2011).

7. Early on, the design team led a workshop with the entire museum team and staff to chart a wide range of potential museum users and to understand the ways they might use the museum and the kinds of effects the museum might have on them, both during an initial visit and through the more sustained contact of repeated visitation and use. From this initial exercise, which was intended to open each member of the team to a range of perspectives beyond his or her own, as much as it was to actually document specific uses, we developed a strategic framework that encompassed both the goals of the museum and the means by which it would accomplish them. The primary purpose was to "enable people to better comprehend a complex world, realize themselves within it and value their own contributions to it."

8. It has also been termed the "*après coup*" by Lacan (Laplanche & Pontalis, 2012).

9. In grief complicated by trauma, people don't remember or even enact so much as disconnect from or disavow, feelings and memories. This can lead to a collapse in the capacity to mentalize, or reflect on one's own and others' intentions and emotional states (Fonagy & Target, 1996). It is reflected at its extremes either in overly imaginative or abstract thinking, or in the overly literal perception of reality called concrete thinking (Pivnick, 2010, 2013b).

10. This was an idea advanced in the nineteenth century by art historians and reaffirmed in the twenty-first century by neuroscientific research (Kandel, 2012; Pivnick, 2013a).

11. A representation is like a schema, but it is about "doing" or "being." It is a procedural process for reexperiencing, not, as was previously believed, a mental structure or habit. Representations of experiences of participating include many elements—sensations, perceptions, affects, actions, thoughts, motivations, contextual elements—all capable of being held in isolation or integrated. When integrated they form a schema of "being with another" because they always involve two or more people (Stern, D. N., 1995; Lyons-Ruth, 1999).

12. Some scholars and editorial writers also criticized the quote beginning in 2011, then again in 2012 and 2013 (cf. Allen, 2012; Alexander, 2011; Dunlap, 2014). Other classical scholars came to the quote's defense. In the end, the quote remained in place.

13. See note 1.

14. "Mentalization" is a form of thinking that functions to predict and make sense of other people's actions by inferring and attributing to them causal intentional mind states (such as beliefs, intentions, and desires). Because the beliefs are not in themselves visible, inference and monitoring and testing one's hypotheses is necessary. This ability to test social reality is disrupted by trauma. As a result, the ability to (abstractly) imagine and the ability to (concretely) maintain continuity with the past fail to function in tandem, leading to distorted thinking and remembering.

15. Arousal creates the force, timing, shape, and directional intent of movement. Together, these emergent properties enhance perceptual experience and stimulate spontaneous interaction. Beginning in mother-infant interactions, particular states of affective mutuality also constitute developing aesthetic forms called "forms of vitality" (Stern, D. N., 2010). These vitality forms include dynamic features of experience such as intensity, contour, rhythm, and duration, as well as how people use kinesic qualities (e.g., strong vs. light, direct vs. indirect, quick vs. sustained), and auditory and visual modalities. The same mechanisms that shape our experience of arousal in infancy underpin what moves us to respond to the temporal arts of music, dance, cinema, and theater (Dissanayake, 2000)—and for museum design purposes, procession, encounter, display, and containment.

16. Anticipatory structures are the focus of relational trauma treatment (Bromberg, 2011).

17. See note 15.

REFERENCES

Al Ramiah, A., & Hewstone, M. (2013). Intergroup contact as a tool for reducing, resolving, and preventing intergroup conflict: Evidence, limitations, and potential. *American Psychologist, 68*(7), 527–42.

Alexander, C. (2011). Out of context. *New York Times*. Retrieved April 6, 2011, from http://www.nytimes.com/2011/04/07/opinion/07alexander.html.

Allen, J. (2012). Plan for 9/11 remains disturbs relatives of the dead. *Reuters*. Retrieved 03.09.2012, from http://www.reuters.com/article/2012/03/09/us-sept11-memorial-idUSBRE82813G20120309.

Beebe, B., McCrorie, E., & Pivnick, B. (December 2013). Poetry of 9/11: Trauma, grief, and imagination. *Clio's Psyche: Understanding the "Why" of Culture, Current Events, History, and Society. (Special Issue on Poetry and Psychohistory), 20*(3), 314–23.

Bernstein, J. W. (2000). Making a memorial place: The photography of Shimon Attie. *Psychoanalytic Dialogues, 10*, 347–70.

Blanchot, M. (1980/1995). *The writing of the disaster.* Paris: Edouard Guillarme.

Bollas, C. (1989). *The shadow of the object: psychoanalysis of the unthought known.* New York: Columbia University Press.

Boulanger, G. (2007). *Wounded by reality: Understanding and treating adult onset trauma*. New York: Routledge.
Bromberg, P. (1998). *Standing in the spaces: Essays on clinical process, trauma, and dissociation.* New York: Analytic Press.
Bromberg, P. (2011). *The shadow of the tsunami: And the growth of the relational mind.* New York: Analytic Press.
Caruth, C. (1996). *Unclaimed experience: Trauma, narrative, and history.* Baltimore: Johns Hopkins University Press.
Civitarese, G., & Ferro, A. (2013). The meaning and use of metaphor in analytic field theory. *Psychoanalytic Inquiry*, *33*(3), 190–209.
Connerton, P. (1989). *How societies remember.* Cambridge, UK: Cambridge University Press.
Damasio, A. (2012). *Self comes to mind: Constructing the conscious brain.* New York: Random House LLC.
Davoine, F., & Gaudillière, J. M. (2004). *History beyond trauma*. Other Press, LLC.
Dissanayake, E. (2000). Antecedents of the temporal arts. In N. L. Wallin, B. Merker & S. Brown, (Eds.), *The origins of music* (pp. 389–410). Cambridge, MA: MIT Press.
Dunlap, D. (2014). A memorial inscription's grim origins. *New York Times.* Retrieved April 2, 2014, from http://www.nytimes.com/2014/04/03/nyregion/an-inscription-taken-out-of-poetic-context-and-placed-on-a-9-11-memorial.html?_r=0.
Falk, J., & Dierking, L. (2000). *Learning from museums: Visitor experience and the making of meaning.* Berkeley, CA: Alta Mira Press.
Felman, S., & Laub, D. (1991). *Testimony: Crises of witnessing in literature, psychoanalysis and history*. New York: Routledge.
Ferrell, D. (1995). The unmourned wound: Reflections on the psychology of Adolf Hitler. *Journal of Religion and Health*, *34*(3), 175–95.
Fonagy, P., & Target, M. (1996). Playing with reality: I. Theory of mind and the normal development of psychic reality. *International Journal of Psycho-Analysis*, *77*, 217–33.
Freedman, N. (1985). The concept of transformation in psychoanalysis. *Psychoanalytic Psychology,* *2*(4), 317–39.
Freud, S. (1914). Remembering, repeating and working-through (Further recommendations on the technique of psycho-analysis II). *Standard edition of the complete psychological works of Sigmund Freud, Volume XII (1911–1913)*: *The case of Schreber, papers on technique and other works*, 145–56.
Freud, S. (1917). Mourning and melancholia. *Standard edition of the complete psychological works of Sigmund Freud, Volume XIV (1914–1916): On the history of the psycho-analytic movement, papers on metapsychology and other works*, 237–58, 1961.
Freud, S. (1919). The uncanny (J. Strachey, Trans.). In *Standard edition of the complete psychological works of Sigmund Freud, Volume XVII*, 218–52.
Freud, S. (1920). Beyond the Pleasure Principle. *Standard edition of the complete psychological works of Sigmund Freud, Volume XVIII (1920–1922),* 7–64. London: Hogarth, 1955.

Freud, S., & Breuer, J. (1895). Studies on hysteria. *Standard edition of the complete psychological works of Sigmund Freud, Volume II (1893–1895),* 3–305, 1955.

Gerson, S. (2009). When the third is dead: Memory, mourning, and witnessing in the aftermath of the Holocaust. *International Journal of Psychoanalysis, 90,* 1341–57.

Greenwald, A. M. (2010). "Passion on all sides": Lessons for planning the National September 11 Memorial Museum. *Curator: The Museum Journal, 53*(1), 117–25.

Halbwachs, M. (1941/1992). *On collective memory.* Chicago, IL: University of Chicago Press.

Heidegger, M. (1927/2008). *Being and time.* New York: Harper Perennial Modern Thought

Hein, G. (1998). *Learning in the museum.* New York: Routledge.

Hein, G. (2012). *Progressive museum practice: John Dewey and democracy.* Walnut Creek, CA: Left Coast Press.

Hennes, T. (2010). Exhibitions: From a perspective of encounter. *Curator: The Museum Journal, 53*(1), 21–33.

Huyssens, A. (2003). *Urban palimpsests and the politics of memory.* Stanford, CA: Stanford University Press.

Kafka, J. S. (2008). Psychoanalysis and democracy. *American Imago, 65*(4), 547–65.

Kandel, E. (2012). *The age of insight: The quest to understand the unconscious in art, mind, and brain.* New York: Random House.

Krupp, G. R. (1965). Identification as a defense against anxiety in coping with loss. *International Journal of Psychoanalysis, 46*, 303–14.

LaMothe, R. (1999). The absence of cure: The core of malignant trauma and symbolization. *Journal of Interpersonal Violence, 14*(11), 1193–210.

Laplanche, J., & Pontalis, J. B. (2012). *The language of psychoanalysis.* London: Karnac Books.

Langan, R. (2000). Someplace in mind. *International Forum of Psychoanalysis, 9,* 69–75.

Lear, J. (2007). Working through the end of civilization. *International Journal of Psycho-Analysis, 88*(2), 291–308.

Lichtenstein, D. (2014). An other ethic. *Division/Review, 9,* 1–2.

Lyons-Ruth, K. (1999). The two-person unconscious: Intersubjective dialogue, enactive relational representation, and the emergence of new forms of relational organization. *Psychoanalytic Inquiry, 19*(4), 576–617.

Margalit, A. (2002). *The ethics of memory.* Cambridge, MA: Harvard University Press.

Ochs, E., & Capps, L. (2001). *Living narrative: Creating lives in everyday storytelling.* Cambridge, MA: Harvard University Press.

Olin, M. (2003). The winter garden and virtual heaven. In R. Nelson & M. Olin. (Eds.), *Monuments and memory, made and unmade* (pp. 133–53). Chicago: University of Chicago Press.

Ornstein, A. (2010). The missing tombstone: Reflections on mourning and creativity. *Journal of the American Psychoanalytic Association, 58,* 631–48.

Pivnick, B. (March, 2010). *Trauma in translation: The effect of threatened object loss on discourse, reflective functioning, and symptomatic behavior during psychotherapy in literature and clinical practice*. Trauma: Intersections among Narrative, Neuroscience, and Psychoanalysis. Conference presented at George Washington University, Washington, DC.

Pivnick, B. (2011). Enacting remembrance: Turning to memorializing September 11th. *Journal of Religion and Health, 50*(3), 499–515.

Pivnick, B. A. (2013a). The beholder's share: An intersubjective review of Bromberg's Shadow of the Tsunami. *Psychoanalytic Quarterly, 82*(1), 179–92.

Pivnick, B. A. (2013b): What the living did: September 11th and its aftermath. In A. Adelman, & K. Malawista, (Eds.), *The therapist in mourning: From the faraway nearby*. New York: Columbia University Press.

Ravven, H. (2013). *The self beyond itself: An alternative history of ethics, the new brain sciences, and the myth of free will*. New York: New Press.

Ricoeur, P. (1970). *Freud and philosophy: An essay on interpretation* (D. Savage, Trans.). New Haven, CT: Yale University Press.

Ricoeur, P. (1984). *Time and narrative* (K. McLaughlin & D. Pellauer, Trans.). Chicago: University of Chicago Press. (Original work published 1988).

Rounds, J. (2012). The museum and its relationships as a loosely coupled system. *Curator: The Museum Journal, 55*(4), 413–34.

Rynearson, E. K. (2005). The narrative labyrinth of violent dying. *Death Studies, 29*, 351–60.

Sen, A. (2006). *Identity and violence: The illusion of destiny*. New York: W.W. Norton.

Shabad, P. (2000). The most intimate of creations: Symptoms as memorials to one's lonely suffering. In P. Homans (Ed.), *Symbolic loss: The ambiguity of mourning and memory at century's end*. Charlottesville, VA: University Press of Virginia.

Spitz, E. H. (2005). Loss as vanished form: On the anti-memorial sculptures of Horst Hoheisel. *American Imago, 62*(4), 419–433.

Stern, D. B. (2013). *Unformulated experience: From dissociation to imagination in psychoanalysis*. UK: Routledge.

Stern, D. N. (1995). *The motherhood constellation: A unified view of parent-infant psychotherapy*. Karnac Books.

Stern, D. N. (2010). *Forms of vitality: Exploring dynamic experience in psychology, the arts, psychotherapy, and development*. Oxford, UK: Oxford University Press.

Ulanov, A. B. (2010, August). The one in the many and the many in the one. In *Facing multiplicity—Psyche, nature, culture: 18th Congress of the International Association for Analytical Psychology*. Montreal, Canada.

Winnicott, D. W. (1953). Transitional objects and transitional phenomena—A study of the first not-me possession. *International Journal of Psycho-Analysis, 34*, 89–97.

Winnicott, D. W. (1971). *Playing and reality*. New York: Basic Books.

Afterword

Marilyn Charles

In his *Four Quartets*, Poet T. S. Eliot reminds us of the inexorability, the undeniability of history. History imprints itself upon us. We can consciously or even unconsciously attempt to avoid it but we cannot escape it. Psychoanalysis has shown us that evasion can diminish the quality of life, cripple us, and make it more difficult to confront life's challenges as they come. Psychoanalysis has also shown the futility of such efforts, as attempts to escape the lessons of history make us more vulnerable to enactments through which those unrecognized lessons make themselves manifest once again. Unresolved, the tragedies of life haunt us, like hounds at our heels, impeding our ability to engage fully and deeply in our experience.

Trauma involves a cut, a disjunctive moment when life, as it has been, is forever changed. Whereas working through the trauma can enhance the quality of life, evasion diminishes it. That failure to mourn is compounded when we become parents. The attachment literature shows that the preoccupation and dissociation linked to unresolved mourning impedes the parent's ability to attend to the child's needs, thereby taking a terrible toll on successive generations. In this way, the pattern is doomed to repeat itself until the ghosts from the past are faced, recognized, and worked through. The current volume can be seen as a consideration of the subject of traumatic memory and also as an exposition of the dilemma, as the authors struggle to both theorize the dilemmas at stake regarding remembering and forgetting, and also to personalize the dilemma such that the reader can find him or herself implicated in the weight and complexity of these matters.

Trauma is both elusive and compelling, in that by definition it eludes encoding into verbal memory. What cannot be digested and incorporated into narrative memory not only remains inchoate but tends to persist in both intensity and affective tone, thereby insisting on recognition. History haunts us to the extent that we have forgotten to remember. Ironically, it may be that only that which can be remembered can be forgotten, so that we may only be truly able to forget that which has been remembered sufficiently to have been worked through and integrated. Otherwise, the forgetting tends to be a dissociative exclusion of memory rather than a true forgetting that presumes the freedom to move beyond where we have been caught. Highly charged affective experience that cannot be explicitly remembered, in contrast, lingers, haunting us by its ineffable presence. The price of remembering and of forgetting, not only for the individual but also for the social groups in which they reside, are vividly illuminated by the contributions contained in this volume.

One theme that comes up repeatedly in the current volume is the issue of individual versus collective trauma. As Stipsits notes, collective history is embedded in individual history, and yet, as Truscott's account suggests, we may lose something through our empathy with the individual that might also be important to take into account. Demonizing one person or group fails to take seriously the potential for evil that resides within us all, making it more likely for those aggressive and regressive urges to emerge unrestrained. Ultimately, suggests Ainslie, collective trauma makes a unique demand for memorialization, perhaps in part because of the dehumanization that must, somehow, be repaired or at least marked as wrong and also so that the collective trauma does not become an excuse for invoking trauma in others.

Collective trauma is particularly difficult to work through. Although trauma can pull people together, sustained trauma over time tends to disrupt the transmission of the narratives that might engender pride in one's ethnic identity, and also disrupts the cultural legacies that facilitated mourning in previous generations. Shame is often the result, an affect that is so virulently inhibiting that it makes it difficult to sustain the type of curiosity necessary for new learning, experiences of mastery, and the development of healthy social relationships. Shame invites a sense of internal badness and a tendency to project that badness onto others, thereby perpetuating the type of *othering* that insists on keeping the badness at bay. We can see this thread in many of the chapters in this volume, in which the disruptions have been complicated by projection, denial, and silence, impeding recognition of precisely that which needs to be confronted and worked through.

Because of the difficulties entailed in painful remembering, we need ways of offering tribute to collective experiences that have been shrouded in painful silence, so that we can recognize meanings that have been reduced to the level of symptom. Derrida (1995), after Lacan (2004), writes of symptoms in terms of an archive that becomes a living museum of meanings that are difficult to take in and therefore must be marked so that they can be encountered and reencountered. This volume may be seen as such an archive, in which the authors mark memories that otherwise might reside only in unmarked graves, specters of a past that haunts us to the extent that we are unwilling to recall it. These memories mark for us uneasy passages in our individual and collective histories, places where we might stumble over the gaps unless we can catch ourselves sufficiently to heed the lessons held in these reminiscences, to recognize that we are inevitably implicated in the possibility of suffering.

Increasingly, in this global age, we can recognize ways in which we are each marked by the traumatic experiences depicted in the media, to which we too easily become complicit bystanders, and also ways in which we are haunted by trauma encountered by our ancestors over the generations. Whether our forebearers have been relegated by history to the side of "victim" or "persecutor," hero or villain, we are each implicated in what it means to be human—the capacity for good, for evil, and for causing and feeling suffering. The ghosts of those who have suffered silently echo along the generations, and it is left to the living to hear their cries and to take a stand that recognizes that we are all more human than otherwise and that, at some level, another's suffering decreases the quality of life for us all.

How do we locate ourselves and our common humanity in this globally interconnected world in which we each are increasingly implicated in one another's trauma? I can well recall the moment in a public shower when, ruminating on vicarious memories of the Holocaust, it suddenly occurred to me that if I had been living in Nazi Germany at that time, I might not have been a Jew but rather might well have been a German. Where, then, might I have located myself? Would I have been able to take a stand for what I thought was right against that type of tyranny? Even if I could have put my own life in danger, what if I had children? Would my fear for their well-being have silenced me? Would I even have been able to ask myself these questions or might I have blindly followed the current zeitgeist? Am I doing that now, in relation to whatever I am blind to in my own culture? These questions are not so easy to answer. We hope to be able to be true to our sense of right and wrong, to be able to live with integrity, but we cannot be certain of how we will fare if tested, or precisely what tests might take us beyond our capacity for endurance. As noted, these questions become further complicated by what becomes invisible within the cultural contexts in which we reside, what cannot be seen because we have become blind to it.

For example, I recall reading Lalita Tademy's (2001) fictionalized account of her research into her maternal ancestry, having left a job in a Fortune 500 company to discover what she could about her roots in slavery in the American South. I imagine that in part it was the strength of her writing but also the fact that my daughter was pregnant with a child who would be biracial that made this story so compelling to me. *Cane River* pulled me beyond the familiar story into a chilling encounter with what it might have been like for me to have no control over such essentials as keeping my family together or even whether I could raise my own children. As compelling for me as my encounter with *Sophie's Choice,* I transcended space and time and felt myself intolerably in shoes that seemed beyond human endurance to bear.

At a certain point in the novel, I could recognize the relentless surge toward whiteness that had been invisible to me because it seemed, somehow, "right." That comfort was suddenly broken into when one of the biracial young men, having been rejected and wounded by his white father, took a stand in the opposite direction and married a woman who epitomized, not the white aesthetic and social values that had been adopted within his own family but rather a dark beauty that stood in stark contrast to the promotion of white values that had been hidden insidiously in the text. In the disorientation that accompanied that shift, I could see myself ensconced in white presumptions of beauty and value in ways that have lingered, as I recognize the layers of prejudice and denial built into the fabric of American culture in which I am inextricably implicated.

For as long as I can remember, I have felt a kinship with African Americans because of a shared sense of what it means to be rejected, persecuted, and demonized historically, my own history having been haunted by unaspirated memories from ghosts whose voices were silenced during the Holocaust. My resonance, however, was not reciprocated. I found myself isolated and alienated by my white exterior that obscured from the external view the internal haunting from ancestors who had been hunted down and annihilated. That disjunction makes me especially grateful to my son-in-law, who seems to accept the whole of me, particularly the heart that reaches out to him and his children.

I find myself with a heightened awareness of color and how it is read in the United States, aware of both the beauty of the variousness of skin tone and features we find here, but also the ugly prejudice that festers and manifests at times. Riding in the car the other day, I was playing *I* Spy with my grandson to pass the time. "I see something brown," he said. I failed to guess correctly what was on his mind. "Daddy's skin," he said, delighted to have foiled me. "What color is your skin," I asked. He thought a minute. "Light caramel," he replied. "And your Mom's skin?" I asked. "light caramel," he said definitively. Apparently, we were all light caramel, aside from his father. I wonder how his views will change over time, to what extent we can be cappuccino together in a world in which subtle gradations tend to disappear into stark and inaccurate dichotomized categories. Caught by my love for these children who are both me and not-me, I now feel implicated in race in ways that are much more entangled than before. Our children and grandchildren's pain is personal, deeply personal, in many ways hitting harder than our own. I would imagine that the most difficult part of Sophie's choice was not making it but having to live with it. And yet, that is the challenge with which we are faced, to *learn to live with it,* whatever *it* is.

Thinking about these issues, I recall the fallout that occurred in the wake of my initial attempt to publish an article considering Don DeLillo's *Falling Man* as a traumatic narrative. Reviewers reacted strongly and negatively to my willingness to view the terrorist in the novel as caught up in his own traumatic history, one going so far as to call me "un-American." This type of willingness to "other" those with different values and experiences seems to be the dangerous ground from which wars are built. Failing to recognize ways in which hatred, fear, and distrust feed one another keeps us all unsafe, making it essential to recover the essential ties that bind us to one another. I trust that readers will have discovered further threads of their own humanity in this current volume, while also being offered conceptual frameworks to better understand the importance of carrying our histories mindfully forward, lest we continue to be haunted by echoes of the past not yet reclaimed.

The archive, as a representation of the repository of human experience, can also be seen as a labyrinth, one of the oldest and most mysterious representations of life, death, and the human spirit. Traditionally, the labyrinth has referred to the place in which the darker side of man's nature might be held and captured, but also to a path to divine wisdom. The labyrinth may be seen as another manifestation of the apple eaten from the tree, the dangerous wisdom that might hold the key to salvation or the seeds of destruction. As such, the labyrinth marks the oedipal challenge as described by Bion (1977) in terms of the tendency to turn a blind eye or even the perceived admonition to do so, to remain a child deferring to an external authority rather than facing that challenge and standing on our own internal sense of right and wrong.

The labyrinth is a profound metaphor for the inherent dialectic between order and confusion that is a function of being human (Charles, forthcoming). Like the archive that compiles the data of human experience, the labyrinth holds an overall pattern that is not visible from within. From that perspective, the archive as labyrinth becomes the place where what is hidden is kept, the place where we might become lost and found or, perhaps more fundamentally, revealed in our essential lostness. Perhaps that is the site of both our particularity and our collectivity—the place where we can join together at a site of recognition of the vulnerability that lies at the core of humanity, that very vulnerability and utter transience that makes life both fleeting and precious.

In classical Greek mythology, the labyrinth stood at the threshold of the underworld, at the edge of potential transformation or annihilation. Although there is the hope of safe passage, there is no solution to the maze. The yearning for ultimate transformation seeks something that cannot be attained in life. In spite of whatever transformations we might be able to attain, we are still human and therefore subject to the perils, paradoxes, and difficulties of daily existence, including the inevitability of that final transformation into death. Lacan (1977) has noted ways in which we avoid the confrontation with lack, with limit, and yet, we each stand in our own place, a place that can be indexed in relation to space, time, culture, and heritage. It may be in our willingness to stand in our own place and yet move beyond our own particularity, to try to imagine that of another, that we may hold the hope of the planet.

REFERENCES

Bion, W. R. (1977). *Seven Servants.* New York: Jason Aronson.

Charles, M. (forthcoming). *The stories we live: Psychoanalysis, literature, and life.* New York: Rowman & Littlefield.

Derrida, J. (1995). *Archive fever: A freudian impression.* E. Prenowitz (Trans.). Baltimore: Johns Hopkins University Press.

Eliot, T. S. (1934). Collected Poems: 1909–1962. New York: Harcourt, Brace and World.

Lacan, J. (1977). Écrits*: A selection.* A. Sheridan (Trans.). New York: W.W. Norton.

Lacan, J. (2004). *Le Séminaire livre X: L'angoisse, 1962–1963.* Paris: Éditions du Seuil.

Tademy, L. (2001). *Cane river.* New York: Warner Books.

Index

About the Editors and Contributors

Ricardo Ainslie is a psychologist-psychoanalyst who uses books, documentary films, and photographic exhibits to capture and depict subjects of social and cultural interest. A native of Mexico City, he teaches at the University of Texas at Austin and also has a private practice where he sees adult patients. His books include *No Dancin' in Anson: An American Story of Race and Social Change* (1995), *The Psychology of Twinship* (1997), *Long Dark Road: Bill King and Murder in Jasper, Texas* (2004), and *The Fight to Save Juárez: Life in the Heart of Mexico's Drug War* (2013). His films include *Crossover: A Story of Desegregation* (1999); *Looking North: Mexican Images of Immigration* (2006); and *Ya Basta! Kidnapped in Mexico* (2007).

In 2002 Ricardo Ainslie received the Texas Psychological Association's "Outstanding Contribution to Science Award." And in 2004 he was a recipient of the American Psychoanalytic Association's (APAs) "Outstanding Contribution to Psychoanalytic Education Award." In 2009 the APA's Division of Psychoanalysis recognized his work with its "Science Award," and the Psychoanalysis and Social Responsibility section of Division 39 awarded him it's "Achievement Award" in 2011. Ricardo Ainslie was inducted into the Texas Institute of Letters in 2006. In 2010 he was named a Guggenheim Fellow and also awarded a Rockefeller Foundation Bellagio Center Residency. In 2014 he was inducted into the Texas Philosophical Society.

Claude Barbre, MS, MDiv, PhD, LP, is associate professor, the Clinical Psychology Psy.D. Department, the Chicago School of Professional Psychology. He is Course Stream Coordinator of the Psychodynamics Concentration at the Chicago School, and also teaches in the Psychology and Spirituality Concentration, and the Child and Adolescent Track. Dr. Barbre has counseled children and families for over twenty-five years, and served for twelve years as Executive Director of the Harlem Family Institute, a New York City school-based, psychoanalytic training program working with children and families in low-income, high-needs neighborhoods. He also taught psychology and religion at Manhattan College and Fordham University before his appointment at the Chicago School. A former associate editor of the *Journal of Religion and Health: Psychology, Spirituality, and Medicine* for fifteen years, Dr. Barbre is a six-time nominee, and four-time recipient of the international Gradiva Award, presented by the National Association for the Advancement of Psychoanalysis (NAAP). He is a certified hospital chaplain and a licensed psychoanalyst in private practice.

Scott Boehm is assistant professor of Spanish at Michigan State University where he teaches twenty- and twenty-first century Spanish Peninsular Studies in a global context, specializing in Spanish cinema. In 2007, he helped launch the Spanish Civil War Memory Project while a PhD student at UC San Diego. That digital archive is now the world's largest collection of unedited testimonies of survivors of the genocidal violence carried out during the war and under the Francoist dictatorship. In 2008, while serving as a fellow at the UC Berkeley Human Rights Center, Scott also participated in several mass grave exhumations in conjunction with the Association for the Recovery of Historical Memory.

Marilyn Charles is staff psychologist at the Austen Riggs Center and a psychoanalyst in private practice in Stockbridge, MA. She is affiliated with Harvard University and several psychoanalytic institutes, and serves as contributing editor of *Psychoanalysis, Culture, and Society* and on the editorial boards of a number of psychoanalytic journals. As the cochair of the Association for the Psychoanalysis of Culture and Society (APCS) and president-elect of Division 39 (Psychoanalysis) of the American Psychological Association, she is actively engaged in mentoring and promoting community involvement for those in the helping professions, and supports psychoanalytic training, outreach, and research initiatives. Her own research focuses on creativity, psychosis, and resilience. Marilyn has presented her work nationally and internationally, publishing over eighty articles and book chapters and four books: *Patterns: Building Blocks of Experience*; *Constructing Realities: Transformations through Myth and Metaphor*; *Learning from Experience: A Guidebook for Clinicians*; and *Working with Trauma: Lessons from Bion and Lacan*. Currently in progress: *The Stories We Live: Life, Literature, and Psychoanalysis*.

Naama de la Fontaine, PhD, is post-doctoral psychology associate at the Yale University Child Study Center, where she specializes in treatment and research related to child, family, and community trauma. She grew up in Israel and completed her PhD in clinical psychology at Adelphi University's Derner Institute of Advanced Psychological Studies in New York. Her independent research focus has been on political trauma and particularly the effects of war trauma on soldiers. Over the past few years, she collected and analyzed narratives of Israeli soldiers who participated in the Second Lebanon War. Clinically, she has provided research-informed, trauma-focused psychotherapy to 9/11 first responders at New York University/Bellevue Hospital. She has also treated children exposed to potentially traumatic events at Mount Sinai Hospital. As an adjunct professor, she taught a course on trauma in the Adelphi University Mental Health Counseling Program. In her current work at the Yale Child Study Center, her research has expanded to complement the clinical work she has been engaged in through the Child Development-Community Policing (CD-CP) Program with the New Haven Police Department. She is currently collaborating with Yale faculty to investigate the effectiveness of this mental health and law enforcement collaboration in responding to children and communities exposed to violence.

Justina Kaminskaitė Dillon is currently a doctoral student in clinical psychology at the Institute of Advanced Psychological Studies at Adelphi University. She was born and lived in Lithuania until coming to the United States for higher education. While growing up and especially after arriving in the United States, when she was immersed in a different culture, she observed certain cultural idiosyncrasies in Lithuanian society that seemed to be remnants of the Soviet occupations. The study of trauma narratives with Lithuanian women survivors of the Soviet deportations is part of Ms. Dillon's predissertation project, supervised by Michael O'Loughlin and facilitated by the Genocide and Resistance Research Center of Lithuania as well as by the deportee survivor community "Lapteviečiai" in Lithuania.

Minh Truong-George came to New Zealand as a child refugee from Vietnam thirty-four years ago. She is married to her husband, who is from Vanuatu, and they have three children. Her life is interwoven with the different threads of diverse cultures such as Chinese, Vietnamese, Ni-Vanuatu, and New Zealand. She was trained as a psychosynthesis psychotherapist and is an associate of the Institute of Psychosynthesis, NZ. She has been working for the last seven years in private practice as well as in the state sector and is especially interested in the dance between Eastern and Western psychology and the holding of clients that includes both "height" and "depth." She is passionate about her work and brings to it her aspiration to deeply know herself as an individual and at the interface with others. She has an art-making background, with numerous exhibitions, including exhibiting at an international conference *The Poetics of Exile* at Auckland University in July 2003.

She also recently produced and edited a documentary called *Journey Home,* which premiered at the recent *Alike-Different: Navigating the Divide,* the 6th International Joint Conference, held in Auckland, New Zealand, August 2012. She is engaged in her Buddhist practice and helps lead meditation/Buddhist classes as well as lead family retreats over the past sixteen years.

Hannah Hahn, PhD, has been in full-time private practice in New York City for sixteen years, providing psychotherapy to adults, adolescents, and children. She received her doctorate in clinical psychology from Columbia University and her psychoanalytic training from the Institute for Contemporary Psychotherapy. She is on the faculty at the New York Institute for Psychotherapy Training in Infancy, Childhood, and Adolescence and is a training supervisor at the Institute for Contemporary Psychotherapy. Recent professional presentations include "A Cross-Cultural Study of Dissociation and Altered States of Consciousness in Healing Rituals"; "A Safe Place to Stand: The Holding Environment with Child Patients and Their Parents"; and "If You Get Any Closer, I'm Going to Run: Engagement and Psychotherapeutic Action with a Schizoid Patient."

Tom Hennes is the founding principal of Thinc Design, a leading exhibition design firm located in New York, serving clients across North America and around the globe in Asia, Africa, and Europe. His scholarly writings promote the transformation of exhibitions into powerful places of personal experience and learning. He has published articles in *Informal Learning Review* and *Curator: The Museum Journal*, for which he has also served as exhibitions editor since 2007. He has presented papers and lectured about his work to an array of audiences, including the American Alliance of Museums, the Gravity Free Multidisciplinary Design Conference, the Chicago Humanities Festival, the International Aquarium Congress, the Inclusive Museum Conference, the American Psychological Association, and INTERCOM.

Prior to launching Thinc, Hennes designed for theater and opera as well as corporate events and theme park attractions. He also designed the stage for the TED conference for nine consecutive years. Hennes has taught at Rhode Island School of Design and for Pratt Institute's summer program at Boisbuchet. He has lectured at New York University's Interactive Telecommunications Program and the Department of Architecture at the University of California, Berkeley. He is a member of the New York theatrical design union, United Scenic Artists Local 829, and holds multiple patents for immersive theaters and 3-D projection techniques.

Luis Martín-Cabrera is associate professor in the Department of Literature, director of the University of California Education Abroad Program in Chile and affiliated faculty of ethnic studies, the Center for Latin American Studies, and critical gender studies at the University of California San Diego (UCSD). Professor Martín-Cabrera is the author of *Radical Justice: Spain and the Southern Cone beyond Market and State* (2011), a study of the politics of memory in Spain, Argentina, and Chile and the director of the Spanish Civil War Memory Project, a UCSD initiative to collect testimonies of the survivors of Fascist violence in Spain. Martín-Cabrera has published extensively on topics related to psychoanalysis, Marxism, migration, and the politics of memory.

Michael O'Loughlin, PhD, is professor in the School of Education and clinical and research supervisor in the PhD program in clinical psychology at Adelphi University. He is cochair of the Association for the Psychoanalysis of Culture and Society (apcsweb.net). He published *The Subject of Childhood* in 2009 and edited *Imagining Children Otherwise: Theoretical and Critical Perspectives on Childhood Subjectivity* with Richard Johnson in 2010. He is coeditor with Cora Smith and Glenys Lobban of *Psychodynamic Psychotherapy in Contemporary South Africa: Contexts, Theories, and Applications* (2013), and in 2013 he also edited two books on children's emotions: *The Uses of Psychoanalysis in Working with Children's Emotional lives* and *Psychodynamic Perspectives on Working with Children, Families and Schools.* With Marilyn Charles he co-edited a companion volume to this book: *Fragments of Trauma and the Social Production of Suffering, Trauma, History, and Memory,* also published by Rowman & Littlefield. He has a private practice for psychotherapy and psychoanalysis on Long Island, New York. Website: michaeloloughlinphd.com.

Nirit Gradwohl Pisano, PhD, is a clinical psychologist working in private practice in Scarsdale, NY. Her psychodynamically informed practice provides individual, family, couples, and group psychotherapy to children, adolescents, and adults. Dr. Pisano earned her degrees from Tufts University and Adelphi University's Derner Institute of Advanced Psychological Studies, and was trained at Bellevue Hospital, Jacobi Medical Center, and Bronx Psychiatric Center. Dr. Pisano recently published her first book, *Granddaughters of the Holocaust: Never Forgetting What They Didn't Experience* (2012), which informs her work with survivors of atrocities. She has presented her findings at conferences in the United States and abroad, and conducted related workshops at Jewish Community Centers in the New York Metropolitan area.

Billie A. Pivnick, PhD, clinical psychologist, is faculty and supervisor at the William Alanson White Institute and Columbia University Teachers College, as well as faculty for the Institute for Contemporary Psychotherapy and the New Directions Program in Writing with a Psychoanalytic Edge. In her private practice, she specializes in treating patients suffering from loss and trauma and their families. She has served as consulting psychologist to Thinc Design partnered with the National September 11 Memorial and Museum as well as on Thinc Design's exhibitions at the Connecticut Science Center and at Chicago's Museum of Science and Industry. Formerly, cofounder of the Denver Learning Community, head of the Dance Movement Therapy Department at New England Rehabilitation Hospital, and coordinator of the Dance Therapy Training Program in the Pratt Institute Graduate Creative Arts Therapy Program, she is now on the board of directors of the Association for the Psychoanalysis of Culture and Society (APCS), and the editorial review boards of the *Journal of Religion and Health* and *Contemporary Psychoanalysis* and has authored numerous academic articles. Her 1990 study, "Symbolization and Its Discontents: The Impact of Threatened Object Loss on the Discourse and Symptomatology of Hospitalized Psychotic Patients," won IPTAR's Stanley Berger Award for its contribution to the field of psychoanalysis.

Mari Ruti is professor of critical theory at the University of Toronto, where she teaches contemporary theory, continental philosophy, psychoanalysis, and feminist and queer theory. She is the author of *Reinventing the Soul: Posthumanist Theory and Psychic Life* (2006); *A World of Fragile Things: Psychoanalysis and the Art of Living* (2009); *The Summons of Love* (2011); *The Singularity of Being: Lacan and the Immortal Within* (2012); and *The Call of Character: Living a Life Worth Living* (2013).

Reinhold Stipsits is associate professor of social pedagogics and humanistic education at the University of Vienna, Austria. He teaches social pedagogics in the Department of Education at the University of Vienna. His research interest is in minorities in Central Europe, migration, counseling, and biography. He is a guest lecturer at the IES, Institute of Education of Students abroad (formerly Institute of European Studies). There he teaches psychoanalysis and contemporary approaches to humanistic education. He is also a licensed person-centered therapist. He had the privilege of working with outstanding people such as Carl R. Rogers, Douglas A. Land, and John M. Shlien, mainly in Europe and in the United States. As a descendent of the Croatian minority in Austria—without being able to speak the Croatian language—he discovered very late that there is also a relatively unknown area close to Austria, namely Central Eastern Europe. He served as guest professor at the University of Cluj-Napoca in Romania at the German Department of Journalism. To keep his inner balance it has been important for him to stay in touch with East and West, e.g., during a scholarship stay at the University of Texas in Austin. Recent study visits have led him to Lithuania and Moldova.

Kate Szymanski is associate professor at the Derner Institute of Advanced Psychological Studies at Adelphi University, New York. She is a clinical and research supervisor in the PhD program in clinical psychology who specializes in acute and chronic trauma and studies mechanisms behind resilience and post-traumatic growth. She is particularly interested in a sense of identity, affect regulation, and object relations in trauma survivors. She coedited (with M. Stroinska and V. Cecchetto) *The Unspeakable: Narratives of Trauma* and published a number of journal articles and book chapters on trauma. She has also presented at numerous national and international conferences and was a consultant to Tuesday's Children, a non-profit organization that works with 9/11 families. She is currently developing group therapy treatment for traumatized adolescents. Szymanski is in private practice with specialty in trauma in Garden City, NY.

Graham Toomey is a proud Aboriginal man belonging to the Wiradjuri and Wongaibon language groups of Western NSW. Since 2010 Graham has been on a journey to learn more about his Aboriginal heritage. Graham studied at the Sydney TAFE Institute in 2010 where he studied the Diploma of Aboriginal Studies at the Eora TAFE College. Graham had a very successful year and was awarded the Sydney Institute Aboriginal Student of the year. The following two years saw Graham study the Aboriginal and Torres Strait Cultural Arts course where he was named Aboriginal Art Student of the year for both 2011 and 2012. Since graduating Graham has seen his artworks exhibited throughout Sydney, Africa, and Japan. His artworks and sculptures are now found in some famous homes, galleries, and organizations, such as, Prince Harry of Wales; the Governor, Marie Bashire; the African Embassy; Price Water House Coopers; Amnesty International; 2014 Vivid Festival Sydney. With the knowledge Graham gained while studying he has begun writing short children's stories as a way of telling stories about his culture. Graham also dedicates his valuable time to various community organizations and committees, which allow him to share his cultural knowledge, passion, and skills. Whether Graham is painting or writing he considers his work as creating awareness and educating people about his beautiful and dynamic culture. See website grahamtoomey.com.

Norma Tracey is senior member of the NSW Institute of Psychoanalytic Psychotherapy. She was social work assistant to the professor of child health at Sydney University, Children's Hospital Unit, and later a senior social worker and psychotherapist in the Department of Family Psychiatry. Her special area of expertise has always been in work with mothers, fathers, and infants. She has been in private practice for many years. She founded the Gunawirra organization which works with Aboriginal preschools in thirty-five outlying areas in rural and regional NSW. Gunawirra studies trauma in the preschool child and creates programs in the preschool for healing trauma. In Redfern, Sydney, Gunawirra works with pregnant and young Aboriginal mothers with drug and alcohol abuse and domestic violence problems, resulting from transgenerational dispossession of their land, family, community spiritual basis, and culture. She is the author of many internationally published papers, books, and booklets. Her special area of interest is the aesthetics of art, drama, literature, and music people have used since ancient times to heal internal pain and trauma since ancient times.

Ross Truscott is currently a postdoctoral associate in women's studies at Duke University. While writing his chapter, he was a postdoctoral research fellow working under the National Research Foundation SARChl Chair for Social Change at the University of Fort Hare in East London, South Africa, and a visiting fellow at the Center for Humanities Research, University of the Western Cape, South Africa. Ross has published on post-apartheid popular culture, nationalism, race, gender, psychoanalysis, and postcolonialism.

Clara Valverde is professor of nursing in Barcelona, Spain. She specializes in therapeutic relations and biopolitics and lectures and offers workshops on transgenerational trauma in Spain, especially on the impact of political violence of the twentieth century. Through her work with Aboriginal communities in Canada, Valverde deepened her understanding of transgenerational trauma and the healing process that work. Valverde also lectures and publishes extensively on neoliberalism and the uses of language, chronic illness, and invisibility, and strategies against the privatization of health care. Her latest books include *No nos lo creemos: Una lectura crítica del lenguaje neoliberal* (2013), *La sanidad está en venta* (2013), and *Pues tienes buena cara. Síndrome de Fatiga Crónica: Una enfermedad políticamente incorrecta* (2009). Valverde is an activist in the 15M and other social movements. She coordinates Equipo Aquo, a training team for mental health workers, doctors, and nurses.

Angie Voela is senior lecturer in psychosocial studies, University of East London. Her research focuses on gender; feminist and psychoanalytic approaches to identity; space, politics, and identity; myth in contemporary culture and philosophy; art and psychoanalysis. Her recent publications appear in the *European Journal of Women's Studies; Subjectivity; Somatechnics, the Journal for Cultural Research and Psychoanalysis of Culture and Society*. She is currently working on a book on gender and myth in contemporary culture, entitled *After Oedipus: Psychoanalysis, Philosophy and Myth in Contemporary Culture*. She is coediting a special issue on *Feminism* *and Social Movements* for the *Journal Gender and Education* and a book on families and neoliberalims entitled *We Need to Talk about Families: Essays on the Family, Popular Culture, and Neoliberalism.*

Nigel Williams is senior lecturer in psychosocial studies at the University of the West of England, UK. He is a psychotherapist and organizational consultant. He is engaged in a wide-ranging piece of research into how therapists, educators, and activists think about and use intergenerational memory as part of their work. He is particularly interested in unwritten histories, and has for many years been interested both in histories from below, and histories of the long term.

www.ingramcontent.com/pod-product-compliance
Ingram Content Group UK Ltd.
Pitfield, Milton Keynes, MK11 3LW, UK
UKHW012034150926
475560UK00001B/11